Andreas Langegger

Ontology-based Information Integration

Andreas Langegger

Ontology-based Information Integration

A Flexible Approach for Ontology-based Virtual Information Integration Building on Semantic Web Technology

Südwestdeutscher Verlag für Hochschulschriften

Impressum / Imprint
Bibliografische Information der Deutschen Nationalbibliothek: Die Deutsche Nationalbibliothek verzeichnet diese Publikation in der Deutschen Nationalbibliografie; detaillierte bibliografische Daten sind im Internet über http://dnb.d-nb.de abrufbar.
Alle in diesem Buch genannten Marken und Produktnamen unterliegen warenzeichen-, marken- oder patentrechtlichem Schutz bzw. sind Warenzeichen oder eingetragene Warenzeichen der jeweiligen Inhaber. Die Wiedergabe von Marken, Produktnamen, Gebrauchsnamen, Handelsnamen, Warenbezeichnungen u.s.w. in diesem Werk berechtigt auch ohne besondere Kennzeichnung nicht zu der Annahme, dass solche Namen im Sinne der Warenzeichen- und Markenschutzgesetzgebung als frei zu betrachten wären und daher von jedermann benutzt werden dürften.

Bibliographic information published by the Deutsche Nationalbibliothek: The Deutsche Nationalbibliothek lists this publication in the Deutsche Nationalbibliografie; detailed bibliographic data are available in the Internet at http://dnb.d-nb.de.
Any brand names and product names mentioned in this book are subject to trademark, brand or patent protection and are trademarks or registered trademarks of their respective holders. The use of brand names, product names, common names, trade names, product descriptions etc. even without a particular marking in this work is in no way to be construed to mean that such names may be regarded as unrestricted in respect of trademark and brand protection legislation and could thus be used by anyone.

Verlag / Publisher:
Südwestdeutscher Verlag für Hochschulschriften
ist ein Imprint der / is a trademark of
OmniScriptum GmbH & Co. KG
Heinrich-Böcking-Str. 6-8, 66121 Saarbrücken, Deutschland / Germany
Email: info@svh-verlag.de

Herstellung: siehe letzte Seite /
Printed at: see last page
ISBN: 978-3-8381-1569-6

Zugl. / Approved by: Linz, JKU, Diss., 2010

Copyright © 2010 OmniScriptum GmbH & Co. KG
Alle Rechte vorbehalten. / All rights reserved. Saarbrücken 2010

Acknowledgements

I would like to express my gratitude to my supervisors a.Univ.-Prof. Dipl.-Ing. Dr. Wolfram Wöß and o.Univ.-Prof. Dipl.-Ing. Dr. A Min Tjoa for their support and time spent to judge my work. Very special thanks go to my love Claudia, for assisting and motivating me after short nights, and my parents, for their kindness to let me stay at their place during workweek after I had moved to Vienna.

I would also like to thank Richard Cyganiak and Jürgen Umbrich from DERI Galway, Andy Seaborne from Talis (formerly HP Labs), Bernhard Haslhofer and Bernhard Schandl from the University of Vienna, Olaf Hartig from HU Berlin, and many other people I have met at conferences for their input, kind support, and time for discussions. In particular I want to thank Richard for coming to Linz and introducing us to the internals of D2R-Server and Herwig Leimer for optimizing D2R-Server and for being the most passionate and committed master student I supervised. I would like to thank all my colleagues at the institute, especially Thomas Leitner, Christina Feilmayr, and Stefan Anderlik for being very friendly, passionate, and humorous office mates.

Finally, I would like to thank again Prof. Wolfram Wöß for spending so much time reading and correcting my work. Special thanks go also to Freddy Priyatna from Universidad Politécnica de Madrid for sending me corrections for this book edition of my thesis.

Contents

List of Figures   ix

List of Tables   xiii

Listings   xv

List of Algorithms   xvii

1 Introduction   **1**
- 1.1 Contribution 2
- 1.2 Challenges 4
- 1.3 Outline of the Thesis 5

I Background   7

2 Capturing the Real World   **9**
- 2.1 Information and its Structure 9
  - 2.1.1 Unstructured Data, Structured Data, and Metadata 10
  - 2.1.2 Data Structures and Data Models 10
- 2.2 Data Modeling 11
  - 2.2.1 Metamodels and Information Representation 11
  - 2.2.2 Symbols, Concepts, and Real World Things 14

3 Information Integration   **19**
- 3.1 Definition of Information Integration 19
- 3.2 Applications of Information Integration Technology 20
- 3.3 Challenges 21
  - 3.3.1 Distribution 22
  - 3.3.2 Heterogeneity 23
  - 3.3.3 Further Aspects 24
- 3.4 Typical Architecture of Information Integration Systems 25

Contents

    3.5   Introduction to Model Mapping 27
           3.5.1   Integrated Global Model 29
           3.5.2   Generation and Representation of Mappings 30
           3.5.3   Interpretation of Mappings Based on Logical Views 31
    3.6   Interoperability and Standardization 33

4 Semantic Web Primer   35

    4.1   Introduction 35
           4.1.1   Origins of the Semantic Web 36
           4.1.2   Overview – The Semantic Web Layer Cake 36
    4.2   Resource Description Framework (RDF) 38
           4.2.1   RDF Concepts and Abstract Syntax 38
           4.2.2   Formal Definition of an RDF Graph 42
           4.2.3   Summary of RDF Core Features 42
           4.2.4   RDF Serializations 43
           4.2.5   RDF Schema 44
           4.2.6   XML versus RDF 47
    4.3   Web Ontology Language 48
           4.3.1   Ontologies 48
           4.3.2   Introduction to OWL 50
           4.3.3   Features of OWL 52
    4.4   SPARQL Protocol and RDF Query Language 54
           4.4.1   Graph Pattern Matching 54
           4.4.2   Query Forms 58
           4.4.3   SPARQL Definitions 59
           4.4.4   Representation of SPARQL Algebra Plans 62
    4.5   Linked Data 63

II Related Work   67

5 Overview   69

6 Early Projects and Fundamental Concepts   71

    6.1   Mediators in Future Information Systems 71
    6.2   IBM Garlic 73
           6.2.1   Architecture 73
           6.2.2   Global Metamodel and Query Language 74
           6.2.3   Query Processing in Garlic 76

	6.2.4	Wrapper-specific STARs	83
	6.2.5	Cost-Model	84
	6.2.6	Browsing Information with PESTO	84
6.3		Other Mediator Systems	85
	6.3.1	TSIMMIS	85
	6.3.2	DISCO	89
	6.3.3	InfoSleuth	91
6.4		Discussion	95

7 Information Integration based on Semantic Web Technologies 97

7.1		Materialized Information Integration	100
7.2		Generic Architectures	101
	7.2.1	Yacob – RDF on Top of an XML-based Mediator	102
	7.2.2	Yuan et al. – Extending a Commercial Of-The-Shelf EII Product	105
	7.2.3	ISENS – Integration with OWL-based Mapping Ontologies	106
	7.2.4	DARQ – SPARQL Query Federation	108
	7.2.5	Discussion	111
7.3		Applied Research Projects	113

III The SemWIQ Approach 117

8 Overview 119

8.1	Concept-based Information Integration	119
	8.1.1 Advantages of Using RDF as a Global Metamodel	121
	8.1.2 Ontologies for Information Integration	122
8.2	Architecture of SemWIQ	123
8.3	Query Federation Based on Statistical Data Summaries	126

9 SemWIQ Mediator 129

9.1		Definitions	130
	9.1.1	SemWIQ Queries and the Virtual Global Graph	130
	9.1.2	Algebra Modifications	131
	9.1.3	SPARQL Extensions	131
	9.1.4	SemWIQ Data Source Description	133
9.2		Query Processing Overview	135
	9.2.1	Parser	136
	9.2.2	Pre-optimizations	137
	9.2.3	Federation	139

Contents

	9.2.4	Post-optimizations	141
	9.2.5	Query Execution	142
	9.2.6	Data Provenance	145
9.3	Triple-based Federator		146
9.4	Instance-based Federator		148
	9.4.1	Type Detection	151
	9.4.2	Generation of sub plans	154
	9.4.3	Subsumption Reasoning at Query Time	156
9.5	Implementation Notes		159

10 SemWIQ Wrappers — 163

- 10.1 General Considerations 164
  - 10.1.1 Implementing Wrappers Based on Jena ARQ ... 165
  - 10.1.2 Required Optimizations ... 165
- 10.2 Wrapping Relational Databases ... 166
  - 10.2.1 D2RQ Mappings ... 167
  - 10.2.2 D2RQ-Map Capabilities ... 170
- 10.3 Wrapping Spreadsheets ... 171
  - 10.3.1 Information Representation in Spreadsheets ... 171
  - 10.3.2 Definition of Spreadsheet Applications ... 173
  - 10.3.3 XLWrap Mappings ... 174
  - 10.3.4 Example ... 177
  - 10.3.5 Processing SPARQL Queries ... 177
  - 10.3.6 Capabilities of XLWrap ... 179

11 Query Pattern Cardinality Estimation with RDFStats — 181

- 11.1 RDFStats Approach ... 181
- 11.2 Generation of RDF Statistics ... 183
  - 11.2.1 Histogram Generation Process ... 184
  - 11.2.2 Order-preserving String Histogram ... 186
  - 11.2.3 Persisting Statistics ... 187
- 11.3 Using and Accessing Statistics ... 187
  - 11.3.1 Graph Statistics ... 188
  - 11.3.2 Cardinality Estimation for Query Plans ... 191

IV Results — 195

12 Demonstration and Evaluation — 197

12.1	Case Study – Virtual Solar Observatory		197
	12.1.1	Data Sources and Vocabularies	198
	12.1.2	Setup Tasks	203
12.2	Evaluation		206
	12.2.1	Sample Queries	206
	12.2.2	Performance	221
	12.2.3	Navigation based on Linked Data Principles	222

13 Conclusion 227

14 Future Directions 231
14.1 Graphical Query Builder and Results Visualization 231
14.2 Query Optimization 233

Appendix 237

A Mapping Specifications for the Use-Case Demo 237
A.1 D2RQ Mapping for the KSO Sunspots Database 237
A.2 XLWrap Mapping for the Scientists Spreadsheet 243
A.3 XLWrap Mapping for the Sunspots Relative Numbers Spreadsheet 244

Bibliography 245

Contents

List of Figures

1.1	Thesis outline.	6
2.1	OMG Meta Object Facility (MOF).	13
2.2	Semiotic triangle.	15
2.3	Example of classifying sets.	16
2.4	Extension and intension of names in a model.	17
3.1	Related fields of research.	19
3.2	Orthogonal aspects of information integration.	22
3.3	Common architecture of information integration systems.	26
3.4	Model mapping overview.	28
3.5	Different mapping approaches addressing metamodel heterogeneity.	29
3.6	Two-phase mapping from a relational database to a target ontology.	30
3.7	Two XML trees with a high degree of structural heterogeneity.	34
4.1	Semantic Web layer cake.	37
4.2	RDF graph examples.	39
4.3	Example of a large RDF graph (FOAF social network).	41
4.4	Definition of FOAF Person as part of the FOAF vocabulary.	46
4.5	Meaning of XML information set.	48
4.6	Ontology spectrum.	49
4.7	Visual representation of SPARQL graph pattern matching.	56
4.8	A SPARQL query and its corresponding algebra plan.	61
4.9	Current Linked Data infrastructure.	64
6.1	Mediators as interfaces for information flow.	72
6.2	Garlic system architecture.	74
6.3	Wrapper interfaces for the discussed example.	76
6.4	One possible Garlic query plan for the discussed example query.	79
6.5	Different join STARs produced by `JoinRoot`.	83
6.6	Architecture of TSIMMIS.	86
6.7	OEM example query.	88

List of Figures

6.8	Architecture and processes in DISCO.	90
6.9	Overview of InfoSleuth.	93
6.10	Classification of the discussed mediator-based approaches.	96
7.1	Ontological expressiveness of virtual and materialized paradigms.	99
7.2	Virtuoso Sponger.	101
7.3	Architecture of the Yacob Mediator.	103
7.4	Semantic information integration based on a COTS EII product.	106
7.5	ISENS Mapping Ontologies.	107
8.1	SemWIQ approach: distributed data sources mapped to distributed ontologies.	121
8.2	Mediator-Wrapper architecture of SemWIQ.	126
9.1	SemWIQ mediator component.	129
9.2	Query processing overview.	135
9.3	SPARQL algebra operators relevant to SemWIQ.	137
9.4	Query execution iterators.	143
9.5	Example of a federated algebra plan.	144
9.6	Execution plan for the algebra plan depicted in Figure 9.5.	145
9.7	SPARQL query with two different subject nodes.	149
9.8	Type detection of the instance-based federator.	154
9.9	SemWIQ mediator UML class diagram.	160
10.1	Mapping from several data models to a common RDF model.	164
10.2	D2RQ-Map example mapping.	168
10.3	A SPARQL query and its corresponding D2RQ query plan.	169
10.4	SQL queries for D2RQ operators of Figure 10.3.	169
10.5	Information representation in spreadsheets.	172
11.1	RDFStats generation process.	183
11.2	RDFStats Histogram API and class hierarchy.	185
11.3	RDFStats vocabulary.	188
11.4	RDFStatsModel and RDFStatsDataset API.	189
11.5	Range coverage for filter expression example.	192
12.1	Solar observation datasets used for the case study.	198
12.2	Domain ontologies for solar observation.	199
12.3	ER diagram of the Kanzelhöhe solar observatory's sunspots database (DS1).	201
12.4	Example exposures from the Kanzelhöhe solar observatory.	202
12.5	Plan for Query 1 (using triple-based federator).	208

List of Figures

12.6 Plan for Query 2 (using instance-based federator). 210
12.7 Plan for Query 3 (using triple-based federator). 212
12.8 Plan for Query 4 (using triple-based federator). 213
12.9 Plan for Query 5 (using triple-based federator). 215
12.10 Plan for Query 6 (using triple-based federator). 216
12.11 Plan for Query 7 (using triple-based federator). 219
12.12 Plan for Query 8 (using instance-based federator). 220
12.13 Browsing Linked Data with SemWIQ (screenshots). 224
12.14 DBpedia page for `http://dbpedia.org/resource/H-alpha`. 225

14.1 SPARUI – A Graphical Query Builder for SemWIQ (Rambichler 2009). 232

List of Figures

List of Tables

2.1	Similarities between data representation languages.	12
4.1	Results of the discussed union query represented as a table.	58
10.1	Source data for discussed XLWrap example.	177
12.1	Sizes of the case study data sources DS1–5.	198
12.2	Example queries.	207
12.3	Results of Query 1.	209
12.4	Results of Query 2.	209
12.5	Results of Query 3.	211
12.6	Results of Query 4.	213
12.7	Results of Query 6.	217
12.8	Results of Query 7.	218
12.9	Query execution time measures.	221

List of Tables

Listings

3.1	XQuery used to transform from the left to the right model shown in Figure 3.7.	34
4.1	Example of SPARQL S-Expression notation.	63
4.2	Grammar of SPARQL S-Expressions.	63
7.1	Example of a DARQ service description.	109
9.1	Modifications to the SPARQL grammar of ARQ.	132
9.2	EXPLAIN query results example.	133
9.3	DESCRIBE SERVICE query results example.	134
9.4	DESCRIBE DATASET query results example (in Notation3 syntax).	134
9.5	Definition of a SemWIQ data source based on voiD	135
10.1	Grammar of XLWrap expressions	176
10.2	Example mapping specified in TriG syntax.	178
10.3	RDF graph for the given example spreadsheet and XLWrap mapping.	178
12.1	Excerpt of the publications data source.	203
12.2	Results of the DESCRIBE variant for Query 4.	214

Listings

List of Algorithms

1	Plan transform algorithm of the federator.	140
2	Triple-based federation algorithm – called by Algorithm 1.	147
3	Instance-based federation algorithm – called by Algorithm 1.	150
4	Algorithm for creating BGP subject groups – called by Algorithm 3.	151
5	Algorithm for detecting BGP subject types – called by Algorithm 3.	152
6	Algorithm for generation of sub-plans – called by Algorithm 3.	155
7	Collects subtypes a data sources has instances for – called by Algorithm 6.	157
8	Algorithm for generation of subsumption plans – called by Algorithm 6.	157
9	Generates permutations for conjunctive sub-type sets – called by Algorithm 8.	159
10	Algorithm for building an order-preserving string histogram.	186

List of Algorithms

1 Introduction

It is a well-known fact, that the IT revolution, led in by the introduction of computers and continuing with the spreading of the internet all over the globe, caused a rapid shift in the way we work, think, and live today. There is hardly any company, organization, research institution, or public administration that does not store and manage a majority of the information it requires to run the daily business with the help if IT systems. Moreover, with the advent of mobile computing and the decline in prices for laptops, PDAs, smart phones and other neat devices masses of people have started managing personal information of their daily life with the help of IT. Because of the fact, that today there is so much information stored in various isolated devices and applications, sustaining the interoperability of software, services, and information has become one of the most important tasks not only for the industry and businesses, but also for research institutions, public administration, and even for private persons (Franklin et al. 2005).

Typically, interoperability between two or more systems can be achieved by introducing common communication protocols like CORBA or Web services and standards for representing information like XML, KIF[1], or the *Resource Description Framework*, which is used on the Semantic Web as a decentralized, graph-based, extensible data model with the expressiveness of description logics. Because all applications have very specific use cases and requirements, they all use different *models* (and *meta-models*) to represent parts of the *real world*.

Sometimes it is required to access the information stored in multiple distributed information systems from a single point of access. Such an approach of a virtual view over distributed information systems is traditionally called *information integration*. From the user's point of view, there is just one integrated information system providing all the information from the sub-systems which, for instance, may be database systems, multimedia servers, document repositories, spreadsheet collections, expert systems, or Web services. Different levels of heterogeneity have been addressed by researchers. Basically, research towards information integration originates from the database domain, where distributed, federated, and multi-database systems had been developed during the eighties to provide access to information stored in different databases. With the growing range of different information management systems the mediator-wrapper architecture introduced by Wiederhold (1992) became very popular.

Traditionally, information interoperability had mainly been a matter for enterprises and that is also

---
[1] *Knowledge Interchange Format* – It provides the expressiveness of a first-order predicate logic and has been developed as an interchange format for knowledge-based systems during the nineties (Kifer et al. 1995).

1 Introduction

why technologies in this area have been developed to solve the specific problems of enterprises in the first run. While enterprises are applying *Enterprise Information Integration* (EII) to virtually integrate information from different subsidiaries, many research projects have been started since the late nineties to apply these techniques with a special focus on semantics and ontologies in various interdisciplinary research domains. With the advent of the Semantic Web around the millennium (Tim Berners Lee et al. 2001), a passionate community has evolved, addressing information integration issues with a more general approach in a Web-scale setting. Semantic Web technologies have already proven to be well suited for information integration in numerous scientific and industrial projects as will be shown in the related work part. Nevertheless, there are still numerous issues to address, not only regarding architectural concepts, but also concerning the flexibility, performance, and scalability of implementations.

Beside several architectural approaches, there has also been a great amount of research in the fields of schema management and model reconciliation. A significant progress in solving heterogeneity issues at the syntactic, schematic, and structural level has been achieved. However, solving semantic conflicts is still an open issue which has gained more and more attention during the last years, especially within the Semantic Web community. Furthermore, the Web plays a very important role today and there has been a big shift in architectural styles since the nineties.

1.1 Contribution

The main contribution of this work is a novel approach for information integration based on ontologies and Semantic Web technologies. SemWIQ (*Semantic Web Integrator and Query Engine*), the integration system developed as part of this thesis is based on RDF graph statistics, which enables scalable query federation as will be shown in Part III. Moreover, it provides a very flexible architecture since the maintenance of an explicit global schema is not required as opposed to existing relational systems.

SemWIQ has been deployed in a scientific project for the integration of solar observation data as will be demonstrated in Part IV. The integration of scientific data or knowledge bases is sometimes more demanding than business information, because it often requires a higher level of expressiveness. Especially within life sciences like biomedicine, pharmaceutics, biology and also in astronomy and space science there are many information systems that have to be integrated with complex data models and logical knowledge bases. Because SemWIQ is based on RDF and every RDF-based ontology can be integrated with SemWIQ, it is able to represent any knowledge that can be represented with OWL and other RDF-based languages. Although the query processor is not a full-fledged distributed description logic reasoner, it is capable of query-time subsumption reasoning. Of course, SemWIQ can be applied to business use-cases also, as pointed out in a presentation for the *Arbeitskreis Semantic Web* and *ebSemantics* at the Austrian Federal Economic Chamber (Langegger 2007).

Because information integration is a rather large topic with many different directions and research fields, the aims of the presented work will be sketched by summarizing the following aspects and goals:

Flexibility and low entry cost – The system can be applied for a broad range of information integration scenarios and is very easy to setup. The mediator does not maintain a fixed global ontology, instead, *RDFStats* (a sub-project of SemWIQ) is used to fetch the required meta-data including statistics from registered data sources. Each data source may use any ontology to describe its data and the mediator is automatically loading published ontologies from the Web. Low entry costs are a very important aspect for the success of an innovation. Unfortunately, research projects very often do not address this aspect at all. It is possible to add a new data source within a very short time (hours–a day, depending on the size and complexity of the local schema and whether existing vocabularies can be used or have to be extended).

Virtual integration – The presented system is based on a *virtual* integration approach which means, that all data is retrieved and processed on-the-fly based on formalized schema mappings and a declarative query language. This approach is best suited for the integration of a large number of data-intensive information repositories as it is very common in science.

Distributed information systems – The system is capable of integrating distributed information systems. Several optimizations have already been implemented for the global query processing engine. Research in the fields of distributed query processing and parallel query processing may be integrated in future to improve the performance especially for costly join operations.

Heterogenous information systems – The presented system is basically designed to cope with all levels of heterogeneity described in Section 1.2. The existing implementation so far supports relational database systems, any ODBC-capable information system, and Microsoft Excel spreadsheets. In Chapter 10 it will be shown how new wrappers can be easily developed by implementing basic triple pattern matchers. The higher level operations of the query engine are already provided.

Leverage Semantic Web concepts – The proposed approach is fully compliant with the latest Semantic Web specifications. It will be shown, how information integration can be achieved based on a *RESTful*[2] architecture and open standards for expressive and extensible data representation developed by the Semantic Web community during the last years.

Holistic query processing approach – It is very important that the integration process is based on a holistic approach which enables the optimization of queries like in a database system

---

[2]REST is an acronym for *Representational State Transfer*, introduced by Roy Fielding in his doctoral dissertation (Fielding 2000). Roy was one of the principal authors of the HTTP specification. He had already envisioned that HTTP can be used as a light-weight communication protocol for loosely coupled distributed systems.

1 Introduction

and traditional mediator-wrapper systems. In order to achieve this, the system is based on the SPARQL algebra, which has been extended query federation. Thus, it is possible to adapt many optimization concepts from the database domain and apply them to distributed RDF graphs.

Performance and scalability – When creating an information integration system, performance is a very important factor for the success of the system, otherwise it will not be usable in real-world applications. Unfortunately, many prototypes which have been developed and announced in the Semantic Web community are nice and originally, but not usable in practice.

The *Resource Description Framework* (RDF) is a powerful and highly extensible data representation framework which is perfectly suited for the integration of data from different sources on the Web. Moreover, it provides the infrastructure for interlinking distributed information on the Web in a scalable manner as will be outlined in Chapter 4 and also in Section 8.1.1. In Section 12.2.3 of Part IV novel ways of navigation and information access based on *Web of Data* principals will be presented.

1.2 Challenges

Beside the challenges which all distributed systems have to cope with (like reliability, concurrency, security, resource discovery, provenance, etc.), the main challenge of information integration is to overcome the heterogeneity of the systems to integrate, especially when it comes to fully autonomous systems. Leser and Naumann (2007) classified different kinds of heterogeneity in information systems regarding the access interfaces and data representation. According to them, heterogeneity can be of syntactical, structural, schematic, or semantic nature and it may occur due to the usage of different metamodels (details will be discussed in Section 3.3.2). Usually, many of these aspects occur at once. If the system should provide a powerful interface, that is a declarative, parameterized query language, this makes a formalized approach and a holistic query processing workflow very difficult. Compared to the traditional data warehouse, the implementation of a virtual information integration system is much more demanding because all the transformation of data has to be performed on the fly. In order to do so, the system has to use formal mappings that support all levels of heterogeneity and maintain the original semantics as detailed as possible.

Several projects have been undertaken to address semantic information integration, especially in life sciences like biology, biomedicine, astronomy, etc. For some of the latest projects RDF and OWL ontologies have been used to integrate various distributed data sets (discussed in Section 7.3). However, many of the approaches have a processing pipeline which involves several transformation steps that have not been developed in a holistic way. Without a holistic query processing pipeline, the performance becomes often very bad, because operations like selections and joins cannot be executed directly in the source systems to benefit from index structures. To achieve an acceptable performance, the presented system has been designed in a holistic manner which enables the implementation of several optimization concepts from the database domain. Additional challenges are discussed in Section 3.3.

1.3 Outline of the Thesis

Apart from this introduction, the rest of the thesis is structured in four parts as outlined in Figure 1.1: *Background*, *Related Work*, *The SemWIQ Approach*, and *Results*. Each part consists of several chapters. Readers with a background in information integration can safely skip Chapter 3. Similarly, Chapter 4 may be skipped if the reader is already familiar with Semantic Web concepts.

The related work part is structured in an overview chapter, and two others. Chapter 6 is about fundamental concepts, introducing Gio Wiederhold's mediator-wrapper architecture and early projects of the nineties. In Chapter 7 some newer approaches are presented which are based on ontologies and Semantic Web concepts.

The approach developed as part of this thesis, is presented in Part III. The part is structured in an overview chapter and three other chapters describing the SemWIQ mediator, wrappers, and the RDF graph statistics and query pattern cardinality estimation component which is called RDFStats. The query processing approach is sketched in the overview chapter, details regarding query federation are given in Chapter 9 and details concerning the wrappers are provided in Chapter 10.

Part IV, finally, contains a demonstration of the integration system, the conclusion, and a chapter on future directions. In order to demonstrate the system, a case study has been developed in the area of solar observation. For the demo application several heterogeneous solar observation data sources have been integrated in order to provide a *Virtual Solar Observatory* as described in Chapter 12. For different example queries, the execution plans are printed and discussed.

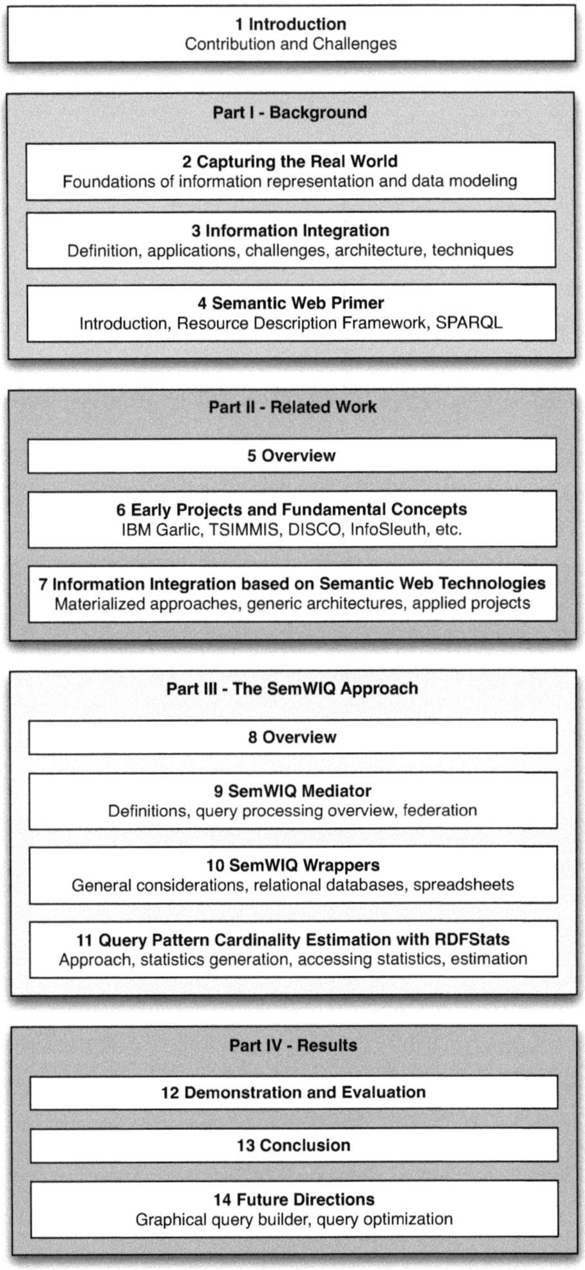

1 Introduction
Contribution and Challenges

Part I - Background

2 Capturing the Real World
Foundations of information representation and data modeling

3 Information Integration
Definition, applications, challenges, architecture, techniques

4 Semantic Web Primer
Introduction, Resource Description Framework, SPARQL

Part II - Related Work

5 Overview

6 Early Projects and Fundamental Concepts
IBM Garlic, TSIMMIS, DISCO, InfoSleuth, etc.

7 Information Integration based on Semantic Web Technologies
Materialized approaches, generic architectures, applied projects

Part III - The SemWIQ Approach

8 Overview

9 SemWIQ Mediator
Definitions, query processing overview, federation

10 SemWIQ Wrappers
General considerations, relational databases, spreadsheets

11 Query Pattern Cardinality Estimation with RDFStats
Approach, statistics generation, accessing statistics, estimation

Part IV - Results

12 Demonstration and Evaluation

13 Conclusion

14 Future Directions
Graphical query builder, query optimization

Figure 1.1: Thesis outline.

Part I

Background

2 Capturing the Real World

The subject of this chapter is a brief discussion on how information from the real world is captured and stored in IT systems and what the common features of heterogeneous data models are. It will not be an in-depth discussion of data modeling in general, since this can be found in most database textbooks such as Kemper and Eickler (2006) or UML modeling books. This chapter should help to get a better understanding of the basic problems with heterogeneity and semantic conflicts in particular.

2.1 Information and its Structure

Because in the following, the terms *data* and *information* will be used rather frequently and sometimes synonymously, a short definition follows. The popular *Data–Information–Knowledge–Wisdom*[1] (DIKW) pyramid is part of many standard textbook of information engineering and knowledge management. While *data* is considered as being in a raw, plain format (i.e. bits and bytes such as stored in a database system), *information* is acquired as soon as plain data gets some meaning. This can happen by explicitly knowing the meaning of some conceptual term or by deducing the meaning based on logical reasoning. In the context of an information system, the distinction depends on the perspective of the viewer and thus, the terms are often used synonymously in the literature. Generally, a machine cannot *understand* information and therefore any information to a machine is mere data. However, if a machine is able to act intelligently because it can interpret specific data correctly, mere data become information even to the machine. *Knowledge* is generated when the information is absorbed, remembered, and integrated into the current state of knowledge which may impose actions or manipulate the state of knowledge. Because expert systems use formal logics to represent data, the typical terminus is not information, but even *knowledge* (a specific model is further called knowledge base or just KB). *Wisdom* is created through the use of knowledge and reflection. It is not further used in the context of information systems, since machines are typically not really *understanding* their knowledge. While the distinction between data and knowledge is mostly clear, distinguishing between information and knowledge is still a subject of discussions among computer scientists.

---

[1] Although the author is not officially known, the origins go back to poet T.S. Eliot in 1934 and even to Frank Zappa's song *Packard Goose* in the album *Joe's Garage: Act II & III* (Tower Records, 1979). Other authors picked it up or invented it again: Harlan Cleveland (1982), Milan Zeleny (1987), and Russell L. Ackoff (1989) (Sharma 2008).

2.1.1 Unstructured Data, Structured Data, and Metadata

The process of capturing information which is generated in the *real world* and storing it in a digital system is hardly straight-forward. For instance, it heavily depends on the desired structural complexity, ranging from unstructured data (e.g. audio and video streams, raw data generated by scientific devices) over semi-structured data (e.g. HTML documents), to highly structured data (e.g. databases and knowledge bases). Additionally, information of the real world is heavily cross-linked. Storing this referential information *in-between* is difficult and not always possible. Today, structured data is typically stored in some sort of *relational database management system* (RDBMS). Other information systems include XML and object databases, expert systems, multimedia/video servers, document repositories, or some highly specific scientific data management systems like DNA databases for instance. The interfaces to information systems with natively expressive languages like SQL or XQuery are sometimes restricted by middleware components like Web services or through HTML forms which allow the execution of *canned queries* only.

Unstructured or raw data may also contain information which is important to an application. This information is commonly denoted as *metadata*. For instance, many multimedia files include file headers with metadata (e.g. MP3's ID3 tags). Metadata may be stored during the capturing (digitizing) process and possibly manually entered by humans, or they can be extracted later using feature extraction algorithms. In order to systematically access and process metadata, it has to be available in a materialized form and usually indexes are used like in a database system to optimize data access. Similarly, when storing plain texts, an information system may extract relevant keywords or even higher level entities occurring in the text (such as people, events, cities, etc.) and store them separately as metadata. Thus, depending on an application's requirements, more or less metadata is usually stored jointly with unstructured information assets.

2.1.2 Data Structures and Data Models

Digitally storing information requires the explicit understanding of common structures of *real world* entities and how to systematically classify and describe them. The more structure and semantics is required, the more expressive data models are needed. In this context, *structure* is regarded as the structure of the real world information which is important to users of the application. For example, the stock, customers, and sales of a subsidiary or the structure of a chemical molecule. For the purpose of this thesis, only structured data are relevant, although unstructured and semi-structured data can be integrated by SemWIQ via appropriate wrappers.

To systematically store structured data an innumerable amount of different concepts and algorithms have been developed by computer scientists and mathematicians, some of them already before there were any computers at all. At the data level, there are conceptual basic data structures like lists, sets, multisets (bags), stacks, queues, maps, trees, graphs, kinds of multi-dimensional structures, etc. each with a range of different actual implementations with varying algorithmic properties. The elements of these structures are typically a range of native data types and the possibility to add pointers which are references in memory basically. With these essentials and the possibility of recursively using these native data structures, it is already possible to store most kinds of information and in fact these are the underlying essentials used by all kinds of information systems.

With the introduction of data management systems, which are used to systematically store data with similar structures, the methodologies of storing structured data changed significantly. For example, when designing a relational database, a *data model* is created at a higher level which is already a bit closer to human understanding. While the *relational model* used by RDBMS is still not very intuitive to human understanding (for instance, so-called join tables are specific constructs to realize $n : m$-relationships), a conceptual model such as the *Entity-Relationship Model* (ER model) or the *Universal Modeling Language* (UML) are more apparent. Interestingly, all kinds of information systems share many commonalities regarding how they store structured data. These commonalities are based on human understanding and have already been explored by the ancient Greeks (*semiotics*). The process of finding an appropriate *data model* to represent real world data is known as *data modeling*.

2.2 Data Modeling

Several conceptual modeling languages exist, like the ER model or UML. To some certain extent, conceptual models can be automatically transformed by CASE (*Computer-Aided Software Engineering*) tools into the logical models used by specific applications and information systems. For example, an ER model can be transformed into the relational model and deployed in a relational database system. Because UML also allows to model behavioral aspects, a UML CASE tool may even generate the complete skeleton for a software program[2]. However, for most of the information systems, the resulting logical model has to be refined by the designer (at least index structures have to be created and tuned accordingly).

2.2.1 Metamodels and Information Representation

The concepts which can be applied to create a specific data model or schema can be abstracted into a *metamodel*. Typical metamodels have the following concepts: *classes*, *objects* (being instances of classes), *properties*, *data types*, possibly *functions* with *arguments*, and *relationship types* such as *is-a* or *part-of*, which can be applied to denote relations between classes. Some metamodels such as the ER model allow to denote *constraints* like for example cardinality constraints on relationships or set-

---

[2]While UML is heavily used for modeling software and also other processes, using it for automated model-driven software engineering is very controversial. UML tools require full support for reverse-engineering and may slow down the development process because of the growing complexity in practice. In fact, it depends on the kind of software whether CASE tools can be successfully applied or not.

2 Capturing the Real World

disjointness, which is often applied to sub-types in *is-a* relationships. Details about ER and UML can be found in text books such as (Kemper and Eickler 2006, Hernandez 2003) and will not be discussed any further.

In Table 2.1 some popular metamodels and similarities of their schema elements are shown. Basically, there are languages that define explicit schemas to which the actual data structure must adhere and on the opposite there are languages such as first-order logics, frame-based languages, and OWL, which just define the basic elements of the language and how they can be combined. However, instances can be created without an explicit schema. In case of RDF Schema and OWL, both approaches are valid: instances can either be explicitly typed, or they can be classified based on inference. Furthermore, RDF and OWL Full support meta modeling (Motik 2007): resources can be classes, properties, and instances of other classes at the same time.

Table 2.1: Similarities between various data or knowledge representation languages. Primitive data types such as strings, numbers, boolean values for the concrete description of entities or *things* are common to all languages.

Metamodel	Schema	Typing by	Concrete description	Associative description	Further features
ER model (databases)	explicit	relation	attribute	relationships	constraints, is-a, disjoint, etc.
UML (Software Engineering)	explicit	class	attribute	associations	methods, visibility, inheritance, etc.
First-order logic (AI, expert systems)	implicit	unary predicate	binary predicate	n-ary predicate	FOL assertions
Frame-based languages (AI)	prototype	frame	slot, facet	component relationships	methods
RDF Schema/OWL (Semantic Web)	implicit and explicit	class	datatype property	object property	DL assertions summarized in Section 4.3.2

OMG Meta Object Facility

While concrete data models are instances of their corresponding metamodel (e.g. a specific relation EMP is an instance of *relation*, which is an element of the relational model), the nature of a metamodel itself can be abstracted and metamodels can be seen as instances of a *meta-metamodel*. This sounds rather complex, but it helps to map and translate the primary elements between different metamodels. Already in the eighties, the American *Electronic Industries Association* started efforts, together with companies like IBM, Oracle, and Boeing, to enable the exchange of heterogenous models created with different CASE tools (Flatscher 2002). The former CDIF framework already introduced the four model levels M0–M3, which were later adopted in the OMG *Meta Object Facility* (MOF) depicted in Figure 2.1. The meta-metamodel defines the concepts available for creating metamodels.

2.2 Data Modeling

These metamodels in turn define the concepts required to create models and as long as pre-defined metamodel definitions are shared by the implementers of CASE tools, models can be exchanged as being instances of metamodels. For different subject areas such as conceptual data modeling, business process modeling, or data-flow modeling specific metamodels have been defined.

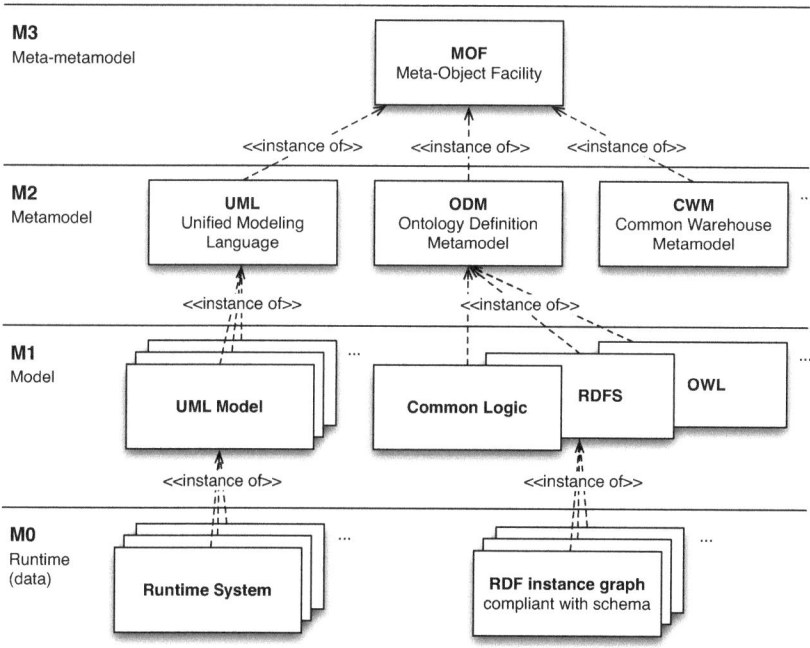

Figure 2.1: OMG Meta Object Facility (MOF).

When two or more information sources using different metamodels need to be integrated, one approach to bridge the data model heterogeneity can lead via the meta-metamodel and corresponding mappings. The levels in detail:

- Level M0 represents the runtime system of some application or the actual data of an information system as instances of the model in level M1.

- Level M1 represents the *model* of the application (e.g. a model as an instance of the UML metamodel) or the traditional *schema* of a database[3].

---
[3]Note that the term *model* in the software engineering and metamodeling domain is slightly different to the terminology in the database community where M1 is usually called *database schema* and M2 would be the *relational model* (a metamodel actually).

13

- Level M2 abstracts the concrete model of M1. It is called the *metamodel* because it represents a common, predefined *model* for the concrete *model* at M1 used to finally realize the concrete run-time system at level M0. This level is the key-level of the MOF. There are multiple pre-defined metamodels available in MOF like the UML, the *Ontology Definition Metamodel* (ODM), or the *Common Warehouse Metamodel* (CWM).
- Level M3 is the closure of the MOF. It features the MOF *meta-metamodel*, which provides a minimal, fixed set of concepts which allow the definition of metamodels at M2. The meta-metamodel is reflexive and defined by itself.

The key of the *Meta Object Facility* is the M3 meta-metamodel on top of different M2 metamodels. All the elements of M2 metamodels (e.g. classes, attributes, etc. – see Table 2.1 for similar metamodel elements) are described by the M3 meta-metamodel and thus, metamodels can be aligned. This mechanism allows to solve the data model heterogeneity to some certain extent. However, once the metamodels are aligned, traditional schema mapping tools are required to solve other levels of heterogeneity.

In practice there are many problems when using this metamodeling approach for information integration. Firstly, it requires that for each M2 metamodel used in the system, a corresponding mapping to a the M3 meta-metamodel exists. Secondly, the MOF-approach does not provide a solution to solve schematic heterogeneity: for example, if instances of one source have to be mapped to classes of another source which requires breaking the *instance-type dichotomy*.

2.2.2 Symbols, Concepts, and Real World Things

In order to introduce a meta-metamodel, similarities between different metamodels are essential. Fortunately, these similarities – as depicted in Table 2.1 – are not arbitrary. Things can be classified into groups of similar things (classes) and they can be described based on their properties. This is where the similarities are grounded. While for a database schema *attributes* are used, a UML domain model uses *properties* and predicate logics use *predicates*. The abstraction from real world things during the data modeling process is closely related to human perception of the world and semantics in communication.

The ancient roots of *semiotics*, which was founded in the 19th century as the *science of signs* by Charles Sanders Peirce et al., already dates back to Platon and Aristoteles. The idea of the *semiotic triangle* (depicted in Figure 2.2) is that there are *things* in the real world. When perceiving these things a thought is generated which is an abstract *concept* representing those things in our imagination. Things can be material or abstract. In order to communicate, we are using *symbols* (i.e. words) to denote things in the real world.

To run through an example, the English word *snow* (which may also be represented by a symbol) produces the corresponding thought or concept snow in our brain, which represents the snow we

2.2 Data Modeling

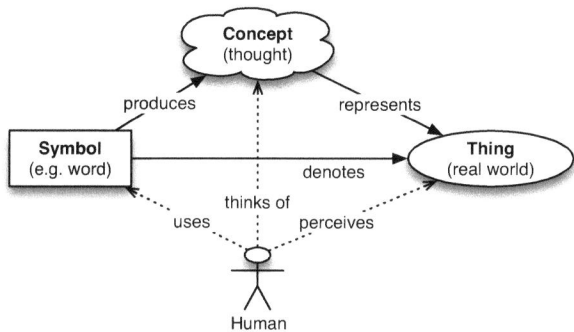

Figure 2.2: Semiotic triangle.

formerly perceived in the real world, i.e. *snow* denotes the wet white compound we can use for our snowball fights in winters.

Problems of semantic interoperability may arise in the following cases:

1. The receiver or user of the data model (can be a person trying to use a database which has been created by someone else) cannot decode the symbol, because he has never perceived the thing *snow* (he comes from a tropical region).

2. The receiver cannot decode the symbol, because he does not know the English language (although he would know the German word *Schnee*).

3. The receiver produced the wrong thought, because he was thinking of the stream-cipher called *SNOW*.

4. The receiver produced the wrong thought, because he could not disambiguate between the different meanings of the word *snow*.

Although the last two cases seam to be very similar, there is still a difference. While in case 4 the receiver could not get any result, in case 3 he got the wrong result.

A closely related and also important aspect is the *instance-type dichotomy*, which appears in most of the data models and information systems. Before it is discussed, a closer look at human perception follows.

Matching Things in the Real World

In the previous section the semiotic triangle was introduced and it was discussed how humans are using symbols to denote real world things. In Figure 2.2 arrows are shown representing the actions *denotes*, *produces*, and *represents*. In the following, the opposite process is discussed: how humans

2 Capturing the Real World

perceive things in the world and match them to previously defined symbols (the feedback loop of a learning process).

In fact, most of the symbols we are using are abstract classifiers that do not denote single things, rather *sets of similar things*: mammals, carnivores, tigers, bears, man, woman, employees, companies, etc. A simple example of such classifying sets is shown in Figure 2.3. Sets are depicted as elliptic shapes, instances are written in quotes and may be members of multiple sets. For instance, *Jim Smith* is a man and also *employee* (an instance of the abstract concept *employee*) at *Fun Corporation* (an instance of *company* or more specifically an *IT company*). It is important to differentiate between strict mathematical sets and sets of things matching a classifier symbol in human communication.

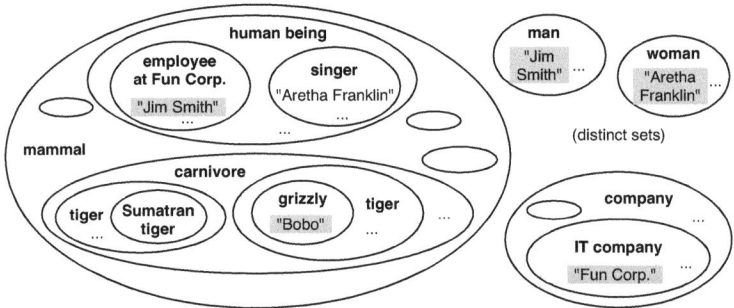

Figure 2.3: Example of classifying sets.

On the one hand we are able to abstract from real world things to *define* classifying symbols[4], and on the other hand we are able to match real world things to existing classifying symbols according to their shapes and specific properties we observe. Sometimes this matching process may even fail. For example when watching a cartoon, some unreal creature may look like something between a dog and a rabbit: we cannot actually find a match or we may have matched wrong (e.g. the artist's intension was a dog while we thought about a rabbit). A real world thing may be an instance of an unlimited set of possible classifiers. For example, Jim is not only employee at Fun Corporation, he is also a *man*, a *human being*, a *mammal, a man born in the year 1943*, etc. Not all of these classifiers can be depicted in a simple Venn diagram like shown in Figure 2.3. In fact, a Venn diagram is very limited. It does not allow to depict disjunctive sets like *the owner of a car*, which may be a *human being* OR a *company*. This set cannot be depicted in Figure 2.3.

The previous example contains many logical implications and constraints. Because Jim is a *man*, he cannot be a *woman* and it would be sufficient to state he is a *human*: we could then infer he is a *mammal* also, because all human beings are mammals. While Aristoteles called these logical connections *syllogisms*, today we have very powerful mathematically founded logical frameworks which

---

[4]In real life this defining process hardly occurs. In fact, it would require us to find some unexplored species or invent something. However, when creating data models or programming we often require some very specific identifiers.

16

2.2 Data Modeling

can be used for automated reasoning. A logical framework may help us to check our information for consistency, but also to derive information to make machines more intelligent and significantly improve their usability.

Instance-Type Dichotomy

By contrast to human communication, information systems use strict classes with sharp boundaries. Although fuzzy logic methodologies can be used to integrate probabilities and confidence, regarding the interpretation of information, there is no room for paraphrasing or pragmatics. Compared to human understanding, the set of classes in a data model is very small. Actually, it is minimally small and includes only those classes which are required to fulfill the requirements of the application. In case of an expert system application the set of classes is typically higher than in case of a database system which use strict schemas.

The semiotic triangle shown in Figure 2.4 has slightly been modified to depict the relationship between named elements of a data model (e.g. relation names) and its *intension* and *extension* (Leser and Naumann 2007). Regardless of the data model, we use names to denote concepts which we intend to represent real world things in our application. This can be either nouns, but also verbs or adjectives and sometimes identifiers are just abstract letters (e.g. in many Prolog programs). Letters have no semantic information at all and some documentation will be required to interpret such a model. A name is supposed to generate semantically equivalent *thoughts* for all people working with this particular model.

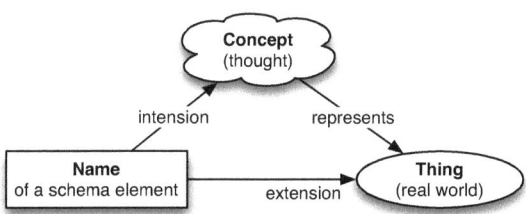

Figure 2.4: Extension and intension of names in a model.

In Figure 2.4 the concept is denoted as the *intension* of the name. It is, what the author of the model intended to denote when choosing the name. The set of real world objects (either the complete set in the world or the sub-set represented in the information system), is called the *extension* of the name.

In many data models, the set of intensions and the union of all extensions are mutually exclusive. This bipartition is often referred to as the *instance-type dichotomy*. In this case, an element in the information system cannot be an intensional concept *and* an instance at the same time. For example, in a relational database system, concepts represented by tables and tuples are mutually disjoint. Similarly, attribute names and tuple values are mutually disjoint. This bipartition is also a characteristic of first-order logics, description logics, and hence OWL-DL ontologies (see Section 4.3). However, it does not apply to plain RDF graph and OWL Full. Reflexive data models with unique identification of elements do not have this dichotomy. Instances of an RDF graph can also be classes of other instances at the same time.

If the instance-type-dichotomy applies to a model, it is usually difficult to address schematic heterogeneity if two or more information systems need to be integrated. To give an example, the following database models are considered:

1. In an encyclopedia about historic Audi models, different car models are stored as tuples (instances) *A3*, *A4*, *TT*, etc. in a table named `cars`.

2. An Audi dealer stores all the cars he offers and sells as instances of several database tables `a3`, `a4`, `tt`, etc.

Although the stored information contains common concepts, the data models follow two different approaches: while for the encyclopedia, the car model and its attributes (horse power, fuel consumption, seats, etc.) are of major interest, for the dealer all further instances of a specific model and their attributes (horse power, seats, age, kilometer reading, condition, etc.) are of interest. Despite there is only a small semantic overlap regarding the attributes (horse power, seats), the real problem is the schematic heterogeneity. Usually, it depends on the subject of discourse, whether to model things as intentional concepts (types) or instances. Many existing information integration systems do not support formal mappings to overcome schematic heterogeneity. Furthermore, it is impossible to solve, if the instance-type dichotomy applies for the target metamodel.

Singletons and Domain of Discourse

In some cases, real world things may behave as singletons: they do not have further instances, they are just the only instance representing a single real world thing. Such examples are *god*, *earth*, or *snow*. However, if the context or *universe of discourse* is changed, even these singletons may become concepts with further instances: there may be none or multiple gods in other religions. In the context of a science fiction novel there may be more then one earth and Eskimos use a large number of different kinds of *snow*.

3 Information Integration

Developing an information integration system is often a task within an interdisciplinary setting and a broad range of different areas in computer science have to be covered. The research areas relevant for this dissertation have been visualized in Figure 3.1. They include distributed systems, mediator-wrapper systems, distributed query processing, metamodeling, and model mapping. Ontologies and description logics provide an alternative global metamodel to traditional relational schemas of database-centric systems. On the right hand side of the picture, Semantic Web related fields of research are depicted. They include SPARQL query processing, generation and maintenance of RDF statistics and histograms, linked data as well as ontology-specific model mapping. The core concepts of the Semantic Web will be discussed in Chapter 4 and as part of the presentation of SemWIQ in Part III. The importance of information integration today has already been pointed out during the introduction. As part of the background of this thesis an introduction into information integration seems to be evident.

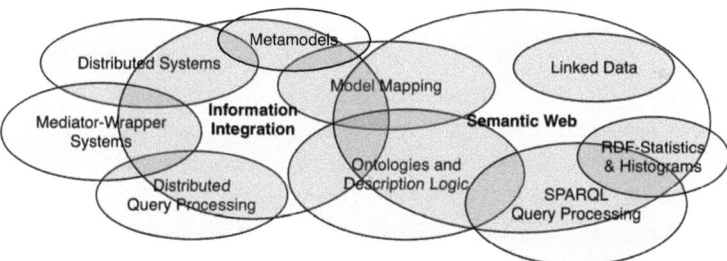

Figure 3.1: Related fields of research.

3.1 Definition of Information Integration

Information integration is the process of enabling transparent access to multiple heterogenous, distributed information systems. Because the most important application field is in business informatics, nearly all definitions in the literature directly relate to *Enterprise Information Integration* (EII). According to Alon Halevy, who is one of the protagonists in this research field, "The vision underlying this industry (EII) is to provide tools for integrating data from multiple sources without having to first load all the data into a central warehouse" (Halevy et al. 2005). Following from that, data warehousing and information integration are considered to be distinct approaches. However, nowadays such a clear separation has become difficult. After the battle between DWH and EII solutions during the nineties, many data warehouses now have support for virtual data integration (*Virtual Data Warehouses*, VDWs) and EII solutions support materialization and integrate DWH features. According to Halevy et al. (2005), successful EII systems have reached the markets in the late 1990's whereas data warehouses (DWH) have already been commonly used by enterprises. It is evident, that without the fast expansion of the internet bandwidth, EII would not have been able to compete with DWH solutions.

Studying the literature, it seems there is no clear distinction between data and information integration. Both terms are frequently used synonymously as pointed out in Section 2.1. But it can be observed that *information integration* has been used more frequently during the last years and also the term *Enterprise Information Integration* prefers *information* over *data*. It obviously shows, that the focus in traditional data integration starting in the database community three decades ago, has shifted to a better understanding of the actual data.

3.2 Applications of Information Integration Technology

There are several reasons why the integration of information systems is gaining more and more importance today. During the last decades, businesses and also research organizations have developed IT systems rather autonomously based on very specific application requirements. With the growing importance of corporate IT infrastructures, companies began either to migrate or integrate isolated systems into common enterprise IT systems. The spreading of the World Wide Web enabled totally new business opportunities and outlets (e.g. E-Commerce, E-Procurement, etc.) as well as new business models (e.g. *Software-as-a-Service*). Additional needs require the development of new software systems and because software development is a rather costly effort, those new systems still have to work with legacy information systems. Furthermore, mergers and acquisitions require the migration or integration of foreign IT systems into corporate IT infrastructures. As a consequence, information integration has become one of the most important factors in enterprise IT of today. Indeed, EII is just one part of the efforts undertaken to make heterogenous systems work together. Especially within business IT, the generic term for these efforts is called *Enterprise Application Integration* (EAI).

However, information integration is not only an important task in businesses and enterprise IT. It is also a very important requirement for global scientific collaboration today. Compared to business IT, the data models and affordances within research are often much more complex and demanding, especially within life sciences. For instance, managing information of bio-medical research requires a very high level of semantic expressiveness. It is very important that the software is able to understand[1] as well as possible what researchers in the past or at different locations have already found out and provide rich user interfaces to support the collaboration process across institutional boundaries. In scientific information systems, it is also very usual to use inference engines to derive new facts out of the existing facts gathered so far. Developing such specialized knowledge-based systems is a complex process which usually takes a long time and costs a lot of money. Scientific information systems are also very heterogenous and even more difficult to integrate. In this regard, they just obey the same rules than other IT developments: they are usually developed autonomously and if no appropriate standards exist (the more specific, the less the chance), they grow in isolation.

While there exist many highly-specific and complex scientific information systems, there are also many research-targeted IT systems which have been developed by the researchers themselves. For example, MySQL databases or directories of ordinary text files in which results of research experiments are stored. These ad-hoc setups and sometimes quite inconsistent prototypes, have often grown to significant large data repositories and essential applications. Using the information stored in those systems with state-of-the-art applications requires a lot of work transforming data and migrating applications. Because a complete migration and re-implementation is too expensive, it is often preferred to virtually integrate legacy systems. Similarly, within enterprises a complete rewrite of applications is often impossible at all because customers and partners still need to use those legacy applications. The only way to access and use the information from these heterogeneous, isolated systems is *information integration*.

Today even *personal information integration* is an issue with growing importance (Franklin et al. 2005). Current research efforts towards semantic desktop solutions, like the EU-funded Nepomuk project (Groza et al. 2007) indicate this. In spring 2009, Leo Sauermann, one of the principal project leaders of the Nepomuk project has founded a startup company in Vienna. Although semantic desktop technology may benefit from the presented approach in some way, it is not discussed further in this thesis.

3.3 Challenges

The main challenges for information integration are the orthogonal aspects of *distribution*, *heterogeneity*, and *autonomy* depicted in Figure 3.2. The three aspects will be discussed in this section based on Özsu and Valduriez (1999) and Leser and Naumann (2007). Within all these dimensions different problems will occur during the integration process. Although they are basically independent of each other, there are correlations. For instance, the higher the autonomy of two or more information sources, the higher is usually the level of distribution and heterogeneity.

---

[1] In the sense of acting intelligently by interpreting additional information represented as logical facts and rules and defining the semantics of data.

3 Information Integration

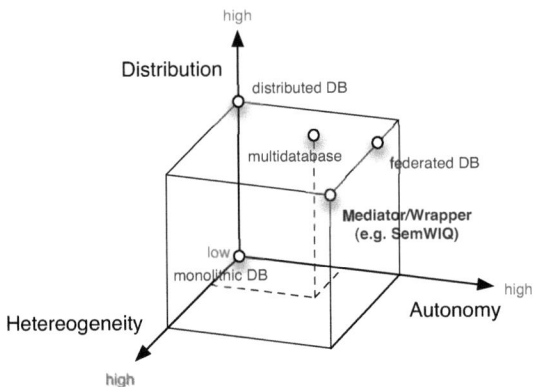

Figure 3.2: Orthogonal aspects of information integration, derived from Özsu and Valduriez (1999).

In the figure several labels for typical information integration architectures are shown. Classical monolithic databases are located at the origin of the graph. No integration is happening at all, but it could have happened before feeding data into the monolithic system like it is the case for a data warehouse where information is extracted, loaded, and transformed (ETL process) into the monolithic warehouse. On the way out of the graph to the highest level of distribution, heterogeneity, and autonomy there are architectures like distributed databases, multi-databases, federated databases which are all out of scope. Based on the aims sketched in the introduction, only the mediator-wrapper architecture is of interest. In the following, all three dimensions of the graph will be discussed with a special focus on the mediator-wrapper case. The architecture itself will be explained in Section 6.1 of Part II.

3.3.1 Distribution

When dealing with information integration it is obvious that information is distributed. Information can be *logically* or *physically* distributed. Throughout this work it is assumed, information is physically distributed at a high level (at least regionally and even globally). In order to deliver information, data has to be localized and transmitted from remote information systems to the user. The localization of data sources can be achieved very easily based on DNS and URIs. To provide the transparency required for the virtual approach some sort of registry catalog is required.

Transmitting data is costly because WAN bandwidth is many times smaller than LAN or even internal data bus bandwidth (e.g. 2–6 Mbit/s WAN vs. 100–1,000 Mbit/s LAN vs. 6,399 Mbit/s 100 MHz-PCI which are factors of approximately 1 : 100 : 1000). The I/O throughput of secondary storage devices (i.e. harddisks, ≈100 MB/s) which is a major factor in monolithic database systems is still very high compared to WAN bandwidth (approximately 200 : 1). Especially when distributed information needs to be joined, the shipping costs become even worse. Joining and combining data requires to transfer all relevant data which needs to be compared to one or the other host. As a consequence, regarding the query processor's implementation and the optimizer's cost model different heuristics and metrics have to be used compared to local query processing.

Autonomous distributed information systems may lead to inconsistent states caused by duplicates and ambiguous information. Some systems allow to impose some final consistency constraints to the integrated data. Their validity can then be checked when data is delivered.

There are many other issues which need to be addressed when implementing a distributed system. These include problems of (un-)availability, concurrency, and security issues. They will not be discussed in this context. SemWIQ addresses ad-hoc unavailability of data sources and is implemented in a multi-threaded style in order to process concurrent queries. A basic level of security can be achieved through HTTP Authentication and Transport Layer Security (SSL/TLS).

Because of the existing internet infrastructure and middleware like the OSI layer protocols, Web services, etc. it has become easier to implement a distributed system. Thus, many general issues arising when dealing with distributed systems will be ignored in this context. Further challenges of distributed systems and their solutions have been discussed in (Coulouris et al. 2005).

3.3.2 Heterogeneity

Heterogeneity is probably the most difficult part to deal with. As explained in the previous chapter, capturing the real world and storing information systematically in an IT system requires *data modeling*. Systematically storing means, that the structure of the information to store is somehow represented in the digital data representation (implicit or explicit schema) which enables a more systematic access to the data by means of a query language.

Depending on the scenario and requirements, different information systems are used with different metamodels (a) and different models (b) are typically used to describe similar domains of the real world. Each different model (b) is an instance of a metamodel (a). Leser and Naumann (2007) have classified different kinds of heterogeneity in information systems:

1. **technical heterogeneity** of interfaces to the information systems (full SQL access, *canned queries*, simple keyword search, etc.)

2. **syntactical heterogeneity**, e.g. incompatible character sets or different representation of logically equal data values (usually easy to cope with by appropriate conversion functions)

3. **heterogeneity of metamodels** used to represent the concrete data models or schemas (relational model, XML, spreadsheets, RDF, etc.)

4. **structural heterogeneity**, i.e. heterogeneity between concrete instances of a data model (e.g. different database schemas for similar application domains)

5. **schematic heterogeneity** occurs if different schema elements (e.g. relational model: relation, attribute, tuple) are used to model the same concept; this is also a problem in first order predicate logic based information integration systems

6. **semantic heterogeneity,** which occurs if the intensions and/or extensions of the same concept are not in sync across different information systems

Until now, mainly aspects 1–5 have been addressed especially in the database community. Research in this area was traditionally known as *schema management*, which involves *schema matching* (the process or finding equivalent or corresponding elements between schemata) and *schema mapping* (the specification and evaluation of these mappings at runtime). A basic introduction into these techniques will be given in Section 3.5.

To solve issues of *semantic heterogeneity*, ontologies have been used since the nineties to explicitly describe the semantics of the integrated information. More recent approaches are based on the Semantic Web, which enables the setup of a distributed ontological framework based on the Web. Furthermore, description logics such as OWL DL and rules are used in the Semantic Web to enable inference and to provide an even better understanding of the information.

Also the third aspect, *metamodel heterogeneity*, is still an important research topic. Research in this area started in the 90ies in the area of mediator-wrapper systems (Wiederhold 1992). In general, the more of the heterogeneity aspects apply to an application, the more sophisticated methodologies are required and the higher a system has to be ranked on the heterogeneity axis in Figure 3.2. In Section 3.5 a basic introduction into schema and ontology mapping is provided and in Section 8.1.1 it will be demonstrated why RDF is well suited as the global data model for an information integration system such as SemWIQ.

3.3.3 Further Aspects

Beside the main aspects of *distribution*, *heterogeneity*, and *autonomy* there are a few other general aspects of information integration systems which are enumerated in short:

Required level of semantic expressiveness and accuracy – This usually depends on the target application scenario and compared to EII, the required semantic expressiveness is often higher in a scientific application. The semantic expressiveness can be improved by the introduction of more specific relationship and property types (e.g. functional, transitive, symmetric, inverse functional) as well as constraints on values, cardinalities, relationships, and generic rules (see OWL description logic, which is explained in Section 4.3).

Required level of transparency – Another aspect concerns the extent to which the integrated system hides the details of the source systems. While some systems hide the complete details of concrete data sources at query time, other systems are more similar to multi-database systems and require explicit addressing of integrated data sources within queries. Common to all approaches is transparency regarding technical interfaces and location.

Read-only vs. propagation of updates over integrated data sources – For an integrated information system it makes a big difference if information is only integrated for the purpose of transparent query access, or if it should also be possible to manipulate information. If updates are required it also means that the system must support some sort of distributed transaction management. Furthermore, a storage and replication manager has to decide at which data source new information should be stored.

Materialized vs. virtual integration approach – Finally, the integrated information can either be loaded into a central store (e.g. data warehouse) or it can be integrated on-the-fly when a query is executed (virtual integration). This aspect is mentioned for completeness. The topic of this thesis is about virtual integration.

A data warehouse is the typical approach for materialized integration of data from various sources. Because all information is available at a central point, the system can much better react on arbitrary user queries against the integrated information set. Furthermore, this enables the application of *Business Intelligence* (BI) and *Online Analytical Processing* (OLAP), which today are essential requirements within large enterprises. However, the data set in a data warehouse is possibly not always up-to-date. A data warehouse also requires a large amount of storage capacity and substantial computational power. In many cases, the virtual integration approach is better suited, although it involves federation of queries and costly shipping of data across the internet.

Depending on all of these aspects and specific requirements of a situation, a range of different architectures has been presented by Leser and Naumann (2007). They include monolithic database systems, distributed databases, multidatabase systems, federated database systems, mediator-wrapper systems, and peer data management systems. In the context of this thesis only the mediator-wrapper architecture is relevant. The fundamental concept of mediators are described in the related work part, in Section 6.1.

3.4 Typical Architecture of Information Integration Systems

A general architectural overview of information integration systems is presented in Figure 3.3. The depicted architecture is a bit more detailed than reference architectures found in the literature such as (Özsu and Valduriez 1999, Leser and Naumann 2007). The following components are common to all systems:

- a central access *interface*, which is used by applications of the integrated system either via an interoperable middleware (ODBC, Web Service, SPARQL, etc.) or API

3 Information Integration

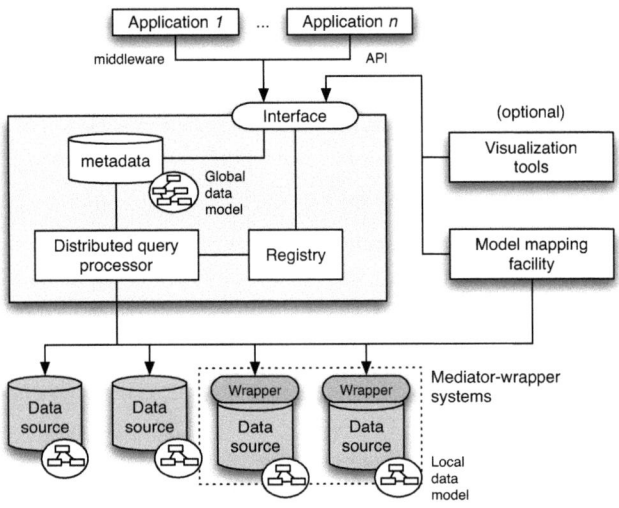

Figure 3.3: Common architecture of information integration systems.

- a central *metadata catalog* (or knowledge base in case of ontology-based systems) storing the *global data model*, which can be either explicitly defined and maintained or implicitly as the union of all local data models. Typically, the metadata catalog also stores statistics such as selectivities or histograms.

- a *query processor*, which is responsible for federation, optimization, and execution of queries issued to the system

- a *registry* component for the registration and de-registration of data sources (typically the registration requires metadata about the source and a model mapping to be submitted)

- in case of mediator systems, *wrappers* are attached to data sources. As will be explained later, they are used to solve technical and metamodel heterogeneity. Depending on the mapping approach, wrappers may additionally tackle other levels of heterogeneity (Sect. 3.5).

Optionally, an information integration system may integrate a model mapping facility, supporting the model mapping task with a GUI and related features such as model matching, data inspection, and cleansing. Some systems also provide a graphical data explorer, query results browser, and other kinds of visualization tools.

Finally, beside these components, a mediator-wrapper based information integration system which addresses metamodel heterogeneity is additionally characterized by

- the *global metamodel* used – Basically the expressiveness of the global metamodel should be as powerful as the local metamodel with the highest expressiveness. But there are also other factors such as the intended target applications and use cases. For example, if only keyword search is required over the integrated data sources, the global metamodel may also be simpler (e.g. just a flat full-text index) than the local metamodels.

- the *global query language* used to formulate global queries – The query language is tightly coupled with the global metamodel. For example, in case of a relational global metamodel the global query language will probably by SQL and in case of RDF, SPARQL would be a good choice.

- the *interface and protocol between wrappers and the mediator* – Based on the query execution approach information integration systems use different strategies to delegate sub-queries to wrappers. For example, in case of Garlic (Carey et al. 1995) the protocol is fine-grained because it is based on algebraic operators. Sub-plans are compiled dynamically by wrappers based on high-level operators created by the mediator. In case of SemWIQ, the protocol is rather coarse-grained since it is based on SPARQL itself.

3.5 Introduction to Model Mapping

Heterogeneity between different concrete models can be solved with *model mapping* techniques. Because a complete overview of existing approaches would be out of scope, only some examples and the fundamental concept are explained. In the database community this field is traditionally called *schema mapping* and regarding ontology-based systems, similar approaches are known on *ontology mapping* (Staab and Studer 2004, Predoiu et al. 2006). The specification of correspondences between different model elements is very similar for different metamodels. Thus, in the following the term *model mapping* will be used to refer to all kinds of similar techniques. Analogous examples for the database domain can be found in (Leser and Naumann 2007).

An important concept in model management is the concept of *mappings*, which relate elements of one model to elements of another model based on their intensional equivalence. Such a mapping is a set of *correspondences* between model elements of the source and the target model. The methodologies of model management are very difficult to formalize in the general case. According to Leser and Naumann (2007, Section 5.1.3), after thirty years of research in the area of database schema management, there is still no methodology flexible enough to be able to cope with all possible mapping

3 Information Integration

situations and heterogeneity aspects. For example, it is not trivial to formulate a mapping from a class of one model to an instance of another model because of the *instance-type dichotomy* discussed in Section 2.2.2.

An overview of a mapping framework is depicted in Figure 3.4: the manually or (semi-) automatically defined *correspondences* are interpreted as a *logical mapping* from the source to the target model by the runtime system. When a query according to the target model (e.g. a virtual global model) is issued, the system uses the logical mapping to *generate local queries* and to transform all source data accordingly.

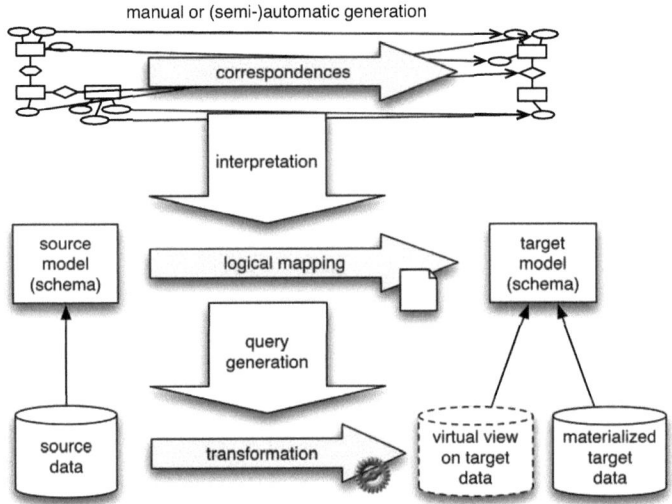

Figure 3.4: Model mapping overview (based on Leser and Naumann (2007)).

In case of metamodel heterogeneity, there are two approaches depicted in Figure 3.5.

Two-phase approach: In the first step, a straight-forward mapping is applied possibly based on a metamodel framework such as the OMG *Meta Object Facility*, which has been described in Section 2.2.1. The metamodeling approach maps the elements of different metamodels (M2) to a common meta-metamodel (M3). However, since the metamodeling approach only aligns models at the metamodel level, in the second step the remaining levels of heterogeneity have to be solved using schema or ontology mapping techniques. The approach is depicted in Figure 3.5(a) and an graphical example mapping is depicted in Figure 3.6.

Direct or single-phase approach: Specification of a dedicated formal mapping framework for specific pairs of metamodels. For instance, XML-to-RDF, SQL-to-RDF, Spreadsheets-to-RDF, etc. This approach is typically more efficient since at runtime, the translation process can be done within a single phase. Other levels of heterogeneity can be solved in the same step. The runtime system can better exploit existing index structures and capabilities of the underlying information system. The approach has been chosen by Chris Bizer and Richard Cyganiak (2006) for the D2RQ-Map wrapper. This approach is depicted in Figure 3.5(b) and a corresponding D2RQ example mapping is shown in Figure 10.2 on page 168.

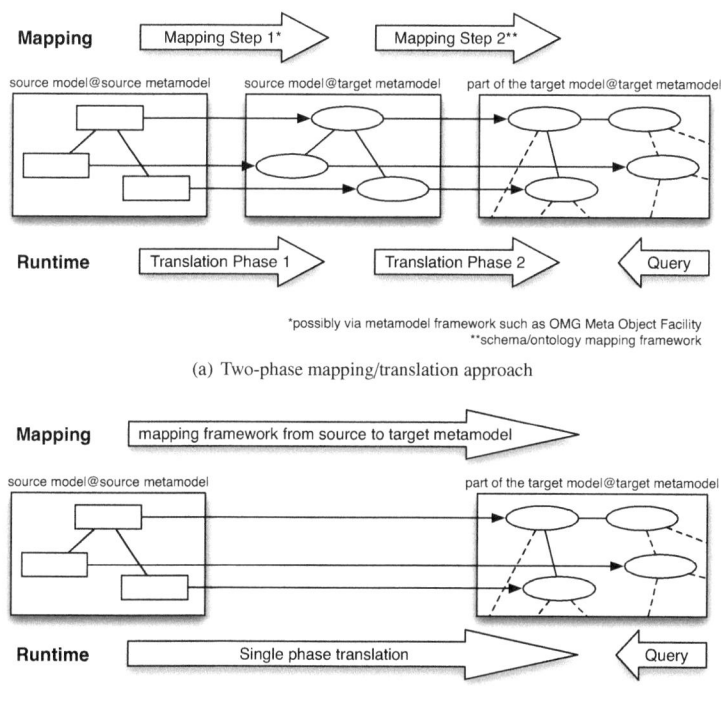

(a) Two-phase mapping/translation approach

(b) Direct or single-phase mapping/translation approach

Figure 3.5: Different mapping approaches addressing metamodel heterogeneity.

3.5.1 Integrated Global Model

Depending on the application scenario, it may be necessary to create a global integrated model based on a given set of source systems to be integrated. While some systems require the explicit definition of the integrated model, other systems are more flexible – SemWIQ, the integration system developed as

3 Information Integration

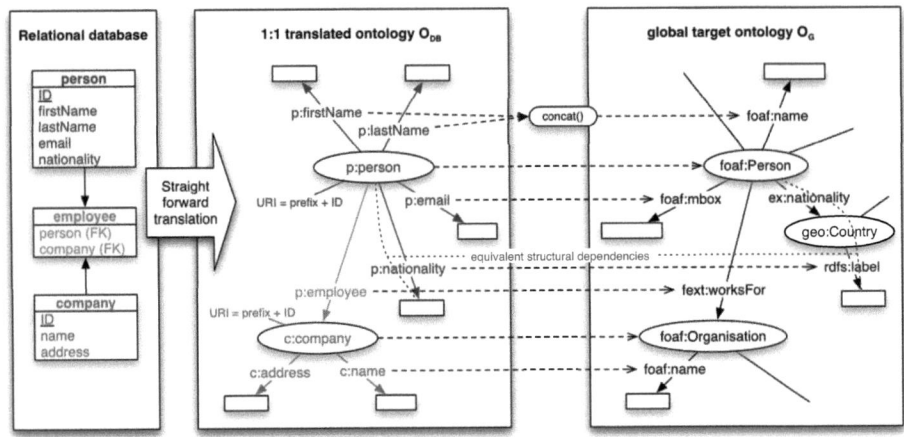

Figure 3.6: Two-phase mapping from a relational database to a target ontology.

part of this work is one of them. In case of SemWIQ, the global ontology is dynamically composed by the source systems. Otherwise, different methodologies exist to support the process of generating an integrated model based on several input models (Batini et al. 1986, Spaccapietra et al. 1992, Schmitt and Saake 2005). In most cases they are also based on correspondences. The global model has to be expressive enough to represent the information from all data sources.

An integrated system with one global target model and n source models requires n logical mappings. The inverse mappings are not required because the information flow is typically unidirectional: from all the sources to the integrated virtual model. A mediator-wrapper system usually does not support the manipulation of data.

3.5.2 Generation and Representation of Mappings

A logical mapping is either created manually or semi-automatically using *schema* or *ontology matching* algorithms. Such algorithms can also be used to facilitate the creation of the integrated global model. They are based on lexical similarity matching (e.g. *Levenshtein* metric, *n-gram models*, phonetic algorithms), graph-based matching such as similarity flooding proposed by Melnik et al. (2001), and may also use taxonomies and thesauri of specific domains. Because the algorithms are based on heuristics, a fully automatic approach does not work precisely enough. One of the first tools supporting a semi-automatic mapping approach for at least relational databases and XML document was *IBM Clio* (Haas et al. 2005). While Clio was a research project at the IBM Almaden research center started in 1999 in cooperation with the University of Toronto, its capabilities have been integrated into *IBM Rational Data Architect*. Model mapping is a very complex process which requires a lot of experience by the data architect.

The term *model mapping* has basically two meanings: on the one hand, it is the process of creating mappings after matching the elements of two different source models. On the other hand, it denotes the set of correspondences which are created as a result.

The formal representation of correspondences or of the logical mapping, respectively, actually depends on the meta-models and the capabilities of the integration system as a whole. A formal approach has been proposed by Legler (2005). In the case of relational databases, the mapping language can be SQL since the mappings can be represented as SQL views. In order to overcome schematic heterogeneity extensions may be necessary in order to allow querying the database metadata catalog with SQL. IBM Clio is able to generate corresponding SQL queries, XQueries, and XSLT code based on logical mappings. Another mapping language will be discussed in Section 10.2 where D2RQ-Map will be described. D2RQ-Map is the mapping language used by D2R-Server for mapping from the relational model to RDF. D2R-Server is used by SemWIQ as a wrapper for relational databases. Another mapping representation which has been developed as part of a spreadsheet wrapper called XLWrap will be described in Section 10.3 of Part III.

Once, the mappings have been created, they can be used during the query execution process to transform data accordingly. Of course, they can also be used to dump all source data for materialization into an integrated storage. However, in this case a formal mapping approach would not have been necessary. The traditional ETL (*extract-transform-load*) process could have been applied instead. In case of virtual integration, a query processor accepts a global query, interprets the mappings accordingly to formulate local queries or to execute local API calls and to transform the source data into the global data model.

3.5.3 Interpretation of Mappings Based on Logical Views

At runtime a query processor may use different techniques in order to interpret mappings and generate a global query plan which is capable of answering a given query. Typically, the specified mappings are compiled into *views*, which can be evaluated by the query processor by *unfolding* or *rewriting* (Ullman 2000, Lenzerini 2002). In the following two approaches called *Local-as-View* (LaV) and *Global-as-View* (GaV) will be discussed.

Lenzerini (2002) describes a data integration system $\mathcal{T}$ formally as a triple $\langle \mathcal{G}, \mathcal{S}, \mathcal{M} \rangle$ with

- $\mathcal{G}$, the *global schema* expressed in a language $\mathcal{L}_\mathcal{G}$ over an alphabet $\mathcal{A}_\mathcal{G}$, which consists of symbols for schema elements in $\mathcal{G}$[2]

---
[2]This definition is not restricted to the relational model, i.e. an RDF-based integration system would use RDF concepts such as classes, properties, and data types as schema elements.

- $\mathcal{S}$, the *source schema* expressed in a language $\mathcal{L}_S$ over alphabet $\mathcal{A}_S$, which includes symbols for the elements of all sources

- $\mathcal{M}$, the mapping between $\mathcal{G}$ and $\mathcal{S}$ expressed in the form of *assertions*[3]:
$$q_S \leadsto q_\mathcal{G} \text{ and } q_\mathcal{G} \leadsto q_S$$

Although there are actually multiple sources and, hence, source schemata, the definition of Lenzerini (2002) uses combined sets for $\mathcal{S}$, $\mathcal{L}_S$, and the source schema alphabet $\mathcal{A}_S$, which contains unique symbols for all source schema elements.

The assertions q_S and $q_\mathcal{G}$ can be formulated as queries over the source schema $\mathcal{S}$ and the global schema $\mathcal{G}$, respectively, expressed in the query languages $\mathcal{L}_{M,S}$ over the alphabet $\mathcal{A}_S$ and $\mathcal{L}_{M,\mathcal{G}}$ over the alphabet $\mathcal{A}_\mathcal{G}$. An assertion of the form $q_S \leadsto q_\mathcal{G}$ states that the concept represented by q_S over the sources corresponds to the global concept represented by $q_\mathcal{G}$ (and vice versa for $q_\mathcal{G} \leadsto q_S$).

Global queries are formulated in a global query language $\mathcal{L}_Q$ over the global schema alphabet $\mathcal{A}_\mathcal{G}$. Apart from this generic definition, the nature of a specific integration system depends on the expressiveness and characteristics of the mapping, schemata, and query languages. A detailed formalization of the semantics of information systems can be found in (Lenzerini 2002). From a logical point of view, answering a global query is in fact a logical implication problem. The system has to produce result tuples which satisfy the global query by logically combining intermediate tuples from a range of sources based on the mapping. Special care is required if an information system enforces additional global constraints. If the information system integrates data from autonomous sources, global constraints may lead to unanswerable queries (Lin and Mendelzon 1998).

Local-as-View

In a *Local-as-View* (LaV) based information integration system, the mapping $\mathcal{M}$ contains assertions of the form
$$s \leadsto q_\mathcal{G}$$
which means, that *single* elements of the source schema are described in terms of a global query (view) over possibly multiple global concepts. Formally, the language $\mathcal{L}_{M,S}$ is restricted to expressions constituted by only one symbol from $\mathcal{A}_S$.

The LaV approach is well suited, when the global data model (and therefore $\mathcal{A}_\mathcal{G}$) is already defined and stable. Adding a new data source is just a matter of adding additional assertions. None of the existing assertions has to be changed. However, query processing based on the LaV approach is substantially more challenging than the GaV approach as shown by Ullman (2000). In order to evaluate queries in LaV based information integration systems such as *Information Manifold* (Kirk et al. 1995), it is required to synthesize a feasible query plan using query containment algorithms which are generally NP-complete.

---

[3] In this context, *assertions* conform to *correspondences* described in Section 3.5.

Global-as-View

In information integration systems following the *Global-as-View* (GaV) approach the mapping $\mathcal{M}$ contains assertions of the form

$$g \rightsquigarrow q_S$$

which means, that *single* elements of the global schema are described in terms of source queries (views) over possibly multiple source concepts. Formally, the language $\mathcal{L}_{\mathcal{M},\mathcal{G}}$ is restricted to expressions constituted by only one symbol from $\mathcal{A}_\mathcal{G}$.

In case of the GaV approach, query processing is just a matter of unfolding views based on the mapping which is straight forward since the assertions already contain source sub-plans q_S. The resulting query plan just has to be simplified after unfolding. However, the downside of the typical GaV approach is its inflexibility. By contrast to the LaV approach, if a new data source is added, it is usually required to update some of the existing assertions.

Most of the existing information integration systems are based on some sort of GaV approach. Also for the SemWIQ integration system a GaV approach is used. Since SemWIQ is based on federated ontologies published on the Web and RDF-wrappers placed directly at the data sources, there is no need to explicitly update any global assertions when adding and removing sources.

Some Notes on Structural Heterogeneity

If there exists a high degree of structural heterogeneity between two data models, which is often the case when XML data is involved, it may be difficult for the mapping framework to create a valid query (e.g. XQuery) based on the defined value correspondences. To give an example, two differently structured XML models are depicted in Figure 3.7. On the left hand side, several companies are listed with employees in a sub structure and on the right hand side, persons are listed with companies in a sub structure. At runtime, the wrapper has to create the correct XQuery as shown in Listing 3.1 in order to correctly transform data between those models.

In such situations the mapping facility may allow or even require partly hard-coded, procedural assertions and let the user specify concrete (sub) queries (e.g. XQuery statements) instead of specifying correspondences. A similar case is a mapping from arbitrary spreadsheet representations to an RDF domain ontology as it is the case with XLWrap. In order to address this difficulties, XLWrap supports the specification of procedural transform operations as will be shown later in Section 10.3.

3.6 Interoperability and Standardization

Standardization is the most important approach to gaurantee interoperability. Standards may even prevent systems from becoming incompatible instead of having to solve heterogeneity a posteriori. The

```
<companies>                               <people>
  <company name="Example, Inc.">            <person name="Tom Hanks"
    <emp>Tom Hanks</emp>                            company="Example, Inc." />
    <emp>Elvis Presley</emp>                <person name="Elvis Presley"
    ...                                             company="Example, Inc." />
  </company>                                <person name="Mickey Mouse"
  <company name="Another Corp.">                    company="Another Corp." />
    <emp>Mickey Mouse</emp>                 ...
    ...                                   </people>
  </company>
  ...
</companies>
```

Figure 3.7: Two XML trees with a high degree of structural heterogeneity.

```
<people>
{
  for $comp in doc('/Users/dorgon/_Phd/latex/4-concept/misc/left.xml')/companies/company
    let $cname := $comp/@name
    for $emp in $comp/emp
      return
        <person name="{ $emp/text() }" company="{ $cname }" />
}
</people>
```

Listing 3.1: XQuery used to transform from the left to the right model shown in Figure 3.7.

inherent entropy causing an increasing level of disorder in the world does also apply to IT systems. Retaining interoperability has always been an important task in the ICT industry.

There are basically three important aspects of heterogeneity in IT systems where interoperability is crucial and standards have been developed: (1) software and processes, (2) communication and protocols, and (3) representation of data. Regarding the first aspect, examples are COBOL, ANSI C, or J2EE, examples for the second aspect are CORBA, Web services, but – at a lower level – also all the internet protocols of the OSI stack. To address the third aspect there are basically runtime standards and data exchange standards like XML, which is closely related to the second aspect. Regarding the interoperable runtime representation, the break-through and spreading of relational databases and the standardization of ANSI SQL has helped to keep systems rather compatible. Also XML is used at runtime in many applications today. Within the Semantic Web, the *Resource Description Framework* is the standard for information and knowledge representation. It is not only used natively by runtime systems, but also during the exchange of data on the Semantic Web.

Referring again to the *Meta Object Facility* (MOF) described as part of Section 2.2.1 and depicted in Figure 2.1, standardization can be issued at different levels: there are standards for M2 metamodels like the *Unified Modeling Language* (UML) or the *Ontology Definition Metamodel*, standards for M1 models like the *Dublin Core Metadata Element Set* (ISO Standard 15836-2003) or the *Friend-of-a-Friend* vocabulary (Brickley and Miller 2007), and standards at the M0 level like the *Dewey Decimal Classification* system used in libraries.

4 Semantic Web Primer

This chapter provides an overview of the core Semantic Web concepts including the *Resource Description Framework* (RDF), RDF Schema, the *Web Ontology Language* (OWL), and the *SPARQL Protocol and RDF Query Language*.

4.1 Introduction

The vision of the Semantic Web is about making information on the Web machine-processable (Tim Berners Lee et al. 2001). Depending on the interpretation of this vision, it may be claimed to have already succeeded or that the breakthrough is still out of sight. Some people claim that the expected impact has never taken place and that the vision will hardly be possible to realize at all. Because of the different (mis-)interpretations and expectations of the Semantic Web, it has always been a very controversial research area. In fact, there are many analogies to *Artificial Intelligence* research, which promised to solve many problems and introduce a new era in which computers will be able to act rationally or even humanly. These misunderstandings may have arisen due to over-exaggeration of researchers, journalists, and columnists but also because the Semantic Web is a very interdisciplinary research community attracting researchers from many different areas with many different problems, perspectives, and expectations.

Therefore, it is required to separate among different goals and applications of Semantic Web technology. It is obviously impossible to develop software agents which act humanly (no Semantic Web application has passed the Turing test) and it is certainly impossible for computers to really *understand* information on the Semantic Web. However, today the Semantic Web and its related research communities have developed a powerful stack of very important and powerful concepts and standards which can be used to significantly improve information-centric applications and software. One of the most fatal misconceptions in public is that the Semantic Web will once replace the traditional World Wide Web. In fact, most of the applications where Semantic Web technology has been successfully applied are within restricted domains and do not scale towards the whole Web: domain-specific knowledge management, semantic wikis, ontology-based information integration, and semantically-enabled service-oriented computing (Semantic Web services).

Whether the Semantic Web will ever improve the accessibility to the global information available on the traditional hypermedia Web remains rather unclear. As long as publishers and content providers do not have any benefit from semantically enabling their content (by means of RDF annotations, providing plain RDF data or SPARQL endpoints), they will not make any effort to do so. Although the *Linking Open Data* SWEO community project could motivate many publishers to open their data sets and to provide RDF to the public as part of the so-called *Web of Data*, this will not happen at a large scale until there is no clear benefit in general. Thus, until now Semantic Web technology is typically applied whenever a rich data model is needed to manage large amounts of decentralized information.

4.1.1 Origins of the Semantic Web

Although the origin of the Semantic Web is typically linked to the Scientific American article published by Tim Berners Lee, James Hendler, and Ora Lassila in May 2001 (Tim Berners Lee et al. 2001), the history can be tracked back to the early days when Tim Berners-Lee developed the World Wide Web at CERN in the 90ies. The idea to add semantics to Web pages and links was already part of the original design plans (Berners-Lee n.d.). However, the idea to combine RDF with description logics to realize the Semantic Web was formulated ten years later.

The *Platform for Internet Content Selection* (PICS) was established by the W3C to add content rating metadata to Web pages (Resnick and Miller 1996). Originally it was designed to let parents and educators control what children may access on the internet. The architecture was de-centralized and PICS services could provide labels about Web resources identified by their URLs. This simple concept of decentralized information management using globally unique URIs for merging different information sets is one of the most crucial concepts of RDF today. However, the PICS infrastructure was never really used in practice and the W3C Metadata Activity, which had developed PICS was finally superseded by the Semantic Web Activity in February 2001. During that time, PICS led to the development of the Resource Description Framework, because it soon was realized that the framework should support treatment of more generic metadata (Swick 2002). While PICS labels where only referring to actual Web resources (URLs), the URI-concept was extended in order to additionally support abstract entities. With RDF, any object that has a URI can be described, but the presence of a Web resource at the given URL is not necessarily required. This enabled RDF to become the core data model for ontologies on the Web usable even for non-Web applications.

Since 2001, the Semantic Web core concepts like RDF, RDF Schema, OWL, and SPARQL have been standardized by the W3C. A Working Draft for OWL 2 has been published in December 2008 and a new version of SPARQL supporting aggregates and insert/update/delete is also in progress.

4.1.2 Overview – The Semantic Web Layer Cake

The Semantic Web layer cake (Horrocks et al. 2005) depicted in Figure 4.1 is an informal stack frequently used to illustrate the different core concepts of the Semantic Web. Starting from the bottom,

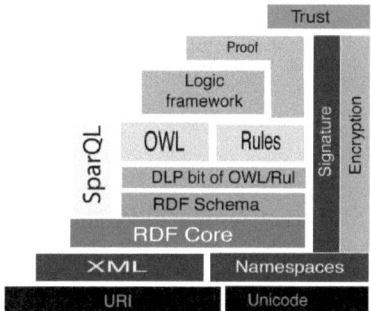

Figure 4.1: Semantic Web layer cake (Horrocks et al. 2005).

two basic concepts are *Unique Resource Identifiers* (URIs) and the *Unicode* character encoding standard to guarantee character set compatibility with all global languages. It should be noted, that the abbreviation IRI is newer and used to denote an *international* Unicode-encoded URI. Next, XML and namespaces are shown as part of the layer cake because the original serialization of RDF was in XML. This was mainly because XML had already become a wide-spread standard for data interchange. Later on, more compact serialization formats have been proposed to express RDF graphs (e.g. Turtle, Notation 3, and N-Triples) which will be presented in Section 4.2.4. These alternative serializations are not shown in Figure 4.1. Like in XML documents, namespaces and prefixes enable the modularization of RDF graphs. They are also applicable to the alternative serialization formats. Any resource described in an RDF graph is uniquely identified by a URI. This allows descriptions about the same resource to be distributed on the Web and merged into a single RDF graph later on.

On top of the RDF Core, RDF Schema can be used to declare predefined classes. These classes can be used to add type assertions to RDF resources. For example, a resource can by typed as being the description of a person or blog post. RDF Schema will be described later in Section 4.2.5. The introduction of a schema is required for systematic data management. While RDF Schema can be used to explicitly type resources, the Web Ontology Language (OWL) can be used to classify resources based on description logic. OWL, which is the successor of DAML+OIL, comes in three variants with different levels of expressiveness: OWL Light, OWL-DL, and OWL Full. OWL will be described in Section 4.3.

Because ontological constraints in OWL DL are based on description logic, it is not possible to use constraints which involve multiple classes. For example, with OWL it is not possible to express: a *car* is something which has twice as many wheels as a *bicycle*. In order to support global Horn-like rules, the Semantic Web Rule Language (SWRL), which is actually a subset of RuleML, has been proposed (Horrocks et al. 2004). The unifying logic framework includes the ontological framework (RDF, RDF-S, OWL) and *Rules* as subsets. Reasoners can deduce additional knowledge based on pre-

4 Semantic Web Primer

defined entailment regimes (which are basically axioms and rules) and the terminological assertions defined in an ontology. Depending on the reasoner's capabilities, RDF resources can be automatically classified and the ontology can be checked for consistency.

Beside the ontological framework, there is the SPARQL query language (explained in Section 4.4) which is stacked on top of the RDF Core. It enables the retrieval of information from RDF datasets based on graph pattern matching. To include inferred information provided by reasoners into query results, query processors can also work upon inferred RDF graphs. However, this behavior is rather specific to available implementations at the moment and also depends on the application scenario. The *Proof* layer illustrates that there should be means of tracing and explaining the logical reasoning processes. Finally, there is the *Trust* framework at the top of the overall stack. Generally, trust can be established by public key infrastructures. Several authorities including some root authorities may issue certificates to all the actors in the trusted application. RDF data can then be signed and encrypted based on certificates. These layers are not explicitly defined and there are also no recommendations or standards regarding the proof and trust at the time of writing.

4.2 Resource Description Framework (RDF)

The Resource Description Framework is the core data model of all Semantic Web-based applications. Any information added by higher-level components like RDF Schema and OWL is modeled within RDF. The current RDF specification is split into six W3C Recommendations: RDF Primer, RDF Concepts and Abstract Syntax, RDF/XML Syntax Specification, RDF Semantics, RDF Vocabulary Description Language (RDF Schema), RDF Test Cases. The most important document is the RDF Primer, which introduces the basic concepts of RDF. It is a summary of the other documents and contains the basic information needed to effectively use RDF. Although the syntax for RDF models is not restricted to XML, the XML representation is used for examples in the documents. The XML serialization is also the standard format when publishing ontologies on the Web. The RDF Primer also describes how to define vocabularies using the RDF Vocabulary Description Language (also called RDF Schema). Finally, an overview of some deployed RDF applications is given.

In the following sections several topics addressed by the aforementioned documents will be discussed. Examples will be provided in the *Turtle* (Beckett 2007) serialization format, since it is more readable and also more compact than RDF/XML.

4.2.1 RDF Concepts and Abstract Syntax

Before discussing the formal definition of an RDF graph, some examples should already give an impression of how RDF graphs are used to represent information. The strength of RDF is obviously its simple core data model based on sets of RDF statements of the form (s, p, o) denoting *subject, predicate, object* similarly to natural language sentences. A statement like:

4.2 Resource Description Framework (RDF)

The website at http://scott.com/ was created by John Scott.

can be represented by the RDF graph shown in Figure 4.2(a). In this example, the subject is the resource with the URI http://scott.com/, the predicate is dc:creator (the predefined Dublin Core property with the URI http://purl.org/dc/elements/1.1/creator), and the literal "John Scott" is the object. Figure 4.2(b) depicts another example of a graph with the following four statements (shown in the *Turtle* serialization format):

```
@prefix foaf:     <http://xmlns.com/foaf/0.1/> .
@prefix ex:       <http://example.org#> .
<http://scott.com/>              dc:creator      <http://scott.com/foaf.rdf#me> .
<http://scott.com/foaf.rdf#me>   foaf:homepage   <http://scott.com/> .
<http://scott.com/foaf.rdf#me>   foaf:name       "John Scott" .
<http://scott.com/foaf.rdf#me>   foaf:mbox       <mailto:js@gmx.com> .
```

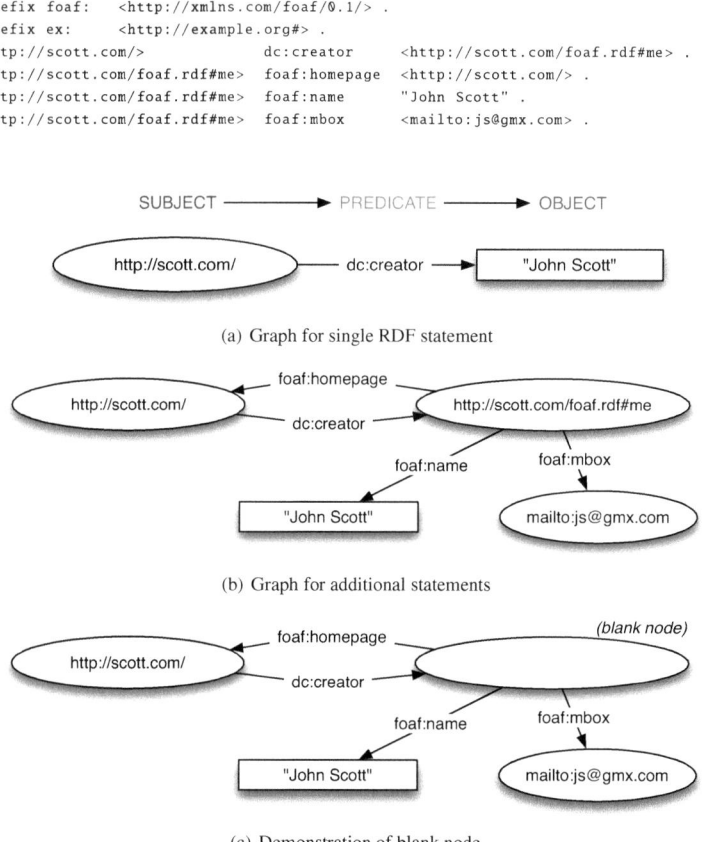

(a) Graph for single RDF statement

(b) Graph for additional statements

(c) Demonstration of blank node

Figure 4.2: RDF graph examples – Resources are usually depicted as elliptic shapes and literals in rectangles. Edges are labeled with the predicate's URI using namespace prefixes. Each edge represents a sentence, where the source node is the subject, the label is the predicate, and the target node is the object of the sentence.

4 Semantic Web Primer

For each of the four sentences, the graph in Figure 4.2(b) contains one directed edge. Note that `foaf:` and `ex:` have been introduced as namespace prefixes following the syntax

```
@prefix [prefix-name]: <[namespace-uri]>
```

Hence, `foaf:name` is a shortcut to `http://xmlns.com/foaf/0.1/name`. FOAF is the *Friend-of-a-Friend* vocabulary, which provides the vocabulary to describe persons and social networks between people. Each namespace uniquely identifies a specific RDF vocabulary. A vocabulary defines several concepts for some specific domain of discourse (e.g. RDF Core, RDF Schema, Friend-of-a-Friend, Dublin Core Metadata, etc.). From now on, the following prefixes and namespaces will be used and not specified further in code listings:

```
@prefix dc:    <http://purl.org/dc/elements/1.1/> .      # Dublin Core system
@prefix rdf:   <http://www.w3.org/1999/02/22-rdf-syntax-ns#> . # RDF Core
@prefix rdfs:  <http://www.w3.org/2000/01/rdf-schema#> . # RDF Schema
@prefix owl:   <http://www.w3.org/2002/07/owl#> .        # Web Ontology Language
@prefix foaf:  <http://xmlns.com/foaf/0.1/> .            # Friend-of-a-Friend
@prefix ex:    <http://example.org#> .                   # used for examples
```

The information contained in the graph is the conjunction of all four sentences.

To be able to add further information about the creator, it needs to become another resource instead of the plain literal "John Scott". Only resources can be used as subjects in RDF statements. The URI `http://scott.com/foaf.rdf#me` has been introduced for a new RDF resource representing the person with `foaf:name` "John Scott" and `foaf:mbox` URI `<mailto:js@gmx.com>`.

Using URIs for Real World Objects

Using the URI `http://scott.com/foaf.rdf#me` to represent a person may seem a bit odd for newcomers. Why should the person be identified by an HTTP-URI? However, using HTTP URIs is one of the core principles: basically everything that should be describable by somebody else on the Web should get a URI and to be able to retrieve information about the resource, its URI should also be resolvable by HTTP clients (Sauermann and Cyganiak 2007). In some cases, it may occur that a resource does not require an explicit URI. For that purpose RDF provides so-called *blank nodes*: a resource node which just has no globally unique URI. When serializing RDF graphs which contain blank nodes, the node gets a random but locally unique blank node identifier which allows to re-allocate and merge blank nodes during parsing later on. Figure 4.2(c) demonstrates the usage of a blank node.

Merging Distributed RDF Data

When RDF statements from different locations are merged, the graph can be easily extended because the URIs used to identify resources are globally unique. For example, if another RDF dataset provides information about the social network of "John Scott", an existing graph can be easily extended by new

4.2 Resource Description Framework (RDF)

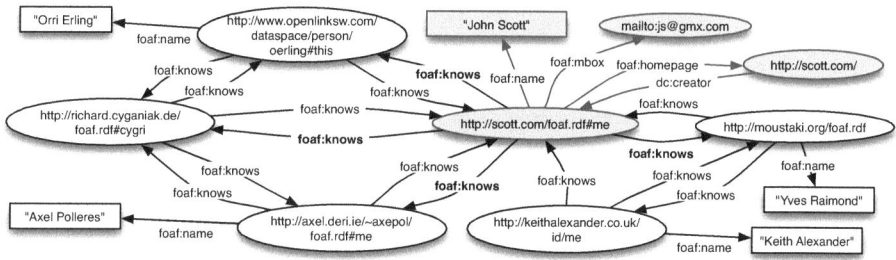

Figure 4.3: Example of a large RDF graph (FOAF social network).

edges and nodes. An example of a larger graph representing a simple FOAF-based social network is depicted in Figure 4.3. The shaded part on the top right of the graph was already known and shown in Figure 4.2(b), the other part was added from some other RDF graph. Because both sources where using the same URI http://scott.com/foaf.rdf#me to denote the person *John Scott*, the graphs can be merged correctly.

Explicitly Classifying Resources

To state that a resource is an instance of some class, i.e. has a specific type, the property rdf:type is used in a statement:

   <http://scott.com/foaf.rdf#me>   rdf:type   foaf:Person .

This sentence states that John is a foaf:Person, which represents a human person as will be explained later in Section 4.2.5. The property rdf:type is defined in the RDF Core vocabulary as reflected by the namespace prefix. Because this property is fundamental to RDF and used very frequently, in Notation 3 and Turtle syntax it is allowed to just write "a" like *something is a something*.

URI Resources, Blank Nodes, and Literals

The elements used so far are *RDF resource* and *literal*. If a resource is identified by a URI, it is called *URI resource*, otherwise it is an anonymous *blank node*. The predicate in a sentence is always a URI resource. Later on it will be shown, that RDF properties are actually more specific RDF resources. They have the special type rdf:Property defined in RDF Schema, which explicitly classifies them to be used as predicates in a statement.

Regarding RDF literals, there are either *plain literals* (simple strings interpreted as-is), or *typed literals*. Typed literals have a *data type tag* and may be used to represent numbers, dates, boolean values, etc. RDF uses XML datatypes but also allows to define custom datatypes which will not be further discussed. For example, in Turtle syntax the typed literal `"23.21"^^xsd:float` represents the real number 23.21. Plain literals can additionally have a *language tag*. For example, in Turtle syntax the literal `"Persönliche Website von John Scott"@en` indicates that the language of the plain literal is German. This allows adding multiple literals in different languages to the graph.

4.2.2 Formal Definition of an RDF Graph

An RDF graph is a directed labelled graph formed by an unordered set of RDF triples also called RDF statements. An RDF triple has three components (s, p, o) where s is called the *subject*, p the *predicate*, and o the *object* of the RDF triple. They can be considered as *roles* of RDF elements.

Given I as the set of IRI references, B as the set of blank nodes, and L as the set of literals (all mutually distinct), the domains of the three components are defined as:

$$s \in I \cup B$$
$$p \in I$$
$$o \in I \cup B \cup L$$

In order to simplify the notation of objects, an *RDF term* is defined as follows.

Definition 1 *The set of RDF terms RDF-T is defined as RDF-T $= I \cup B \cup L$.*

Definition 2 *An RDF graph G is a directed labelled graph defined by an unordered set of RDF triples of the form $G = ((I \cup B) \times I \times RDF\text{-}T) = ((I \cup B) \times I \times (I \cup B \cup L))$.*

IRI references and blank nodes used as subject or object are denoting RDF resources, which are the nodes of the corresponding RDF graph. Predicates, which must be IRI references, are also called *properties* with associated objects as their values. Properties are the edges connecting the graph's nodes. Typically, objects of one statement become subjects of other statements in a graph.

Also a property IRI of one statement can also be used as the subject of another statement. By doing so, properties can be defined and described reflexively with the same core concepts of RDF.

4.2.3 Summary of RDF Core Features

Beside the basic elements and the notation of RDF graphs as set of triples, the RDF Core provides many useful concepts for data modeling which will not be covered in detail. To give a quick overview, the most important capabilities are summarized below. For more information, the six documents of the W3C RDF Recommendation mentioned earlier may be consulted. The RDF Core provides

4.2 Resource Description Framework (RDF)

- support for structured property values and modeling of *n-ary* relations by means of blank nodes (e.g. for splitting a postal address into street name, zip code, city and country)

- custom datatypes, beside the pre-defined XML datatypes, to type literals

- a special XML datatype, which allows to embed XML documents into RDF

- *RDF Containers*, which can be used to create *bags*, *sequences*, and sets of alternative items – Especially sequences are very important because the set of triples which forms an RDF graph is unordered. A container is created by adding the type rdf:Bag, rdf:Seq, or rdf:Alt to a resource and adding the elements with multiple enumerated predicates of the form rdf:_i where $i = 1, 2, 3, \ldots$

- *RDF Collections*, which can be used to create finite lists of elements – This is done by using blank nodes to interlink sequences of sublists similar to lists in Prolog. Each sublist has two predicates: rdf:first linking the list element resource, and rdf:rest pointing to the next sublist (*tail* in Prolog). To terminate a collection, the rdf:rest of the last element is pointed to the predefined rdf:nil resource.

- *RDF Reification*, which allows to add statements about statements[1]

4.2.4 RDF Serializations

There are multiple serialization formats to represent an RDF graph. The initial format developed at W3C was RDF/XML. It is still the standard syntax for publishing and exchanging RDF vocabularies and data on the Web. Because the XML syntax is rather bulky and difficult to read for humans, alternative syntaxes have been proposed like *Notation 3* (N3) by Tim Berners Lee (1998) and its subsets of whose *Turtle* (Beckett 2007) has become the most popular. The syntax of N3 and Turtle respectively are intuitively readable and more compact compared to RDF/XML. While N3 adds some features that are not expressible as RDF/XML, Turtle is used for examples throughout this thesis.

A first example written in Turtle syntax has already been given at the beginning of Section 4.2.1. Very useful features of Turtle (and also N3) are the abbreviations of lists of objects by commas and lists of (p, o)-pairs sharing the same subject by semicolons. The following additional statements will also show, how a blank node can be described inside a bracketed block:

```
<http://scott.com/foaf.rdf#me>   ex:address [
                ex:street        "Webgasse 101" ;
                ex:postalcode    "1060" ;
                ex:city          "Vienna"@en ;
                ex:city          "Wien"@de
```

---
[1] However, RDF reification has many drawbacks mainly regarding performance within triples stores and query engines. It is partly considered as deprecated in the community and many people prefer to use named graphs instead (Gibbins and Shadbolt 2009).

4 Semantic Web Primer

```
          ] ;
          foaf:knows     <http://www.openlinksw.com/dataspace/person/oerling#this> ,
                         <http://richard.cyganiak.de/foaf.rdf#cygri> ,
                         <http://axel.deri.ie/~axepol/foaf.rdf#me> ,
                         <http://moustaki.org/foaf.rdf> .
```

Note that the ex:address of http://scott.com/foaf.rdf#me is a blank node and all (*p, o*)-pairs with the same subject (the blank node) can be enumerated using the semicolon. Similarly, multiple foaf:knows properties are listed using commas. The same information in RDF/XML syntax would be more complex:

```
<rdf:RDF xmlns:rdf="http://www.w3.org/1999/02/22-rdf-syntax-ns#" xmlns:foaf="http://xmlns.com/foaf
    /0.1/" xmlns:owl="http://www.w3.org/2002/07/owl#" xmlns:dc="http://purl.org/dc/elements/1.1/"
    xmlns:rdfs="http://www.w3.org/2000/01/rdf-schema#" xmlns:ex="http://example.org#">
  <rdf:Description rdf:about="http://scott.com/">
    <dc:creator rdf:resource="http://scott.com/foaf.rdf#me"/>
  </rdf:Description>
  <rdf:Description rdf:about="http://scott.com/foaf.rdf#me">
    <foaf:knows rdf:resource="http://www.openlinksw.com/dataspace/person/oerling#this">
    <foaf:knows rdf:resource="http://moustaki.org/foaf.rdf"/>
    <foaf:knows rdf:resource="http://axel.deri.ie/~axepol/foaf.rdf#me"/>
    <foaf:knows rdf:resource="http://richard.cyganiak.de/foaf.rdf#cygri"/>
    <ex:address rdf:nodeID="A0"/>
    <foaf:mbox rdf:resource="mailto:js@gmx.com"/>
    <foaf:name>John Scott</foaf:name>
    <foaf:homepage rdf:resource="http://scott.com/"/>
  </rdf:Description>
  <rdf:Description rdf:nodeID="A0">
    <ex:city xml:lang="de">Wien</ex:city>
    <ex:city xml:lang="en">Vienna</ex:city>
    <ex:postalcode>1060</ex:postalcode>
    <ex:street>Webgasse 101</ex:street>
  </rdf:Description>
</rdf:RDF>
```

Note that the serializer has introduced the anonymous ID A0 to be able to identify the blank node of the address. The ID is, however, only required for parsing and serializing. It has no external meaning at all, the resource has no URI.

4.2.5 RDF Schema

RDF Schema extends the RDF Core vocabulary. It contains several pre-defined concepts such as rdfs:Class, rdfs:Property, etc. which are used to define custom classes and properties.

Classes and Properties

Within RDF, basically every resource can be used as a predicate or as a class (which is assigned using the rdf:type property). For example:

4.2 Resource Description Framework (RDF)

```
<http://scott.com/foaf.rdf#me>   rdf:type     foaf:Person .
<http://scott.com/>              dc:creator   <http://scott.com/foaf.rdf#me> .
```

However, to be able to understand the semantics of `foaf:Person` and `dc:creator`, these resources must be described somewhere. The definition of `foaf:Person` is part of the *Friends-of-a-Friend* vocabulary (Brickley and Miller 2007) published at `http://xmlns.com/foaf/0.1/`. Creating an RDF class is just a matter of stating, that a resource is member of the pre-defined class `rdfs:Class`:

```
@prefix vs:       <http://www.w3.org/2003/06/sw-vocab-status/ns#> .
foaf:Person
   a                    rdfs:Class , owl:Class ;
   rdfs:comment         "A person." ;
   rdfs:isDefinedBy     foaf: ;
   rdfs:label           "Person" ;
   rdfs:subClassOf      foaf:Agent , <http://xmlns.com/wordnet/1.6/Agent> , <http://www.w3.org
      /2000/10/swap/pim/contact#Person> , <http://www.w3.org/2003/01/geo/wgs84_pos#SpatialThing> , <
      http://xmlns.com/wordnet/1.6/Person> ;
   owl:disjointWith foaf:Document , foaf:Organization , foaf:Project ;
   vs:term_status "stable" .
```

Line 3 states that the concept `foaf:Person` is an RDF Schema class and also an OWL class (OWL will be explained later in Section 4.3). It additionally states, that a FOAF Person is a sub-class of other concepts as for instance, `foaf:Agent` and `http://xmlns.com/wordnet/1.6/Agent`[2]. The same information can be depicted as a graph as shown in Figure 4.4. The gray arrows in the back indicate, that there are many other relations between the depicted concepts. The definition of `foaf:Person` in this picture is a very small subset of a huge interlinked RDF graph.

Similarly to the class `foaf:Person`, the definition of the RDF property `dc:creator` is part of the *Dublin Core* vocabulary published by the *Dublin Core Metadata Initiative* at `http://purl.org/dc/elements/1.1/`:

```
http://purl.org/dc/elements/1.1/creator
      rdf:type          rdsf:Property ;
      rdfs:label        "Creator"@en-US ;
      rdfs:comment      "An entity primarily responsible for making the resource"@en-US ;
      dcterms:description "Examples of a Creator include a person, an organization, or a service.
         Typically, the name of a Creator should be used to indicate the entity."@en-US ;
      rdfs:isDefinedBy  <http://purl.org/dc/elements/1.1/> ;
      dcterms:issued    "1999-07-02"^^xsd:date ;
      dcterms:modified  "2008-01-14"^^xsd:date ;
      dcterms:hasVersion <http://dublincore.org/usage/terms/history/#creator-006> ;
      skos:note         "A second property with the same name as this property has been declared
         in the dcterms: namespace (http://purl.org/dc/terms/). See the Introduction to the
         document 'DCMI Metadata Terms' (http://dublincore.org/documents/dcmi-terms/) for an
         explanation."@en-US ;
      .
```

---

[2] *Wordnet* is an ontology for the English language (Fellbaum 1998). It contains more than 115.000 concepts (*synsets*) which are interrelated with various associations. In order to integrate Wordnet into Semantic Web applications, the complete database is available as an RDF ontology.

4 Semantic Web Primer

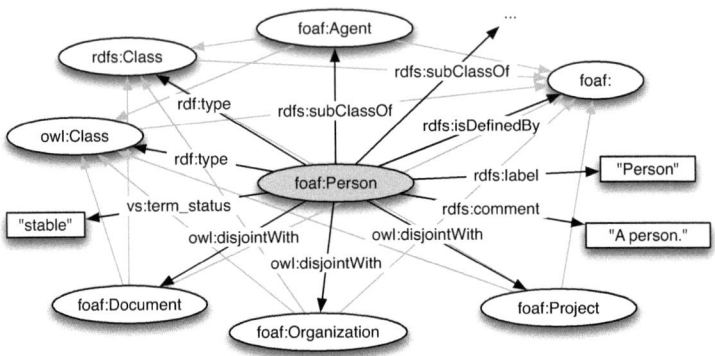

Figure 4.4: Definition of FOAF Person as part of the FOAF vocabulary.

The code fragment shows all statements of the vocabulary with dc:creator as the subject. Line 2 states, that the resource dc:creator is an rdfs:Property.

The RDF Schema vocabulary defines several properties which can be used to accurately describe concepts and provide detailed information like a short, descriptive label, and a more extensive comment. It also features several properties for version control. Note that all literal values may be specified in multiple different languages. Moreover, it is always possible to use further vocabularies by means of different namespaces. For instance, for the description of dc:creator, *Dublin Core Terms* and the *Simple Knowledge Organization System* (Miles and Bechhofer 2009) have been used.

Domain and Range of Properties

Given a specific property p', the set of RDF statements (s, p', o) can be interpreted as a binary relation $p'(s, o)$, which associates a value o to some subject s. Using this notation, the domain $D_{p'}$ denotes the set of all possible values of s and the range $R_{p'}$ denotes the set of all possible values of o. RDF Schema provides two properties which can be used to define the domain and range of an RDF property. For example, the property rdf:type is defined as:

```
rdf:type                                                                          1
    rdf:type           rdf:Property ;                                             2
    rdfs:label         "type" ;                                                   3
    rdfs:comment       "The subject is an instance of a class" ;                  4
    rdfs:domain        rdfs:Resource .                                            5
    rdfs:range         rdfs:Class ;                                               6
    rdfs:isDefinedBy   <http://www.w3.org/1999/02/22-rdf-syntax-ns#> ;            7
```

This example should also point out, that the RDF Core and RDF Schema vocabularies are defined reflexively within RDF itself. Line 2 contains a statement to describe rdf:type, which itself contains an rdf:type property. The statement defines rdf:type as an instance of the class rdf:Property. The domain of rdf:type is any RDF resource (line 5) and the range is the set of all classes (line 6). This seems reasonable, since an instance is supposed to be the instance of a *class*.

Properties in RDF are globally defined. If they have no defined domain and range, they can be used with any resource regardless of the class membership. This is a major difference to a database schema, where attributes are defined in the context of a specific relation.

Type System

In Section 4.2.1 it was shown, how the rdf:type property is used to make resources instances of a class. RDF provides a type system which allows to model class hierarchies similar to the concept of *specialization* in UML. Classes can be defined as subclasses of other classes. In order to define such a relationship, the property rdf:subClassOf is used. For example:

```
foaf:Person    rdfs:subClassOf    foaf:Agent .
```

According to the RDF-S entailment rules specified in Section 7 of (Hayes and McBrien 2004), any instance of foaf:Person is also a member of foaf:Agent. Similarly, it is possible to define subproperties. For example, to indicate the corresponding author of a conference paper who should be contacted by the reviewer, a more specialized dc:creator can be defined:

```
ex:primaryAuthor    rdf:type              rdf:Property ;
                    rdfs:subPropertyOf    dc:creator .
```

As a consequence of RDF-S entailment, if some paper has ex:primaryAuthor *Mike*, it is entailed that its dc:creator is *Mike*.

4.2.6 XML versus RDF

While XML is perfectly suited for the exchange of structured data, it lacks three important aspects. Firstly, the defined schema elements, attributes, and entities indicate no more semantics than their encoded names reveal. For instance, if an attribute is called tempValue, it could mean *temperature* (arguably it could be degree Centigrade or Fahrenheit) or it could denote some *temporary value*. To interpret XML data correctly, human reasoning is required and usually some additional documentation to the XML schema must be provided. Secondly, XML has a limited capability to describe relationships between elements with respect to objects. Although it is possible to use ID and IDREF attributes to give elements identity and refer to other elements, these references do not have any special associative meaning. An element reference is simply a meaningless symbolic link to an already existing element. Thirdly, XML is based on the *closed world assumption* and hence, it is impossible to augment additional information to already existing XML documents and it is further impossible to merge distributed XML information sets.

Regarding the first point, the lack of semantics could be described using a simple example shown in Figure 4.5. The difference to RDF is, that it is reflexive and thus, each schema concept can be described like any other resource. XML Schema is only reflexive with respect to its syntactic notation, but not the XML information set (the information entailed in an XML document).

```
<ex:Person ID="2312" name="Tom">
  <ex:email>tom@example.org</ex:name>
  <ex:phone>+43 0123 4567890</ex:phone>
</ex:Person>
```
To a human reader

```
<element1 attrib1="2312" attrib2="Tom">
  <element2>tom@example.org</element2>
  <element3>+43 0123 4567890</element3>
</element1>
```
To a machine

Figure 4.5: Meaning of XML information set.

4.3 Web Ontology Language

In Section 2.2.2 it was discussed, how humans use abstract symbols to denote real world things when communicating and creating abstract models. Given a set of known symbols, while perceiving the world we are able to match things to our personal collection of known symbols. This methodology of classification is basically the idea behind description logics. Instead of explicitly stating that some thing has a specific type, the set of matching types can be deduced by a description logic reasoner based on logical entailment. The Web Ontology Language has been developed to enable knowledge representation in a decentralized manner across the Web. Recent research is also investigating towards distributed description logic reasoning (Collet et al. 1991).

Before an introduction into OWL and description logics is provided, a terminology of *ontology* is given.

4.3.1 Ontologies

The term *ontology* can be derived from the greek words οντος (ontos), which means *of being* and λογος (logos), which can be translated to *science* or *theory*. Thus, ontology means *the science of being*. In this context *being* is not centered around mankind; this would be *anthropology*. Instead, it means *being* in a much broader sense: the being of things in the world. Traditionally, ontology is part of *metaphysics*. Its role is to find out what entities are there in the world, the nature of their properties, and how they are related to each other, i.e. exactly what was described as *data modeling* in Chapter 2 of Part I.

This definition, allows for quite a wide scope of the term. For example, an ontology can be a natural language like the German language, a database model of some real-world domain, or the classification of conference papers. As can be seen, there is a broad range of different examples with

4.3 Web Ontology Language

a varying degree of expressiveness. Finding *the* ontology that is capable of describing the whole world or universe is obviously impossible. On the other hand, there should be some boundary, some minimal criteria that has to be fulfilled.

Ontology Spectrum

McGuinness (2003) came up with a linear categorization for ontologies ordered by the levels of expressiveness depicted in Figure 4.6. According to this categorization the simplest form may be a controlled vocabulary, i.e. a finite set of terms represented by some *catalog*. It provides an unambiguous interpretation of terms which have an *unique ID*. A slightly more expressive form is a *glossary*, which may describe terms and incorporate semantic information for humans. *Thesauri* introduce hierarchical narrower/broader relationships. With an *informal is-a* relationship the authors mean taxonomies, which are often used in Web sites and shopping portals to classify content or products. Informal is-a relations usually mix sub-class, super-class, instance and other relations in a term hierarchy. Examples for such taxonomies are the *Open Directory Project* (Netscape Communications Corp. 2009) or Wikipedia categories. Usually, they can be interpreted correctly by human beings only.

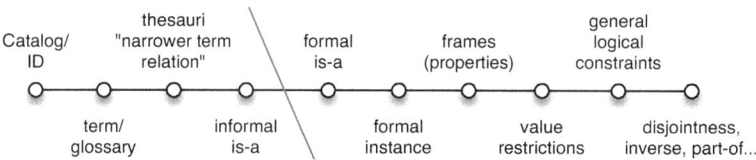

Figure 4.6: Ontology spectrum according to McGuinness (2003).

The bar splits the figure into a left and a right hand side. While the knowledge organization schemas on the left hand side can only be used with human interpretation and help, ontologies of the right hand side are formally defined and can be used for reasoning. *Formal is-a* relations enable strict sub-class hierarchies. For instance, if *human being* is a *mammal* and *mammal* is an *animal*, *human being* is also an *animal*. With the introduction of *formal instances* we can deduce that Tom, as an instance of *human being*, is an *animal*, just because of the fact that *human being* is a sub-class of *animal*. The next point introduces *frames* (Minsky 1974). They have *slots*, which defined the properties common to similar instances. For example, *products* have a *producer* and may have some *price*. In the original logics-based frames system, products would be matched based on their properties rather than explicitly defined as being products. It was a first approach towards description logics, which hide complex logical rules and provide a more human-friendly way of formally describing things in the world.

Even more expressivity can be achieved by *value restrictions* on properties. For example, the *price* may be restricted to the range of decimal numbers, the *producer* property to instances of *producer*.

The last two points in the figure refer to *general ontological constraints* and further features like expressing disjointness, inverse relations, compositions, etc. Such expressive ontology languages which are typically based on first-order logic are *F-Logic* (Kifer et al. 1995), *OntoLingua* (Farquhar et al. 1997), *CycL*, and also OWL.

According to McGuinness (2003), an ontology must have

1. a controlled vocabulary,

2. unambiguity in the interpretation of classes and term relationships,

3. and strict hierarchical sub-class relationships.

Ontologies fulfilling these conditions are depicted on the right hand side of Figure 4.6.

Another popular definition of ontology has been coined by Gruber (1993) as the "specification of a conceptualization". This is less precise than the definition used in the previous section, however, it includes another important term: *specification*. In many projects ontologies are introduced as commonly used, standardized conceptualizations of some specific domain with the goal of enabling *semantic interoperability*.

Application of Ontologies

Maybe the different interpretations of *ontology* is a good example to demonstrate that semantic conflicts are so inherent in human communication that chances are extremely low to ever find a way to fully eliminate them. However, since communication is such a significant and dominant process of our every-day lives, the ultimate ambition must still be the improvement of existing techniques to cope with these issues. In other words, there is no other way to succeed.

During the last decade ontologies have gained more and more interest from many different research areas including life sciences, astronomy, mathematics, applied informatics, etc. Especially for life sciences, a formal representation of the complex knowledge acquired in thousands of laboratory tests and experiments is crucial. Many companies and research organizations have started to experiment with ontologies and Semantic Web technology to manage their knowledge produced at different branch offices. The international collaboration between researchers has become more and more important to increase the efficiency of global research activities.

4.3.2 Introduction to OWL

The *Web Ontology Language* (OWL) is a modern knowledge representation language which has been developed based on the Resource Description Framework to enable an expressive representation of distributed information on the Web and reasoning across that information. The language is similar to Marvin Minskey's *Frames* language (Minsky 1974). The most important differences and characteristics will be explained in the following (Wang et al. 2006):

4.3 Web Ontology Language

No Unique Name Assumption

The UNA is a general concept of description logics, which states that different names always refer to different entities in the world. By contrast to *Frames*, OWL does not make this assumption. For example, in OWL it cannot be assumed by default that the two resources `<http://scott.com/foaf.rdf#me>` and `<http://people.org/JohnScott>` are distinct entities. Actually, it could be that they refer to the same entity and hence, the information about both resources could be merged from different sources on the Web. Asserting equality of resources is done with the `owl:sameAs` property. Explicitly asserting inequality for different resources is possible with the `owl:differentFrom` property.

Open World Assumption

The OWA is a general concept of formal logics, which admits that the given knowledge is incomplete and everything is true unless it is asserted otherwise. For example, given only the fact

```
<http://scott.com/foaf.rdf#me>  rdf:type  foaf:Person .
```

it cannot be assumed, that `<http://scott.com/foaf.rdf#me>` is not an `ex:Employee` also. SQL would return *false* when asking whether the resource is an employee. With the OWL entailment the result is just *unknown*.

The UNA and the OWA are fundamental principles of the Semantic Web. Within the Semantic Web it is always assumed that local information is not complete. There may be some more information somewhere else. Together with URIs as global identifiers for things in the real world and the simple RDF graph model, this core data model of the Semantic Web is very powerful and enables us to merge information from an arbitrary number of distributed resources. This is also the reason why Semantic Web concepts can be successfully used for information integration.

Axioms and Entailment Rules

The RDF Semantics and the OWL Semantics W3C Recommendations (Patel-Schneider et al. 2004) define the entailment regimes for RDF-S and OWL ontologies. The specifications also include the axioms and rules that a reasoner needs to know in order to correctly produce inferred facts. All predefined statements of the RDF Core and RDF Schema are axioms. For example

```
rdf:type    rdf:type    rdf:Property
```

is an axiom. To also provide an example for a rule, the rule identified as *rdfs9* will be explained. Given the RDF graph E:

```
u rdfs:subClassOf x .
v rdf:type u .
```

51

with u, v for any URI reference or blank node identifier and x for any URI reference, blank node identifier or literal, the following triple can be inferred:

```
v rdf:type x .
```

Depending on the required expressiveness of an application, there are basically three different OWL variants (McGuinness and van Harmelen 2004):

- OWL Lite
- OWL DL (Description Logic)
- OWL Full

This separation was introduced, because the more expressiveness is required, the more rules have to be applied by reasoners and the worse are the resulting computational properties. OWL Lite has the lowest formal complexity. It adds a few features to RDF Schema as for example equality and inequality constraints for classes and individuals or cardinality constraints for properties (but only values of 0 or 1). OWL DL was designed for maximal expressiveness while retaining computational completeness and decidability (reasoners will terminate in finite time). OWL Full does not add any restrictions to the available language constructs (for example, classes can be instances of other classes at the same time which is not allowed in OWL DL). It provides the maximum expressiveness but does not guarantee decidability. It is rather unlikely that there will ever be a reasoner supporting any feature of OWL Full.

4.3.3 Features of OWL

The discussion of all features of the Web Ontology Language is certainly out of scope for a Semantic Web primer. In the following some of the most interesting features of OWL will be mentioned without concrete examples. For a detailed study of OWL, it is suggested to consult the introductive OWL Overview (McGuinness and van Harmelen 2004) or the slightly more detailed OWL Guide (Smith et al. 2004), which also contains many code examples.

The following enumeration contains all features which are basically supported by all three OWL variants. OWL Lite has some minor restrictions on some of them.

RDF Schema elements: classes, individuals (instances), and properties; domain and range of properties, subclass and subproperty relationship, datatypes

Equality/Inequality: equivalent class/property/individual assertions; different individuals (equality/inequality has to be explicitly asserted because of the *Open World Assumption* explained before)

Property characteristics: inverse, transitive, symmetric, functional, inverse functional property relationship[3]

Restriction on quantification of property values: universal (all values from ...) and existential (some values from ...) quantification – Note that this restriction is defined on a property used with a specified class. For a general restriction on a property's range, the range construct of RDF Schema can be used.

Cardinality restriction: similar to the quantification of property values in combination of a specified class, the cardinality can be restricted by a lower and upper bound (min/max) as well as an exact value (for example, to specify that a soccer team exactly requires 11 players to be valid).

Class intersection: additional classes can be defined as the intersection of other classes (e.g. the class *scientist who is acting as a reviewer* can be defined as the intersection of *scientist* and *reviewer*)

Further features are available in OWL Full and (with minor restrictions) in OWL DL:

Enumerated classes: definition of a class based on an enumeration of individuals, e.g. the class *weekdays* = (*monday, tuesday, wednesday, thursday, friday, saturday, sunday*)

Property value restriction: property restriction on a specific value, e.g. the class *Austrian* are all *persons* that have a property *country* with the value *Austria*

Disjointness of classes: it is possible to assert the disjointness of classes

Set-based class definition: definition of a class based on set-combination of other defined classes (union, intersection, complement)

Given this rich set of features, OWL ontologies can be used to represent complex knowledge rather precisely. A reasoner can be used to infer additional triples based on the predefined entailment rules as explained before. This can be done by forward-chaining and adding the entailed information into the model. If there is any contradiction in the asserted graph the reasoner will detect this and may provide a backlog of the tracking process so that the user can fix the invalid assertion which led to the contradiction.

---

[3] Inverse functional properties are very important. For example, it is possible to indirectly identify a person via his/her e-mail address based on `foaf:mbox` because it is defined as *inverse functional* (i.e. the same object value can only occur in triples with identical subjects) (Golbeck et al. 2009).

4.4 SPARQL Protocol and RDF Query Language

Since January 2008, SPARQL is the standard query language of the Semantic Web. It can be used to retrieve information contained in RDF graphs in a structured way. The acronym stands for *SPARQL Protocol and RDF Query Language*. Thus, it does not only define a declarative query language like SQL does for the relational model, in addition, it defines a RESTful protocol which is used to send queries and retrieve results via the Hypertext Transfer Protocol (HTTP).

SPARQL is the result of several preceding approaches and proprietary implementations for an RDF graph pattern matching language. Since 2001 there have been Squish (Bristol University, UK), RQL (from ICS-FORTH, GR), RDQL (a W3C Submission by Andy Seaborne, HP Labs UK), SeRQL (used in the popular *Sesame* framework and now maintained by Aduna Software, NL), iTQL used in the *Mulgara Semantic Store* project (which was formally known as *Kowari*). One of the first implementations fully conforming with the final W3C Recommendation was *ARQ* as part of the *Jena Semantic Web Framework for Java* (Jena Community 2009a, Carroll et al. 2004). Jena had originally been developed at HP Labs in Bristol and has become a fully independent Open Source community project in fall 2009. The SPARQL W3C Recommendation was co-authored by Andy Seaborne, who implemented ARQ and also the Jena RDF stores SDB, which is backed by a relational database, and a non-transactional native store called TDB. Tool support is crucial for a standard to be accepted by the industry and SPARQL has successfully been implemented in all major Semantic Web software frameworks.

In order to understand the SPARQL algebra used for SemWIQ, the query methodology of SPARQL is very important. In the following section, the concept of *graph pattern matching* is explained.

4.4.1 Graph Pattern Matching

The concept of *graph pattern matching* is best described starting with the simple matching of triples of a graph. For example, given the RDF graph for the FOAF network depicted in Figure 4.3 (page 41), we could be interested in people John Scott knows. To get this information, it is sufficient to select all those triples from the source graph that have the subject `<http://scott.com/foaf.rdf#me>` and the predicate `foaf:knows`. The object is a free variable which can be instanced with any valid value entailed in the graph. This can be done by a simple *triple pattern*:

```
<http://scott.com/foaf.rdf#me>   foaf:knows   ?person
```

Where `?person` represents a variable for the object of such triples. In SPARQL variables are prefixed by the question mark. The syntax for triples is the same syntax which Turtle and Notation 3 use for representing triples. If all triples of the graph are matched subsequently against this pattern, the following triples remain:

```
<http://scott.com/foaf.rdf#me>   foaf:knows
```

4.4 SPARQL Protocol and RDF Query Language

```
                                <http://www.openlinksw.com/dataspace/person/oerling#this> .
<http://scott.com/foaf.rdf#me>  foaf:knows  <http://richard.cyganiak.de/foaf.rdf#cygri> .
<http://scott.com/foaf.rdf#me>  foaf:knows  <http://axel.deri.ie/~axepol/foaf.rdf#me> .
<http://scott.com/foaf.rdf#me>  foaf:knows  <http://moustaki.org/foaf.rdf> .
```

The variable ?person is bound to four different resources which are the objects of the remaining triples. The solution *s* forms a *multiset* or *bag* containing four *solution mappings* from query variables (here only ?person) to their bound values:

$$s = ((?\text{person} \leftarrow \texttt{<http://www.openlinksw.com/dataspace/person/oerling\#this>}),$$
$$(?\text{person} \leftarrow \texttt{<http://richard.cyganiak.de/foaf.rdf\#cygri>}),$$
$$(?\text{person} \leftarrow \texttt{<http://axel.deri.ie/ axepol/foaf.rdf\#me>}),$$
$$(?\text{person} \leftarrow \texttt{<http://moustaki.org/foaf.rdf>}))$$

The triple pattern restricts the graph to a subset of triples that match the pattern. The least restrictive triple pattern possible is just { ?s ?p ?o }. It selects the entire graph and can be used to retrieve all entailed information.

Basic Graph Patterns

Coming back to the FOAF example, the URI of resources is not very meaningful. What is much more interesting, is the name of the selected persons. In order to retrieve the full names, it is necessary to add another triple pattern which selects the foaf:name property of each ?person. This can be achieved by the following *basic graph pattern* (BGP), which consists of two *triple patterns*:

```
{ <http://scott.com/foaf.rdf#me>   foaf:knows   ?person .
  ?person                          foaf:name    ?name . }
```

Note that a BGP is a block delimited with braces. Similar to a set of RDF triples, the BGP can be represented as a graph shown in Figure 4.7(a). The matching parts from the source graph are shown below in 4.7(b).

Compared to the previous single triple pattern, the BGP above can also be seen as a further restriction on the source graph: it will only match those persons ?person, who also have an associated foaf:name (second triple pattern). After a closer look onto the graph in Figure 4.3, it can be seen that <http://richard.cyganiak.de/foaf.rdf#cygri> does not have a foaf:name property. As a consequence, matching the second triple pattern for the intermediate solution mapping (?person ← <http://richard.cyganiak.de/foaf.rdf#cygri>) will fail. Hence, the result of the BGP contains only three solution mappings with two variables, ?person and ?name:

55

4 Semantic Web Primer

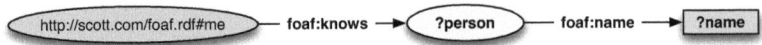

(a) Example of a SPARQL *basic graph pattern* (BGP) represented as a graph.

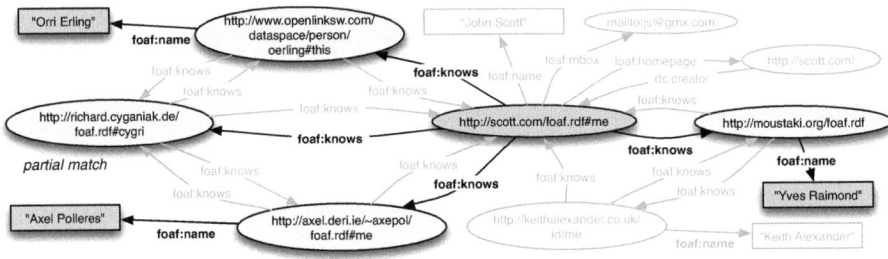

(b) Matching parts of the source graph from Figure 4.3.

Figure 4.7: Visual representation of SPARQL graph pattern matching.

$S = ((?\text{person} \leftarrow \texttt{<http://www.openlinksw.com/dataspace/person/oerling\#this>},$

$\quad ?\text{name} \leftarrow \text{"Orri Erling"}),$

$\quad (?\text{person} \leftarrow \texttt{<http://axel.deri.ie/ axepol/foaf.rdf\#me>}, ?\text{name} \leftarrow \text{"Axel Polleres"}),$

$\quad (?\text{person} \leftarrow \texttt{<http://moustaki.org/foaf.rdf>}, ?\text{name} \leftarrow \text{"Yves Raimond"}))$

When matching a BGP against an RDF graph, each triple pattern of the BGP has to match the graph. This is equivalent to the inner join in SQL algebra. Formally, solution mappings of the first triple pattern are *merged* against solution mappings of the second triple pattern and so on. *Merging* means, that two compatible solution mappings (one from the first and one from the second triple pattern) are combined to a single solution mapping if they are *compatible*, i.e. all their shared variables have equal values (see Section 4.4.3, Definition 9). If the solution mappings are not compatible, they are dropped (*join semantics*) and if there are no shared variables at all, the outcome of the join is the *cross product* of both solution sequences.

Combining Basic Graph Patterns

It is also possible to combine multiple BGPs. When concatenating multiple BGPs, three different semantics can be achieved:

- *join* semantics, unless there is no operator specified in-between of the BGPs

56

- *left join* semantics, if the OPTIONAL keyword is specified
- *union* semantics, if the UNION keyword is specified

Optional Matches

In the previous example, there are only three solutions, because one of the persons in the source graph does not have an associated foaf:name. If the result should *optionally* include the person's name, but still contain the person's URI, the OPTIONAL keyword can be used:

```
{ <http://scott.com/foaf.rdf#me>    foaf:knows   ?person . }
OPTIONAL { ?person                  foaf:name    ?name .   }
```

The solution mappings produced by the first BGP are *merged* with the solution mappings produced by the second BGP based on *optional* semantics, which means that if two bindings are not *compatible*, the left bindings are still streamed through as results:

$s =$ ((?person ← <http://www.openlinksw.com/dataspace/person/oerling#this>,

?name ← "Orri Erling"),

(?person ← <http://richard.cyganiak.de/foaf.rdf#cygri>),

(?person ← <http://axel.deri.ie/ axepol/foaf.rdf#me>, ?name ← "Axel Polleres"),

(?person ← <http://moustaki.org/foaf.rdf>, ?name ← "Yves Raimond"))

Alternative Matches

The UNION operator allows to combine BGPs with *union* semantics. However, there are some differences to SQL. In SQL the schemes (i.e. columns) of both sides of the union have to be compatible. This is not obligatory in SPARQL. When combining BGPs with the union operation, both BPGs may share common variables, but they can even have distinct sets of variables. The union in SPARQL is just the union of the solution mappings from the first and the second BGP, i.e. the solution sequences are just combined independent from any shared variables. To give an example (and to finally show the full syntax of a SPARQL SELECT query), the following query is used and executed against the graph in Figure 4.3:

```
SELECT * WHERE {
   { <http://scott.com/foaf.rdf#me>   foaf:knows   ?knows ;
                                      foaf:name    ?name }
   UNION
   { ?knownBy                         foaf:knows   <http://scott.com/foaf.rdf#me> ;
                                      foaf:name    ?name }
}
```

4 Semantic Web Primer

The result of this query is the union from both BGP results. The first BPG selects persons known by John Scott including their names and the second BGP selects all persons and names John is known by.

Although SPARQL is a query language for RDF graphs and the source data sets of a query are graphs, the result of a SPARQL SELECT query is a multiset which can easily represented as a table like SQL result sets. To display a SPARQL SELECT result, it is very common to use a table with all the query variables written as column header. For each solution mapping, a new row is filled with all available variable mappings. The query solution for the above example query can be represented as shown in Table 4.1.

Table 4.1: Results of the discussed union query represented as a table.

?knows	?knownBy	?name
	`<http://www.open...oerling#this>`	Orri Erling
	`<http://moustaki.org/foaf.rdf>`	Yves Raimond
	`<http://axel.deri.ie/...#me>`	Axel Polleres
`<http://richard.cyg...#cygri>`		Richard Cyganiak
	`<http://keithalexander.../me>`	Keith Alexander
`<http://axel.deri.ie/...#me>`		Axel Polleres
`<http://moustaki.org/foaf.rdf`		Yves Raimond
	`<http://richard.cyg...#cygri>`	Richard Cyganiak
`<http://www.open...oerling#this>`		Orri Erling

Note that the order of the solution mappings is irrelevant, it is an unordered mutliset. By contrast to SQL, empty rows are not *null*, the corresponding variables are just *unbound*.

4.4.2 Query Forms

All the queries shown so far are SELECT queries. A SELECT query is used to select concrete elements like the values of nodes and edges of an RDF graph and obtain a bag of solution mappings. However, there are three additional query forms: DESCRIBE, CONSTRUCT, and ASK. All forms are based on graph pattern matching, however, the form determines how the obtained solution mappings are post-processed and finally represented. For example, the DESCRIBE query can be used to obtain any information about resources that have been selected by a graph pattern in the form of another RDF graph. The CONSTRUCT query can be used to construct an alternative graph based on a construct template which is filled by solutions from the graph pattern. ASK queries are the simplest form. They are used to check the entailment of parameterized subgraphs and return *true* if there are any possible solutions and *false* otherwise.

Since SELECT queries are most frequently used, the majority of the examples throughout this thesis will be of this form. However, SemWIQ basically supports all of the four query types. More

4.4.3 SPARQL Definitions

From a query processing and implementation perspective, a formal algebra for a query language like SPARQL is crucial. Otherwise it is very likely that different implementations behave differently. The SPARQL algebra (*compositional semantics*) has been developed not until the early *operational semantics* of the SPARQL draft yielded ambiguities and inconsistencies after the first implementations. There have been long discussions concerning the correct semantics of SPARQL (Richard Cyganiak 2005, Newman 2006, Arenas et al. 2007) until the W3C Recommendation was finally published in January 2008 with the help of Pérez et al. (2006). The SPARQL algebra is now defined as part of the recommendation (Prud'hommeaux and Seaborne 2008, Section 12) and will be discussed in short to provide a basis for query processing in SemWIQ.

Triple patterns and Basic Graph Patterns

The following definitions are used to formalize the query pattern of a SPARQL query (which has been explained in Section 4.4.1).

Definition 3 *V defines the set of all query variables. It is infinite and disjoint from the set of RDF terms, $V \cap RDF\text{-}T = \emptyset$.*

Definition 4 *A triple pattern tp is a member of the set $TP = (RDF\text{-}T \cup V) \times (I \cup V) \times (RDF\text{-}T \cup V)$*[4].

Definition 5 *A basic graph pattern (BGP) is a set of triple patterns $bgp = (tp_1, tp_2, \ldots, tp_n)$ where $tp_i \in TP$. If $bgp = \emptyset$ the BGP is called* empty graph pattern.

Basic graph patterns can be compared to low-level selection operators in RDBMS query processing. They are the basis of the query processing workflow since all intermediate solutions going through the query execution pipeline are created based on BGPs. Higher level operators combine and filter intermediate solutions until they are returned as final query solutions by the query engine. In most SPARQL implementations, the basic graph pattern is actually a join over intermediate solutions produced by triple patterns as will be shown.

Basic Graph Pattern Matching

By contrast to SQL, where selections are based on attributes of relations, selections in SPARQL are based on the active RDF graph, which is formally a set of (s, p, o)-triples[5]. Instead of referring to

---
[4]SPARQL explicitly allows literal subjects although they are not allowed in RDF graphs (Tim Berners Lee 2000).
[5]Or (g, s, p, o) quads when using named graphs, which is not relevant in case of SemWIQ.

attributes as part of a fixed database schema, a SPARQL query may contain arbitrary variables that are instantiated when evaluating the query.

The SPARQL W3C Recommendation defines basic graph pattern matching in a rather generic form, where the complete BGP is matched against the *active graph* (Prud'hommeaux and Seaborne 2008, 12.3.1). While some implementation may evaluate BGPs efficiently based on graph-based data structures, most SPARQL implementations are actually based on *triple pattern matching*, especially when the dataset is a scalable RDF store. A triple pattern may contain arbitrary variables (Definition 4) and when evaluating the triple pattern, a *solution sequence* is created by matching the triple pattern against the *active graph* of the query's dataset and instantiating any variables with corresponding values of the graph (Prud'hommeaux and Seaborne 2008, Sect. 12.3.1).

Definition 6 *A solution mapping μ maps RDF terms to variables. It is a partial function $\mu : V \to RDF\text{-}T$. The domain $dom(\mu)$ is the subset of V where μ is defined.*

Definition 7 *A list of possibly unordered solution mappings is called solution sequence.*

A BGP can be regarded as a conjunctive query where all triple patterns must match the active graph. This is effectively equivalent to a join over the solution sequences obtained from matching the BGP's triple patterns. When joining two solution sequences, all their solution mappings are pairwise compared and *compatible* mappings are *merged* into single mappings as a result which is similar to SQL join semantics.

Definition 8 *The function $merge(\mu_1, \mu_2)$ is defined as:*

$$merge(\mu_1, \mu_2) = \begin{cases} \mu_1 \cup \mu_2, & \text{if } \mu_1, \mu_2 \text{ compatible,} \\ \{\}, & \text{otherwise.} \end{cases}$$

Definition 9 *Two solution mappings μ_1 and μ_2 are compatible if, for every $v_i \in dom(\mu_1) \cap dom(\mu_2)$ the bound RDF terms are equal, $\mu_1(v_i) = \mu_2(v_i)$. In the special case of $v_i = \emptyset$, μ_1 and μ_2 are still compatible (in case of cross product).*

A solution mapping is sometimes also called *solution binding* (this is mainly in context of the Jena ARQ implementation).

Algebra Operators, Query Plans, and Queries

For the compositional semantics of SPARQL as defined in (Prud'hommeaux and Seaborne 2008, Sect. 12) a set of algebra operators is defined including the basic graph pattern (BGP) as a low-level (leaf) operator with zero sub-operators. Higher level operators may have either one or two sub-operators and an optional list of arguments (e.g. the *Project* operator defines a set of projection

4.4 SPARQL Protocol and RDF Query Language

variables, *Filter* defines a filter expression, etc.). They operate on solution sequences previously initialized by a BGP. Any operator may be the root of a query plan.

Definition 10 *An algebra operator p is defined as a (A, P, s)-tuple with a sequence of arguments A, $|A| \geq 0$, a sequence of sub-operators $P = (p_1, p_2, \ldots, p_n)$, $0 \leq |P| \leq 2$, and a special algorithm s defining its semantics (e.g. filter solutions produced by p_1 according to expression a_1).*

Besides the *BGP*, higher level algebra operators include *Filter*, *Join*, *Optional* (left join), *Union*, and *Graph* as well as the solution modifiers *Order-by*, *Project*, *Distinct*, *Reduced*, and *Slice*. *Join*, *Optional*, and *Union* define two different sub-plans, *BGP* defines none and the others define one sub-plan.

Definition 11 *For each valid SPARQL query string q_{lex}, there exists a formally defined query plan q, which is recursively defined by a composition of single algebra operators p.*

In this thesis, the term *algebra plan* is often used instead of *query plan* although there is no difference at all. The order in which a query string is parsed and the corresponding algebra plan sequence is built is defined in Sect. 12.2.1 and the evaluation semantics of higher level operators is defined in Sect. 12.4 of the W3C Recommendation (Prud'hommeaux and Seaborne 2008). To give an example, the algebra plan for a lexical example query is shown in Figure 4.8.

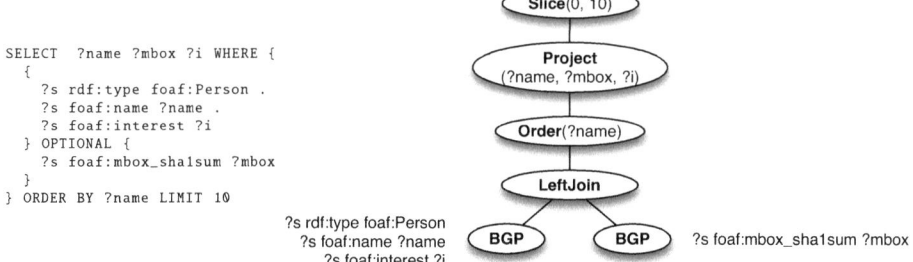

Figure 4.8: A SPARQL query and its corresponding algebra plan.

A SPARQL query is always executed against an *RDF dataset*, which is defined as follows.

Definition 12 *An RDF dataset DS is a set $DS = (G, (u_1, G_1), (u_2, G_2), \ldots, (u_n, G_n))$ where G and G_i are RDF graphs and u_i are distinct IRIs used to assign names to G_i. G is called* default graph *and graphs G_i are called* named graphs.

This definition of the RDF dataset was introduced by the *RDF Data Access Working Group* to make SPARQL capable of processing queries over multiple graphs and quad-based RDF stores. The graph which is currently subject of graph pattern matching is called *active graph*. If a SPARQL query does not contain any GRAPH keyword, the default graph is always the active graph and none of the named graphs will be taken into account.

Definition 13 *A SPARQL query is defined as a tuple (q, DS, R) where q is an algebra plan as defined in Definition 11, DS is an RDF dataset as defined in Definition 12, and R is one of the query forms described in Section 4.4.2.*

4.4.4 Representation of SPARQL Algebra Plans

Query plans are often depicted as graphs where operators are drawn as nodes connected by edges (as shown in Figure 4.8). However, sometimes it is useful to describe query plans based on a compositional notation. In order to discuss the SemWIQ approach in Part III, a compositional notation based on Definitions 10 and 11 is used. For example, the query plan depicted in Figure 4.8 can be written as:

Slice((0, 10),
  Project((?name ?mbox ?i),
    Order((?name),
      LeftJoin(
        BGP((?s rdf:type foaf:Person), (?s foaf:name ?name), (?s foaf:interest ?i)),
        BGP((?s foaf:mboxsha1_sum ?mbox))
)
)
)
)

An operator may specify a list of arguments, followed by a list of sub-operators.

SPARQL S-Expressions

Another serialization of query plans called *SPARQL S-Expressions* has been suggested by Seaborne (2007). It is used in *Jena ARQ* to print algebra plans. Since this notation is also used for the EXPLAIN query extension (introduced in Section 9.1.3), an example for the query plan depicted in Figure 4.8 is shown in Listing 4.1. The corresponding BNF grammar is printed in Listing 4.2 (note that tokens are not separated by white spaces, instead <SPACE> and <NEWLINE> tokens are placed explicitly). OperatorType is a valid algebra operator such as *Join*, *Filter*, *Union*, *Project*, etc. and Argument may be of any type (e.g. a list of projection variables for *Project*, a filter expression list for a *Filter*, a named graph IRI for a *Graph* operator, etc.). Arguments are separated by whitespaces, set-vales are enclosed in brackets. Each `Operator` defines a specific list of valid arguments and either zero, one, or two sub-operators as indicated by comments in the above grammar.

```
(slice _ 10
  (project (?name ?mbox ?i)
    (order (?name)
      (leftjoin
        (bgp
          (triple ?s <http://www.w3.org/1999/02/22-rdf-syntax-ns#type> foaf:Person)
          (triple ?s foaf:name ?name)
          (triple ?s foaf:interest ?i)
        )
        (bgp (triple ?s foaf:mbox_sha1sum ?mbox))))))))
```

Listing 4.1: Example of SPARQL S-Expression notation.

```
Operator ::= "(" OperatorType (<SPACE> Argument)*
            (
              ( <NEWLINE> Operator ) |   // single sub-operator
              ( <NEWLINE> Operator        // left/right sub-operator
                <NEWLINE> Operator )
            )?                            // possibly no sub-operator
            ")"
```

Listing 4.2: Grammar of SPARQL S-Expressions.

4.5 Linked Data

Similarly than the World Wide Web provides a global network of documents connected by hyperlinks, Semantic Web concepts can be combined with traditional hypermedia technology in order to provide a global network of browsable *Linked Data*. In July 2006 Berners-Lee (2006) published an article on the Web about the idea of *Linked Data*. While the WWW consists of HTML documents and multimedia resources connected by hyperlinks, the Semantic Web consists of resources (things) of any kind connected by properties (or *semantic links*). In order to make RDF graphs intuitively accessible and browsable, he suggested four design rules (Berners-Lee 2006):

1. URIs should be used to identify things.

2. More specifically, HTTP URIs should be used so that people can look up things.

3. If someone looks up a URI, useful information should be provided using standards (RDF, SPARQL).

4. Further semantic links should point to other URIs so that people can discover more things.

4 Semantic Web Primer

In the year 2007 several projects have been launched to support this idea and promote the wide adoption of the *Linked Data* paradigm (W3C SWIG 2009, Auer et al. 2007). Lots of publicly available, user-generated, and open governmental datasets have been published since then. On the one hand there is the great idea of building a globally scaled public *Web of Data* in additional to the traditional World Wide Web. On the other hand, the same principles are perfectly suited for corporate solutions in the area of information integration.

In Figure 4.9 the current infrastructure of the Web of Data is depicted. The Figure shows a client application (usually a browser or a specialized *Linked Data* browser such as Tabulator (Berners-Lee et al. 2006)) in the middle, some simple RDF resources distributed over the Web, some RDF datasets with a SPARQL endpoint and possibly a *Linked Data Interface*, a Semantic Web search engine (e.g. Swoogle (Ding et al. 2004) or SWSE (Harth et al. 2006)), a look-up service (e.g. Sindice (Tummarello et al. 2007)), and a mediator (e.g. SemWIQ, the system presented in this thesis). All these components will be described in the following.

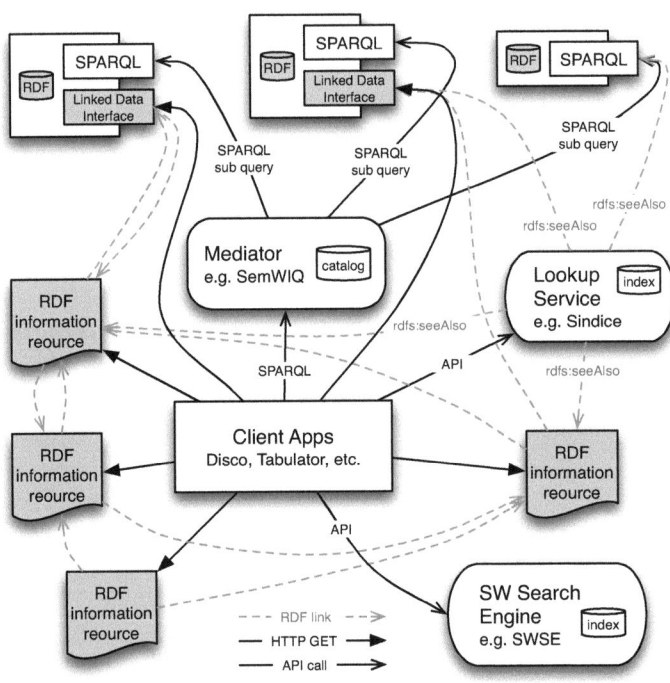

Figure 4.9: Current Linked Data infrastructure.

4.5 Linked Data

Client applications – Currently, the most popular clients are linked data browsers[6]. They parse plain RDF data and provide a well-organized, structured view of the information, usually as groups of subjects, properties and values (literals or linked resources).

RDF information resource – According to the findings of the W3C Technical Architecture Group (TAG) it is a Web document containing RDF data. It is identified by an absolute HTTP URI. It may also be dynamically generated out of a database but it appears as a single Web document. It contains a set of RDF statements describing one or more *information* or *non-information* resources, possibly with external RDF links[7].

SPARQL endpoints – They provide access to usually bigger RDF datasets via SPARQL, a declarative query language and HTTP-REST based protocol. To prevent intentional or even unintentional denial-of-service attacks, some endpoints have limit constraints on the result sets returned. It can be assumed that a good portion of available data will be provided through public SPARQL endpoints.

Linked Data Interface – Because SPARQL endpoints only provide declarative access it is not possible to browse over resources described behind the endpoint without wrapping the information by executing DESCRIBE queries, for instance. Such a *Linked Data Interface* is actually an RDF-to-HTML wrapper attached to the endpoint (e.g. Pubby (Cyganiak and Bizer 2009)). It resolves resource URIs, executes the corresponding query and returns the HTTP response (possibly being a 303-redirect) on-the-fly.

Semantic Web search engine – Such a search engine uses a specialized crawler which looks for RDF data on the Web, usually identified by the Content-type header of the HTTP response. It also provides a Web interface and/or API with several search options. For example, SWSE provides a keyword search which returns a list of RDF resources (both, informational and non-informational). In a second step the user may restrict the RDF resources displayed based on known types.

Sindice, a look-up service – While search engines usually keep all data (mainly RDF and OWL files) they have crawled in a cache, the idea of Sindice is to use specialized indices to store only partial but relevant information. For instance, currently they only keep an index for resource URIs, inverse functional properties and their values, and keywords. Sindice can also be integrated into linked data browsers or similar clients. An API is provided which returns a list of rdf:seeAlso properties with target URIs as values.

---

[6] A complete list of browsers and client libraries can be found at http://esw.w3.org/topic/TaskForces/CommunityProjects/LinkingOpenData/SemWebClients (as of January 2008).

[7] A complete guide on how to publish linked data on the Web is provided in (Bizer et al. 2007)

Mediator – A mediator like SemWIQ can be used to query distributed RDF datasets from a single point of access. It can be seen as another service as part of the Web of Data infrastructure which can be used by other clients and applications. Mediator-like services such as the *Semantic Web Client Library* (Bizer et al. 2009) or *SQUIN* (Hartig et al. 2009), which supports automatic link-traversal over a distributed RDF graph can be accounted to this type of services.

A user session usually begins either with entering or clicking some resource URI or with an initial query against a search engine or look-up service returning URIs to start with. This is rather similar to the traditional hypermedia Web: either one is in the know of a URL, or one uses a search engine to get a list of directions to start with. After a resource has been resolved, the user can click on related resources or things and continue with browsing.

The infrastructure so far is a good basis for the emerging Web of Data. However, the amount of available datasets and public SPARQL endpoints is still very small compared to the traditional Web. Beside several single RDF resources spread over the Web, the *Linking Open Data* initiative has already achieved a substantial growth. Examples of available datasets are dbpedia.org, geonames.org, dbtune.org, the Semantic Web port of the *Digital Bibliography & Library Project* at http://www4.wiwiss.fu-berlin.de/dblp, or governmental datasets such as the US census. It can be expected that during the next years further datasets will be provided by public endpoints and more and more Web pages will contain semantic annotations which can be wrapped to RDF. Because the Web of Data is deep per se, it will be a challenge to maintain search engine indexes over this vast amount of world knowledge. While the goal of the search engine SWSE is to index all RDF data available on the Web (even some microformats are wrapped and indexed), Sindice does not completely crawl the hypermedia Web. Instead, a catalog of interesting datasets and services like www.pingthesemanticweb.org are used to bootstrap an RDF-crawler which only follows RDF links.

Part II

Related Work

5 Overview

In the previous part the necessary background to information integration and Semantic Web concepts was presented. The related work part is dedicated to related research projects including the concepts and architectures as well as the implementations of existing systems.

As highlighted in Section 3.3 of Part I, there are three dimensions which can be used to classify information integration systems: *autonomy*, *distribution*, and *heterogeneity*. For the context of this thesis, only those systems are interesting that enable the integration of autonomous, distributed, and *heterogeneous* information sources. This includes systems which are heterogenous regarding their metamodels. Hence, *mediator systems* are discussed in more detail in this chapter.

Mediator systems became very popular during the nineties and have not lost their interest until today. However, the focus has changed and today, the Web and semantic interoperability have gained the predominant role. During the nineties, research in information integration faced a convergence of database-centric approaches and logic-based approaches originating from the artificial intelligence (AI) community. Database-centric approaches typically used some object-oriented data model for the global representation of integrated information (e.g. ODMG-93). Logic-based systems were typically based on some kind of first-order logic (e.g. Loom, KIF, KL-ONE, F-Logic, etc.). In 1990, the DARPA (*Defense Advanced Research Projects Agency*) initiated the *Knowledge Sharing Effort* (KSE), with the goal of building tools, protocols, and languages to enable sharing knowledge. One of the KSE projects was *Ontolingua* (Farquhar et al. 1996), with the goal to create a unified space for knowledge represented in the same language (KIF). At least since that time, the term *ontology* has become more and more popular to denote formally defined knowledge bases to create semantics-aware information integration systems (Gruber 1993). At the end of the nineties, RDF and the Semantic Web vision came into play and caused on the one hand a shift from former approaches to a more Web-centric view of the problem and on the other hand, the revolutionary vision became very popular and attracted many researchers from other domains.

Another important development during the nineties was the *eXtensible Markup Language*, XML, which was published as a W3C Standard in February 1998, after more than two years of hot discussions via mailing lists and teleconferences. XML soon became an industry standard for data exchange. While it is well suited for applications with clearly defined interfaces, it has several disadvantages outlined in Section 4.2.6. Scientists working on the implementation of XML databases soon came up with concepts for XML-based mediator-systems (Baru et al. 1999, Sattler et al. 2005).

5 Overview

The related work part is structured as follows. In the first chapter, early projects and fundamental concepts of information integration based on the mediator-wrapper architecture are discussed. The chapter includes a section about the mediator paradigm as articulated by Wiederhold (1992). The discussed systems include Garlic (Carey et al. 1995), TSIMMIS (Chawathe et al. 1994), DISCO (Tomasic et al. 1996), and the InfoSleuth agent framework (Bayardo et al. 1997). Newer approaches based on Semantic Web technology are discussed in Chapter 7.

6 Early Projects and Fundamental Concepts

The development of database systems during the eighties was accompanied by the development of wide-area networking technology. It was self-evident that the storage and retrieval and hence, the integration of distributed information became more and more important for enterprises and decentralized organizations. With the continuously growing expansion of WAN technology and the internet, the significance has even more increased. Especially when the information to be integrated is maintained in highly autonomous and heterogenous systems, traditional approaches developed for multi-database and distributed database systems are not adequate anymore. Although many of the fundamental algorithms are similar, they have been extended and combined with new concepts in order to address the new challenges. If information is supplied by various sources like different kinds of database systems, XML document collections, or websites and different kinds of interfaces like SQL, XQuery, or Web services, the *mediator-wrapper* approach is typically applied.

6.1 Mediators in Future Information Systems

One of the proponents of the mediator approach, Gio Wiederhold has formulated the concept of a *mediator* as follows (Wiederhold 1992):

> "A mediator is a software module that exploits encoded knowledge about some sets or subsets of data to create information for a higher layer of applications."

This quotation can be taken as a high-level definition of the mediator architecture. According to Wiederhold, in 1992, the community was facing two types of problems:

1. "for single databases a primary hindrance for end-user access is the volume of data that is becoming available, the lack of abstraction, and the need to understand the representation of data"

2. "the major concern when combining information from multiple databases is the mismatch encountered in information representation and structure"

6 Early Projects and Fundamental Concepts

The first class of problems has been well addressed during the last couple of decades: today, it is not a real problem to manage and retrieve information from large volumes. OLAP technology is powerful enough to be able to abstract from fine-grained data and provide more meaningful information very fast. What still remains an issue today is the correct interpretation of the data represented in databases.

The second type of problems is, in short, the focus of current Semantic Web research activity. When combining (i.e. integrating) information from various sources, it is usually a problem to correctly match the semantics, even more if the underlying data should be combined and processed automatically. Wiederhold lists some of the problems encountered when combining autonomous sources including naming conflicts, abstraction grain, temporal context, domain semantics, value semantics, etc. Furthermore, he defines an abstract *model of information processing* referring to the popular article *"As We May Think"* by Bush (1945). Wiederhold calls the process of obtaining, processing, and communicating information *planning*, because data is taken from the past, with the objective of affecting the future. He argues, that the interfaces of future information systems must take on an active role supporting the user during this *planning*. He calls the *mediator* "a module occupying an explicit, active layer between the user's applications and the data sources" and defines its architecture as depicted in Figure 6.1. This understanding of a mediator is similar to the theory of *software agents*, which are acting on behalf of their users and carry out diverse tasks. For example, the goal of *Carnot* (Collet et al. 1991) and *InfoSleuth* (Bayardo et al. 1997) was the development of a generic agent-based framework with specialized software agents being responsible for resource discovery, brokering, and integration of information and services in dynamic environments. The vision of intelligent software agents fulfilling sophisticated tasks which usually require some kind of human intelligence are rather ambitious in fact and difficult to realize.

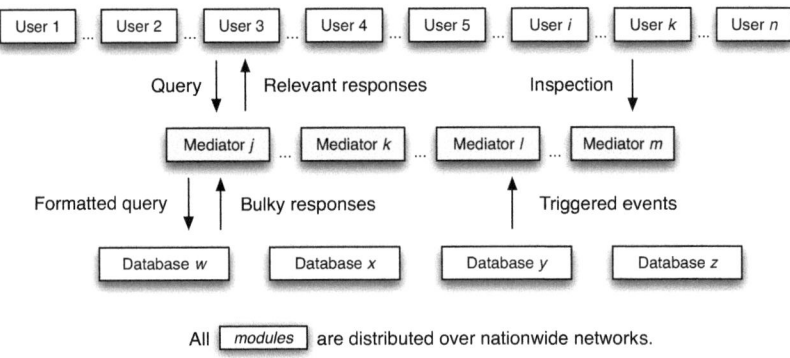

Figure 6.1: Mediators as interfaces for information flow (Wiederhold 1992).

In the context of information integration, a mediator should be capable of answering queries by consulting an arbitrary number of different known information sources. This is typically achieved by placing a wrapper at each data source which is responsible of local query processing and data transformation. In the following sections concrete implementations of such mediator-based information integration systems are discussed. Basically, the approaches can be divided into projects originating from the database community (like IBM Garlic), and projects originating from the *artificial intelligence* (AI) and *agent-based computing* (ABC) domain (e.g. InfoSleuth).

The IBM Garlic project will be described first, because it already incorporates many important aspects of a typical mediator-wrapper system introduced in Section 3.4 of Part I.

6.2 IBM Garlic

One of the first and historically most popular mediator system aiming at the integration of heterogeneous distributed multimedia data was *Garlic*. It was developed by IBM at the Almaden research center during the nineties (Carey et al. 1995, Laura M. Haas et al. 1997)[1]. At that time, distributed and federated RDBMS had already been popular. However, Garlic was an innovative approach to enable the integration of *heterogeneous* data sources with a focus on multimedia data.

6.2.1 Architecture

Figure 6.2 shows the typical mediator-wrapper architecture in the case of Garlic. In the middle of the figure, there is the Garlic mediator including query services and a runtime system as well as a metadata repository. Garlic could be integrated into C++ applications via an API. The interactive query/browser component, called *PESTO* (Carey et al. 1996), provided a more convenient way of accessing the integrated information for end-users. PESTO was a new approach of querying called *query-by-graphical-example* paradigm. In fact, it was very similar to the upcoming hypermedia browsers dedicated to realize the vision of Vannevar Bush (Bush 1945). Compared to the World Wide Web, which applied a much less restrictive and uncoordinated way of putting links and anchors, the information in Garlic came from databases and was compiled based on algebraic rules.

On the bottom of the figure, there are several data repositories, each one with an attached wrapper connected to Garlic. The job of the wrappers is to translate information about data types and schemas and to transform queries in the native query language or execute a sequence of API calls at the remote repository. All the information about the global Garlic schema and other translation-related information is maintained in the metadata repository. One of the repositories is special: the *Complex Object Repository* is used to *glue* information together. It may reside in a remote repository or inside Garlic

---

[1] *Garlic* is not an acronym. The name was obviously chosen because of the Gilroy garlic fields nearby. As of April 2009, IBM still maintains the project website of Garlic with a summary and list of publications at http://www.almaden.ibm.com/cs/garlic/.

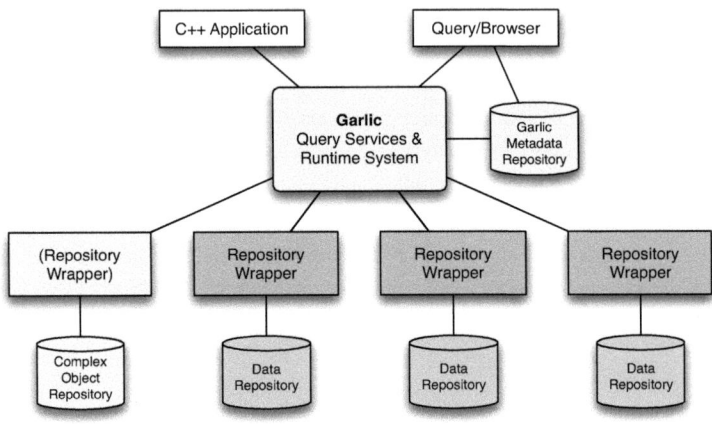

Figure 6.2: Garlic system architecture.

and it is used to augment additional information to join related but previously unconnected objects from different repositories.

The architecture of Garlic is based on the following assumptions:

- for any kind of data source (relational databases from various vendors, older, non-relational databases like IBM's IMS, record-based file systems, multimedia databases with media-specific capabilities for searching, etc.) it should be possible to write a wrapper

- a wrapper should exploit the capabilities of the underlying information system (e.g. selection based on keywords, ranges-queries, boolean expressions, similarity matching, etc.)

- it should be as easy as possible to write a new wrapper or to extend existing wrappers with new capabilities (e.g. as remote capabilities evolve)

- adding a new wrapper to the architecture should be independent of other components

6.2.2 Global Metamodel and Query Language

The global data model used in Garlic is the ODMG-93 object database standard (Cattell 1993), which had been slightly modified, especially regarding the treatment of object identifiers and references. Garlic does not provide a formal model mapping approach for wrappers. It is up to the wrappers' implementations, how they translate native data into instances of the exported ODMG-93 interfaces. A wrapper may also use a formal mapping framework, but no information into this direction could be found in the literature. Another research project initiated by IBM in the area of schema mapping was CLIO (Haas et al. 2005).

Basically ODMG-93 is very similar to the definition of *Java Data Objects* (JDO) today. The basic building blocks are *objects* and *values*. Objects have a unique *identity* and they are strongly typed by means of an *interface*. An interface has *attributes*, *relationships*, and even *methods*. Additionally, it can inherit from another interface realizing the concept of sub-typing. Each attribute of an object stores a value. A value can be a *base value* (i.e. a primitive like a number) or *structured* with built-in collection interfaces like sets, lists, bags, etc.

To describe the concept and query processing workflow of Garlic, the example from Carey et al. (1995) will be used. The example describes an insurance case. There are four distributed repositories:

1. `ClaimRep`, a relational database storing policies and claims
2. `ImageRep`, an image repository storing images of incidents using IBM's historic QBIC image database which provided methods for similarity matching
3. `TextRep`, a text repository storing text documents
4. the special `Complex Object Repository`, which stores *claim folders*

A claim folder *glues* all the distributed objects together: claims, pictures, and reports (documents). The wrapper interfaces for all four repositories are depicted in Figure 6.3. There is one relationship inside the RDBMS repository between `Policy` and `Claim`. The other relationships are between distributed objects. As already mentioned, the interfaces also specify methods. For example, the image repository is capable of executing similarity matches based on predicates like color, patterns, etc. The method `matches` returns true or false based on some implicit threshold. It can be used in queries inside conditional predicates.

Because Garlic was designed to integrate information from various independent sources, it has to take care for correct identification and referencing of distributed objects. Wrappers are responsible for correctly translate reference values between the global ID format and repository-specific IDs. Otherwise global joins would not be possible.

The query language of Garlic (also called GQL for *Garlic Query Language*) is basically SQL with several extensions to support the object-oriented features of ODMG-93[2]. It had been extended with features for traversing paths based on inter-object relationships, querying collection-valued attributes of objects, and invoking methods of objects within queries.

For example, the following query taken from Carey et al. (1995) can be used to obtain a list of customers with a red car, which had an incident due to "fatal speeding" during the first 60 days of insurance. The query will return the customer names and additionally pictures of the incident:

---

[2] Although the *Object Query Language* (OQL) did already exist, they decided to use SQL because at that time OQL was still in its infancy.

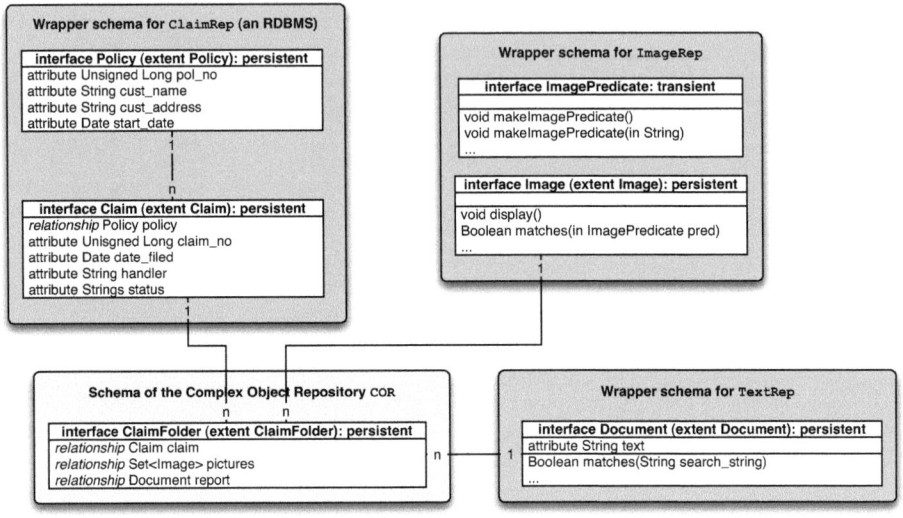

Figure 6.3: Wrapper interfaces for the discussed example.

```
select P.cust_name, {C.pictures}
from Policy P, P.claims C, C.pictures X
where (C.date_filed - P.start_date) < 60 and
      c.report.matches("fatality_speeding") and
      X.matches(["color", RED, .15])
```

6.2.3 Query Processing in Garlic

IBM was a leader in early database research. They contributed many architectural concepts and algorithms and came up with *System R*, the first implementation of Codd's relational model in 1975 (Astrahan et al. 1976). IBM was already experienced with federation techniques and distributed query optimization after developing the federated R* optimizer (Mackert and Lohman 1986) and the revolutionary *Starburst* optimizer (Lohman 1988). Much of the research effort during that time was focused on building extensible query optimizers based on some kind of rules instead of being hard-coded which involved expensive code refactoring each time new operators or better algorithms had to be tested (Graefe and DeWitt 1987, Freytag 1987). Instead of using a rule engine, Lohman proposed a compositional rule grammar known from compilers which could be recursively descended and was actually much faster. For Garlic, beside other changes to the existing optimizer, these rules where extended with additional ones for the operators of wrappers. They could build the system upon the existing DB2 CS system and make use of the already existing distributed Starburst query optimizer.

Although Garlic has been developed twenty years ago, the fundamental concepts are sill highly relevant. Actually, most concepts of the early prototypes can be found in IBM software of today. Some years ago, a major version of Garlic has been integrated into DB2 UDB (Josifovski et al. 2002). Details about Garlic's query processor have been published by Laura M. Haas et al. (1997). The major extension to the Starburst optimizer was the introduction of generic wrapper STAR operators. To be able to understand the concept, is is necessary to explain the basics of Starburst first.

The Starburst Query Optimizer

The first step of any query processor is parsing a lexical query into an internal representation which is the basis for logical and physical optimizations and the construction of a *query evaluation plan* (or *plan* in short). A plan consists of several operators each of which is consuming tuples from one (e.g. table scan or projection) or two (e.g. join, union, etc.) input operators. The output of one operator is the input to another such that the query execution engine can stream result tuples from the leave nodes which select physical data to the root node which produces the overall results. A query can be rewritten into alternative plans which are logically equivalent and a query engine may implement different physical operations for each logical operator (e.g. sequential or indexed access or different join algorithms). Typically, a query optimizer is therefore enumerating different equivalent plans to find the best plan in terms of costs (i.e. execution time). As already mentioned before, it was common to use a rule engine and declarative rules to specify the behavior of the optimizer. The key concept in Starburst was the introduction of grammar-like functional rules used to enumerate alternative plans (Lohman 1988). Because these rules were similar to grammar rules of a programming language, compilers could generate the optimizer code automatically without hard-coding the optimizer's behavior. In the following, the grammar of Starburst will be explained, example rules and productions will be shown in the next section.

A formal grammar consists of terminal symbols, non-terminals, production rules, and an initial non-terminal symbol. The terminals of Starburst's grammar are LOLEPOPs, which stands for *LOw-LEvel Plan OPerator*. The LOLEPOP is also called POP in the context of Garlic, obviously because they are not really low-level – they still get translated by wrappers into native queries/API calls as will be explained. LOLEPOPs are interpreted by the query engine at runtime during the execution process. They are a variation of the relational algebra (e.g. there is a Join, Union, etc.) with some additional LOLEPOPs like Access, Sort, Ship, etc. Ship is required for distributed queries which are supported by the Starburst optimizer. All LOLEPOPs may have different variants, i.e. there are different joins implemented like a *merge-join*, *nested-loop join* (NLJ), *bind-join*, etc. Each valid query evaluation plan produced by Starburst is a directed graph of different LOLEPOPs.

The non-terminals of the grammar are called STARs for *STrategy Alternative Rules*. Within the literature, the authors make no clear distinction between non-terminal symbols and the corresponding

6 Early Projects and Fundamental Concepts

production rules. Both are called STAR. To make things clearer, in the following a production rule is called a STAR rule, whereas the non-terminals will be called STAR. Once a STAR rule fires (i.e. gets visited during descending the grammar), it subsequently creates different *incomplete* sub-plans including further STARs and LOLEPOPs. A STAR rule may have a conditional function including several dynamically evaluated pre-conditions for a STAR rule to fire. Strictly spoken, in Starburst there is no single initial non-terminal. The initial state consists of a small number of *root* STARs. These root STARs basically resemble the canonical query plan after basic logical optimizations like push-down of filters, etc. There is an `AccessRoot` for single-collection accesses, a `JoinRoot` for producing joins, a `FinishRoot`, which adds root projections, sorting, etc. to the final query, and some others. The parsing of the grammar is done bottom-up starting with all the `AccessRoot`, `JoinRoot`, etc. and finally the `FinishRoot`. After evaluating all rules only one final plan will remain which consists of terminals only, i.e. LOLEPOPs. The evaluation is done in a dynamic programming fashion with more expensive plans pruned as early as possible (Selinger et al. 1979).

The STAR algorithm of Garlic differs from the original Starburst version in that the wrapper STARs are *generic*. A generic wrapper STAR consults the corresponding wrappers to build sub-plans. Depending on the registered repositories and thus, the existing wrappers, a generic STAR may be expanded into plans defined by the wrapper's STAR rules. Each generic STAR produces a generic P D [3] POP, which contains wrapper-specific instructions. Neither Garlic nor any other wrapper needs to understand the sub-plan of a P D POP. The only information available to Garlic are some parameters including costs. In the following, generic wrapper STARs will be prefixed with Repo.

Plan Generation with STARs – An Example

To explain the whole process more visually, given the repositories in Figure 6.3, the following simple query will be discussed in detail:

```
select F.claim
   from ClaimFolder F, F.report D
   where (D.matches("Interstate_101"))
```

The query selects all claims where the corresponding report mentions the "Interstate 101". As explained before, it is assumed that each wrapper exploits the capabilities of the underlying repository. However, at least a wrapper has to support two access functions: returning the list of OIDs and returning all attribute values for a given OID. To demonstrate such a scenario, it is assumed that the text repository called `TextRep` has only these two capabilities. The only other capability is retrieving OIDs based on the defined method `matches(String)`. One possible query plan is shown in Figure

---
[3] Although printing bold letters in the middle of continuous text is usually discouraged, POPs will be printed bold to differentiate them from STARs in the text.

6.4. The initial state may look like the following:

```
FinishRoot(
    JoinRoot(
        RepoAccess(ClaimFolder F, {F.claim, F.report}, ∅)
        RepoAccess(Document D, {D.OID, D.text}, { D.matches("Interstate 101") })
        { F.report = D.OID ∧ D.matches("Interstate 101") },
    ),
    proj, order, ...
)
```

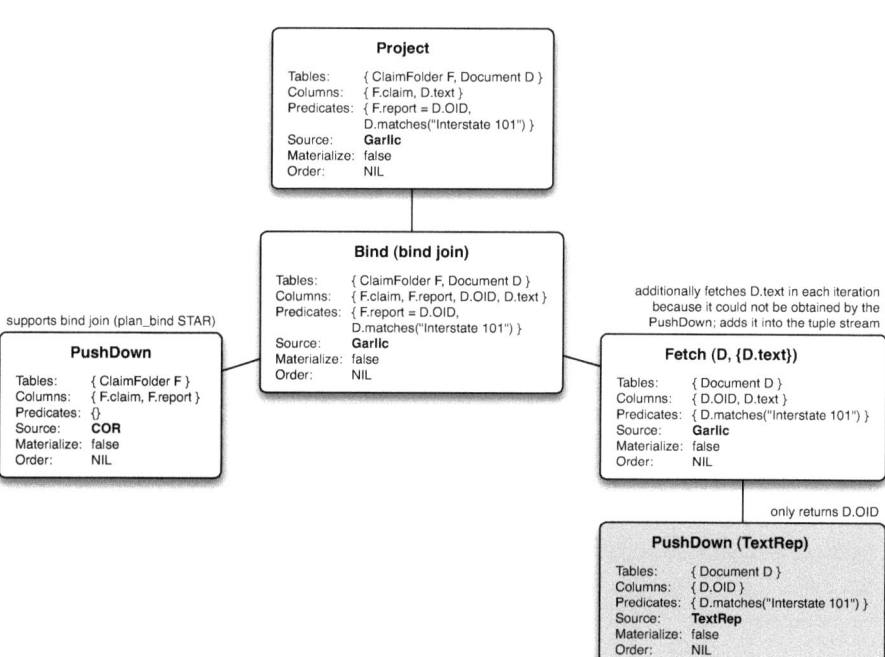

Figure 6.4: One possible Garlic query plan for the discussed example query.

6 Early Projects and Fundamental Concepts

There is actually no explicit STAR rule for the initial state in Garlic. Instead, the root STARs are combined programatically by the optimizer. The configuration above is only theoretically to visualize the initial state. In the example there is only one join. However, if there are multiple joins, the optimizer applies JoinRoot iteratively, passing it two plans and join predicates each time to get all possible join combinations. The STARs for the example and their arguments will be explained in the following.

Generation of Access Plans

The evaluation of STARs is performed bottom-up, starting with the access plans. Because Garlic does not store any data itself, the original AccessRoot introduced before is initially replaced with the generic Garlic-specific wrapper STAR RepoAccess. Thus, all access sub-plans are remote sub-plans (where data is coming from). Each one of both RepoAccess STARs shown above will produce sub-plans for accessing ClaimFolder and Document respectively. The arguments are the involved table[4], the set of columns, and any select predicates (e.g. D.matches("Interstate 101") for the Document access). These sub-plans are further combined by a JoinRoot STAR producing all possible join combinations of permutations of access sub-plans. The arguments of JoinRoot are all the sub-plans generated by the access plans and all join predicates. The FinishRoot STAR has further arguments specifying the projections, order attributes, etc. For each root STAR, except for FinishRoot (which is a pure Garlic STAR) there is a generic wrapper STAR rule. The following STAR rules are used to descend into RepoAccess:

$$\text{RepoAccess}(T, C, P) ::= \forall p \in \text{plan\_access}(T, C, P) : P \quad \supset \quad (p)$$

Condition: plan_access(T, C, P) defined by wrapper of $T.Source$

$$\text{RepoAccess}(T, C, P) ::= \forall p \in \text{plan\_access}(T, C', P) : \text{FetchCols}(T, C, P \quad \supset \quad (p))$$

Condition: plan_access(T, C', P) defined by wrapper of $T.Source$

with $C' = \{c \in C \mid c.name = \text{"OID"}\}$

Like all STARs with the prefix plan_, plan_access is a generic wrapper STAR, i.e. only wrappers provide further rules for these STARs. In each of the rules above, the plan_access rule is fired at the wrapper of the corresponding repository with the arguments T (the corresponding table), its attributes or columns C, and any predicates P. If a wrapper has no matching rule (e.g. missing capabilities), it returns an empty list. In the worst case, there may be no final query plan at all and hence, no results. In the normal case, a wrapper returns a list of wrapper plans, which are encapsulated and represented by the generic P $\supset$ POP. As explained earlier, this is a generic wrapper POP which encapsulates plan p^5 obtained from plan_access. p is only understandable by the wrapper and

---
[4]The terms *table* and *collection* as well as *columns* and *attributes* are used synonymously.
[5]Please note that p has nothing to do with P, which is the set of predicates for an access plan.

6.2 IBM Garlic

irrelevant to Garlic.

The first RepoAccess STAR rule is straight-foward: it pushes down sub-plan p, which was generated by the wrapper's plan_access rule. If a wrapper only provides the minimal capabilities, after obtaining OIDs, additional attributes have to be fetched in a second phase by the F POP. The second RepoAccess STAR rule shown above submits a reduced set C' to plan_access which only contains values $c \in C$ that are OIDs. The FetchCols STAR further produces a F POP according to the following rule:

$$\text{FetchCols}(T, C, Plan) ::= F \quad (T, C', Plan)$$
$$\text{Conditions: } C' \neq \emptyset, C' = C \setminus Plan.Columns$$

Whereas C' is computed as C without the columns already present in *Plan*. If $C' \neq \emptyset$ the F POP fetches the missing attributes for a given OID.

In case of the example given, for the ClaimFolder stored at the COR, direct access is possible and thus, the first RepoAccess STAR rule will produce the cheapest plans. The second RepoAccess STAR rule would also produce plans, but because of the separate fetching of attributes they are more expensive and will be pruned.

Regarding the access plans for Document, the repository TextRep only supports the minimum set of capabilities plus the matches(String) method. As a consequence, the first RepoAccess rule will not produce any plans and the best plan produced by the second rule introducing F will be used. After that, the state looks like this:

```
FinishRoot(
    JoinRoot(
        P    D    (wrapper-specific plans)
        F    (Document D, {D.text}, P    D    (wrapper-specific plans)
        { F.report = D.OID ∧ D.matches("Interstate 101") },
    ),
    proj, order, ...
)
```

POP Properties

Each POP provides any information Garlic requires via its properties. Property values are shown in Figure 6.4. There are properties for the set of retrieved tables and columns, predicates which must apply (e.g. for selections or theta-joins), the repository where the POP is executed ("Garlic" or any other repository name), a flag to indicate materialization, and a set of attributes to specify interesting orders of retrieved tuples. The order of tuples is interesting for merge-joins or order-by operations. An additional property not shown in the figure is *cost*. Every POP provides a cost estimate, which is used to calculate overall costs of alternative plans during plan optimization. Based on this cost model and an *dynamic programming* algorithm, expensive plans can be pruned as early as possible which significantly reduces the search space of possible query plans. Especially for the P D POP, properties are important. They are the only information Garlic may obtain from the encapsulated plan. A wrapper may use any custom POP inside such a plan that is not known by Garlic.

Join Enumeration

In the next step, JoinRoot is evaluated. Although in this example there is only one join, the optimizer usually enumerates all possible combinations of access plans by joining two sub-plans each time starting with 2-way joins, 3-way, and so on. The optimizer considers all possible *bushy* joins[6], which is very important for parallel distributed query execution. As Garlic supports different join methods, there are several STAR rules to evaluate a root join STAR:

$$\text{JoinRoot}(T_1, T_2, P) ::= \text{RepoJoin}(T_1, T_2, P)$$
$$\text{JoinRoot}(T_1, T_2, P) ::= \text{NestedLoopJoin}(T_1, T_2, P)$$
$$\text{JoinRoot}(T_1, T_2, P) ::= \text{BindJoin}(T_1, T_2, P)$$

The arguments submitted to a join STAR are T_1 and T_2 for two sequences of access plans generated by the AccessRoot STAR, and the set of join predicates P. Further STAR rules for the three different join STARs are shown in Figure 6.5. When evaluating a RepoJoin as shown in the figure, a wrapper will only generate any plan, if it defined a rule for plan_join. Additionally, the rule has a condition which is true, if all information is obtained from the same repository except from Garlic itself: $T_1.Source = T_2.Source \land T_1.Source \neq \text{"Garlic"}$.

The two other join operations are distributed joins executed at Garlic: NestedLoopJoin (NLJ) and BindJoin. The NLJ rule defines the required POPs and STARs to realize the nested loop join algorithm: fetching (FetchCols) and materializing (T POP) the inner plan results which are iteratively scanned (S POP) and joined (NLJ POP) with tuples fetched by the outer plan.

BindJoin is similar to a NLJ, but more efficient if one side has a lower cardinality. Each intermediate tuple from the outer plan fetched by FetchCols, is submitted to the bind-join capable wrapper executing the inner iteration. The wrapper constraints the access plan for the next tuple to fetch by the already obtained values from the outer tuple. This way, the join predicates can be applied locally and less data has to be shipped over the network. The *bind join* does not work well with cross-products

---

[6]*Bushy* means balanced join trees by contrast to *left-deep* join trees. There have been long discussions about pros and cons of left-deep and bushy joins in the database community (Ioannidis and Kang 1991).

```
RepoJoin(T₁, T₂, P) ::= ∀p ∈ plan_join(T₁, T₂, P) : P    D    (p)
```
Conditions: $T_1.Source = T_2.Source \wedge T_1.Source \neq \text{``Garlic''} \wedge$
   plan_join(T_1, T_2, P) defined by the wrapper of $T_1.Source$
Functions: none

```
NestedLoopJoin(T₁, T₂, P) ::= NLJ(FetchCols(T₁, NeedAttr(T₁, P), P),
       S   (T   (FetchCols(T₂, NeedAttr(T₂, P), P))), P)
```
Conditions: none
Functions: NeedAttr(Plan, Preds) computes the attributes of collections of sub-plan *Plan*
   that are needed to compute the predicates in *Preds*.

```
BindJoin(T₁, T₂, P) ::= ∀p ∈ plan_bind(T₁, T₂, P) :
       B   (FetchCols(T₁, NeedAttr(T₁, P), P), P    D    (p))
```
Conditions: $T_2.Source \neq \text{``Garlic''} \wedge$ plan_bind(T, P) defined by the wrapper of $T_2.Source$
Functions: NeedAttr(Plan, Preds) as above

Figure 6.5: Different join STARs produced by `JoinRoot`.

(which are a big problem in distributed query processing anyway) and is only favorable if one join side has a low cardinality.

Coming back to the example, the join between `ClaimFolder` and `Document` is a distributed join. Because $T_1.Source \neq T_2.Source$, `RepoJoin` will not produce any plans, even if `TextRep` defined a STAR for `plan_join`. However, `NestedLoopJoin` always produces at least one plan and `BindJoin` may produce further plans, depending on the wrappers' STAR rules for the generic `plan_bind`. It is assumed that the COR, where the claim folders are stored supports the bind join and that the cheapest plan was one of them. The optimizer recognizes, that the access plan for `Document` already produced a `FetchCols` STAR whose *Predicates* property contains the required join predicates (`D.OID`). Thus, the additional `FetchCols` generated by the bind join is not required and after applying the `FinishRoot`, a final query plan might look as depicted in Figure 6.4.

6.2.4 Wrapper-specific STARs

The generic wrapper STARs like `plan_access` or `plan_bind` can be arbitrarily implemented by a wrapper. The only interface is the production rule and the properties of the produced POP. Due to this generic concept the requirements concerning the mediator-wrapper architecture can be fulfilled in a very elegant manner. The wrappers can be independently and incrementally developed for a broad range of different information systems.

For example, a relational database system can provide many different access plans for the generic `plan_access` STAR passing through the underlying capabilities like indexed access or keyword search to the mediator. Because each STAR may also specify cost functions, the mediator can use dynamic programming to chose the best sub-plan (e.g. indexed access instead of a full-table scan). Also the possibility of executing joins remotely can be achieved by providing the appropriate join STARs.

6.2.5 Cost-Model

To track the costs of a plan, each POP provides three different cost estimation formulas: *total cost*, *re-execution cost*, and *result cardinality*. Also wrappers should provide these properties when the corresponding P D POP is instantiated. Otherwise, a default function will be used. Additionally, for each method a wrapper supports, it is asked to provide two additional cost functions: *total method cost* (for executing the method once) and *re-execution method cost* (for further executions of the method). Because the generic wrapper STARs define an abstract interface to the wrappers, the mediator does not need detailed statistics used for physical access plans such as histograms. Physical access to information is hidden by the wrapper implementation. The mediator only needs high level statistics like cardinalities, the number of distinct values for an attribute, and the second highest and second lowest values. Wrappers may use further physical statistics for their private cost formulas.

Similar to SemWIQ, Garlic provides a generic facility to compute statistics from source data by executing a workload of queries and use the results to calculate various statistics. The base workload can be extended and modified according to the wrapper's capabilities and specific methods.

6.2.6 Browsing Information with PESTO

The PESTO query browser (*Portable Explorer of Structured Objects*), which has been developed by IBM in cooperation with the University of Wisconsin, is a very innovative way of providing a rich user interface to less experienced users. While the typical graphical interfaces of that time separated between tabular views, SQL source views, SQL design views, etc. PESTO provided an integrated browser putting all these features in place. Carey et al. (1996) declared the goal of PESTO as "to provide a similarly friendly browsing interface, also based on hypertext-style navigation, and to augment this interface with an equally natural paradigm for integrating querying and query refinement with browsing".

6.3 Other Mediator Systems

Garlic was probably one of the most sophisticated approaches towards integration of heterogenous distributed data sources with a strong focus on scalability and performance. The Starburst-based architecture which allows to hook-in wrapper specific operators and cost functions can be seen as a reference architecture for relational-based mediator-wrapper systems aimed at the integration of multimedia repositories. It allows wrappers to expose very specific access functions and very fine-granular query optimization. The possibility of defining methods as part of repository interfaces provides a high level of freedom for supporting very specific capabilities as part of the global query language.

Already in the nineties, a broad range of different architectures, prototypes, and production systems have been developed. It is impossible to include a full overview of the related work in this area. Additional literature and further approaches can be found by inspecting the references of the cited examples. During the nineties, among others, there was SIMS (Arens and Knoblock 1993), TSIMMIS (Chawathe et al. 1994), Information Manifold (Kirk et al. 1995), IRO-DB (Gardarin et al. 1997), DISCO (Naacke et al. 1998), COIN (Goh et al. 1999), and the agent-based computing approaches Carnot (Collet et al. 1991) and InfoSleuth (Bayardo et al. 1997).

In the following TSIMMIS, DISCO, and InfoSleuth will be described in short. TSIMMIS is interesting, because its authors introduced a more flexible data model which does not require the explicit specification and maintenance of a global schema. DISCO is more fault-tolerant and can deliver partial results when data sources become unavailable. Additionally, the authors also addressed the task of model mapping. Carnot and InfoSleuth are larger frameworks with the goal of integrating distributed information and services based on autonomous software agents.

6.3.1 TSIMMIS

TSIMMIS, which is an acronym for *The Stanford-IBM Manager of Multiple Information Sources*, was a cooperative project between the IBM Almaden Research Center and Stanford University right at the same time when Garlic was conducted at Almaden (Garcia-Molina et al. 1997, Chawathe et al. 1994). However, TSIMMIS' architecture is different in many ways.

Architecture

Firstly, multiple stacked mediators are used, each of which takes the input from multiple wrappers or other mediators and does some processing in order to contribute some added-value. Within TSIMMIS, a wrapper is called *translator*. An overview of the architecture of TSIMMIS is depicted in Figure 6.6. As the figure shows, users may chose one of the existing mediators (and also wrappers directly) to execute queries. Mediators have a fixed behavior which is hard-coded as part of their implementation. For example, mediators may combine two wrapped data sources with a join, union or

6 Early Projects and Fundamental Concepts

other procedural operation (Chawathe et al. 1994). While a wrapper may provide information about a library, a mediator may contribute book covers obtained from another wrapper into the intermediate results. Another mediator may include extended information about the author or user reviews in a third step. Each query interface is like a more or less rich specific view onto available data items. As will be explained later, the query language used in TSIMMIS does not explicitly provide operators like the relational algebra and other declarative query languages. The user has no direct possibility to formulate a join or union operation, it is only possible if there is a mediator providing that specific view over two other sources which may be mediators or wrappers (Papakonstantinou et al. 1995).

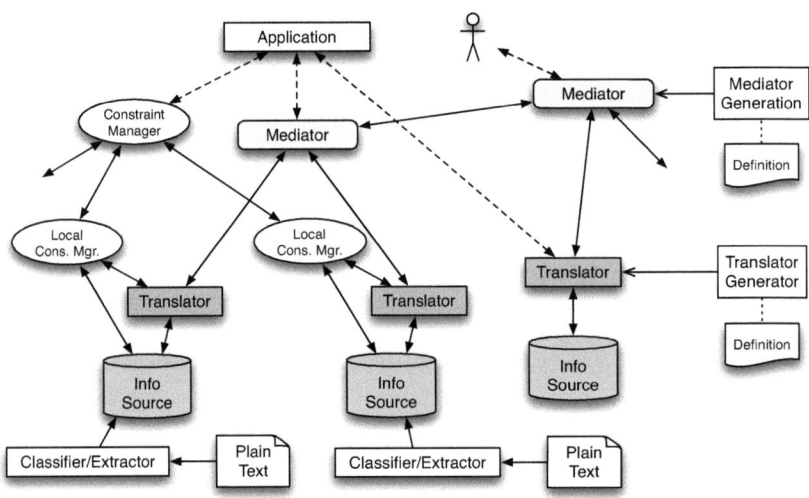

Figure 6.6: Architecture of TSIMMIS.

The TSIMMIS approach very clearly reflects the vision of Gio Wiederhold explained in Section 6.1, although, it may be argued, that the possibilities are rather limited because joins and other typical operations have to be provided explicitly by mediators. The need for a broad range of different mediators was also the reason for the authors of TSIMMIS to develop generators for both, wrappers and mediators. Based on rules and a software library, mediators and wrappers can be generated.

Secondly, TSIMMIS wrappers have been extended by classifiers and extractors, which are able to extract structured data from unstructured sources like plain text and HTML documents. Garlic also supports the integration of multimedia data sources, but compared to TSIMMIS, it is assumed that the multimedia system provides a specific wrapper which exposes the STARs and POPs to use the specific access functions directly. TSIMMIS provides classifiers and extractors independent of a wrapper. However, this feature can also be regarded as an add-on which is basically independent from the mediator-wrapper system. A multimedia data source may also provide native metadata in which case, no explicit extractor is required. Compared to the Garlic approach for integrating multi-media sources, TSIMMIS' classifiers and extractors could be attached to wrappers of any other integration system and are as such not an integral part of the architecture.

TSIMMIS has support for maintaining global logical constraints by means of global and local constraint managers. However, when integrating *autonomous* information sources, there is usually little possibility to fix inconsistencies if constraints are violated. Assuming local constraints are enforced and checked by the data sources, any global constraint should be defined such that it cannot become invalid anyway[7].

Concerning the global data model, there is another difference to Garlic. While data source descriptions (interfaces) are fixed in Garlic, the TSIMMIS architecture is a bit more flexible.

Object Exchange Model as a Flexible Global Metamodel

Papakonstantinou et al. (1995) introduced a self-describing global data model called *Object Exchange Model* (OEM). The model can be used to describe data without the need for an explicit schema layer. This facilitates the management of available mediators and wrappers, because a mediator is not required to maintain a pre-defined global schema. OEM is based on a structured graph which is formed by nested tuples of the form < *label, type, value* >, where *value* can be a leave node's value or a reference to a nested tuple. An example is shown in Figure 6.7. The semantics of the value is based on the label. Modeling semantics within OEM is not more advanced than in the relational model: self-descriptive names are used for properties in-line when describing data. There is no possibility to model explicit class relationships, hierarchies, nor is there a way to add additional logical constraints compared to RDF-Schema and OWL. The global query language in TSIMMIS is OEM-QL. From a structural perspective, both, OEM and OEM-QL are even similar to XML and XPath/XQuery (without using an explicit XML Schema). An example for an OEM-QL query and corresponding source model is given in Figure 6.7.

As the example query may reveal, query processing in TSIMMIS is based on matching graph paths. For the query in Figure 6.7, the mediator named Biblio would find all paths to the sub-object structure defined by the sequence {bib, doc, authors, authors-ln}, where the last object has the value "Ullman". For each of these paths, the sub-structure of bib.doc is expanded to retrieve all values for bib.doc.topic.

---

[7]For example, consider a reservation system for theater rooms with a cardinality constraint on reservations (seats). The system should be designed in a way, that the same room is not handled by different data sources, which implicitly fulfills the global constraint anyway.

S :

< bib, set, $\{doc_1, doc_2, \ldots, doc_n\}$ >
   doc_1 :   < doc, set, $\{au_1, top_1, cn_1\}$ >
      au_1 :   < authors, set, $\{au_1^1\}$ >
         au_1^1 :   < author-ln, str, "Ullman" >
      top_1 :   < topic, str, "Databases" >
      cn_1 :   < local-call#, integer, 25 >
   doc_2 :   < doc, set, $\{au_2, top_2, cn_2\}$ >
      au_2 :   < authors, set, $\{au_2^1, au_2^2, au_2^3\}$ >
         au_2^1 :   < author-ln, str, "Aho" >
         au_2^2 :   < author-ln, str, "Hopcroft" >
         au_2^3 :   < author-ln, str, "Ullman" >
      top_2 :   < topic, str, "Algorithms" >
      cn_2 :   < dewey-decimal#, str, "BR273" >
. . .

Q :

```
SELECT bib.doc.topic
       FROM Biblio
       WHERE bib.doc.authors.author-ln = "
             Ullman"
```

Q :

< answer, set, $\{o_1, o_2\}$ >
   o_1 :   < topic, str, "Databases" >
   o_2 :   < topic, str, "Algorithms" >

Figure 6.7: OEM example query (Chawathe et al. 1994).

Query Processing in TSIMMIS

Similarly to Garlic, the native query capabilities of wrapped information systems can be exploit. However, the methodology is different and based on *query containment*. The capabilities of a wrapper are specified by parameterized rules (Garcia-Molina et al. 1997). Capabilities in this sense also specify which tuples a data source provides. During query processing, these rules are matched against the received query. By contrast to Garlic, the rules are not as fine granular as the specification of algebraic operations. In the worst case, a wrapper (or mediator) may only support very specific queries and if some part of the query is missing, the wrapper cannot answer it. However, if multiple rules have been defined and the query cannot be answered directly, the wrapper tries to combine rules to find an equivalent. This process is similar to query containment calculation used for resolving views in relational database systems. An optimizer for the runtime system of TSIMMIS mediators has been introduced by Papakonstantinou et al. (1996). There is an algebraic optimizer which is part of the view expander and a cost-based optimizer which determines what queries are sent to the sources and in which order they are sent. It follows a rather different approach than typical cost-based optimizers for relational algebra plans (e.g. Starburst). This is basically because the query processing approach is rule-based and more related to logical programming. The optimization is more challenging, because of OEM uses nested objects which have an unknown structure. For example, when a mediator is executing a join, it is not possible to predict, if a specific value will be obtained from one or the other source which makes a push-down of selections impossible. The flexible architecture of TSIMMIS based on OEM and OEM-QL clearly has a bottleneck regarding the implementation and application of sophisticated query optimization. This is the main reason, why the approach is only adequate to some certain extent.

Web-based Browsing of OEM Answer Graphs

It is also rather interesting, how first approaches have been proposed during the nineties, to use the World Wide Web as a basis for user interfaces of distributed systems. As part of the TSIMMIS project, the *Mosaic-based Information Explorer* (MOBIE) has been developed. Although it was very simple compared to the interfaces we have today, at least it was a first approach towards navigating in a graph of interlinked information based on the hypermedia paradigm. To explain the meaning of an OEM label, MOBIE had a special *help* button which could be used to recall a human readable description. This is very similar to the rdfs:comment property used to describe RDF schema elements with natural language. Compared to the extensible Resource Description Framework, the expressiveness of OEM is low. OEM-QL queries are starting with a root node, which is not required when querying RDF graphs. RDF is better suited for the description of distributed information because it does not have the *unique name assumption* and it is based on the *open world assumption*.

6.3.2 DISCO

DISCO (Naacke et al. 1998, Tomasic et al. 1996), an acronym for *Distributed Information Search COmponent*, was a European project conducted at the late nineties. Some of the researchers had already taken part in the former EU Esprit project called IRO-DB (Gardarin et al. 1997), one of the first EU-funded cross-national IT projects actually – with the goal to develop a federated object-oriented multi-database system. The authors of DISCO could benefit from the lessons learnt in the IRO-DB project (Naacke et al. 1998). Compared to the multi-layered IRO-DB architecture, DISCO is designed more compact and simpler.

The architecture of DISCO is depicted in Figure 6.8. The numbers indicate the order of actions starting with the registration (1) of a new wrapped data source at the DISCO mediator, the provisioning of all required information such as exported schema, capabilities, and cost functions by the wrapper (2) and a query execution process (numbers 3–6). The figure also shows, that the global query language OQL is processed based on the relational calculus, however, the sub-queries are based on single algebraic operations. For instance, a wrapper may provide an access function, but no join operation as part of its capability specification. The results are always tuples.

A special focus was put on the problem of unavailability of data sources. DISCO can provide partial results when a data source becomes unavailable during query execution. The remaining results are stored in the form of another query and can be executed later on to complete the overall result. Like Garlic, DISCO uses the ODMG-93 standard for the specification of the global data model.

6 Early Projects and Fundamental Concepts

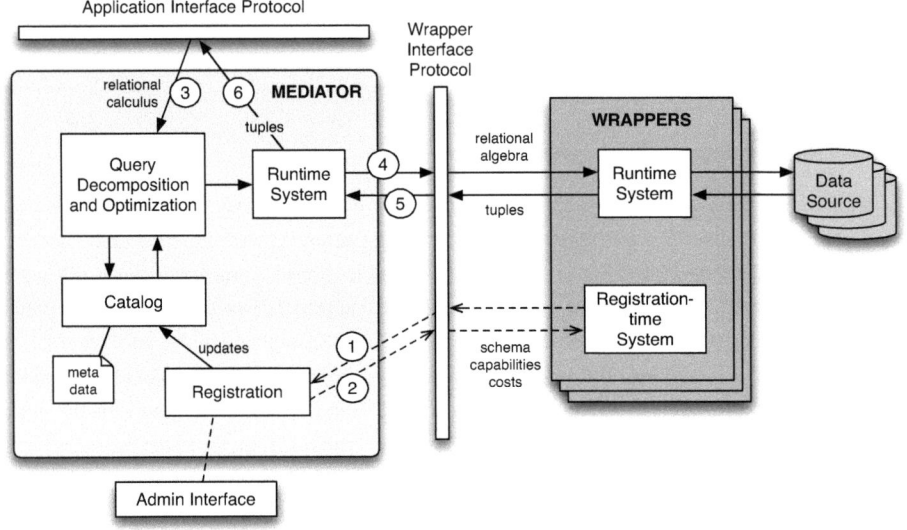

Figure 6.8: Architecture and processes in DISCO.

However, instead of inventing a proprietary query language, global queries in DISCO are formulated in ODMG's OQL (*Object Query Language*). As a special feature, DISCO exposes the metadata about registered wrappers, which can be queried using OQL like a wrapped data source.

Support for Model Mapping

In the DISCO project the task of model mapping was also addressed. DISCO provides three methods to integrate data sources having a local schema which does not match the global schema definition. However, the approach only works between ODMG schemas. Thus, it is assumed, that in a first phase, the wrapper already provides an ODMG schema for the legacy data of the underlying information system. The three methods are *subtyping* for modeling similar substructures, *maps* for modeling similar structures, and *views* for modeling dissimilar structures (Tomasic et al. 1996, Sect. 2.2).

The sub-typing method already comes with ODMG and works well for objects with a different type, but similar structure. For instance, if the global data model only defines the interface Person and a data source has an interface Student with similar substructure, the wrapper only needs to define a sub-class relationship to subsume Student with the global Person. A global query for persons will include all exposed students of the data source. Sub-typing is typically used together with a mapping (i.e. *local transformation map*).

A mapping in DISCO is specified as part of an interface definition. There are two different kinds of mappings: mappings between a local type (e.g. relation) and a global type and mappings between a field of a local type and a field of a global type. For example, if the field representing a student's name in the Student type (e.g. student_name) is different from the name in the Person type (e.g. pName), a 1:1 mapping can be used to map the name fields. Mappings in DISCO are flat only. There is no possibility to map between different nested structures and there is no way to resolve conflicts of schematic heterogeneity. Also the support for functional mappings (e.g. value translations) has been announced only and obviously is not realized.

However, in many cases of dissimilar type structures, the concept of *views* is a very powerful approach to align types. Views are actually query definition expressions in OQL which may generate the necessary virtual interface to conform with the global type definition. A view can, furthermore, reference other views. Apart from performance issues, this provides a powerful approach when the simpler mappings are not sufficient.

Query Processing and Cost Functions

Especially regarding query processing and optimization, the authors of DISCO could benefit from the lessons learnt in the IRO-DB project before. The architecture of IRO-DB requires each wrapper (called *adapter*) to support full OQL to answer local queries. As a consequence, an OQL query processor has to be implemented for each wrapper on top of native information sources[8]. For local queries issued to wrappers, DISCO uses algebraic operators similar to Garlic, instead of a full declarative query language. This approach allows for a more fine-grained cost model and improved query optimization. The optimizer is based on standard relational database optimization techniques. All plans have a global part and multiple local sub-plans which are directed to the corresponding wrappers. The equivalent operator for Garlic's PushDown is called *submit* in DISCO. Much of the research in the DISCO project was dedicated to the improvement of the cost model (Naacke et al. 1998).

6.3.3 InfoSleuth

The *InfoSleuth* project was initiated by the former *Microelectronics and Computer Technology Corporation* (MCC) in 1995 as a follow-up project of *Carnot* (Collet et al. 1991). The Carnot project was a very early approach (and probably the first one) towards a large-scale multi-agent enterprise information integration software. The ideas and the proposed and implemented concepts can be regarded as ground-breaking at that time. Both, Carnot and InfoSleuth use ontologies to support the semantic integration of heterogeneous data sources. In case of Carnot, the low-level ontology *Cyc* (Lenat 1995) is used to map real world entities with so-called *articulation axioms* to formally define concepts of the

---

[8]Please note, that also SemWIQ requires wrappers to support a full query language (SPARQL). But as will be shown in Chapter 10, based on the Jena/ARQ query engine, it is only necessary to implement a single triple match function and provide a cost estimate for the expected cardinalities.

Cyc ontology. Several prototype applications have been developed for Carnot in the areas of workflow management, heterogenous database access, knowledge discovery in large databases, and integrated access to text repositories and structured databases.

The InfoSleuth project was sponsored by large companies like Andersen Consulting, Bellcore, Boeing, NCR/AT&T, etc. and the US Department of Defense, who were interested in a fail-safe, scalable solution to integrate information maintained in a variety of geographically distributed sources. The idea of *autonomous software agents*, which are acting on behalf of humans to achieve some particular task, originates from the artificial intelligence (AI) community and became rather popular during the 90ies (Russell and Norvig 2003, Ch. 2). A software agent is basically an autonomous software program which is communicating over a network (e.g. the internet) with other software agents.

In Figure 6.9, an overview of the InfoSleuth architecture is depicted. In a multi-agent framework like InfoSleuth, there are basically two kinds of agents: *user agents* and other, fully independent agents with very specific capabilities. For example, there are *monitor agents, broker agents, task execution agents, task monitoring agents, association mining agents, multi-resource query agents, resource agents*, and others. A *user agent* serves as an intelligent interface for human users. The system was implemented in Java to provide platform independence. The user agent could also be integrated into Websites as Java applets. Like all other agents, it advertises its existence and capabilities to a broker agent, which is acting as a super-peer in the network and routes messages to other agents. The location of the user agent is fully independent from the users' location which makes it possible to use the system from any computer or device connected to the internet. At the time when InfoSleuth was developed, there was no existing peer-to-peer middleware as for example JXTA, which has been introduced by Sun in 2001 (Gong 2001). Thus, InfoSleuth can also be seen as a pioneering project towards peer-to-peer networking, which became very popular at the millennium (and especially after the Napster lawsuit filed by the RIAA).

A resource agent can be seen as a gatekeeper to an information source. Its task is to respond to queries whose answers are entailed in the attached information source. This can be some kind of database (relational, object, XML), a multimedia repository or a simple collection of texts. All information sources in InfoSleuth are regarded as fully autonomous. It is viewed at the level of its relevant semantic concepts, hence, its local schema, format, and representation is fully independent. The resource agent is the equivalent of a wrapper in the mediator-wrapper architecture. It also maintains a mapping from the common domain ontologies to the local schema and language native to its underlying resource. The resource agent advertises its capabilities – i.e. what it knows and what kind of answers it can respond to – and accepts queries specific to the resource.

The equivalent of the mediator is not easy to identify, because the sub-components of a mediator like Garlic, TSIMMIS, or DISCO are separated and executed by different agents. A mediator in the sense of Garlic could be comprised of a broker agent, a task execution agent, an ontology agent, a multi-resource query agent, and a task monitoring agent.

6.3 Other Mediator Systems

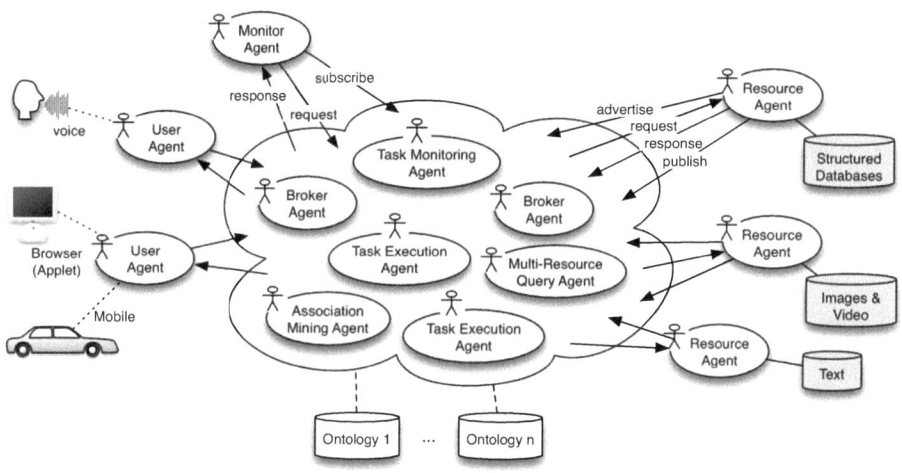

Figure 6.9: Overview of InfoSleuth including agents relevant for information integration.

Ontologies in InfoSleuth

While the Carnot prototype Cyc was used to accurately map various entities to a formal ontology, in case of InfoSleuth, an arbitrary number of different domain ontologies are used. A low-level ontology like Cyc may be adequate as a basis for interlinking distributed objects based on their meaning, however, in general it is not sufficient for specialized applications with a very specific domain of discourse. As a communication language between agents, the *Knowledge Query and Manipulation Language* (KQML) is used (Finin et al. 1994). It specifies several performatives for querying agents (*ask, ask-all, evaluate*), informational performatives (*tell, untell*), and capability-related performatives (*advertise, subscribe, monitor*). KQML is actually an envelope for the actual content of a message, which may be represented in different languages. It can be compared to the SOAP envelope of XML-based Web service calls containing arbitrary XML data which is typically not required to be readable by the middleware. The language used for the content is specified as part of the KQML envelope. The standard language in InfoSleuth is the *Knowledge Interchange Format* (KIF)[9], a LISP-style logical representation language which was developed for the purpose of sharing knowledge between distributed systems with different internal knowledge representation formats.

---

[9]Both, KQML and KIF have been developed as part of the *DARPA Knowledge Sharing Effort* during the early nineties (Patil et al. 1992).

Information Integration in InfoSleuth

As already mentioned, all agents advertise their existence and capabilities to agent brokers (by means of a *tell* performative). A user agent is acting on behalf of a human user and communicating with other agents to fulfill the assigned tasks. It serves as a portal into the agent framework which is independent of the user's location (*ubiquitous access*). A resource agent accepts queries specific to the resource it is attached to. It maintains a mapping from the stored information to global domain ontologies. Alternatively, such mappings can also be managed by dedicated *value mapping agents* (Fowler et al. 1999). The InfoSleuth architecture is rather generic. Some agents are pre-defined, but depending on the applications, more or less specific agents can be added to fulfill the required tasks and sub-tasks.

In the following, it is assumed that a user wants to acquire information stored in several resources of different kinds (e.g. databases, text repositories, multimedia servers, etc.). A multi-resource agent, which is able to answer such queries has already advertised itself to all brokers. The user agent sends the query, which may be formulated in any language understandable by the multi-resource query agent, encoded as a KQML performative (e.g. *ask*) to a broker agent. The broker matches the performative to its knowledge base which includes information about other agents, their types, capabilities, load, state, etc. and returns the reference to a task-execution agent. The task-execution agent coordinates the workflow of high-level information gathering tasks. It will delegate parts of its process to other agents, such as the multi-resource query agent. A query may also involve data mining sub-tasks or query decomposition in which cases, the task-execution agent will consult further agents during the task execution. Because the assumed example query is a global query merging information from multiple resources, the task-execution agent delegates the task to the multi-resource query agent. The query contains a domain context, which is typically the name of a domain ontology. The multi-resource query agent decomposes the original (e.g. SQL) query and requests the necessary ontological model from the ontology agent. Parts of the ontologies are typically cached for later re-use to speed-up the whole process. The multi-resource query agent is only capable of executing union combinations. For global joins and other operations, the *query decomposition agent* is used (Bayardo et al. 1997). The multi-resource query agent requests matching resource agents at the broker and sends multiple KIF queries to relevant resource agents. Each resource agent translates the corresponding KIF query into the native language of the attached information source based on the mappings it maintains. It executes the native queries and translates the answers back into the KIF language. The results are composed by the task-execution agent and incrementally delivered to the user agent using a streaming protocol.

Although in the existing literature, many ideas and concepts have been explained, only a few of them have actually been implemented in InfoSleuth. For instance, it is unclear whether the query-decomposition agent has been implemented. Regarding the resource agents, the authors have developed a wrapper for JDBC and ODBC which was tested with Oracle, MS Access, and SQL Server.

Any other wrapper may have been implemented by specific applications of InfoSleuth like the US *Environmental Data Exchange Network* (EDEN).

6.4 Discussion

The early mediator-based approaches already addressed many typical issues of information integration. The focus in the Garlic project was towards distributed query optimization and exploitation of the native capabilities of information systems. TSIMMIS, on the other hand, was more flexible due to the self-describing, schema-less data model. However, it lacked sophisticated distributed query optimization. In the DISCO project issues of unavailability and tuning wrapper cost models had been addressed and for the InfoSleuth project the focus was put on semantic interoperability and scalability. But while InfoSleuth was scalable, used ontologies, and provided support for model mapping, it would have been a huge overhead to set it up for small to medium-sized scenarios. Below the line, in none of these projects all issues have been addressed at the same time.

An attempt to classify the presented mediator-based information integration systems is shown in Figure 6.10. Please note that, due to the range of different properties and concepts, a strict classification is not feasible. The figure should give a vague impression of the general strengths of the approaches. In order to classify them, four dimensions are used: *query processing and optimization*, *global data model expressiveness*, *ease of use*, and the *origin or underlying paradigm*, which is database or AI and agent-based computing (ABC).

IBM Garlic probably had the best performance, however, it was rather inflexible due to the globally maintained fixed data model. Today, information is changing frequently and thus, its representation and schema in various sources. Changes in a local information source, should not affect the entire integration system. Garlic has found its way into the product line of IBM DB2 and Information Server and the metadata management has been improved much as part of the enterprise-targeted software package. However, its focus has ever been in the area of relational database systems since all enterprises are using RDBMS. Within the literature about Garlic, there was no attempt to represent semantics of data and integrate them into the integration workflow. As a consequence, the semantics of attributes were only defined by their names, which is even weaker than in relational database systems which additionally know about inclusion dependencies and integrity constraints. By contrast, RDF/OWL ontologies are an integral part of SemWIQ, which allow an explicit specification of the semantics of the integrated information.

It is interesting, that the authors of the PESTO query browser for Garlic argued, that the strict schema-centric approach of Garlic and PESTO was superior compared to the schema-less hypertext approach of that time (Carey et al. 1996). On the other hand, assumed that the schema of a data source evolves because attributes and relations are added, altered, or removed frequently in a distributed environment, the system was far to inflexible. By contrast to Garlic, within SemWIQ the global data

6 Early Projects and Fundamental Concepts

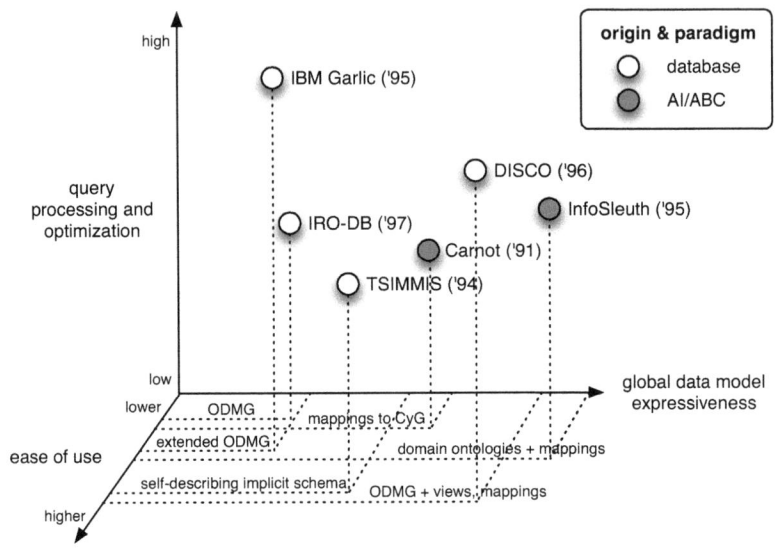

Figure 6.10: Classification of the discussed mediator-based approaches.

model is purely virtual. There is no need to specify interfaces or types for the global virtual view. It is the union of the integrated data sources which can register and abandon freely.

Regarding the user interface, there are many parallels to the Semantic Web and especially *linked data browsers* of today: we are now integrating structured information, declarative query support via SPARQL, the facetted-search paradigm, and semantic links into ordinary web browsers. In Section 4.5 these new paradigms of linked data and semantic links have been presented.

InfoSleuth serves as a scalable base architecture which can be extended as required, although the performance for information integration tasks is not comparable to that of Garlic or DISCO, which are dedicated systems for that purpose. It has been used in the late nineties as a basis for various applied research projects in the areas of health care, genome mapping, environmental monitoring (Fowler et al. 1999), crisis management, distributed traffic monitoring, satellite data dissemination, or battlefield applications (Telcordia Technologies, Inc. 2005).

One must admit, that Garlic has been developed 20 years ago. During the last two decades many things have changed and especially the World Wide Web has gained a momentum. Today, Semantic Web based approaches have become very popular. Based on Semantic Web concepts, fragments of information can be described in a distributed fashion and globally identified by means of URIs. Because RDF does not rely on a unique name assumption and is based on the open world assumption, information can be merged and extended very flexibly based on the existing WWW infrastructure.

7 Information Integration based on Semantic Web Technologies

In this chapter, Semantic Web-based approaches for virtual information integration will be discussed. The majority of the projects that were initiated since the millennium – and especially after Tim Berners Lee et al. (2001) have published an article about the Semantic Web vision in the *Scientific American* – are based on RDF ontologies and Semantic Web concepts. The discussion of further non-Semantic Web approaches of the nineties is out of the scope of this thesis. Although, ontologies have already been used during the nineties to address issues with semantic interoperability the concepts developed recently in the Semantic Web community are different and very promising with respect to scalability and flexibility[1].

By the vast amount of SW-based information integration projects initiated during the last years, it is impossible to keep track of all of them. To get an overview of the various characteristics, the following orthogonal dimensions for a comparison can be identified:

(A) applied vs. generic approach

(B) expressiveness of the ontologies used

(C) materialized vs. virtual paradigm

(D) comprehensive vs. narrow approach

Regarding (A), on the one hand, there are applied projects which have a specific goal in a usually interdisciplinary setting (e.g. healthcare, life sciences, environmental science) and on the other hand, there are projects towards fundmantal and generic architectures for a broader range of similar applications. Because SemWIQ is a generic information integration system, only related generic systems are discussed in detail in Section 7.2. It will be shown, how the approaches differ with respect to the their methodologies. Actually, there are only a few generic approaches that are applicable for real-world use cases, SemWIQ is one of them. The majority of related projects is undertaken in application-specific domains and has been developed with very specific needs and not for general use. For many research disciplines, the requirements and affordances are very specific. For instance, the biomedical

---

[1]The concepts of the Semantic Web are introduced in Chapter 4.

domain requires very specific access methods, matching algorithms (for matching genetic sequences), and for joining information sources it is still rather typical to develop small Perl scripts to do the necessary operations. Some applications also need to integrate services and applications. In Section 7.3 a few application-oriented and inter-disciplinary projects are discussed.

Another distinction (B) can be made based on the expressiveness of the ontologies used. Because RDF supports different ontological layers, it is possible to build rather simple systems with the RDF Core and without any schema layer, and it is possible to build systems which are using DL reasoners and all the language features provided by OWL. As mentioned in the Semantic Web primer, the original vision of Tim Berners Lee et al. (2001) was to make information on the Web machine-processable. In order to achieve this goal, computers need to *understand* data. The Semantic Web is therefore using many concepts developed decades before in the artificial intelligence (AI) community. The knowledge representation language of the SW is the *Resource Description Framework* (RDF). Because of its properties (especially the lack of a *unique name assumption* and the presence of the *open world assumption*), it is well-suited for distributed knowledge representation. As explained in Chapter 4, RDF graphs from multiple sources can be merged very easily and the entailed knowledge will be the union of both knowledge bases. Furthermore, RDF can be extended with ontological layers of increasing expressiveness (RDF-Schema, OWL Lite, OWL DL, OWL Full, Rules, etc.). RDF ontologies can therefore be used, not only as a formally defined terminology, but also as a formal description logic (DL) ontology which enables logical reasoning. Resources can be classified based on DL and new facts can be deduced based on existing assertions.

However, because logics-based systems are usually computationally intensive, nearly all integration systems that are extensively using OWL ontologies and reasoning are based on the materialized – instead of the virtual – paradigm (C). An attempt to visually express this correlation between axis (B) and (C) is shown in Figure 7.1. While the horizontal axis represents the level of expressiveness, the vertical axis represents the integration paradigm: virtual vs. materialized. A simple example of a materialized non-reasoning integration approach is Virtuoso Sponger (Idehen and Blakeley 2007), which will be described in Section 7.1. Many integration systems in the healthcare domain are actually materialized solutions, because reasoning is very important, but also performance and fast response times. The *Semantic Web Client Library* (Bizer et al. 2009) is an example for a semi-materialized, non-reasoning approach. It fetches RDF data on-demand which is materialized before a query is executed locally (no federation). The upper right corner is very difficult to address and even questionable to track in future. The aim of the EU-funded research project, *Large Knowledge Collider*[2] (larKC), is to build a large-scale knowledge and reasoning system that should realize the original vision of the Semantic Web (Fensel and van Harmelen 2007).

Although the Semantic Web is meant to be a decentralized knowledge sharing infrastructure, in fact,

---

[2]The acronym is a wordplay with the popular *Large Hadron Collider* experiment at CERN and should reflect the large-scale character and significance in computer science.

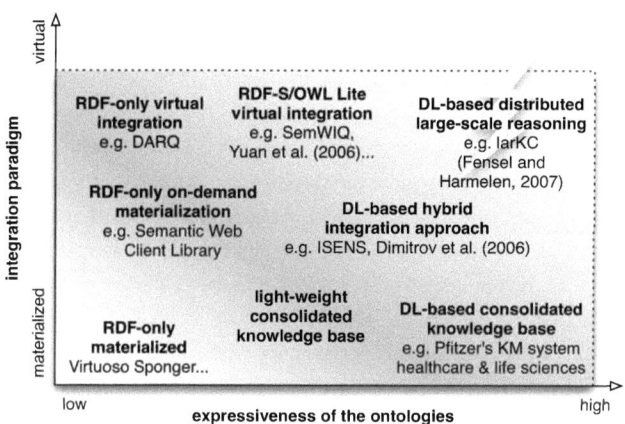

Figure 7.1: Attempt to express the correlation between the expressiveness of the ontologies used for information integration and the virtual and materialized paradigms.

the majority of current SW-based integration approaches are based on the consolidation of distributed RDF data into a central store. But this is not always done, because of the requirements of applied projects. It is often just an inevitable workaround because of a lack of existing virtual integration systems. If fact, the materialized approach has many drawbacks and somehow contradicts to the idea of the Semantic Web as a decentralized, machine-readable information space. Interestingly, the first successful Semantic Web-based applications were actually implemented in corporate and often local settings, and not in a distributed fashion expected by Tim Berners Lee et al. (2001). Especially the bio-medical and healthcare community adopted SW ontologies for building large knowledge bases. But the methods used were similar to traditional data warehouses. Because the materialized paradigm is still rather dominant, some examples will be presented in Section 7.1. The approaches are usually simpler than a virtual approach. Actually, a basic materialized SW-based integration system can be developed within hours. It is more or less a matter of setting up existing tools such as the open source edition of OpenLink Virtuoso.

A fourth distinction of projects can be made, based on their comprehensiveness (D). For example, some projects do not provide a registry or other basic components and lack distributed query optimization. DARQ is based on a simple configuration file which is loaded when starting the server and it does not collect statistics at runtime. On the other side, there are systems which provide facilities for model mapping, visualization, and graphical query browsers. Typically, mature projects with a larger budget and a bigger development team are more comprehensive than small research projects that have a narrow focus on a specific issue.

7 Information Integration based on Semantic Web Technologies

7.1 Materialized Information Integration

In the materialized approach, all source data is dumped into a global RDF store before queries are executed against it. Like a data warehouse, the approach has several advantages. Firstly, the traditional ETL (*extract-transform-load*) approach can be used. Data can be transformed and loaded in a procedural fashion without the need for a formal mapping of heterogenous data models. Secondly, query processing is much faster because all data is available in a central store at one location. Finally, it enables sophisticated reasoning possibilities since all assertions and rules are present at one location. Examples for applied projects in this area are SW-based knowledge management systems developed by Pfizer, Merck and other pharmaceutical, medical, and biotech companies (Feigenbaum et al. 2007, Slater et al. 2008). Pfizer is experimenting with several larger integrated knowledge bases to support researchers maintaining all the existing knowledge. The *Conference on Semantics in Healthcare and Life Sciences* (C-SHALS) and the *Data Integration in the Life Sciences Workshops* are a good place to look for further research in this field. A recent article about how Pfizer and others are applying Semantic Web technology for drug discovery has been published by (Marx 2009).

A representative generic approach is *Virtuoso Sponger* from OpenLink (Idehen and Blakeley 2007). Although it is a commercial product, an open source version is available with most of the features enabled. It is based on the Virtuoso universal server planform which includes an integrated relation database, an RDF quad store, and various enterprise IT features such as federation and replication. However, these features are only available in the commercial version. In Figure 7.2, Sponger is shown as part of the universal server. It features several wrappers, called *cartridges*, for various kinds of data sources. Each cartridge is able to fetch data from the Web or local resources, convert them into RDF and store them into a central RDF store. The consolidated information can then be queried with SPARQL or viewed as rendered HTML pages. The information can also be accessed and maintained by the *Virtuoso Data Spaces* application, which is targeted towards personal information integration. Virtuoso supports reasoning based on forward-chaining rules and materializing the entailed facts into the RDF store again, as well as some query-time reasoning capabilities (e.g. subsumption and `owl:sameAs` equivalence). There are Sponger cartridges for RDFa (*Resource Description Framework (in) attributes*, which is a special XHTML dialect supporting direct integration of RDF fragments into traditional Web pages and a *microformats* cartridge supporting GRDDL translation profiles, which specify how HTML fragments are translated into corresponding RDF triples. GRDDL is a framework used to extract RDF from *microformat* annotations in XHTML pages (Khare and Çelik 2006, Connolly 2007). However, if wrappers like some of the Sponger cartridges are not based on a formal mapping approach, adjusting the transformation code of wrappers is often rather costly, because it is hard-coded. Moreover, the materialized approach fails if there is a large number of data-intensive information sources storing frequently changing information.

To overcome some of these limitations, a mediator could fetch and transform information on-demand, materialize it into a centralized store and query the consolidated dataset (Prud'hommeaux

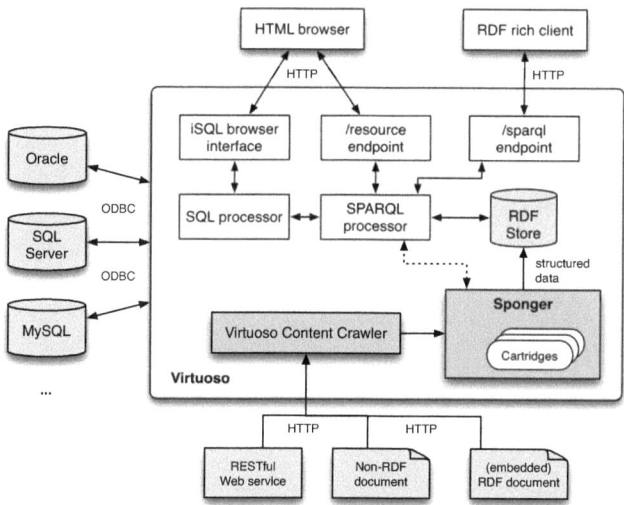

Figure 7.2: Virtuoso Sponger.

2007). Simple SPARQL queries over distributed RDF documents are also possible using the FROM keyword, which can be used to explicitly define the dataset a query is issued against as part of the query. The SPARQL query processor will fetch the required RDF documents from the Web as needed. Since the complete remote document is downloaded, this approach is not optimal and will result in a rather bad query execution performance and even non-terminating queries. Furthermore, it does not work with other SPARQL endpoint as data sources.

In some scenarios, when legacy data should be integrated and a formal mapping is impossible, some materialization will be even required for the virtual integration approach. In this case, a wrapper would use hard-coded procedures to provide the legacy information in the form of an RDF graph (Erling 2008).

7.2 Generic Architectures

In this section, some generic Semantic Web-based approaches for virtual information integration will be discussed, which can be used for a range of different applications. The first approach being presented is the XML-based Yacob mediator proposed by Sattler et al. (2005), which has been extended to use RDF-S ontologies to address the semantic heterogeneity aspect. It has been selected as an example to demonstrate, that some approaches are not entirely based on Semantic Web technologies, but adopted some of the concepts (e.g. RDF ontologies).

7.2.1 Yacob – RDF on Top of an XML-based Mediator

Sattler et al. (2005) proposed an XML-based mediator system called Yacob, which is able to integrate various information systems based on XML and *CQuery*, a variant of XQuery with some necessary extensions. As will be explained, the whole mediator-wrapper system is based on XML technology since at the time when the project started, there was no standardized RDF query language. The authors called the integration approach *concept-based*, because they added an additional intensional layer to the underlying XML/XQuery-based query processor, which maps local XML data to concepts from a global RDF-S ontology. CQuery provides the necessary concept-based operators in addition to the normal XQuery language. Web services are used as a common gateway between the mediator and data sources, and XSLT is used at wrappers to map XML data to the global structure if necessary. Each data source is able to execute simple XPath queries. According to the literature, only XML-based wrappers have been implemented. It would of course be possible to add additional wrappers for other information sources. However, it remains unclear, how optimizations and a cost-model could be integrated into the query processing workflow. Additionally, the fact that wrappers are only executing XPath queries and the rest of a query plan including joins is executed at the mediator, implies that sophisticated query optimization is impossible to implement.

The architecture of Yacob is depicted in Figure 7.3. Like in any other mediator-wrapper system, there is a central mediator including a *query planning* and a *query execution component*, as well as a *concept management, transformation*, and *access component*. At the bottom of the figure, several attached data sources are shown and at the top of the figure, there is the user interface connected to the mediator. The concept management component includes an RDF store for the global RDF-S ontology and an API for querying and maintaining the ontology, which is *Jena* (Jena Community 2009a) in this case. The concept management additionally maintains the mappings for all the attached data sources. Upon registration, XSL templates are automatically generated which are used later to transform results from the local into the global XML representation. The access component includes a cache (an Apache Xindice XML database) which stores partial results and is used to answer certain parts of the query without the need to access a remote data source. The caching mechanism has been described by Karnstedt et al. (2003).

CQuery

The global RDF-S ontology defines the global concept hierarchy and hence, the information that can be queried. The proprietary CQuery language is based on XQuery with additional operators for querying the conceptual layer. This includes the selection of concepts according to specified properties or operations like traversal of relationships and set-operations as well as the selection of instances of concepts which are actually XML elements obtained from the data sources. Of course the extensions are easier to describe giving an example:

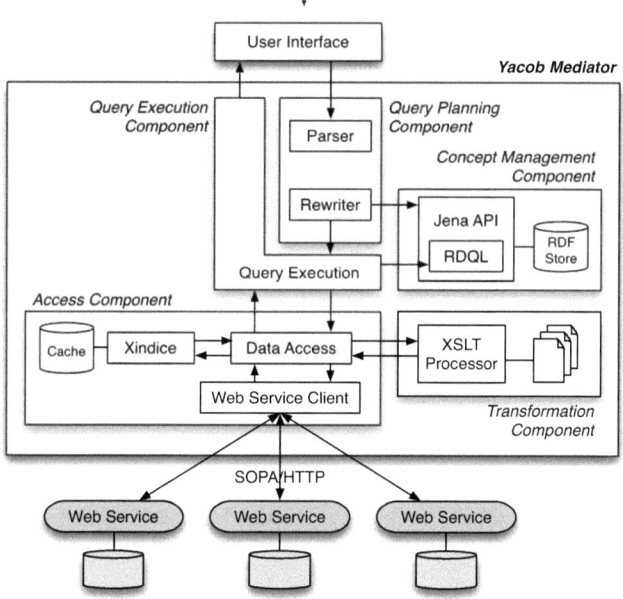

Figure 7.3: Architecture of the Yacob Mediator.

```
FOR $c IN concept[name='painting']/!subClassOf+
LET $e := extension($c)
WHERE $e/artist = 'van_Gogh'
RETURN
  <painting>
    <title>$e/name</title>
    <artist>$e/artist</artist>
  </painting>
```

The FOR clause is used to select instances of specific RDF classes. The pseudo-element concept is interpreted as the class hierarchy with given attributes which can be used to select certain concepts. In this example, the concept *painting* (an RDF class) is selected directly using the pseudo-attribute name, which refers to the rdfs:label attribute in RDF (a hard-coded mapping). Additionally, all sub-classes of *painting* are selected, using the special syntax /!subClassOf+ shown in the example. The exclamation mark indicates that the inverse relationship must be used when evaluating the path expression (i.e. select all classes having *painting* as direct or indirect *super-class*, which is the inverse relationship of subClassOf) and the plus sign specifies that the complete transitive closure must be calculated. Beside these two features, it is possible to use set-operators to build the union, intersection, and difference between selected concept sets. The approach seems a bit awkward, however, it is a simple way to access concepts of an RDF ontology using XQuery. As will be clearer soon, this approach allows to mix the conceptual layer with the instance layer.

The LET clause in the example contains a special pre-defined function `extension()`. This part of a CQuery is where the concept level is mixed with the instance level. The function returns the extension (i.e. instance set) of a concept $c, and assigned it to the variable $e. By specifying multiple extensions, it is possible to denote cross-product and join operations. Unfortunately, all joins will be computed at the mediator. The authors have, however, implemented some optimizations regarding the push-down of filters to local XPath expressions. As a consequence, the filter expression for an instance's `artist` property: `$e/artist = 'van Gogh'` will be pushed down to the corresponding data sources which is generally a very important requirement for a distributed query processor. Finally, the RETURN clause is used to create the result XML fragment including projections of the query result.

The example above demonstrates only the basic features of CQuery. Additionally (not part of the query), for each concept bound to variable $c, it would be possible to obtain all the properties which have an `rdfs:domain $c` from the RDF-S ontology with the pseudo attribute `properties(c)`. In this way, it is possible to select only those paintings that have some special value occurring in *any* of their properties.

Query Processing in Yacob

Sattler et al. (2003) described the query process in detail. It will be sketched in short. A CQuery is sent to the parser first, then it is rewritten into a global query plan including several XPath expressions as leaves which are sent to the wrapped data sources. The global plan can be described using a few algebraic operators defined by Sattler et al. (2003). Concept level operators include expression-based selection, set-operators ($\cap, \cup, -$), and a path traversal operator (including inverse traversal and calculating the transitive closure). Operators of the instance level include selection, projection, cross product, and outer union. The outer union is similar to the SPARQL union operation and very important for an information integration system. Unlike the SQL union operation, it accepts two different input schemas (see Section 4.4).

A CQuery contains two different types of expressions: concept-level expressions (*CExpr*) specified in the FOR clause, and instance-level expressions (*IExpr*) specified in the WHERE clause (actually both expression types can additionally be specified when declaring variables in the LET clause). Queries that include a cross-product or join operation are decomposed into elementary queries and combined later. For each concept *c* occurring in an elementary query, the cache is consulted for already obtained results matching the corresponding *IExpr(c)*. If the lookup is successful, the cached results are added to the overall results. Otherwise, concept mappings are used to transform the *IExpr(c)* into a local XPath query. The local query is executed via the Web service middleware and the XML results are transformed into the global representation using the pre-compiled XSLT.

7.2.2 Yuan et al. – Extending a Commercial Of-The-Shelf EII Product

The approach proposed by Yuan et al. (2006) from Boeing Phantom Works, which is the major research devision of Boeing, is also partly based on Semantic Web technology and adds a semantic layer using ontologies to a *Commercial-Off-The-Shelf* (COTS) EII product. As pointed out by Uschold and Gruninger (2004) and Halevy et al. (2005), almost all COTS EII products lack support for semantic interoperability. This is basically, because most of the products are based on traditional RDBMS architectures and use simple metadata to denote the meaning of data to be integrated. Often the meaning is captured only in the mind of its users. On the other hand, the query processors of commercial EII products are already mature and highly optimized.

When building a semantic information integration system, there is basically the option of augmenting a semantic layer on-top of existing software and benefit from high performance distributed query processors. Such an approach has pros and cons as will be discussed based on the exemplary approach. As a pro, the system may benefit from query optimization, possibly even parallel or Grid-based distributed query processing, and many bundled features addressing automatic schema matching, data cleansing, record linkage, etc. bundled with the COTS EII product. Additionally, implementation cost are of course much lower since the core components of the integration system do not have to be implemented. The most significant drawback is the dependency on the EII product which does not only mean costs in terms of license fees, but also the limited possibilities for customizations, extensions, and further developments. Especially for academic research projects, the availability of the code sources is often very significant. Moreover, such a semantic *overlay-approach* is not hundred percent Semantic Web compatible. For instance, data is just annotated and mapped to ontologies, however, it is not represented and processed as RDF triples. As a consequence, it does not use the Semantic Web query language SPARQL and there is also no SPARQL endpoint which could be used to execute remote queries based on the standardized protocol. The architecture is depicted in Figure 7.4 according to Yuan et al. (2006). The unshaded shapes represent existing components and the bold and shaded shapes represent the components added to enable semantic information integration.

As indicated with numbers in the figure, a system integrator (1) starts with mapping existing information in various attached member systems to several domain ontologies with the help of some integrated or external mapping tool. Three kinds of different metadata are stored in the *Metadata Repository*: a domain ontology, local metadata, and mappings between them. The domain ontology defines the global data model. It encompasses the concepts to capture the complete knowledge of the integrated member systems, but nevertheless, it is independent from any local schema. The local metadata are logical or physical schemas provided by the member systems. The mappings are similar to *D2RQ-Map*, which has been developed for the RDBMS-to-RDF wrapper *D2R-Server* (Chris Bizer and Richard Cyganiak 2006): they are RDF views on relational data. For example, a mapping may define a virtual RDF extension based on SQL queries. Additionally, a mapping may include functions

7 Information Integration based on Semantic Web Technologies

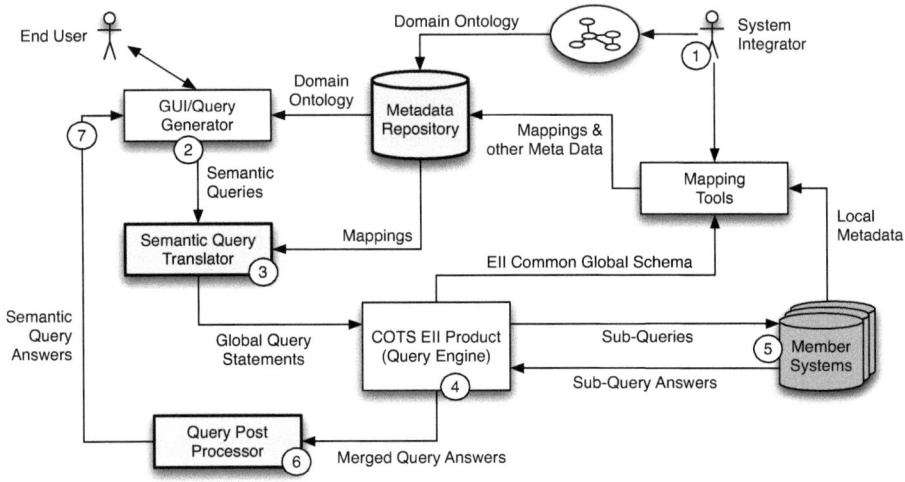

Figure 7.4: Semantic information integration based on a Commercial-Off-The-Shelf EII product.

and even hard-coded procedures (Yuan 2006).

Yuan et al. (2006) developed a proprietary semantic query language with similar features than SPARQL[3]. A graphical query builder (2) can be used to construct a semantic query based on the global domain ontology. The query is translated by the *Semantic Query Translator* (3) into one or more native query statements which can be further processed by the COTS EII query engine (4). The query engine will execute the query in the traditional manner by issuing sub-queries to the member systems (5) and composing the results using distributed query optimization. The *Query Post Processor* (6) translates the results obtained from the COTS EII query engine into a semantic representation based on the global domain ontology and sends the result back to the user's GUI (7).

7.2.3 ISENS – Integration with OWL-based Mapping Ontologies

A completely Semantic Web-based approach called ISENS, has been proposed by Dimitrov et al. (2006). To overcome the heterogeneity of the information sources, they first apply a straight-forward translation from arbitrary data models to RDF ontologies and on top of that, a *local-as-view* (LaV, see Section 3.5.3) mediation approach to reformulate queries and load relevant RDF sub-graphs from the data sources into a central knowledge base (KB). The KB additionally contains all domain ontologies

---
[3] Although the first SPARQL draft was published by the W3C in October 2004, the first *Candidate Recommendation* was released after Yuan et al. (2006) published the approach in April 2006.

and several mapping ontologies. Finally, the original global query is executed against the KB and the results are computed based on DL inference.

The architecture of ISENS consists of three components: the *Web Interface Component* (WIC), a Web-based user interface which allows the submission of SPARQL queries, the *Distributed Querying System* (DQS), the actual mediator which is responsible for processing SPARQL queries and transforming data, and the *Distributed Enabling Component* (DEC), a communication layer providing authentication and security services. The WIC and DEC will not further be discussed. The more interesting part are the mapping approach and the mediator.

Ontologies and Mappings

Within the ISENS approach, it is assumed that each data source provides information of a similar domain described by different RDF/OWL domain ontologies. The information can be stored in any other underlying information system such as a RDBMS or XML repository, however, a wrapper has to provide an RDF/OWL-based view on the information it provides. In the prototype proposed by Dimitrov et al. (2006), only native RDF stores are discussed and no wrapping of other (legacy) information systems is further investigated. For each attached source repository, the DQS contains a source description, which specifies the information stored in the repository. Beside the ontologies used at a repository, the source description may contribute one or more *mapping ontologies*, which are used to glue together different local ontologies as shown in Figure 7.5.

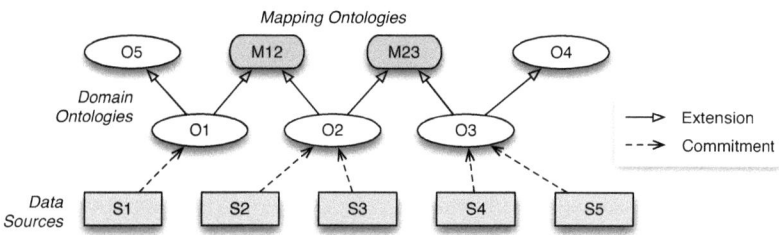

Figure 7.5: ISENS Mapping Ontologies.

At the bottom of the figure, several data sources are depicted (boxes), each one providing information according to one or more domain ontologies (elliptic shapes). A domain ontology may extend other ontologies via OWL's import mechanism. The mapping ontologies (two shapes at the top of the figure) are introduced to provide the necessary mappings between the different ontologies based on a subset of OWL DL assertions. The mapping ontologies are used to decompose a query into a set of sub-queries which can be answered either directly by data sources or indirectly by traversing semantic relationships defined in the mapping ontologies.

For instance, if a query is formulated according to O1 (Figure 7.5), the mapping ontology M12 can be used to construct sub-queries and retrieve data from S2 and S3. Additionally, although there is no direct mapping between O1 and O3, M12 and M23 are combined to retrieve data from S4 and S5. As a consequence, an O1-query can be decomposed to retrieve subsets of data from S1–5. The resulting subsets are processed by the *answering engine*, which is based on the KAON2 knowledge base system. It retrieves the partial results and stores them into a temporary RDF knowledge base (KB). Additionally, it loads all involved domain ontologies and mapping ontologies into the same KB. Finally, the original query is executed against the materialized KB and processed by the KAON2 OWL DL reasoner before the result is returned to the user (WIC). The reasoner further infers all information entailed in the materialized KB.

No Fixed Global Ontology

In case of ISENS, a query can be formulated according to any ontology which becomes the target ontology for the results, i.e. there is no fixed global ontology. Mappings between the local ontologies are used to pull semantically equivalent data from other data sources, translated into the target ontology. The mapping approach is done solely at the Semantic Web ontology layer and also the information of the attached sources is represented in RDF. As a consequence, SPARQL can be used as the global query language.

7.2.4 DARQ – SPARQL Query Federation

DARQ (Bastian Quilitz and Ulf Leser 2008), which is an acronym for *Distributed ARQ*, provides access to multiple, distributed SPARQL endpoints by means of query federation. Although the primary goal of the project has not been the development of a SW-based information integration system, it can also be used for this purpose. For example, a wrapper has been implemented to integrate LDAP endpoints. However, issues regarding heterogeneity have not been addressed. DARQ is only capable of executing queries and does not support manipulation of data although this would have been an interesting direction because of its characteristics which make it also similar to distributed RDF stores such as YARS2 (Harth et al. 2007), 4store (Harris et al. 2009), or Systap BigData (Thompson et al. 2006).

DARQ was actually an internship project at HP Labs Bristol, the home of Jena and ARQ (Jena Community 2009a), and as such its goal was to experiment with SPARQL query federation. DARQ allows to query multiple distributed RDF graphs as if querying a single RDF graph. From that point of view it is similar to SemWIQ, however, the most significant difference is that query federation in DARQ is based on properties of triple patterns which results in very large query plans. While SemWIQ is able to push down complete sub-plans to remote endpoints including joins and left-joins, DARQ is querying relevant data sources per triple pattern based on capabilities configured in a static

```
[] a sd:Service ;
    sd:capability [
        sd:predicate foaf:name ;
        sd:objectFilter "REGEX(?object, '^[A-R]')";
        sd:triples 51 ;
        sd:subjectSelectivity 0.019607843 ;
        sd:objectSelectivity 0.022222222 ] ;
    sd:capability [
        sd:predicate foaf:mbox ;
        sd:triples 51 ] ;
    sd:capability [
        sd:predicate foaf:weblog ;
        sd:triples 10 ] ;
    sd:totalTriples "112" ;
    sd:url "http://example.org/sparql" ;
    sd:requiredBindings [ sd:objectBinding foaf:name ] ;
    sd:requiredBindings [ sd:objectBinding foaf:mbox ] .
```

Listing 7.1: Example of a DARQ service description.

file. Although triple patterns are combined if possible into BGP sub-plans, in real world examples, this is hardly possible. Multiple triple patterns can only be combined into a single local BGP query, if for all triple patterns only one relevant endpoint exists.

Furthermore, DARQ can only execute queries with bound predicates. For instance, it is not possible to execute queries against the conceptual level like: { :s ?p [] }, which would return all properties used to describe a given resource. This is because data source selection in DARQ is based on matching query pattern predicates to predicates in capability patterns.

Query Processing in DARQ

The query interface between the DARQ federator and endpoints is simply based on triple pattern matching. For each triple pattern of a BGP, the federator selects relevant endpoints and executes a triple pattern query against the endpoint even if a complete BGP could be executed remotely. The selection of relevant endpoints is based on *service descriptions*, which are represented in RDF and include information about cardinalities, selectivities, and access limitations based on triples. All the service descriptions are stored in a static configuration file which is loaded by DARQ when it is launched. There is no possibility of updating this information during runtime. Also the statistical information has to be entered manually since there is no statistics generator available. Unfortunately, the project has not been continued and hence only a rudimentary – and regarding the dependent libraries already outdated – prototype exists.

An example of a service description is shown in Listing 7.1. The capabilities describe which triple patterns the service endpoint can answer. A capability consists of a predicate and several constraints on subjects or objects. The constraints are formulated as regular SPARQL filter expressions. For example, the endpoint described in the figure can answer triple patterns of the form { ?s foaf:name ?o }, where the object is a string literal starting with a letter in the range A–R (constraint

REGEX(?object, '[A-R]'). The query will return 51 triples ($n(p)$, $p=$foaf:name). Additionally, it is possible to specify selectivities $ssel(p)$ and $osel(p)$ for the triple pattern if the subject or the object is bound. Based on the example description, the subject selectivity for the example query { :sBound foaf:name ?o } is $1/51 = 0.019607843$ because all persons have a unique URI and one foaf:name property. The default selectivities used in DARQ are $1/n(p)$ if the subject is bound, and 1 if the object is bound.

Query planning in DARQ is done separately for each BGP of the global query. The algorithm in (Bastian Quilitz and Ulf Leser 2008) tries to combine triple patterns into single BGP sub-queries if possible. This is possible, if for multiple triple patterns only one endpoint is relevant based on the capabilities described before. However, in real world scenarios this is hardly the case. For example, properties such as rdf:type, rdfs:label, or foaf:name are used in nearly all RDF graphs.

Optimizations

Joining distributed triple patterns is the major bottleneck of the DARQ approach. For example, given the following SPARQL query which selects all persons knowing Richard Cyganiak and returns their names, optionally the email address and all other persons they know:

```
SELECT ?name ?mbox ?knows WHERE {
        ?s a foaf:Person ;
          foaf:name ?name .
          OPTIONAL { foaf:mbox ?mbox }
          foaf:knows ?cygri ;
          foaf:knows ?knows .
          FILTER (?cygri = <http://richard.cyganiak.de/foaf.rdf#cygri>)
}
```

For each triple pattern, the relevant data sources will be selected based on the service descriptions explained before. If there are multiple data sources storing FOAF data, none of the triple patterns may be combined into single local BGP queries and for each triple pattern, the union of all results for relevant sources are subsequently joined. In order to optimize such queries, triple patterns are re-ordered based on their expected cardinality. The cardinality of a SPARQL triple pattern can be estimated with the help of the base cardinality $n(p)$ and the selectivities for bound subjects and objects $ssel(p)$ and $osel(p)$. Additionally, constant equality expressions in SPARQL filters like FILTER (?cygri = <http://richard.cyganiak.de/foaf.rdf#cygri>) are pushed into the corresponding triple patterns if possible: { ?s foaf:knows <http://richard.cyganiak.de/foaf.rdf#cygri> }. Regarding the example query, the transformed triple pattern with the inserted filter constant will probably have the lowest cardinality. It will fetch URIs of people who now Richard Cyganiak and bind them to ?s. In this case, a *bind join*, as already explained in the context of Garlic (Section 6.2) will be used to subsequently join all the other triple patterns.

The cardinalities for joins are calculated as

$$|R(q_1 \bowtie q_2)| = |R(q_1)| * |R(q_2)| * jsel_{12}$$

with a constant join selectivity of $jsel = 0.5$. Because there are no statistics for all the arbitrary join combinations, it is not possible to use more accurate estimates for the join selectivity. In practice, the cardinality will vary greatly between 0 and $|R(q_1)| * |R(q_2)|$.

In some situations, a bind join is not applicable or more expensive than a nested loop join (NLJ). For that reason, (Bastian Quilitz and Ulf Leser 2008) defined a simple cost model for both, the bind and the NLJ. In order to calculate costs for BGP plans (if a combination of triple patterns is possible), the authors also defined a cardinality estimation function for basic graph patterns which is very similar to that of SemWIQ. Based on a dynamic programming algorithm, the best join alternative is selected.

DARQ is an interesting approach towards SPARQL federation based on properties. However, there are still many issues to solve regarding the query processor. Additionally, it currently lacks a registry component and monitoring service. Setting up DARQ requires the user to explicitly supply a configuration file including service descriptions. It is unclear if there is some facility to generate the cardinalities and selectivities automatically, or if it has to be determined manually indeed. Without such supporting tools, the system cannot be applied to real world use-cases.

7.2.5 Discussion

After a detailed review of the Yacob approach, the architecture appears to be a bit awkward. It is obviously too complex making sophisticated distributed query optimization impossible. For example, a join operation over distributed data sources is executed over the materialized elementary query results. Even a join involving only one data source, which could actually be executed locally at the data source, cannot be pushed down into a local sub-plan. After all, it is questionable whether an XML-based information integration approach is reasonable at all. At least, when using ontologies to achieve semantic interoperability, an XML-based approach seems to be the wrong direction. As explained in Section 4.2.6, XML lacks important capabilities when it comes to information integration. It is perfectly suited for point-to-point data interchange and when the interfaces of both communicating systems can be well defined. However, for a semantic information integration system, it is better to use a more powerful data model like RDF or frame-like knowledge representation languages.

The system developed by (Yuan et al. 2006) is an interesting approach which demonstrates that existing commercial Enterprise Information Integration can be extended with a Semantic Web overlay. This way, existing integration systems which already use robust distributed query processing and are scalable enough for large data sets can be used to semantically integrate distributed, heterogeneous data sources. Most of the pros and cons have already been mentioned. As a concluding remark it should be noted, that such an approach cannot exploit the full power of Semantic Web technology and ontologies in general. For instance, it is cumbersome to integrate reasoning support. The query processor appears like a black box. Although, t-box-only reasoning is possible to extend the global query plan, a fully integrated Semantic Web query processor would be more powerful. Additionally, SPARQL has became a standard and it has been accepted by the community. In order to provide a high level of interoperability with other systems, it is crucial to adopt the standards developed by the Semantic Web community.

The ISENS approach demonstrates an OWL-based mediator system for the integration of distributed RDF data sources. It is a hybrid approach using traditional mediator techniques like the LaV approach and decomposing and rewriting queries, as well as a description logic reasoner to answer global queries. Basically, the approach looks promising. However, there are a few things which seem to become critical issues in practice. Firstly, the final processing of partial query results at the mediator may require loading a large amount of RDF data into the KB. Secondly, as the authors have also mentioned, OWL DL is too weak to be used as a mapping approach without further rules which can be specified in SWRL (the *Semantic Web Rule Language*) or the *Rule Interchange Format* (RIF) currently developed by the W3C RIF Working Group. As described in Section 4.3.2, OWL can be used to express equivalence, sub-class relationships, class definitions based on various constraints, set-based class definitions, etc. However, it comes short when mapping, i.e. expressing the semantic equivalence, between structurally different represented concepts.

To give an example, two ontologies A, B are considered. A represents the maximum thrust of an aircraft engine `Engine` with the property `maxThrust` with `rdfs:domain Engine`. Ontology B uses an additional class `TechSpec` attached to an engine and a `thrustSpec` property with `rdfs:domain TechSpec`. With OWL it is not possible to denote the semantic equivalence of the two relationships because it would require role composition. The mapping could, however, be defined with the following first-order logic rule:

$$A\text{:Engine}(?x) \land A\text{:techSpec}(X,S) \land A\text{:maxThrust}(S,Z) \Leftrightarrow B\text{:Engine}(X) \land B\text{:thrustSpec}(X,Z)$$

The approach In (Qasem et al. 2008) ISENS has been extended with deep web wrappers to build a Semantic Web query system over popular SPARQL endpoints such as DBpedia, Geonames, and NASA SIR-C/X-SAR images. Instead of automatically generating source descriptions, logical statements are introduced in OWL to describe the data provided at a data source. Such a statement is called *REL* and may look like (`http://sourceURL, CinemaDisplay` ∩ ∀ `madeBy` = "Dell"), which specifies that the data source endpoint `http://sourceURL` stores information about *cinema displays* made by *Dell*. By contrast to this approach, the RDFStats processor developed for the SemWIQ mediator automatically computes various histograms from SPARQL endpoints which does not further require the manual notation of REL-like statements. Although, the explicit description using logical statements is more expressive in the general case then the histograms RDFStats generates, with some heuristics, basic histogram data can be combined to calculate usable estimates without much effort. RDFStats will be described in detail in Chapter 11 or Part III. Finally, the ISENS approach requires further research towards the optimization of local queries, as their authors explained.

Although DARQ has not been a dedicated information integration project, it can be used to integrate heterogeneous data sources if there are appropriate wrappers available. The architecture is similar to SemWIQ, however, query processing is based on triple patterns primarily and therefore, there are some limitations as discussed. Using DARQ with a wrapper such as D2RQ may lack performance because in most cases, DARQ will subsequently join all single triple patterns resulting in a heavy load against D2RQ, which itself still has performance problems.

7.3 Applied Research Projects

Applied research projects in the field of Semantic Web-based virtual information integration are typically initiated in an inter-disciplinary setting, such as medical and biological informatics. Many research disciplines have the following problem: knowledge is present at different locations and people, however, in order to be efficient, researchers have to work in an integrated fashion. Another problem is that scientific knowledge is often intuitive and tacit, bound into the brains of researchers. Capturing this knowledge and making it accessible to others is not only an important goal of private companies (e.g. biotech enterprises), and of course, it is also a desirable goal of open communities.

Biomedical Information Integration

Regarding the biomedical domain, Slater et al. (2008) pointed out, that research and development is characterized by "profound and persistent uncertainty", which means that the research departments have to work as efficiently as possible to prevent misspending of investment. They also argue, that currently scientific data repositories in the biomedical domain are characterized by being *siloed*, redundant, and often inaccessible to other researchers. They say, that building large, centralized archival repositories (i.e. materialized approach) are dangerous and unworkable. Thus, the integration of these valuable knowledge is very important for any industry with a high rate of research and development, i.e. the *knowledge industry*. With the advent of the Semantic Web, the biomedical industry was one of the first to adopt the ideas because a more flexible and distributed way of linking knowledge was needed.

A lot of applied information integration projects in the biomedical domain are actually more service than data oriented. Although information is exchanged, access is wrapped by Web service calls. This is, however, not much different from mediator-wrapper systems. For example, *BioMoby* (Wilkinson et al. 2005) is a Web services-based integration platform for various data and analysis tools. It started with a proprietary ontology language, but it is planned to port the whole system to Semantic Web compatible formats. Similarly, *BioPortal* (Noy et al. 2008) is a one-stop-shop for researchers in biomedical informatics providing a range of biomedical ontologies and Web services. It is currently being developed by the *National Center for Biomedical Computing* (NCBC), an interdisciplinary network of research organizations across the United States. The portal is the central gateway to an constantly increasing number of ontologies and tools which are integrated by Web services. Ontologies can be searched, browsed, graphically visualized and interactively navigated, as well as annotated with various objects such as text notes, hyperlinks, and images. Several ongoing projects have been reviewed by Bodenreider (2008).

In (Martín et al. 2008) an EU-funded SW-based information integration project in the area of clinical cancer research is described. The system provides transparent access to integrated clinical, genetic, and image databases using a master ontology on cancer. Although the system looks very interesting: according to the authors it uses SPARQL, OWL DL ontologies, a Locel-as-View approach, D2R-Server for relational databases, a custom wrapper for DICOM image databases, provides a graphical mapping tool, a data cleansing tool and most interestingly, beside the information integration component the complete system use leveraging Grid technology. Unfortunately, the architectural details are not published and therefore it remains unclear what has actually been implemented.

Another biological information integration system based on Web service composition has been developed by (Ayadi et al. 2008). *BiOnMap* is a Web-service based integration system leveraging Semantic Web technology to describe the integrated biological data repositories. It is also capable of integrating workflows based on the Taverna workbench (Hull et al. 2006). Queries are not formulated in a declarative language such as SPARQL, instead, a query is a rule which can be fulfilled by composing and executing various Web services. The service composition approach is based on a RDF-based rule engine. In (Lacroix et al. 2006) some of the authors of BiOnMap propose another integration framework for biological data which is based on a compositional query semantics. Unfortunately, the query language is proprietary although the semantics are actually a subset of SPARQL. They define a *life science data model*, which is actually an RDF-S based metamodel framework used to semantically integrate distributed heterogeneous data sets. It includes a conceptual level and a data level and allows both layers to be queried. The authors also address the issue of ranking query results and propose a relevance algorithm based on RDF graph path distances.

The *NeuroCommons* project (Ruttenberg et al. 2009) has the goal of developing a comprehensive framework to support scientific collaboration in the field of computational biology and particularly neuroscience and neuromedicine with the help of Semantic Web technology. The system is currently based on a central RDF store (OpenLink Virtuoso) which consists of several separately loadable datasets called "bundles". The bundles can be obtained by means of a package manager.

Environmental Science, Earth and Space Observation

Further interesting application areas for Semantic Web-based information integration are ecology and environmental sciences. The *Science Environment for Ecological Knowledge* (SEEK) project is building an infrastructure for ecological, environmental, and biodiversity research. The infrastructure

7.3 Applied Research Projects

includes the setup of a data grid (EcoGrid) which will enable access to various biodiversity and ecological data and analysis tools. It also includes a tool called *Kepler* for building scientific workflows. Such a workflow defines a sequence of tasks a researcher typically needs to perform in order to reach some goal. Tasks include resource discovery, data mining, calculations, conversions, etc. which can be executed via Web services, Grid jobs, scripts, etc. (Berkley et al. 2005).

In (Fox, McGuinness, Raskin and Sinha 2007) the SESDI[4] project is described. The goal of this project is the integration of volcanic and atmospheric data from heterogeneous sources. SESDI supports researchers assessing the atmospheric effects of volcanic eruptions by allocating all related environmental information sources. Some of the authors have also been involved in a similar project towards semantic astronomy called VSTO (*Virtual Solar Terrestrial Observatory*) (Fox et al. 2009). During the last years the NASA began to leverage Semantic Web technology in order to manage the vast amount of environmental information they maintain (Ashish 2005). Among other projects, they created the SWEET ontologies, which stands for *Semantic Web for Earth and Environmental Terminology* (Raskin and Pan 2003). Several ontologies have been developed as part of this project which have been re-used by many other earth science projects and also VSTO and SESDI. Other projects in the field of semantic astronomy are the EURO-VO project *European Virtual Observatory* and the *International Virtual Observatory Alliance* (EURO VO Consortium 2008, Fox, Cinquini, McGuinness, West, Garcia, Benedict and Zednik 2007).

---

[4]http://sesdi.hao.ucar.edu/

Part III

The SemWIQ Approach

8 Overview

In this part of the thesis the fundamental concepts of SemWIQ are presented. This overview chapter serves as an introduction to concept-based information integration. It is explained why the *Resource Description Framework* is well suited as a metamodel for information integration systems and how global domain ontologies are used to describe distributed information contained in a range of different systems and data models. Additionally, the SemWIQ architecture is presented as part of this overview and the idea of scalable query federation based on statistical data summaries is introduced.

In Chapter 9 the SemWIQ mediator will be described and the execution of global SPARQL queries will be explained in detail. It will be shown how RDF graph statistics are used to enable scalable federation and query optimization. Chapter 10 is dedicated to wrappers for SemWIQ. Firstly, general considerations on designing and implementing SPARQL wrappers based on Jena ARQ (Jena Community 2009a) are presented, followed by several sections giving detailed information to wrappers for relational database systems, spreadsheets, and XML datasets. Details on the RDFStats approach and notes on its implementation can be found in Chapter 11.

8.1 Concept-based Information Integration

According to Calvanese et al. (2009), current commercial information integration systems are still based on various extended forms of the relational algebra. It should be noted that with the growing popularity of XML, also some XML-based approaches have been proposed (Baru et al. 1999, Sattler et al. 2005). But because of the complex structure of XML trees which may even aggravate structural heterogeneity and the higher complexity involved with query optimization, XML is not well suited as the global metamodel in information integration. The main problem with current information integration systems is that the global model is expressed in terms of a traditional database model. Instead of designing the global model as a conceptual representation of the application domain, it is designed as a specification of a data structure. The fact that the relational model is not suited for conceptual modeling had already been addressed in the 80ies when several *semantic data models* have been proposed (Peckham and Maryanski 1988). Today many tools exist for conceptual modeling (e.g. based on the Entity Relationship model or UML) to develop database models, but current information integration systems are nevertheless based on integrated relational models and queries have to be formulated in SQL based on these models.

8 Overview

When the SemWIQ project was started, a *concept-based integration approach* such as described by Sattler et al. (2005) and more recently by Calvanese et al. (2009) was the starting point in order to abstract from specific local data structures which may adhere to a range of different metamodels depending on the information systems used by the sources (XML, relational model, semi-structured text, multimedia content, etc.). Because an information integration system should support a wide range of data models, the global metamodel must have enough expressivity and capabilities to capture all the information to be integrated as accurately as possible. Furthermore, it should be possible to add and remove data sources without the need to alter the global model or any mappings. And in case of a large-scale information integration system which is used to globally share information between independent parties, it should be possible to extend the integrated model and domain ontologies in a flexible way.

Instead of following a straight-forward schema integration approach used in current commercial systems, where the global model is more or less the least common sum of all source models, SemWIQ is based on a conceptual model which describes the relevant parts of an application domain in order to provide a system-independent specification. A conceptual approach has many benefits including improved extensibility, better understanding of the application domain, and support for graphical visualization when mapping data sources and when exploring and querying the integrated information.

The SemWIQ approach is depicted in Figure 8.1: data sources known by the SemWIQ mediator are mapped to distributed ontologies. Users of SemWIQ consult the mediator, which further executes sub-queries against relevant data sources in order to compose the query result. The system is scalable with respect to the number of data sources and the number and size of the ontologies.

To give a concrete example, a conceptual model in the area of solar observation is excerpted in Figure 12.2 on page 199 of the results part. The figure contains some of the concepts which are part of several distributed ontologies published on the web. Because distributed RDF graphs can be merged and the entailed information can be combined, ontologies can be extended by anybody who needs more expressiveness in order to contribute a new data source. The example contains specific ontologies developed in cooperation with the Kanzelhöhe Solar Observatory (KSO) in order to integrate solar observation data with SemWIQ in the Austrian Grid (Blöchl et al. 2006). The concepts on the top right in the figure are defined by the popular *Friend-of-a-Friend* (FoaF) vocabulary (foaf: prefix), the concepts with a obs: prefix are part of an observation ontology, the ones with a sobs: prefix are defined by a more specific *solar* observation ontology, and the concepts with a sci: prefix are defined in a science ontology which have been developed for the KSO application.

Compared to the relational model, the concepts defined in RDF ontologies have a global scope by definition. Relational concepts have a local scope. In other words, a relation or attribute such as EMP or EMP_NO has a local scope for the context of a specific database or application. If someone else wants to formulate a query, it may not be clear to him or her what EMP or EMP_NO actually should mean. In order to compensate this shortcomings, commercial systems are using glossaries and centralized

8.1 Concept-based Information Integration

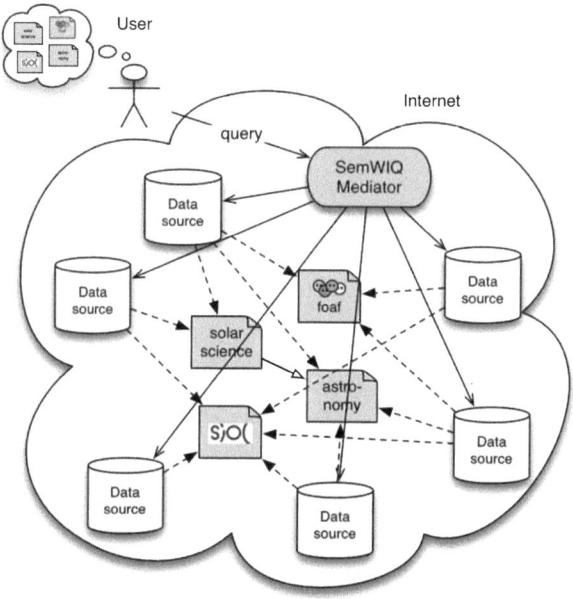

Figure 8.1: SemWIQ approach: distributed data sources mapped to distributed ontologies.

metadata infrastructures on top of relational systems. However, queries still have to be formulated in SQL according to the integrated system-dependent database model. In the next section it will be explained why RDF is well suited to be used as the global metamodel in information integration systems.

8.1.1 Advantages of Using RDF as a Global Metamodel

The Resource Description Framework has many characteristics which make it very well suited to be used as the global metamodel for information integration systems dealing with metamodel heterogeneity.

- RDF is Web-centric per definition and highly scalable because inter-related RDF ontologies may be distributed over the World Wide Web.

- RDF ontologies can be published by everybody on the Web in order to extend existing concepts with new concepts if required (e.g. when adding a new data source to SemWIQ whose infor-

121

8 Overview

mation is not captured by the current global model which is effectively the sum of all published ontologies used to describe data sources).

- URIs are used as global identifiers for all concepts which makes it easy to manage the global URI namespace based on the *Domain Name System* (DNS). Every domain owner, is the owner of a definition space, i.e. (s)he can introduce URIs based on his/her own domain name.

- It does not impose the *Unique Name Assumption* (UNA), which enables concept-based fragmentation, i.e. anybody can add statements about a specific resource and partial RDF graphs can be merged from various locations.

- RDF, RDF-Schema, OWL, and other W3C Recommendations building on top of these are standardized and broadly accepted knowledge representation languages.

- An RDF graph can be described simply by a set of triples which facilitates merging incomplete, fragmented graphs from distributed sources.

- RDF-Schema, OWL and other vocabularies building on top of the RDF Core provide all the typical conceptual design mechanisms known from other frameworks (e.g. Entity Relationship Model or UML) which are required for modeling ontologies.

- RDF-Schema and OWL support terminological (t-box) and assertional statements (a-box) as well as many useful description logic features which can be used to reason over data and to impose restrictions.

- While the RDF metamodel (RDF Core) remains as simple as possible, all RDF Schema and OWL Full features can be described themselves based on the RDF metamodel which allows for metamodeling and breaks the instance-type dichotomy[1].

Unlike other systems which either use RDF only as a metadata layer on top of an existing global schema (see Section 7.2.1 and 7.2.2), SemWIQ leverages RDF and some OWL capabilities in order to provide a powerful, distributed, Web-scale information integration system capable of merging information from a wide range of information systems based on federated SPARQL queries.

8.1.2 Ontologies for Information Integration

The sometimes raised argument, that modeling application-specific ontologies (also called *domain ontologies*) is a costly and tedious task which requires the participation of experts, is absolutely true and also applies to SemWIQ. However, this task needs to be done only once by a core community which may develop and maintain the vocabulary with collaboration tools developed by the Semantic

---

[1]Please note that the instance-type dichotomy still arises when reasoning with OWL DL.

Web community (Auer et al. 2006, Basca et al. 2008). But even for non-experts it is possible to add and map new data sources serving information where well-established ontologies already exist on the Web (e.g. Dublin Core, FOAF, SOAP, DOAP, etc.).

When applying SemWIQ for a specific application domain (e.g. solar observation), it is reasonable to look for existing ontologies in that domain first and then fill the gaps based on a bottom-up approach. Experiences in many applied Semantic Web projects have shown, that a dedicated top-down approach is often not very promising resulting in long philosophical discussions between the collaborators. It is usually impractical to capture a complete domain at once although the initial data sources represent only a small fraction of a domain. Instead, it is typically better to follow a bottom-up approach and model the necessary concepts based on existing ontologies while keeping some degree of generality and possible future extension points in mind.

SKOS – Simple Knowledge Organization System

Sometimes it is useful to use leight-weight ontologies and simple taxonomies of terms instead of comprehensive and detailed DL ontologies. For example, the concepts marked by the circle in Figure 12.2 are SKOS concepts that represent an extensible taxonomy of various solar phenomenona. The *Simple Knowledge Organization System* (SKOS) is based on RDF and enables the representation of taxonomies and classification schemes. It provides several properties that can be used to semantically interlink abstract concepts.

8.2 Architecture of SemWIQ

At the initial stage of the development of SemWIQ, some global requirements have been stipulated. They have already been discussed as part of the introduction on page 2. Basically, the general requirements are: *flexibility* and *low entry cost*, *virtual* integration of *distributed* and *heterogeneous* information systems, leverage *Semantic Web* concepts, application of a *holistic query processing approach* in order to ensure *good performance* and *scalability*.

Regarding the heterogeneity aspect, SemWIQ must be able to cope with all levels of heterogeneity discussed in Section 3.3.2 including *metamodel heterogeneity*. SemWIQ is therefore based on the classical mediator-wrapper approach (see Section 6.1): heterogeneous data sources are virtually integrated via wrappers, and a central federated query processor is responsible for answering queries by delegating sub queries to the wrappers. The query process is based on pipelining, which enables fast response times and ensures the scalability of the system by streaming results through the pipeline from the source information systems up to the requesting client.

Based on the general discussion of the architecture of information integration systems provided in Section 3.4 the following architectural concepts of SemWIQ are highlighted:

8 Overview

Interface – Because SemWIQ thoroughly leverages Semantic Web concepts, the central access interface is based on the *SPARQL Protocol and RDF Query Language* (SPARQL) (Prud'hommeaux and Seaborne 2008). As the name implies, it features both, a query language and interface protocol. The protocol is based on a REST-style Web service which greatly facilitates its usage from JavaScript and other simplistic clients. But SemWIQ can also be embedded into Java applications via the mediator API. Furthermore, SemWIQ supports the *Jena Assembler API* (Jena Community 2009a), which enables the integration of a virtual SemWIQ dataset into any Jena-based application just by means of a configuration file and without the need of re-compiling code.

Metadata catalog – The metadata catalog of SemWIQ is a central RDF store which contains information about the registered data sources (described using *voiD*), their current state of availability, and RDFStats statistics (Langegger and Wöß 2009c). These statistics are used to federate and optimize global SPARQL queries. The metadata catalog can be stored in any *Jena*-based RDF store, but the best performance has been achieved with *Jena TDB* (Jena Community 2009a). SemWIQ integrates a multi-threaded data source monitor which observes the registered data sources based on configurable profiles and updates the availability state and RDFStats statistics in the background.

Query processor – The SemWIQ query processor accepts a global SPARQL query and calculates a federated query plan based on the state of the metadata catalog. It is based on *Jena ARQ* (Jena Community 2009a), which has been extended by a federator and a statistics-based dynamic query optimizer. There are two different federators: the triple-based and the instance-based federator. The federators and the query engine are discussed in detail as part of Chapter 9.

Registry component – New data sources can be registered (and de-registered) at the SemWIQ mediator by means of the registry API and via a REST-style Web service. A data source is registered by the SPARQL endpoint URI provided by the corresponding wrapper. Upon registration, the data source monitor will try to find *voiD* (Alexander et al. 2009) metadata from the Web, which may include the maintainer of the dataset, license information, and subject terms related to the dataset. The monitor additionally fetches RDFStats statistics if natively provided, otherwise it will use the embedded RDFStats component and generate statistics remotely.

Wrappers – For each different source information system and corresponding source metamodel a specific wrapper is used to map and translate data to RDF in a single phase. General considerations towards wrapper development for SemWIQ and descriptions of D2R-Server (Chris Bizer and Richard Cyganiak 2006) and XLWrap (Langegger and Wöß 2009c) are described in Chapter 10.

In terms of the global metamodel, query language, and wrapper interface (Section 3.4) SemWIQ is characterized as follows:

Global metamodel – The global metamodel used by SemWIQ is the *Resource Description Framework* (RDF). In Chapter 8.1.1 the adequacy and advantages of RDF as a global metamodel for virtual information integration have been summarized.

Global query language – As already mentioned, the global query language is SPARQL (see Section 4.4 for a brief description). A global SPARQL query may contain any ontological concept, however, a query will only return results if it can be answered by the global virtual dataset, i.e. by the union of contributed virtual RDF graphs.

Wrapper interface and protocol – The interface between SemWIQ wrappers and the mediator is also SPARQL. Each wrapper is able to process SPARQL sub queries and stream intermediate solution mappings to the mediator[2].

In Figure 8.2 the architecture of SemWIQ is depicted. The basic building blocks are clients on the top, the mediator in the middle, and several data sources at the bottom of the figure. Users of SemWIQ access the mediator by a client (embedded or Web service-based) and submit global SPARQL queries (1). A global SPARQL query may contain any terminological concepts such as classes and properties, but also instances that exist in the global virtual graph. The query parser (2) generates a canonical query plan, which is transformed and optimized by the federator (3) based on information contained in the metadata catalog (4). There are two different federators available in SemWIQ which will be described as part of Chapter 9. The metadata catalog, which is an RDF graph itself managed by *Jena TDB* (Jena Community 2009a), contains a `void:Dataset` (Alexander et al. 2009) and RDFStats statistics (Langegger and Wöß 2009b) for each registered data source. The federated and optimized query plan is finally processed by the query execution engine (5). A global query plan consists of several local sub-plans that are further combined by higher-level algebra operators processed at the mediator. Any operation that can be executed directly by wrappers remotely is part of the local query plan. Remote wrappers are placed directly on top of the remote data source (6). For data sources that are fully autonomous, the corresponding wrappers may be placed in a special container at the mediator (7).

The data source registry (8) is responsible for the registration and de-registration of data sources. A data source can be registered and de-registered by sending an HTTP POST request with the corresponding SPARQL endpoint URI. The data source monitor (9) is periodically checking the availability of registered data sources and fetches *voiD* metadata and up-to-date RDFStats statistics.

---

[2]Streaming SPARQL XML results over HTTP works very well based on the *Streaming API for XML* (StAX), which is used by *Jena ARQ* (Jena Community 2009a).

8 Overview

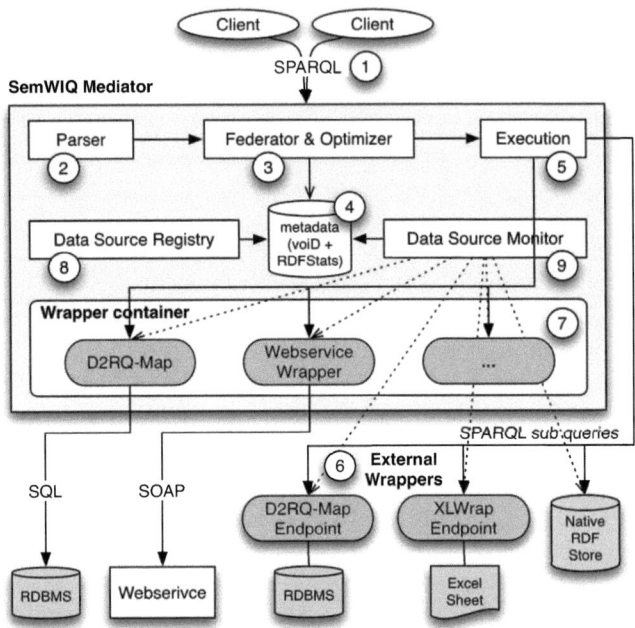

Figure 8.2: Mediator-Wrapper architecture of SemWIQ.

8.3 Query Federation Based on Statistical Data Summaries

As explained in Section 3.4 an information integration system requires special metadata to be able to federate global queries. The general goal is to only include data sources into a global query plan if they are potentially contributing any results. By contrast to traditional integration systems, SemWIQ does not require the explicit notation and maintenance of a global schema. As a consequence the disadvantage of typical *Global-as-View* integration systems, where the global schema must be updated when a data source is added, does not apply to SemWIQ. Instead of maintaining a global schema which describes all the integrated local schemas, SemWIQ is based on statistical data summaries.

Query federation based on data summaries is a key concept of SemWIQ that makes the system scalable. In traditional mediator-wrapper systems, the selection of relevant data sources is based on the global schema definition and not on the actual dataset. For a given query, each data source that is relevant with respect to its exported schema is explicitly accessed in order to determine if it has any data to contribute. This requires the initiation of at least one network connection in order to invoke the data source's cost functions. In SemWIQ it is possible to integrate a large number of data sources, because relevant data sources can be identified *offline*, i.e. without the need to consult the corresponding SPARQL endpoint.

In order to generate statistical data summaries, the RDFStats (Langegger and Wöß 2009b) component has been developed. The component consists of an RDF statistics generator for RDF datasets accessible via SPARQL endpoints and a set of cardinality estimation functions. These functions are used to estimate the expected minimal, average, and maximal number of results for triple patterns, basic graph patterns, and full query plans. Because RDFStats provides the maximum estimation (i.e. upper bound), it is possible to give guaranteed answers whether a given data source will return any results at all (upper bound must be > 0). RDFStats also supports the estimation for range queries specified by means of filtered triple patterns and basic graph patterns.

For each data source, the mediator maintains an RDFStats dataset, which contains a data summary of the sub-graph contributed by the corresponding source. How statistics are generated, what kind of information is collected, and how it is used during federation will be subject of Chapter 9.

Additional metadata about a registered data source, such as its creator, publisher, contributors, license, or subject keywords, is stored in the catalog based on *voiD*, the *Vocabulary of Interlinked Datasets* (Alexander et al. 2009). The vocabulary has been developed to describe interlinked datasets for the Web of Data.

8 Overview

9 SemWIQ Mediator

The SemWIQ mediator is the core component of the presented integration system. As depicted in Figure 9.1, it consists of the parser, federator & optimizer, query execution engine, data source registry, metadata store, and the data source monitor. The data source registry and the monitor manage metadata including RDFStats statistics, which is used by the federator and the optimizer to generate query plans.

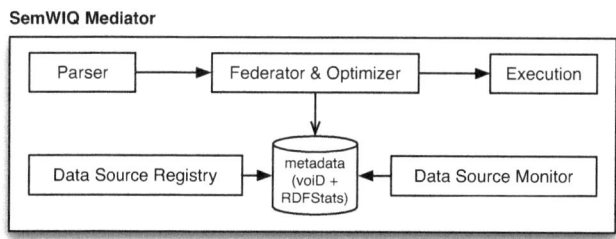

Figure 9.1: SemWIQ mediator component.

Since SemWIQ is based on *Jena ARQ* (Jena Community 2009a, Carroll et al. 2004), many components already existing in the *Jena Semantic Web Framework* can be reused. This basically includes the management of RDF models[1], persistent storage of RDF models, query capability with SPARQL, serialization/de-serialization of models into various formats (RDF/XML, N3, Turtle, etc. as explained in Section 4.2.4), and a broad range of base functionality such as for parsing lexical queries, manipulating algebra plans, and implementing custom query executions.

This chapter is structured as follows. After some definitions (Section 9.1), an overview of the SemWIQ architecture and the query processing work flow is provided in Section 9.2. In Sections 9.3 and 9.4 two different federation approaches are described with different characteristics and computational properties. Finally, some details on the implementation are provided in Section 9.5.

---

[1] Jena wraps plain RDF graphs that contain sets of triples by a special model API, which enables higher-level access to instances, classes, properties, RDF containers, etc.

9.1 Definitions

In this section some definitions are specified which are required to describe the SemWIQ mediator and several extensions to SPARQL. They build upon the SPARQL definitions of Section 4.4.3.

9.1.1 SemWIQ Queries and the Virtual Global Graph

SemWIQ is based on distributed SPARQL graph pattern matching, which means that a global query is formulated in SPARQL. A *global query* in the context of SemWIQ, is a SPARQL query directed to the mediator. By contrast to the definition of the SPARQL dataset (Definition 12, page 61), which consists of a set of graphs with a default graph and multiple named graphs, global SemWIQ queries are executed against a single RDF graph, the virtual global graph $G_\mathcal{G}$.

Definition 14 *A global SemWIQ query is defined as a tuple $(q_\mathcal{G}, R)$ where $q_\mathcal{G}$ is an algebra plan as defined in 11 (page 61) with the algebra modifications defined in Section 9.1.2, and R is one of the query forms described in Section 4.4.2.*

By contrast to the original SPARQL query definition (Definition 13), where the user specifies the target dataset DS as part of the query, the global virtual graph $\mathcal{G}$ is defined implicitly by the current state of the SemWIQ mediator. SemWIQ supports all four query forms: SELECT, ASK, DESCRIBE, and CONSTRUCT. Regardless of the query form, the global query plan $q_\mathcal{G}$ is executed in the same way in the first place. While the result of a SELECT query is the sequence of solution mappings obtained after the graph pattern matching process (Section 4.4.1), the other query forms require some post-processing of the solution sequence in a second step. Because the majority of queries are SELECT queries, the definition of global SemWIQ query given above and the following definition of the global query plan $q_\mathcal{G}$ are sometimes used interchangeably for simplicity.

Definition 15 *The global query plan $q_\mathcal{G}$ is executed against a single graph, the global virtual graph $G_\mathcal{G}$, which is defined as the union of all sub-graphs G_{S_i} contributed by SemWIQ data sources: $G_\mathcal{G} = \bigcup G_{S_i}$.*

During query federation, a global query plan $q_\mathcal{G}$ is decomposed into several local sub-plans $q_{S_i,j}$ and a remaining global part $q'_\mathcal{G}$, which combines the local sub-plans.

Definition 16 *A local sub-plan $q_{S_i,j}$ is a query plan executed against the source graph G_{S_i} of the corresponding data source. The global part $q'_\mathcal{G}$ of the original query plan is executed at the mediator.*

Definition 17 *A SemWIQ data source s is some source of information which contributes a sub-graph G_{S_i} to the virtual global graph $G_\mathcal{G}$. In case of a non-RDF data source, the sub-graph G_{S_i} is virtually defined by the native dataset D_{S_i} of the data source S_i and a mapping specification $\mathcal{M}_i$.*

Because each wrapper used in SemWIQ follows a direct metamodel-to-metamodel mapping approach (as described in Section 3.5), the mapping specification is wrapper-specific. Mapping approaches for different wrappers are discussed in Chapter 10.

Federation Modes

The semantics of query evaluation in SemWIQ depends on the federation approach. There are two different modes available: *triple based* and *instance-based* federation. While the first approach generally evaluates each triple pattern of a BGP against $G_{\mathcal{G}}$, the *instance-based* federator stipulates some specific structure of the global graph $G_{\mathcal{G}}$. Both approaches are described in Chapter 9.

9.1.2 Algebra Modifications

Instead of specifying the target dataset of a global SemWIQ query explicitly, the pattern of a query adheres to the virtual graph $\mathcal{G}$ defined by the current state of the mediator. The integration approach is completely virtual and based on global ontological concepts. Hence, the FROM or GRAPH clauses are not required and the *Graph* operator is not used for SemWIQ.

For SemWIQ queries, all algebra operators of the original SPARQL definition (Definition 10) are available with the following modifications:

- the *Graph* operator has been dropped
- the *Service* operator, which is used to delegate local sub-plans to wrappers, is introduced

Definition 18 *Following Definition 10, the* Service *operator is defined as* $((u), (q_{S_{i,j}}), s_{Service})$, *where the single argument u is the URI of the wrapper's SPARQL endpoint, $q_{S_{i,j}}$ is a local sub-plan (Definition 16), and $s_{Service}$ defines the algorithm that delegates the sub-plan.*

9.1.3 SPARQL Extensions

In addition to the *Service* operator, several extensions to the SPARQL query language have been proposed and implemented in order to support the following features required for SemWIQ. The grammar is based on the ARQ grammar, which already adds several extensions to the W3C Recommendation (Prud'hommeaux and Seaborne 2008). The modified BNF production rules are printed in Listing 9.1.

EXPLAIN queries – SemWIQ supports explanation queries for all four query forms in order to obtain details on the execution plan, e.g. EXPLAIN SELECT * WHERE { ... }. The result of an explain query includes the *Jena*-specific algebra plan encoded in LISP-style syntax as shown in Section 4.4.4 as well as the initial state of query iterators in a *Jena*-specific notation. Similar to explanation queries in SQL, it is probably difficult to propose a standard for explain

9 SemWIQ Mediator

```
Query           ::= Prologue
                    ( <EXPLAIN> )?
                    ( SelectQuery | ConstructQuery | DescribeQuery | AskQuery )
SelectQuery     ::= <SELECT>
                    ( <DISTINCT> | <REDUCED> )?
                    (
                      (
                        Var
                        | AggExpression
                        | BuiltInCall
                        | FunctionCall
                        | ( <LPAREN> Expression ( <AS> Var )? <RPAREN> )
                      )+
                      | <STAR>
                    )
                    ( DatasetClause )*
                    WhereClause
                    ( <BINDINGS> Bindings )?
                    SolutionModifier
Bindings        ::= ( Var )* <LBRACE> ( ( NullVarOrNode )* <DOT> )* <RBRACE>
NullVarOrNode   ::= ( <NULL> | VarOrTerm )
DescribeQuery   ::= <DESCRIBE>
                    (
                      ( <SERVICE> | <SELF> )
                      | <DATASET>
                      | (
                          ( VarOrIRIref )+
                          | <STAR>
                        )
                        ( DatasetClause )* ( WhereClause )? SolutionModifier
                    )
```

Listing 9.1: Modifications to the SPARQL grammar of ARQ.

query results since the query processor and the information obtained are highly implementation-specific. This feature is available for global SemWIQ queries, but also at SemWIQ wrappers for testing purposes. An example in case of the proposed extension implemented for *Jena ARQ* is shown in Listing 9.2.

Initial bindings – In order to efficiently process distributed joins, the substitution algorithm described in Section 9.2.5 is used which performs better if wrappers support initial bindings for sub-queries, a feature also called *row blocking* in SQL query processing (Kossmann 2000). Initial bindings are supported by all SemWIQ wrappers. The feature is best described with an example query:

```
SELECT * WHERE {
   ?s :p ?a ; :p ?b ...
} BINDINGS ?a ?b {
   bsbm:Product "34"^^xsd:int .
   null "23"^^xsd:int .
   foaf:Person . // remaining slots are interpreted as empty (null)
}
```

The query includes three initial bindings for the variables ?a and ?b. Partial bindings are allowed: empty bindings can be specified by the special null keyword.

9.1 Definitions

Service and dataset description – In order to obtain a description of the SPARQL service endpoint or the dataset it serves including RDFStats, all SemWIQ components (mediator and wrappers) support special `DESCRIBE` query forms: `DESCRIBE SERVICE` and `DESCRIBE DATASET`. While the first form returns a description of the service endpoint and its capabilities, the second describe form returns meta data and RDFStats statistics for the served dataset. Example results for both query forms are printed in Listings 9.3 and 9.4. The meaning of the Base64-encoded histogram data as part of the dataset description will be explained in Chapter 11.

```
@prefix spx:       <http://purl.org/NET/sparql-explain#> .
@prefix rdfs:      <http://www.w3.org/2000/01/rdf-schema#> .
@prefix xsd:       <http://www.w3.org/2001/XMLSchema#> .
@prefix rdf:       <http://www.w3.org/1999/02/22-rdf-syntax-ns#> .

[]     a       spx:QueryExplanation ;
       spx:plan """(service <http://semwiqdemo:8909/sparql>
  (bgp
    (triple ?p <http://www.w3.org/1999/02/22-rdf-syntax-ns#type> <http://xmlns.com/foaf/0.1/Person>)
    (triple ?p <http://xmlns.com/foaf/0.1/name> ?name)
  ))
QueryIteratorCloseable/MediatorQueryEngine$3
  MediatorQueryEngine$3/QueryIteratorCheck
    QueryIterRoot
    QueryIterService
"""^^xsd:string ;
       spx:queryString """PREFIX  dc:     <http://purl.org/dc/elements/1.1/>
PREFIX  foaf:  <http://xmlns.com/foaf/0.1/>
PREFIX  rdf:   <http://www.w3.org/1999/02/22-rdf-syntax-ns#>

EXPLAIN SELECT  *
WHERE
  { ?p rdf:type foaf:Person .
    ?p foaf:name ?name
  }
"""^^xsd:string .
```

Listing 9.2: EXPLAIN query results example.

9.1.4 SemWIQ Data Source Description

As part of the SemWIQ metadata catalog, each data source is described as an instance of the OWL class `sdv:Datasource` (Listing 9.5) using the SemWIQ data source vocabulary (SDV)[2], which is based on *voiD*. The definition in Listing 9.5 requires that a data source is at least specified by its SPARQL endpoint URI (qualified cardinality restriction on `void:sparqlEndpoint`). The *voiD* vocabulary can be used to supply additional metadata including the creator, publisher, contributors of the dataset, the linkage to external datasets, licensing information, etc. (Alexander et al. 2009).

---

[2] http://purl.org/semwiq/mediator/sdv#

9 SemWIQ Mediator

```
<?xml version="1.0"?>
<rdf:RDF
    xmlns:rdf="http://www.w3.org/1999/02/22-rdf-syntax-ns#"
    xmlns:sd="http://darq.sf.net/dose/0.1#"
    xmlns:xsd="http://www.w3.org/2001/XMLSchema#"
    xmlns:saddle="http://www.w3.org/2005/03/saddle/#"
    xmlns:rdfs="http://www.w3.org/2000/01/rdf-schema#">
  <sd:Service>
    <saddle:dataSet rdf:resource="http://ramses.faw.uni-linz.ac.at:8900/void/sparql"/>
    <saddle:resultFormat rdf:parseType="Resource">
      <saddle:spec rdf:resource="http://www.w3.org/TR/rdf-sparql-XMLres/"/>
      <saddle:mediaType rdf:datatype="http://www.w3.org/2001/XMLSchema#string">application/sparql-
          results+xml</saddle:mediaType>
      <rdfs:label rdf:datatype="http://www.w3.org/2001/XMLSchema#string">SPARQL/XML</rdfs:label>
    </saddle:resultFormat>
    <saddle:queryLanguage rdf:parseType="Resource">
      <saddle:spec rdf:resource="http://www.w3.org/TR/rdf-sparql-query/"/>
      <rdfs:label rdf:datatype="http://www.w3.org/2001/XMLSchema#string">SPARQL</rdfs:label>
    </saddle:queryLanguage>
    <sd:totalTriples rdf:datatype="http://www.w3.org/2001/XMLSchema#long">40344</sd:totalTriples>
    <rdfs:label rdf:datatype="http://www.w3.org/2001/XMLSchema#string">Joseki SPARQL Endpoint</rdfs:
        label>
    ...
  </sd:Service>
</rdf:RDF>
```

Listing 9.3: DESCRIBE SERVICE query results example.

```
@prefix dc:      <http://purl.org/dc/elements/1.1/> .
@prefix rdf:     <http://www.w3.org/1999/02/22-rdf-syntax-ns#> .
<http://ramses.faw.uni-linz.ac.at:8900/void/sparql>
    a           <http://rdfs.org/ns/void#Dataset> ;
...
:b2    a        <http://purl.org/rdfstats/stats#RDFStatsDataset> ;
       dc:creator "dorgon@ramses.faw.uni-linz.ac.at" ;
       dc:date "2009-10-09T15:07:42.563Z"^^<http://www.w3.org/2001/XMLSchema#dateTime> ;
       <http://purl.org/rdfstats/stats#sourceType>
                <http://purl.org/rdfstats/stats#SPARQLEndpoint> ;
       <http://purl.org/rdfstats/stats#sourceUrl>
                <http://ramses.faw.uni-linz.ac.at:8900/sparql> .

[]     a        <http://purl.org/rdfstats/stats#PropertyHistogram> ;
       rdf:value """ATKQHmrFOrYAAAAyaHR0cDovL3d3dy53My5vcmcvMjAwMS9YTUxTY2hlbWEjZGF0ZVRpbWUUDAAAA
BAAAAkAAAALAAAADQAAABUAAAANAAAAHAAAACAAAAASAAAAIAAAAB8AAAAkAAAALgAAABkAAAA2
AAAALwAAACgAAAA4AAAAQwAAADIAAABLAAAASgAAAEAAAABJAAAASwAAAEsAAABRAAAAOwAAAE0A
AABBAAAAKAAAADsAAAA7AAAAHwAAAD0AAAApAAAAIwAADEAAAoAAAALAAACYAAAAaAAAAGAAAA
ABoAAAANAAAAGAAAABAAAAAMAAAABQAAAYAAAfQAAAAtgAAARbqVc2AAAABGpNkRwAAABAAAAA
QAAAAEA=""" ;
       <http://purl.org/NET/scovo#dataset>
                _:b2 ;
       <http://purl.org/rdfstats/stats#propertyDimension>
                <http://www4.wiwiss.fu-berlin.de/bizer/bsbm/v01/vocabulary/validFrom> ;
       <http://purl.org/rdfstats/stats#rangeDimension>
                <http://www.w3.org/2001/XMLSchema#dateTime> .
...
```

Listing 9.4: DESCRIBE DATASET query results example (in Notation3 syntax).

```
:DataSource            a owl:Class ;
    rdfs:label "SemWIQ data source" ;
    rdfs:comment "data source accessible via the SPARQL protocol - Instead of introducing a new
        data source vocabulary, we assume that each void:Dataset that has a void:sparqlEndpoint
        property is a valid data source" ;
    rdfs:subClassOf void:Dataset ;
    rdfs:subClassOf [
        a owl:Restriction ;
        owl:onProperty void:sparqlEndpoint ;
        owl:cardinality "1"^^xsd:nonNegativeInteger ;
    ] .
```

Listing 9.5: Definition of a SemWIQ data source based on voiD

9.2 Query Processing Overview

An overview of the mediator query engine and a data source query engine is depicted in Figure 9.2. Although the SemWIQ approach shares similarities with traditional SQL-based federated database systems (Özsu and Valduriez 1999, Sheth and Larson 1990), there are important differences due to the SPARQL algebra and the federation approach which is based on *RDFStats* data summaries (Langegger and Wöß 2009b). The mediator query engine is depicted on the top of the figure and the query engine of a data source is shown at the bottom of the figure.

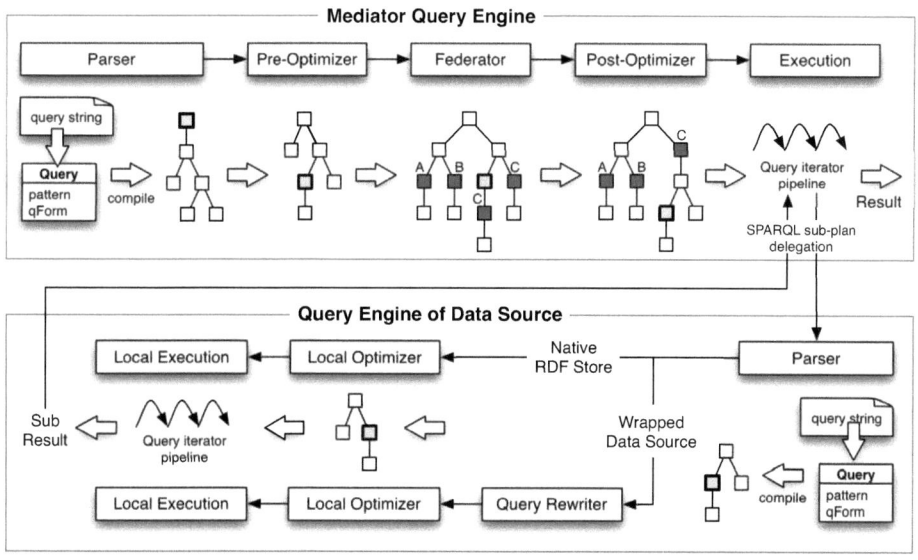

Figure 9.2: Query processing overview.

The figure shows the query process from an initial query string to its executable query iterator pipeline. Query iterators produce consecutive query solutions, i.e. final variable bindings, which can be obtained in a loop by the client. A pipelined approach is required to save resources and ensure good performance and scalability of the system. Both query engines first have to parse a lexical query string into a Java representation before its pattern is compiled into a query plan. In case of the mediator, the pre-optimizer is applying several logical simplifications and optimizations such as push-down of filters (bold boxes) as close as possible to basic graph patterns (leaves). The federator is decomposing the query plan and inserting *Service* operators (gray boxes). All sub-plans of *Service* operators are local sub-plans delegated to data sources (A, B, and C in the example). The post-optimizer is applying further logical optimizations such as merging local sub-plans but also filter-push downs again. The last step is the streamed execution of the compiled query plan.

During query execution, the mediator query engine will open connections to remote query interfaces of data sources and delegate sub-plans to be executed directly at data sources. There are two cases indicated by a branch: the upper path shows the query engine in case of a native RDF store and the lower path represents the query engine of a wrapper which needs to rewrite a query before execution. Additionally, in both cases, local optimizations are applied since the query engine typically has more accurate statistics and metadata (e.g. existence of indexes) than the mediator. The mediator query engine will be discussed in detail now. Query processing in native RDF stores is not discussed in this context, however, several wrapper implementations are described in Chapter 10.

9.2.1 Parser

The existing SPARQL parser of *Jena ARQ* is used to transform a lexical query string into a Java representation which is further transformed by the ARQ `AlgebraGenerator` into an abstract canonical query plan. This is fairly similar to SQL query processing which is typically based on algebra plans or abstract syntax trees also. SPARQL has four different query forms: SELECT, ASK, DESCRIBE, and CONSTRUCT. In any case, the query engine compiles a query plan for the graph pattern of the query. Depending on the query form, the query engine will take other actions and post-process solutions obtained from executing the query plan (e.g. consult a describe handler for information on resources in case of a DESCRIBE query).

All the algebra operators relevant to SemWIQ are shown in the class hierarchy depicted in Figure 9.3. The operator names in the figure correspond to Java class names which have the prefix `Op`. The unshaded operators are standard SPARQL operators defined in (Prud'hommeaux and Seaborne 2008) and the shaded ones with a bold edge are additional operators used to federate and optimize queries. The operators are categorized into four groups based on the number of sub-operators. Any operator extending `Op0` is a leaf node that produces solution mappings from some source of RDF data like a graph or a wrapped data source. `Op1` operators have one, `Op2` operators have two, and `OpN` operators can have multiple sub operators, i.e. sub-plans.

9.2 Query Processing Overview

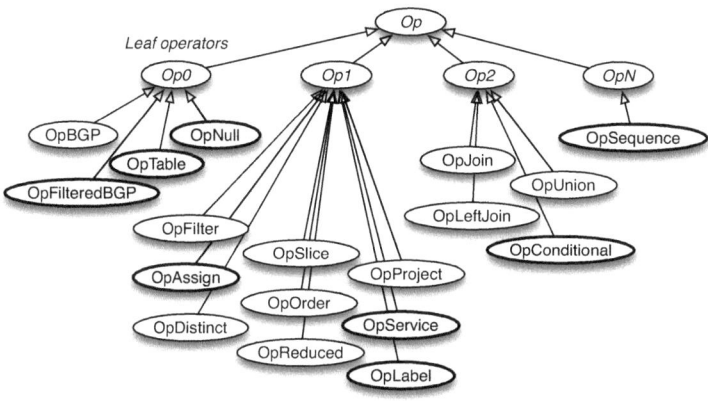

Figure 9.3: SPARQL algebra operators relevant to SemWIQ.

An example for an algebra plan has already been shown in Figure 4.8 on page 61. A serialized form of the same algebra plan using the LISP-style notation proposed by Andy Seaborne is shown in Section 4.4.4.

9.2.2 Pre-optimizations

Before the query plan is federated, several logical optimizations are applied in the pre-optimization phase. They include the following steps:

1. Filters

    The *Filter* operator defines a single argument which is a list of expressions $E = (e_1, e_2, \ldots, e_n)$, where each single expression e_i has to be satisfied (conjunction).

    a) At first, consecutive *Filter* operators in the plan are combined by merging their expression lists, i.e. $Filter(E_1, Filter(E_2, q)) \rightarrow Filter(E_1 \cup E_2, q)$.

    b) Next, for each *Filter*, its filter expressions E are merged into a single conjunctive filter expression $e' = e_1 \wedge e_2 \wedge \ldots \wedge e_n$, such that E' finally contains only one expression: $E' = (e')$, with $|E'| = 1$.

    c) De Morgan's law is recursively applied to the single conjunctive expression e' in order to expand expressions $!(a \vee b)$ into $!a \wedge !b$, where a and b are direct or indirect sub-expressions of e'.

    d) Similarly, the distributive law is recursively applied in order to expand $a \vee (b \wedge c)$ into $(a \vee b) \wedge (a \vee c)$, where a and b are direct or indirect sub-expressions of the single expression.

e) Any consecutive conjunctives $e_1 \wedge e_2 \wedge \ldots \wedge e_n$ in the resulting expression are split into an expression list $E = (e_1, e_2, \ldots, e_n)$ again.

f) Whenever possible, sub-expressions e_i are now pushed down in the query plan as close as possible to *BGP* operators according to the rules described below.

g) Whenever possible, filter sub-expressions of the form $e_i := (v == c)$, where v is a variable and c a constant RDF term $\in (I \cup B \cup L)$, i.e. an IRI reference, blank node, or literal, are merged into basic graph patterns. Additionally, the corresponding *BGP* is wrapped into an *Assign* operator which constantly re-inserts the otherwise missing bindings $v \leftarrow c$ into the solution sequence produced by the *BGP*.

2. Filtered BGPs

Any *BGP* that has a preceding *Filter* is finally transformed into a special *FilteredBGP* operator, which keeps a reference to the preceding *Filter* required for the RDFStats-based federation and optimization later on.

The first optimizer implementation was based on a declarative approach (Langegger et al. 2008a, Langegger et al. 2008b), where all the logical optimizations where expressed in the form of abstract rules. The *JBoss Drools* rules framework (JBoss Community n.d.) was used to formulate and execute the rules and transform query plans accordingly. However, since the performance of this approach was not satisfactory, the current implementation is based on several hard-coded iterator-based plan transformations. Given that query plans are rather small in size (usually 5–50 operators), a repeated and even cascaded traversal of query plans is still very fast.

Filter Push-down Rules

In order to push-down filters, filter expressions are prepared as previously described (e.g. De Morgan and distributive laws are applied). Before step 1f is applied, for all *Filter* operators an expression list of the form $E = (e_1, e_2, \ldots, e_n)$ exists. For a given expression list, *all* single expressions e_i have to be satisfied when evaluating E at execution time. Since the commutativity property applies to E and E can be split into two expression lists: $E = E_1 \cup E_2$, filters can be split in order to apply some filter expressions earlier in the query plan. Filter push-down has been implemented for *Union*, *Join*, *LeftJoin*, and *Service*. Additionally, any occurring subsequent filters are merged again as described in step 1a. Depending on the operator, a filter push-down is possible according to the following rules:

- Join: given a preceding *Filter* with expression list $E = (e_1, e_2, \ldots, e_n)$, let $V_L = (l_1, l_2, \ldots, l_s)$ be the set of variables possibly bound in the left sub-plan, let $V_R = (r_1, r_2, \ldots, r_t)$ be the set of variables possibly bound in the right sub-plan, and let $L = R = K = \emptyset$.

9.2 Query Processing Overview

For each sub-expression e_i, decide whether it may be pushed down left (set L) and/or right (set R), or it must be kept (set K). Let V_e be the set of variables occurring in e_i:

$$L = L \cup \{e_i\} \text{ if } V_e \subseteq V_L$$
$$R = R \cup \{e_i\} \text{ if } V_e \subseteq V_R$$
$$K = K \cup \{e_i\} \text{ if } V_e \nsubseteq V_L \wedge V_e \nsubseteq V_R$$

- LeftJoin: given a preceding *Filter* with expressions $E = (e_1, e_2, \ldots, e_n)$, let $V_L = (l_1, \ldots, l_s)$ be the set of variables possibly bound in the left sub-plan, let $V_R = (r_1, r_2, \ldots, r_t)$ be the set of variables possibly bound in the right sub-plan, and let $L = K = \emptyset$.

For each sub-expression e_i, decide whether it may be pushed down left (set L) or it must be kept (set K). Let V_e be the set of variables occurring in e_i:

$$L = L \cup \{e_i\} \text{ if } V_e \subseteq V_L$$
$$K = K \cup \{e_i\} \text{ if } V_e \nsubseteq V_L \wedge V_e \nsubseteq V_R$$

Note that it is not possible to push-down a filter into the right sub-plan of the *LeftJoin*. Otherwise, the filter will be applied on the *optional* bindings and not the complete joined binding.

- Union: Given a preceding *Filter* with expression list E, the complete expression list can be copied and pushed down both sides: $Filter(E, Union(\emptyset, q_L, q_R))$ becomes $Union(\emptyset, Filter(E, q_L), Filter(E, q_R))$.

- Service: Given $Filter(E, Service((u), q))$, it is always possible to push-down the *Filter* beyond the *Service* operator: $Service((u), Filter(E, q))$.

9.2.3 Federation

The task of the federator is to transform the query plan accordingly, such that the query engine is able to produce correct results given the virtual global graph as $G_\mathcal{G} = G_{S_1} \cup G_{S_2} \cup \ldots \cup G_{S_n}$. It can also be represented as a large set of triples virtually merged from all source graphs:

$$G_\mathcal{G} = (\, t_{s_1,1},\ t_{s_1,2},\ \ldots,\ t_{s_1,k_1},$$
$$t_{s_2,1},\ t_{s_2,2},\ \ldots,\ t_{s_2,k_2},$$
$$\ldots$$
$$t_{s_n,1},\ t_{s_n,2},\ \ldots,\ t_{s_n,k_n}\,)$$

9 SemWIQ Mediator

Given a triple pattern *tp* (see Definition 4, page 59), the federator must determine which of the *virtual* triples t_{s_i,k_j} will match. A data source is relevant, if its source graph G_{S_i} (which is virtual in case of a wrapped data source) contains triples that match the triple pattern *tp*. The necessary information is maintained in the form of statistical data summaries by the *RDFStats* component as described in Chapter 11. For each *BGP* the federator creates a modified sub-plan which contains *Service* operators to delegate local plans to the query interface of registered data sources. The algorithm used to modify a query plan *q* and insert federated sub-plans is printed as Algorithm 1. The output is the federated query plan.

Algorithm 1 Plan transform algorithm of the federator.

---
function F   -P   (*q*)
    q, root operator of query plan to federate (see Definition 11)
    return V   -T -D   (*q*)
end function

function V   -T -D   (*q*)
    q, operator to visit (root of a sub-plan)
    y ← type of *q*
    P ← sequence of sub-operators $p_1, p_2, \ldots, p_n$ of *q*
    if |*P*| = 0 **then**
        if *y* = *BGP* **then**
            q ← F   -BGP(*q*)
        end if
    else if |*P*| = 1 **then**
        sub ← V   -T -D   (p_1)
        q ← C   -O 1(*y*, *sub*)
    else if |*P*| = 2 **then**
        left ← V   -T -D   (p_1)
        right ← V   -T -D   (p_2)
        q ← C   -O 2(*y*, *left*, *right*)
    else if |*P*| > 2 **then**
        Q ← N   -S
        for all $p_i \in P$ **do**
            sub ← V   -T -D   (p_i)
            P   (*Q*, *sub*)
        end for
        q ← C   -O N(*y*, *Q*)
    end if
    return *q*
end function

SemWIQ supports two different federation strategies: instance-based and triple-based federation. To leverage the full power of RDF, the triple-based federation (TF) mode can deal with full fragmentation of instances over multiple distributed locations and untyped resources. In TF mode it is possible to integrate complete distributed RDF sub-graphs into a global virtual graph. There are no restrictions on the local sub-graphs or the ontologies used to represent the distributed information. However, triple-based federation requires more distributed joins and creates more complex queries. Accurate statistics generated by RDFStats are therefore crucial. The instance-based federation (IF) mode has been proposed to reduce the complexity and cost of processing a large number of distributed joins for each triple pattern (Langegger et al. 2008a, Langegger and Wöß 2008). The downside is its limited capability to merge fragmented information. Within the IF approach it is assumed that all the integrated information is organized in sets of instances (extensions). Each subject in the global graph G_G is assumed to have at least one associated type t (which is an RDF Schema class). Depending on the strategy, the function F   -BGP is implemented differently as described in Section 9.3 and 9.4. As shown in Figure 9.2, the interface between the mediator and the query engines of data sources is based on SPARQL also. Hence, it is possible to delegate complete query sub-plans to remote endpoints. The query is serialized back into a SPARQL query string and parsed by the remote query engine.

9.2.4 Post-optimizations

After federation, some of the pre-optimizations (Section 9.2.2) need to be re-applied. The following post-optimizations are applied:

1. Filter optimization (pre-optimization steps 1f and 1g are re-applied)

2. Join optimization

    a) The ARQ-based *Sequence* operator is a specialized join sequence operator which will be explained in the following. In this step, consecutive *Join* operations are combined into a single *Sequence*, which can have n sub-operators as shown in Figure 9.3.

    b) *Filter* operators preceding a *Join* or *LeftJoin* are dropped and their expressions are moved into the *Join* or *LeftJoin* realizing theta-joins.

    c) All *Sequence* operators realizing left-deep n-way joins are now optimized based on cost-based re-ordering of sub-plans.

3. Finally, step 2 from the pre-optimization phase is re-applied.

The most important part of a query processor is typically the optimization of n-way joins, because they are the most influencing factor regarding the computational complexity of a query. Due to the commutativity and associativity of n-way joins, it is possible to re-order them arbitrarily and enumerate alternative plans. The cheapest plan to execute can be determined based on a cost model taking many kinds of elementary costs into account such as loading pages into memory, executing algorithms (e.g. quicksort), and transferring data over network connections. However, an n-way join already gives $n!$ possible permutations, which makes a full enumeration impossible in the general case. Therefore, many systems only consider left-deep joins (Özsu and Valduriez 1999, p. 231), which still have $O(2^n)$ complexity, and use pruning techniques or evolutionary algorithms to find a good compromise between optimization time and outcome. Left-deep join trees have another important property: they allow pipelining. Bushy join trees would enable parallel distributed query processing. Because parallel distributed query processing would require additional preconditions for participating components and because SemWIQ should be flexible and based on Semantic Web standards, another approach was taken as will be explained.

Dynamic Join Optimization

Because SemWIQ is a web-based mediator-wrapper system, the major costs of processing a global query are transfer costs involved with transmitting data over the network. Currently, a very simplistic cost model is used which only takes the expected cardinalities of intermediate query results into account. Instead of join enumeration based on dynamic programming, which is used in many SQL query engines but also DARQ (Bastian Quilitz and Ulf Leser 2008), SemWIQ uses a dynamic query optimization approach similar to INGRES (Özsu and Valduriez 1999). This approach which supports pipelining is also used by *Jena ARQ* for local query processing where it is called *substitute algorithm*.

In post-optimization step 2a, consecutive *n*-way *Joins* are replaced by single *Sequence* operators. When the query plan is executed, the *Sequence* operator realizes the *substitute* algorithm used in *Jena ARQ*. The algorithm will be described in Section 9.2.5. In order to optimize the join sequence, it is required to re-order the joined sub-plans based on the expected cardinality of their intermediate solutions. This estimations are provided by the *RDFStats* component as explained in Chapter 11. The sub-plan with the lowest cardinality will be executed first. For each result obtained from the first sub-plan, the query engine calculates a specific sub-plan at runtime before evaluating the next sub-plan and so on. By replacing already bound variables in subsequent sub-plans by their values, the complexity of a query can be reduced very fast at runtime. Because cross products and join sequences involving a very large number of sub-results from all sub-plans are very costly, it is better to process such queries with a traditional nested-loop join. Additionally, the query engine supports row-blocking which allows to execute batched local sub-queries (see Section 9.2.5).

9.2.5 Query Execution

Once the query plan has been compiled, it can be executed. As shown in Figure 9.2, the query processor initializes a pipeline of iterators, which is called *execution plan* in the following. *Jena ARQ* already provides the base functionality for streamed SPARQL query execution and implements a range of iterators to execute streamed and materialized joins, left joins, unions, filter, etc. The original implementation has been extended with support for row-blocking, distributed semi-joins, and provenance tracking. The iterator concept is used in nearly all query processor implementations and it is explained in many database text books. It is assumed that it is well-known. In Figure 9.4 the most important iterators available in Jena ARQ including the extensions for SemWIQ are depicted. All iterators extend the `QueryIteratorBase` class, which provides methods for the iteration over bindings

9.2 Query Processing Overview

(i.e. intermediate solution mappings). On the left hand side, all iterators extend from `QueryIter1`, which iterates over bindings from a single input iterator. `QueryIterBlocked` and its descendants have been added for the row-blocking feature of SemWIQ. The classes shown at the bottom of the picture are required for data provenance and distributed semi-join support. In the middle of the diagram, iterators with two input iterators are depicted. Only the materialized *Join* and *LeftJoin* use two inputs. Although the *Union* algebra operator actually has two sub-plans, the corresponding execution iterator only has one input iterator. This is because of the nature of the *substitute algorithm* explained below. Miscellaneous iterators are shown on the right hand side. Besides `QueryIterSort`, which implements a merge sort, these iterators are basically utilities to be used for various tasks such as concatenating iterators.

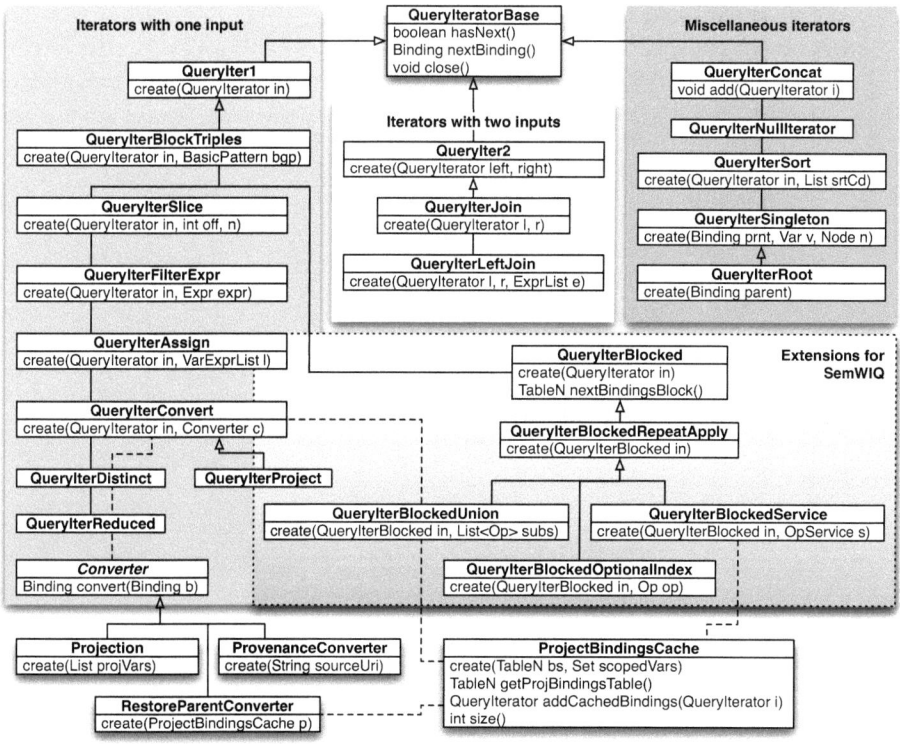

Figure 9.4: Query execution iterators.

`QueryIterRoot`, which extends `QueryIterSingleton` – an iterator that yields a single binding

9 SemWIQ Mediator

– is a special iterator used to initialize iterator pipelines. Each pipeline starts with a root that yields a single empty binding, the so-called *join identity*. The *substitute algorithm* requires that the join sequence is bootstrapped with the *join identity* as will be explained in the following.

Substitute Algorithm

As mentioned in Section 9.2.4, Jena ARQ is based on a dynamic query optimization approach similar to the original INGRES optimizer (Wong and Youssefi 1976, Özsu and Valduriez 1999). In ARQ it is called *substitute algorithm*, because during query execution join sequences are processed by *substituting* variables in sub-plans with already bound values from subsequent stages. Any consecutive join is replaced by a *Sequence* operator during the post-optimizer step 2a. The *Sequence* maintains an ordered list of sub-plans and resembles a left-deep join tree.

Figure 9.5 shows an example of a federated algebra plan. The original *Join* has been replaced by *Sequence*, which has two sub-plans to join (a sequence joins ≥ 2 sub plans actually). There are three *Service* operators and, hence, three local sub-plans delegated to the query interfaces of attached data sources.

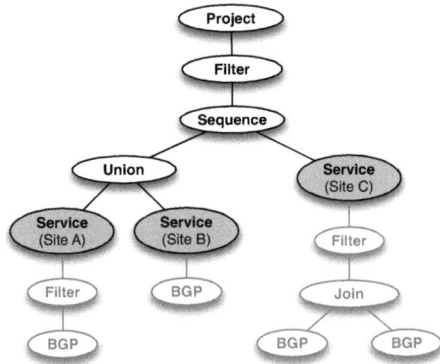

Figure 9.5: Example of a federated algebra plan.

The corresponding iterator pipeline is depicted in Figure 9.6. The query execution plan is created by traversing the query plan bottom-up using a post-order visitor. The visitor creates and initializes the iterator pipeline. The root input for the first iterator is an instance of `QueryIterRoot`, which produces just one empty intermediate solution mapping with no variable bindings: $\mu_0 = \{\}$. This is called the *join-identity*, because $merge(\mu_0, \mu_k) = \mu_k$ (see Definition 8 for *merge*).

Apart from the root iterator, the first iterator in the example is a `QueryIterBlockedUnion`, which extends `QueryIterBlockedRepeatApply` as can be seen in the class diagram in Figure 9.4. This

9.2 Query Processing Overview

kind of iterators is repeatedly executing a complete sub-plan for a given binding from the input. The next iterator in Figure 9.6 also has *repeat-apply* behavior. While this one delegates a *Service* sub-plan multiple times, the *Union repeat-apply* repeatedly executes a set of sub-plans and concatenates the iterators of the resulting execution plans.

In order to support row-blocking, all *repeat-apply* iterators have to consume a block of N bindings from the input iterator. For that reason, they are based on `QueryIterBlocked`. It ensures, that the preceding iterators are able to provide n bindings. All other single-phase iterators can be re-used from Jena ARQ, because they do not break the serial stream of the pipeline as do the *repeat-apply* variants. The block size N of intermediate bindings can be configured and a value between 500–1000 is recommended. All iterators extending `QueryIterBlockedRepeatApply` are represented with a bold box in Figure 9.6. The sub-plan which is applied multiple times is still kept in algebra form and in each stage, it is executed and a new iterator sub-pipeline is inserted into the overall pipeline.

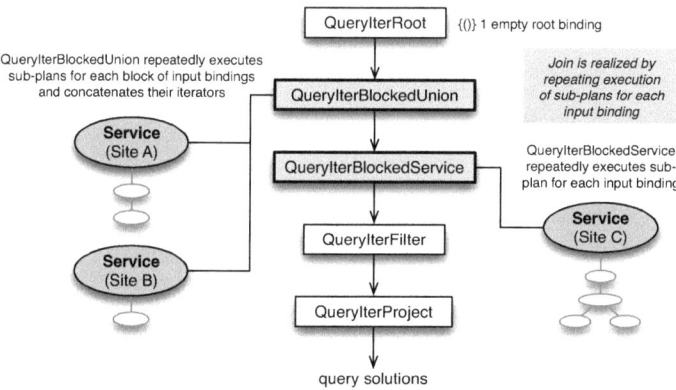

Figure 9.6: Execution plan for the algebra plan depicted in Figure 9.5.

Query execution of local sub-plans works similar as shown in Figure 9.2. Basically, it depends on the SPARQL implementation of data source which may be a native RDF store or a wrapper (see Chapter 10). The output of the iterator pipeline are solutions for the query. They can be iterated by the client. The stream can also be aborted and the query engine will safely clean up any used resources.

9.2.6 Data Provenance

For a virtual information integration approach it is very important for users to be able to track down where information is originating from. However, because data items such as numbers and strings may be calculated based on values from different sources and be post-processed by arbitrary functions, this is not always easy to accomplish. Actually, data provenance is a big topic of its own and a good approach should provide the user with a graphical visualization of the transition path, showing where data is coming from and how it is modified during the query process.

In case of SemWIQ, data provenance is addressed to some certain extent. Basically, the query execution engine stores a source annotation, which is the URI of the remote SPARQL endpoint of a data source, when a variable is initially bound. Because all bound values eventually originate from some data source, this is a good basic approach. It is realized by a `QueryIterConvert`, which is inserted into the pipeline by `QueryIterBlockedService` right after the sub-plan iterator that produces bindings for a local sub-plan. The provenance iterator utilizes the `ProvenanceConverter` (shown at the bottom of Figure 9.4) in order to convert default bindings into annotated bindings. To support these annotations the Jena `Node` implementation has been modified. Any client is finally able to retrieve the source URI via the patched Jena API.

9.3 Triple-based Federator

The triple-based federator (TF) can deal with full fragmentation of instances over multiple distributed locations and untyped resources. In TF mode it is possible to integrate complete distributed RDF subgraphs with no restrictions on the shape of the sub-graphs. But the approach requires more distributed joins.

The triple-based federation algorithm is printed as Algorithm 2. The logical pre-optimizer has already prepared the query plan. All filters have been pushed down as close as possible to basic graph patterns. Function F -BGP(b) is called from Algorithm 1 for each basic graph pattern b. At the beginning, the set of preceding filter expressions E is obtained (if b has a preceding *Filter*, otherwise $E = \emptyset$), and the map P_D is initialized, which will store data source specific BGPs.

For each triple pattern t the federator selects relevant data sources D based on statistical data summaries. A data source is relevant if it will contribute triples for t. The corresponding estimation functions provided by RDFStats are explained in Chapter 11. Regarding the set D, there are three cases:

1. If $|D| = 0$, the algorithm breaks and returns a special `OpNull` operator which return no results. If one of the triple patterns of a BGP cannot be satisfied, the whole BGP has no solution.

2. If $|D| = 1$, i.e. there is just one relevant data source d for t, then t is added to a specific (initially empty) BGP sub-plan b_d. All data source specific sub-plans are stored in the map P_D and added to the overall sub-plan in the end.

3. If $|D_i| > 1$, i.e. there are multiple relevant data sources for t, then a new sub-plan is created as follows:

    - For each $d \in D$ a new BGP b_d is created with t as a single triple pattern.

9.3 Triple-based Federator

Algorithm 2 Triple-based federation algorithm – called by Algorithm 1.

```
function F    -BGP(b)
    b, a BGP to federate
    E ← G  -P       -F    -E    (b), may be ∅
    P_D ← C    -M    D → BGP
    for all t ∈ G  -T    -P    (b) do
        D ← R    -D    (t, E)
        if |D| = 0 then
            return C    -O -N
        else if |D| = 1 then
            d ← G  -F    -E    (D)
            if C    -K    (P_D, d) then
                b_d ← G    (P_D, d)
            else
                b_d ← C    -BGP
                P    (P_D, d, b_d)
            end if
            A    -T    -P    (b_d, t)
        else
            for all d ∈ D do
                b_d ← C    -BGP
                A    -T    -P    (b_d, t)
                q_S ← C    -S    (d, b_d)
                if q_U = ε then
                    q_U ← q_S
                else
                    q_U ← C    -U    (q_U, q_S)
                end if
            end for
            if q_J = ε then
                q_J ← q_U
            else
                q_J ← C    -J    (q_J, q_U)
            end if
        end if
    end for
    for all d ∈ K  -S  (P_D) do
        b_d ← G    (P_D, d)
        q_S ← C    -S    (d, q_S)
        if q_J = ε then
            q_J ← q_S
        else
            q_J ← C    -J    (q_J, q_S)
        end if
    end for
    if q_J = ε then
        return C    -O -N
    else
        return q_J
    end if
end function
```

- The BGP b_d is wrapped by a *Service* operator q_S.
- All q_S sub-plans are combined with subsequent *Union* operators: this is done via q_U, which is initialized with q_S if $q_U = \epsilon$ (meaning *undefined*), and then set to the newly created *Union*.
- All *Union* chains q_U are combined with subsequent *Join* operators: similarly, q_J is initialized with q_U and then set to the previous q_J in a loop.

4. Finally, the data source specific sub-plans are added to q_J. For each d that has a corresponding sub-plan in P_D, b_d is obtained from P_D and wrapped by a *Service* q_S. If q_J should not have been initialized before (because there was no triple pattern with more than one relevant data sources), q_J is initialized with q_S. Otherwise, q_J is chained to the previous q_J with another *Join* over q_S.

5. The result returned by the algorithm is q_J or an OpNull in case there were no relevant data sources to fulfill the basic graph pattern b.

A similar approach has been proposed by Bastian Quilitz and Ulf Leser (2008). The main difference is that SemWIQ is using more accurate statistics based on RDFStats. Because RDFStats provides an upper bound estimate $card_{max}$ for triple pattern cardinalities, the federator can safely ignore data sources if $card_{max} = 0$, because it is guaranteed that the data source would not contribute any results. This is an important property in order to achieve scalability in terms of the number of registered data sources. However, especially if equal properties are used frequently for different kinds of instances (e.g. Dublin Core or RDF/RDF-S/OWL properties), the federator will consider all data sources as relevant for a triple pattern if it provides data described with that property. In the end, the federator will produce very complex query plans with many costly distributed joins. In many cases and application scenarios, the instance-based federator is better suited.

9.4 Instance-based Federator

For the instance-based federation approach it is assumed that all the integrated information is organized in sets of instances. Each subject in the global graph $G_\mathcal{G}$ is assumed to have at least one associated type t (which is an RDF Schema class).

Restriction 1 $G_\mathcal{G} = (s, p, o)$, $\forall s \ \exists (s, \mathit{rdf{:}type}, t)$

When setting up SemWIQ, this stipulation can be satisfied when mapping data sources. If the subsumption reasoning feature is enabled, the approach basically works also with untyped resources, because the reasoner will deduce that a given resource at least is an instance of the RDF class rdfs:Resource. As a consequence, the federator might consider a large number or even all data

9.4 Instance-based Federator

sources, because rdfs:Resource is the least specific type at all and potentially all sub-class extensions are relevant.

As a second restriction, it is assumed that instances are exclusively described by a single data source.

Restriction 2 $G_{S_i} = (s, p, o), \forall s \not\exists G_{S_j} = (s, p', o')$

Based on these restrictions, a global query can be federated based on instance sets of a SPARQL query. Equal subject nodes of a basic graph pattern always refer to the same set of instances. Given the BGP shown in Figure 9.7, the first three triple patterns refer to the same instance set for variable ?s. In total, the BGP refers to two different instance sets, one for variable ?s and one for ?p. For each of them, relevant data sources are selected and individual sub-queries are delegated to the query interfaces of the data sources. The algorithm is printed as Algorithm 3.

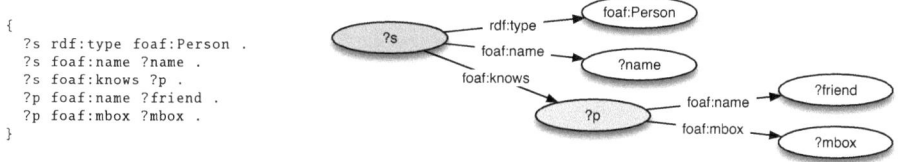

```
{
 ?s rdf:type foaf:Person .
 ?s foaf:name ?name .
 ?s foaf:knows ?p .
 ?p foaf:name ?friend .
 ?p foaf:mbox ?mbox .
}
```

Figure 9.7: SPARQL query with two different subject nodes.

Algorithm 3 works as follows: F   -BGP(b) is called for each basic graph pattern b visited by Algorithm 1. It returns a new sub-plan for b. At the beginning, the set of preceding filter expressions E is obtained (if b has a preceding *Filter*, otherwise $E = \emptyset$), and the maps B and C are initialized. B is created by the function C   -S   -G   (b), printed as Algorithm 4, which groups triple patterns of b by common subjects. For each occurring subject s, the map contains a new BGP with triple patterns (s, p_i, o_i).

C is created by the function D   -S   -T   (b), which is explained in Section 9.4.1 and printed as Algorithm 5 on page 152. The map C contains mappings from S, the set of triple pattern subjects, to the sets of RDF-S/OWL classes. In other words, for each subject $s \in \text{domain}(B)$, C contains a set of RDF-S/OWL classes. An instance of the corresponding subject group for s must be a member of all these classes. That is why it is also called *minimal conjunctive type set* (MCTS): *conjunctive*, because instances need to be member of *all* types and *minimal*, because it does not contain any other classes that are already subsumed by a class. Type detection and the calculation of the MCTS are described in Section 9.4.1.

Once, E, B, and C have been initialized, Algorithm 3 iterates over all subjects s of the compiled subject groups B (K   -S   (B) returns the domain of B, the set of subjects found). The corresponding

Algorithm 3 Instance-based federation algorithm – called by Algorithm 1.

```
function F    -BGP(b)
    b, a BGP to federate
    E ← G -P    -F    -E    (b), may be ∅
    B ← C    -S    -G    (b) // a map: Subjects → BGPs
    C ← D    -S    -T    (b) // a map: Subjects → Sets of classes (MCTS)
    for all s ∈ K -S  (B) do
        b_s ← G  (B, s)
        y ← S    -K    (s)
        if y = Variable then
            D_all ← A  -D
            for all d ∈ D_all do
                C_s ← G   (C, s)
                q_d ← C      -S -P   (d, s, b_s, C_s, E)
                if q_d ≠ ε then
                    q_S ← C     -S       (d, q_d)
                    if q_U = ε then
                        q_U ← q_S
                    else
                        q_U ← C      -U    (q_U, q_S)
                    end if
                end if
            end for
        else if y = URI then
            D ← R       -D       (b_s, E)
            for all d ∈ D do
                q_S ← C    -S       (d, b_s)
                if q_U = ε then
                    q_U ← q_S
                else
                    q_U ← C     -U    (q_U, q_S)
                end if
            end for
        end if
    end for
    if q_U = ε then
        return C       -O -N
    end if
    if q_J = ε then
        q_J ← q_U
    else
        q_J ← C     -J   (q_J, q_U)
    end if
    return q_J
end function
```

9.4 Instance-based Federator

Algorithm 4 Algorithm for creating BGP subject groups – called by Algorithm 3.

function C   -S   -G   (b)
   b, a *BGP* to split into subject groups
   $G \leftarrow$ C   -M   , a map: *Subjects* $\rightarrow$ BGPs
   for all $t \in$ G -T   -P   (b) **do**
      $s \leftarrow$ G -S   (t)
      if C   -K   (G, s) **then**
         $b_s \leftarrow$ G   (G, s)
      else
         $b_s \leftarrow$ C   -BGP
         P   (G, s, b_s)
      end if
      A   -T   -P   (b_s, t)
   end for
   return G
end function

BGP b_S is obtained and depending on the kind of s, which may be a variable or a URI node, the algorithm proceeds differently. Actually, also blank nodes are supported. They behave like variables, but in the end they are projected out by the query engine. In most cases, s will be a variable and refer to an instance set. Then, for each data source $d \in D_{all}$, the algorithm tries to compile a sub-plan q_d by calling C   -S   -P   . If it succeeds, the sub-plan is wrapped by a *Service* operator q_S and inserted into a union sequence. Otherwise, the loop continues with the next data source. The creation of a union sequence is the same as explained before for Algorithm 2 in Section 9.3.

If s is a URI subject, it directly refers to a specific instance with the given URI instead of an instance set. In this case, only data sources that know anything about s (i.e. contribute triples (s, p_i, o_i)) are selected by the function R   -D   (b_s, E). The function is provided by the data source registry component which integrates RDFStats (Chapter 11). Additionally, RDFStats statistics are used to detect whether a data source is relevant for the given BGP b_s and any preceding filter expressions E. For each relevant data source, the corresponding BGP b_s is wrapped into a *Service* operator q_S and inserted into a union sequence q_U.

If no relevant data sources have been found for a given subject group's BGP b_s, then q_U will be undefined (ϵ) and hence, the BGP cannot be answered. In this case, the algorithm returns the special `OpNull` operator, which produces no bindings (i.e. it will cause the creation of an instance of the special `QueryIterNullIterator` when executed). Otherwise, the *Union* sequences q_U created for each subject group are combined in a *Join* sequence q_J. Finally, the instance-based federation algorithm returns q_J as the resulting sub-plan for BGP b.

9.4.1 Type Detection

Knowledge about type membership of instance nodes is crucial in case of the instance-based federation approach. At the beginning of Algorithm 3, the function D   -S   -T   (b) is called, which is printed as Algorithm 5. The algorithm calculates C, the *minimal conjunctive type set* (MCTS)

9 SemWIQ Mediator

for all subjects of BGP b. It is called *conjunctive*, because an instance for s must be a member of *all* classes in C, and it is called *minimal*, because it does not contain any classes that are already subsumed by another class to prevent duplicates when execution the plan.

Algorithm 5 Algorithm for detecting BGP subject types – called by Algorithm 3.

Require: i, global config flag for inference feature – if true, use reasoner to detect implicit types
    function D   -S   -T   (b)
        b, a *BGP*
        $C \leftarrow$ C   -M // a map: $S \rightarrow$ *Sets of classes*, stores MCTS for all subjects in BGP b
        $G \leftarrow$ C   -G   -F -P   (b) // RDF graph representation for BGP b
        if i **then**
            $G_{inf} \leftarrow$ A   -R   (G, O_{cache})
        else
            $G_{inf} \leftarrow G$
        end if
        for all $s \in$ L   -S   (G) **do**
            $C_s \leftarrow$ C   -S // a set of *Classes*
            A   (C_s, rdfs:Resource)
            for all $c \in$ L   -RDF-T   (G_{inf}, s) **do**
                A   (C_s, c)
            end for
            $C_{mcts} \leftarrow$ C   -MCTS(C_s) // remove subsumed classes
            P   (C, s, C_{mcts})
        end for
        return C
    end function

    function C   -MCTS(C_s)
        C_s, classes of a subject instance set
        $C_{mcts} \leftarrow$ C   -S // set of *Classes*, minimal conjunctive type set
        $C_{clos} \leftarrow$ C   -S // set of *Classes*, super type closure
        for all $c \in C_s$ **do**
            for all $c_{sup} \in$ L   -S   -T   (c) **do**
                A   (C_{clos}, c_{sup})
                R   (C_{mcts}, c_{sup}) // more specific type c found
            end for
            if !C   (C_{sup}, c) **then**
                A   (C_{mcts}, c)
            end if
        end for
        return C_{mcts}
    end function

Basically, types can be explicitly specified via triple patterns as part of the query. For example, given the BGP in Figure 9.7 on page 149, the type of instances bound to ?s is explicitly defined by the corresponding triple pattern { ?s rdf:type foaf:Person }. However, there is no explicit type defined for ?p. The instance-based federator is able to detect implicit types based on the query pattern and cached ontologies. Any ontologies used in the query pattern will be imported prior to type detection. Because the reasoner will also include all super-types of a defined class hierarchy, the type detector must minimize the set of types to the MCTS to avoid duplicates when combining sub-plans later (function C   -MCTS(C_s) as part of Algorithm 5).

9.4 Instance-based Federator

The type detection algorithm works as follows. First, an empty map C is created, which will be used to store the MCTS for all subjects that are found in b. Then an RDF graph G is built, which resembles the query pattern of b. If the global configuration flag i is set to true, the type inference feature will be used in order to deduce types based on cached ontologies O_{cache}. For that purpose, a Jena inference model is used for G_{inf} and all the cached ontologies that are managed by the *vocabulary manager* component are attached to G. The result is a union of a number of RDF graphs which can be accessed like a single graph. If inference is disabled, the original graph $G_{inf} = G$ will be used for detecting types.

In the next loop, for each subject s found in G, a new set C_s is created and initialized with rdf:Resource, the super-type of all instances. Next, G_{inf} is queried for all types known for s, which are added to C_s. Because C_s will also include any inferred super-types, the function C -MCTS is called as already explained. All the subject-specific MCTS are inserted into the map C, which is finally returned as the result of the function.

The function C -MCTS(C_s) is iterating over all classes $c \in C_s$. For each class c, the super-class closure is calculated and collected by C_{clos}. All classes c are added to the resulting set C_{mcts} as long as they are not already part of the super-class closure. If C_{clos} is extended, and an already added class $c \in C_{mcts}$ becomes part of C_{clos}, it is removed again from C_{mcts}. The algorithm has polynomial complexity.

The Web Ontology Language has been discussed only briefly as part of the Semantic Web Primer in Section 4.3. Next, it will be shown, how OWL can be used to specify ontological constraints that will be leveraged by the type inference feature. Consider the following basic graph pattern:

```
{ ?obs a obs:ScientificObservation ;
       sci:observedBy ?s .
  ?s a rev:Reviewer ;
     foaf:name ?name }
```

and the following restriction on property sci:observedBy, which is defined as part of a science ontology:

```
sci:ScientificObservation a owl:Class ;
    rdfs:subClassOf [
        a owl:Restriction ;
        owl:onProperty sci:observedBy ;
        owl:allValuesFrom sci:Scientist ;
    ] ;
    ...
```

Besides the explicitly specified type rev:Reviewer, which is represented with a bold solid edge in Figure 9.8, the type detector will also infer that ?s is a member of sci:Scientist (bold dashed edge), because the restriction states, that all values of the property sci:observedBy are members of the type sci:Scientist. Actually, the reasoner will infer that ?s is a member of all the classes shaded gray in Figure 9.8.

9 SemWIQ Mediator

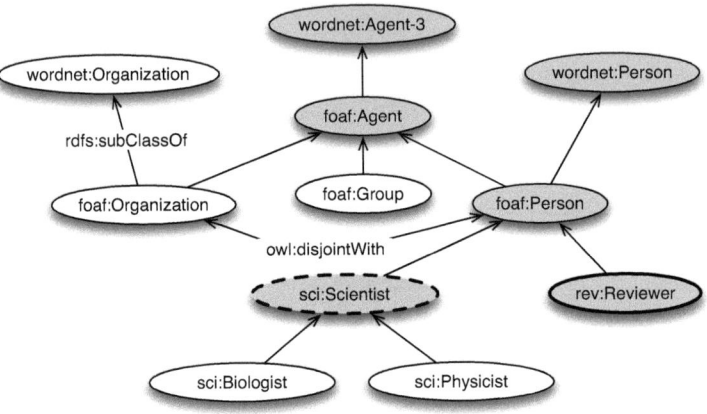

Figure 9.8: Type detection of the instance-based federator.

After the function C   -MCTS of Algorithm 5 has been applied, the set C_{mcts} will only contain sci:Scientist and rev:Reviewer (classes with a bold edge in Figure 9.8), because all other types are already subsumed.

9.4.2 Generation of sub plans

Algorithm 3 does not reveal how sub-plans are actually generated, it only shows how data sources are selected and the generation of sub-plans is delegated to C   -S -P . The function is printed as Algorithm 6 and will be discussed now. The parameters handed over by Algorithm 3 include the data source to consider d, the BGP b_s for subject s, as well as the MCTS C_s, and any preceding filter expressions E.

Basically, the algorithm determines, whether d will contribute any results. If it does, a sub-plan is created which may either be a simple BGP delegated to the data source, or a more complex sub-plan in order to resemble subsumption. If d does not contribute any results, ϵ is returned to F   -BGP, which will ignore d. For the meanwhile the query-time subsumption feature is ignored and only the case where the global configuration flag u is set to *false* and d does not support subsumption reasoning natively is discussed. Query-time subsumption reasoning will be explained later in Section 9.4.3.

Now consider $u \lor S$ -S   -N (d) evaluates to *false*, then the algorithm enters the else branch and creates a new BGP b_c. Then it iterates over the minimal conjunctive type-set C_s and adds triple patterns of the form { ?s rdf:type c } to b_c. It will check whether the data source has any instances that are member of all types in C by querying the RDFStats component. If the function E   -T   -F -P   returns > 0 the function C   -S   -P   is called in

154

9.4 Instance-based Federator

Algorithm 6 Algorithm for generation of sub-plans – called by Algorithm 3.

Require: u, a global configuration flag to enable query-time subsumption reasoning

  function C   -S   -P (d, s, b_s, C_s, E)
    d, a data source
    s, a triple pattern subject
    b_s, a BGP (all triple patterns with subject s)
    C_s, MCTS for instance set of subject s
    E, any preceding filter expressions, may be $\emptyset$
    if $u \vee$ S   -S   -N (d) **then**
      $C_{cts} \leftarrow$ C   -L   // a list of *Sets of classes*, conjunctive type sub-sets
      $x \leftarrow$ true // *exact match flag*
      for all $c \in C_s$ **do**
        $C_{sub} \leftarrow$ C   -S   // a set of *Classes*, sub-classes of c
        C   -I   -S (d, c, C_{sub})
        if $|C_{sub}| = 0$ **then**
          return ϵ
        else
          A (C_{cts}, C_{sub}) // add set of sub-classes C_{sub} to C_{cts}
        end if
        if !C (C_{sub}, c) **then**
          $x \leftarrow$ false
        end if
      end for
      if S   -S   -N $(d) \vee x$ **then**
        return C   -S   -P (s, b_s, C_s)
      else
        return C   -S   -P (s, b_s, C_{cts})
      end if
    else
      $b_c \leftarrow$ C   -BGP // create BGP with typing triple patterns
      for all $c \in C$ **do** // must satisfy all types
        A   -T   -P $(b_c, (\epsilon, \text{rdf:type}, c))$
      end for
      if E   -T   -F   -P $(d, b_c, E) > 0$ **then**
        return C   -S   -P (s, b_s, C_s)
      else
        return ϵ
      end if
    end if
  end function

  function C   -S   -P (s, b_s, C_s)
    s, a triple pattern subject
    b_s, a BGP (all triple patterns with subject s)
    C_s, MCTS for instance set of subject s
    for all $c \in C_s$ **do** // ensure types (e.g. required for left joins over split BGPs)
      A   -T   -P $(b_s, (s, \text{rdf:type}, c))$
    end for
    return b_s
  end function

order to return a simple sub-plan. Otherwise, the algorithm return ϵ to F   -BGP, which will ignore the data source. C   -S   -P   is printed as part of Algorithm 6. It ensures that all types $c \in C_s$ are part of the BGP to be created.

9.4.3 Subsumption Reasoning at Query Time

The instance-based federator is able to calculate query plans that resemble subsumption reasoning at query time. This feature can be optionally enabled by the global configuration flag u and if a data source is already capable of subsumption reasoning, it will not be used for that data source. However, if $u = false$, but a data source natively supports subsumption reasoning, Algorithm 6 will still collect interesting sub-classes and query the RDFStats component in order to check if the data source will contribute results. The global flag has no influence if a single data source supports subsumption reasoning. The process will be explained in detail now.

If $u \vee S$ -S   -N $(d) = true$, a new list C_{cts} is created. It is a list of sets of classes and it is called list of *conjunctive type sub-sets* (CTS). For each $c \in C_s$, it will gather another set of classes whose members are *interesting sub-classes* of c. An *interesting sub-class* is a sub-class of c, the data source d stores instances for. The boolean variable x is initialized with *false*. It will track, if a MCTS can be exactly fulfilled by a data source in which case C_{cts} would contain single-item sets with all $c \in C_s$.

For each class $c \in C_s$, the set C_{sub} is filled with interesting sub-classes of c. In case a data source does not store instances of class c, but instances of c_1 and c_2, which both are sub-classes of c, c_1 and c_2 will be added to the set C_{sub}. To give an example, consider this BGP:

```
{ ?s a foaf:Agent, rev:Reviewer ;
     foaf:name ?name }
```

If a data source does not store any instances that are members of both types, foaf:Agent *and* rev:Reviewer, but it stores instances that are members of foaf:Person *and* rev:Reviewer, the data source may still contribute results, because of the fact (foaf:Person rdfs:subClassOf foaf:Agent) defined in the FOAF vocabulary.

The function C   -I   -S (d, c, C_{sub}) recursively continues with looking for further sub-classes as long as the current class to look at yields no instances. C_{sub} serves as a collector during the recursive iteration as can be seen in the implementation printed as Algorithm 7. If for only one class c, there is no interesting sub-class at all, i.e. $|C_{sub}| = 0$, the algorithm may return ϵ, because the MCTS cannot be fulfilled. Otherwise, C_{sub} is added as a new type sub-set for c into C_{cts}. In case of an exact match, c itself is the only member of C_{sub}. If for any class c during the iteration, $c \notin C_{sub}$ (!C (C_{sub}, c)), the flag x is set to *false* meaning at least one expansion to sub-classes has occurred.

Next, it is checked if d supports native subsumption reasoning *or* if there was an exact match ($x =$

9.4 Instance-based Federator

Algorithm 7 Collects subtypes a data sources has instances for – called by Algorithm 6.

```
function C    -I    -S    (d, c, C_acc)
    d, a data source
    c, a Class to find interesting sub-classes for
    C_acc, accumulator set for sub-classes of c
    if E    -T    -F    -P    (d, (ϵ, rdf:type, c)) > 0 then
        A    (C_acc, c)
    else
        C_sub ← L    -D    -S    -C    (c)
        for all c_s ∈ C_sub do
            C    -I    -S    (d, c_s, C_acc)
        end for
    end if
end function
```

---

true). In both cases, the function C   -S   -P (s, b_s, C_s) creates a simple plan as before. Otherwise, a subsumption plan is compiled by the function C   -S   -P (s, b_s, C_{cts}) printed as Algorithm 8. In the latter case, the list of conjunctive type sub-sets C_{cts} is provided as an argument instead of C_s.

Algorithm 8 Algorithm for generation of subsumption plans – called by Algorithm 6.

```
function C    -S    -P    (s, b_s, C_cts)
    s, a triple pattern subject
    b_s, a BGP (all triple patterns with subject s)
    C_cts, list of Sets of classes, conjunctive type sub-sets fulfilled by instance sets of s
    b_plain ← C    -BGP // new BGP without rdf:type triple patterns
    for all t ∈ G    -T    -P    (b_s) do
        if G    -P    (t) ≠ rdf:type ∨ V    -O    (t) then
            A    -T    -P    (b_plain, t)
        end if
    end for
    C_perm ← G    -S    -C    (C_cts) // permutations of type sub-sets
    for all C_comb ∈ C_perm do
        b ← C    -BGP
        for all c ∈ C_comb do
            A    -T    -P    (b, (s, rdf:type, c))
        end for
        A    -T    -P    (b, b_plain) // add plain triple patterns to b
        if q_U = ϵ then
            q_U ← b
        else
            q_U ← C    -U    (q_U, b)
        end if
    end for
    return q_U
end function
```

A subsumption plan consists of several *BGPs* combined into a sequence of *Union* operators. The function C   -S   -P (s, b_s, C_{cts}) creates a new BGP b_{plain} with all triple patterns from b_s, except all the typing triples of the form $(s, \texttt{rdf:type}, c)$. However, patterns with variable object, { ?s rdf:type ?c }, are still included in order to bind all possible values for ?c.

157

9 SemWIQ Mediator

In the following step, another list of sets, C_{perm}, is compiled by the function G-S-C (C_{cts}). The list C_{perm} contains permutations of sub-types as will be explained next. The list of conjunctive type sub-sets C_{cts} basically looks like this:

$$C_{cts} = (\,(c_{s(1,1)},\; c_{s(1,2)},\; \ldots,\; c_{s(1,k_1)}),$$
$$(c_{s(2,1)},\; c_{s(2,2)},\; \ldots,\; c_{s(2,k_2)}),$$
$$\ldots$$
$$(c_{s(n,1)},\; c_{s(n,2)},\; \ldots,\; c_{s(n,k_n)})\,)$$

where each set $C_{sub} = (c_{s(i,j)})$, with $i = 1\ldots n$, $j = 1\ldots k_n$, (rows) stands for a class c in the former minimal conjunctive type-set C_{mcts} and each entry $c_{s(i,j)} \in C_{sub}$ stands for an interesting sub-class of c (or c itself in case of an exact match as previously explained). In order to compile the subsumption sub-plan, a *Union* sequence must include BGPs with the plain triples from b_{plain} and *typing* triples of the form { ?s rdf:type c } for any permutations between the set elements of C_{sub_n}. For example, consider the query pattern:

```
{ ?s a foaf:Agent, rev:Reviewer ;
     foaf:name ?name }
```

Assuming a data source stores resources that are instances of foaf:Person and foaf:Group, which are therefore *interesting* sub-classes of foaf:Agent, the following sets are calculated:

$$C_{mcts} = (\text{foaf:Agent},\, \text{rev:Reviewer})$$
$$C_{cts} = ((\text{foaf:Person},\, \text{foaf:Group}),\, (\text{rev:Reviewer}))$$

Algorithm 9 calculates the set C_{perm} with the following permutations:

$$C_{perm} = ((\text{foaf:Person},\, \text{rev:Reviewer}),\, (\text{foaf:Group},\, \text{rev:Reviewer}))$$

Algorithm 8 finally iterates over C_{perm} and for all $C_{comb} \in C_{perm}$ it creates a new BGP b, which contains typing triples for each $c \in C_{comb}$ and all triples from b_{plain}. The final subsumption sub-plan will consist of the following simple *Union* sequence (actually only one union):

Union(
    BGP((?s rdf:type foaf:Person), (?s rdf:type rev:Reviewer), (?s foaf:name ?name)*)*,
    BGP((?s rdf:type foaf:Group), (?s rdf:type rev:Reviewer), (?s foaf:name ?name)*)*
)

The computation of C_{perm} in function G-S-C (Algorithm 9) works as follows. The algorithm first initializes the list C_{perm} with n_{perm} sets, whereas $n_{perm} = \prod_{i=1}^{|C_{cts}|} |C_{sub}|$. In the main part, it enumerates all permutations for C_{perm}, which is finally returned.

Algorithm 9 Generates permutations for conjunctive sub-type sets – called by Algorithm 8.

function G-S-C(C_{cts})
  C_{cts}, list of *Sets of classes*, conjunctive type sub-sets fulfilled by instance sets of s
  $n_{perm} \leftarrow 1$
  for all $C_{sub} \in C_{cts}$ **do** // calculate number of permutations
    $n_{perm} \leftarrow n_{perm} * |C_{sub}|$
  end for
  $C_{perm} \leftarrow$ C-L(n_{perm}) // a list of *Sets of classes*, permutations of all $C_{sub} \in C_{cts}$
  for $i \leftarrow 0 \ldots n_{perm}$ **do**
    $C_{perm}[i] \leftarrow$ C-S // initialize
  end for
  $r \leftarrow n_{perm}$
  $s \leftarrow \epsilon$
  for all $C_{sub} \in C_{cts}$ **do**
    $i \leftarrow 0$
    $r \leftarrow r/|C_{sub}|$
    $s \leftarrow n_{perm}/r/|C_{sub}|$
    for $i \leftarrow 0 \ldots s$ **do**
      for all $c \in C_{sub}$ **do**
        for $j \leftarrow 0 \ldots r$ **do**
          A($C_{perm}[i], c$) // add c to C_{perm} at slot i
          $i \leftarrow i + 1$
        end for
      end for
    end for
  end for
  return C_{perm}
end function

9.5 Implementation Notes

A detailed description of the implementation of SemWIQ would be out of scope, but to provide an overview, a UML class diagram of the most important classes is depicted in Figure 9.9. The diagram shows the `Mediator` interface with life cycle methods and several getters for sub-components such as the data source registry and user registry. Queries can be executed by obtaining a `QueryExecution` instance from the mediator. Another possibility would be to create a `SemWIQDataset`, which takes a mediator instance as an argument and then, use this data set to execute queries with ARQ as usual. The Jena Assembler feature is also supported (implemented by `SemWIQDatasetAssembler`).

An instance of `Mediator` has a reference to exactly one instance of `MediatorConfiguration`, `UserRegistry`, `SemWIQDataset`, and `Federator`. The configuration maintains global settings which are loaded from a configuration file during startup. Some of the sub-components have specific configuration objects that are also initialized from the configuration file. Depending on the configura-

9 SemWIQ Mediator

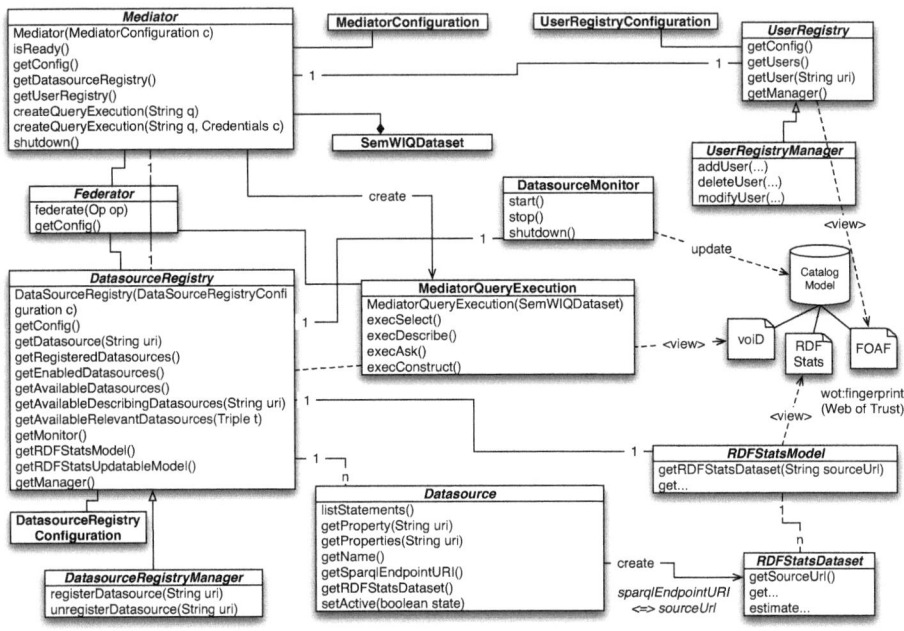

Figure 9.9: SemWIQ mediator UML class diagram.

tion, a specific implementation of the `Federator` interface is created during startup. At the moment, the `InstanceBasedFederator` (as described in Section 9.3) and the `TripleBasedFederator` (as described in Section 9.4) are available.

The federator utilizes the data source registry to access registered data sources and RDFStats statistics. The interface `DatasourceRegistry` provides several methods to access and query for registered data sources and RDFStats models. Basically, a registry such as the user registry and the data source registry, is read-only. In order to obtain a writable implementation, each registry provides the method `getManager()`, which returns a corresponding `*Manager` instance. Managers extend the read-only interface with several methods for modification. For example, `DatasourceRegistryManager` provides methods for registering and unregistering a data source by its SPARQL endpoint URI. Additionally, the data source registry uses a multi-threaded monitor, which is periodically monitoring registered data sources. If a data source becomes inaccessible, it will be marked as unavailable and at the next update, it may become available again.

All meta data used by the SemWIQ mediator are stored in a central catalog, which is a Jena RDF model. Based on the Jena Assembler feature, this model can be persisted in any compatible RDF storage system, which is Jena TDB by default. However, it would also be possible to use a relational database backed RDF store, or a simple RDF file. The catalog contains information about registered data sources based on the *voiD* vocabulary, RDFStats statistics, as well as user information based on an extended FOAF vocabulary.

10 SemWIQ Wrappers

SemWIQ is basically able to integrate data from all standard SPARQL endpoints. However, there are several issues with the current SPARQL standard which make a large-scale integration based on standard SPARQL endpoints impossible. Firstly, RDF statistics are required in order to federate and optimize SemWIQ queries. The RDFStats statistics generator is also integrated into the SemWIQ mediator which makes it possible to create statistics remotely for medium sized datasets. Secondly, SPARQL does not support initial bindings as described in Section 9.1.3. Hence, row blocking for distributed joins is impossible.

For these reasons, several Jena components such as the Jena core library, ARQ, and Joseki have been patched in order to provide the required functionality to wrappers. Each SemWIQ wrapper is able to efficiently process SPARQL sub-queries in order to contribute solution mappings to the results of a global query. An overview of the complete picture has been depicted in Figure 9.2 on page 135.

In Section 3.5 it was shown how model mapping techniques are used to solve several levels of heterogeneity between data models. At runtime, mappings are used to rewrite SPARQL queries and transform native data on-the-fly to RDF in order to realize the virtual integration approach. In this chapter it is shown how heterogeneous data models can be mapped to a common RDF model as depicted in Figure 10.1. The global RDF model consists of all the virtually existing information that has been mapped and the ontological concepts used to describe it. Typically, mappings relate to so-called *vocabularies*, which are ontologies containing mainly terminological statements (also called *T-Box*). The wrapped information is usually instance data, i.e. assertional statements (*A-Box*). But it is also possible to map to non-terminological resources or generate T-Box statements from instance data. For example, a data source may provide a sub-class hierarchy based on relational tuples.

In order to map arbitrary data models to RDF there are basically two approaches which have been presented in Section 3.5 (Figure 3.5): the two-phase or the single-phase approach. In the first approach, the metamodel heterogeneity is solved separately and then traditional schema matching and mapping is applied. The major problem with the first approach is that the transformation of data at runtime and the optimization of queries is more difficult and probably not always possible. In the second approach, a specific mapping framework is used for each specific kind of source metamodel to enable direct mapping and data translation. In case of SemWIQ all wrappers are based on a direct mapping approach.

10 SemWIQ Wrappers

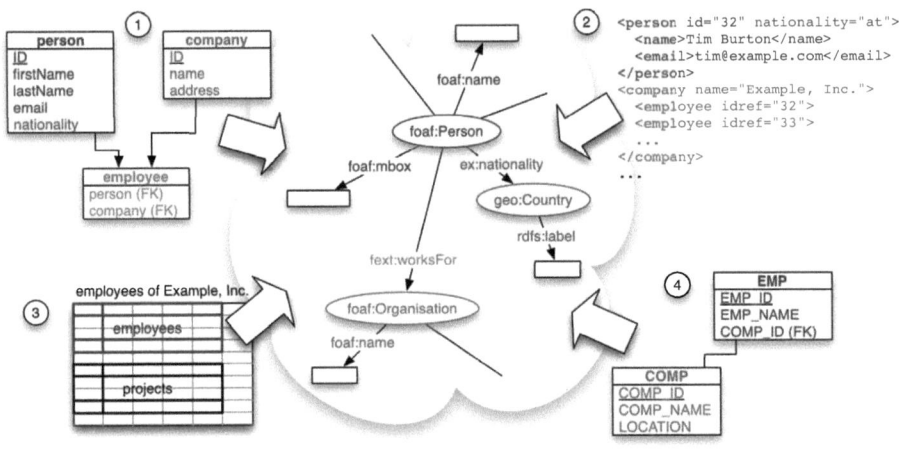

Figure 10.1: Mapping from several data models to a common RDF model.

10.1 General Considerations

A SemWIQ wrapper must be able to simulate an RDF graph $\mathcal{G}_S$ for some other source data model S based on a mapping $\mathcal{M}$. Furthermore, it must be able to answer SPARQL queries against this virtual graph $\mathcal{G}_S$. In order to map arbitrary data structures to an RDF graph, a definition of the RDF metamodel is required. The RDF Core (without RDF Schema semantics) has only structural modeling capabilities such as basic (untyped) relationships, data types, and collections. Higher-level conceptual modeling features provided by RDF Schema and OWL are also based on the RDF Core and thus, the RDF metamodel is actually defined by the RDF graph (Definition 2).

Based on the definitions for SPARQL queries and their evaluation provided in Section 4.4.3, it will be shown how RDF wrappers can be developed. As explained before, the evaluation of a SPARQL query starts with *basic graph pattern matching*. In triple-based implementations, each triple pattern $tp_i \in bgp$ (Definition 5) is matched against the active graph G' of the RDF dataset and any variables in tp_i are instantiated with all possible values from G'. The result is a solution sequence for each tp_i (Definition 7). In order to evaluate a BGP, *compatible* mappings of two solution sequences are subsequently *merged*. The solutions produced by BGPs are further combined by higher level operators as described in Section 4.4.3 and the final output represents the final query result. Typical implementations are based on iterators and a pipelined evaluation technique in order to optimize memory

10.1 General Considerations

consumption and response time.

A general approach for developing virtual RDF wrappers which are capable of answering SPARQL queries is the implementation of a *triple pattern evaluator*. Given a triple pattern tp_i, it must be able to produce solution mappings μ_{tp_i} based on the source database with source schema S and a mapping specification M (see Sect. 3.5.3). Given that basic functionality RDF wrappers can be easily implemented based on an existing SPARQL query engine (e.g. *Jena ARQ* (Jena Community 2009a)) which is responsible for all higher level operations.

10.1.1 Implementing Wrappers Based on Jena ARQ

Since *Jena ARQ* (Jena Community 2009a) is implemented in a highly extensible manner, it is a good starting point for any kind of virtual RDF wrapper. There are many extension points which can be used to hook into the query engine. For example, it is possible to transform the generated algebra plan (by implementing the interface com.hp.hpl.jena.sparql.algebra.Transform) and replace default SPARQL operators with custom operators. Furthermore, it is possible to provide custom implementations of query iterators for both, the default and custom algebra operators (by overriding com.hp.hpl.jena.sparql.engine.main.OpExecutor). In order to hook a custom BGP evaluator into the default ARQ query engine the easiest way is to implement a custom stage generator (interface com.hp.hpl.jena.sparql.engine.main.StageGenerator)[1]. A stage generator is producing root solution bindings for basic graph patterns.

For example, in case of an RDB-to-RDF wrapper a custom stage generator could be provided which generates solutions based on a mapping specification and data obtained from the database by executing SQL queries. Given a triple pattern tp_i, the remaining difficulty is the compilation of a correct and sound SQL query based on tp_i and a mapping M, as well as the translation of the obtained SQL result into corresponding RDF triples for tp_i. The generated SQL query, which is a combination of the existing mapping assertions $g \leadsto q_S$, can be regarded as an *RDF view* on the source schema S according to M.

10.1.2 Required Optimizations

The general approach for implementing wrappers based on *Jena ARQ* and custom BGP evaluation requires several optimizations in order to achieve an acceptable performance for larger amounts of data. These optimizations should include:

- Any filter expression on variables in scope of triple patterns must be taken into account when evaluating patterns. To give an example, for the following query:

  ```
  SELECT * WHERE {
  ```

---

[1] Most of the extension points are documented at http://jena.sourceforge.net/ARQ/arq-query-eval.html

```
            ?s a foaf:Person ; foaf:age ?age .
            FILTER (?age > 30)
}
```

the query engine should take the `FILTER` expression on `?age` into account when matching the triple pattern `{ ?s foaf:age ?age }` against the active graph in order to avoid the needless production of additional intermediate solution mappings.

- When evaluating a BGP, the query engine should re-order triple patterns based on the expected cardinality of their solution sequences to reduce the amount of intermediate bindings and hence, memory consumption and CPU time. For example, if there is a dataset with 1,000 FOAF persons, two persons older than 30, it would be cheaper to match `{ ?s foaf:age ?age }` first and then match the pattern `{ ?s a foaf:Person }` for each `?s` than the other way around.

- Any low-level index structures that are available as part of the source information system should be leveraged by the query engine. For example, given the query above, the pattern evaluator could access a B-tree index over the corresponding source data structure for `?age`.

- In case of `ORDER BY` expressions, the query engine should determine whether a corresponding index can be used to avoid additional sorting of values.

Before filters and order-by expressions can be taken into account at BGP level, they have to be pushed down in the algebra plan wherever possible. Because not all such logical plan optimizations are currently available in *Jena ARQ*, some of them have been contributed to *Jena*.

10.2 Wrapping Relational Databases

Since the introduction of the Semantic Web there has been an increasing interest in mapping relational databases to RDF and enable on-the-fly query execution and transformation of data. It can be safely assumed that the majority of today's information is stored in relational databases. Existing wrapper technology includes D2RQ-Map (Chris Bizer and Richard Cyganiak 2006), R2O (Rodríguez et al. 2004), OpenLink Virtuoso RDF Views (Erling and Mikhailov 2007), the approaches proposed by Chen et al. (2005) and de Laborda and Conrad (2006), and SquirrelRDF (Steer n.d.). While D2RQ-Map, R2O, and Virtuoso RDF Views are domain-semantics driven, which means mappings are used to map an arbitrary relational model to a global domain ontology, SquirrelRDF is generating RDF data from a database in a straight forward manner and does not allow to map to pre-defined ontologies.

In September 2009 the *RDB2RDF W3C Working Group* has been chartered[2], whose mission is "to standardize a language for mapping relational data and relational database schemas into RDF and

---

[2]http://www.w3.org/2001/sw/rdb2rdf/ – The work of the Incubator Group started already in February 2009.

OWL". The formation of this working group may be regarded as rather late, since D2R-Server has been introduced already in 2002, which is seven years ago. The growing importance of scalable RDB-to-RDF mapping technology led to many different tools in that area and different mapping languages. In order to ensure interoperability between mapping tools, the W3C decided to initiate a new working group to propose a standardized mapping language. A first working draft will be published in March 2010 and the final recommendation is scheduled for September 2011. In the meantime, the community has to rely on proprietary mapping languages.

D2RQ-Map is the mapping and translation facility of D2R-Server. While the mapping facility can be used as a library for Semantic Web applications, D2R-Server adds a Web application providing a SPARQL endpoint and a user interface called *Snorql*. Because D2RQ-Map is based on *Jena* and because a good relationship exists to its developers, D2RQ-Map is used as the relational wrapper for SemWIQ. In 2008 several optimizations to D2RQ-Map have been contributed to this Open Source project. The importance of a tool like SemWIQ to the Semantic Web community has been underlined by the report of Bizer and Cyganiak (2007), in which they argued that people also need a possibility to issue queries over distributed relational databases. In the following only the mapping technique of D2RQ-Map will be discussed further, alternative solutions have been analyzed in the master thesis of Herwig Leimer (2009).

10.2.1 D2RQ Mappings

D2RQ-Map is based on a *Global-as-View* mapping approach. Hence, writing a D2R mapping is basically a process of creating assertions of the form $g \rightsquigarrow q_S$ as described in Section 3.5.3. For a single global concept g, which can be an RDF class or property, a query q_S is formulated over the database source schema S. D2RQ-Map does not support SQL queries directly, however, it supports all what is required to create $1:1$, $1:n$ and $n:n$ correspondences including functional correspondences (based on SQL expressions and functions), value translation tables, and conditions (based on SQL expressions).

Property correspondences (called *property bridges*) are grouped into *class maps*. D2RQ-Map follows a concept-based approach, where all resulting resources are generally assumed to be instances of some RDF class, although it is also possible to create untyped resources. A *class map* can be regarded as a group of similar target resources such as *persons* or *documents* that share common properties and thus, common property bridges.

Mappings are represented in RDF themselves which facilities the notation of references to external RDF ontology concepts. In Figure 10.2 an example mapping is shown which wraps the database model introduced in Figure 3.6 (Section 3.5 on page 30) directly to RDF. The D2RQ mapping enables a one-step transformation at runtime and facilities the utilization of low-level indexes and other optimizations at query time.

The mapping example consists of one database resource (1) providing all necessary connection in-

10 SemWIQ Wrappers

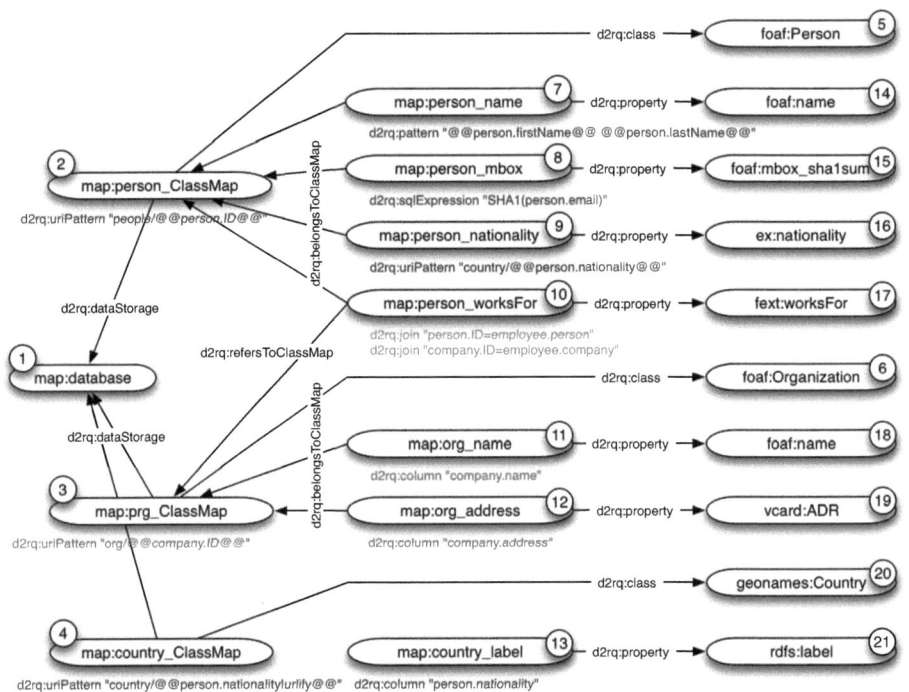

Figure 10.2: D2RQ-Map example mapping based on model (1) of Figure 10.1.

formation (JDBC URI, username, password, etc.) and three class maps (2–4) referring to the database (via property d2rq:dataStorage). For each target class (foaf:Person, foaf:Organization, and geonames:Country) a class map is created. Typically, a concrete RDF class is assigned to a class map using the d2rq:class property as shown in the figure (5–6). At runtime, D2RQ-Map will automatically add a corresponding rdf:type property to the instances of a class map.

The property bridges (7–13) refer to specific class maps (via d2rq:belongsToClassMap). As already mentioned, a class map groups property bridges and at runtime the engine applies all associated property bridges to the instances of the class map's source extension (tuples of the associated database table). Depending on the query pattern, each property bridge may generate potential RDF triples with the pre-defined RDF property specified by d2rq:property as shown on the right hand side of the figure (14–21). A property bridge can be regarded as a virtual statement pattern, which is called *triple relation* in D2RQ. It can be defined as a triple (s', p_i, o'), where p_i is pre-defined by the property bridge and s', o' are instantiated at runtime.

168

10.2 Wrapping Relational Databases

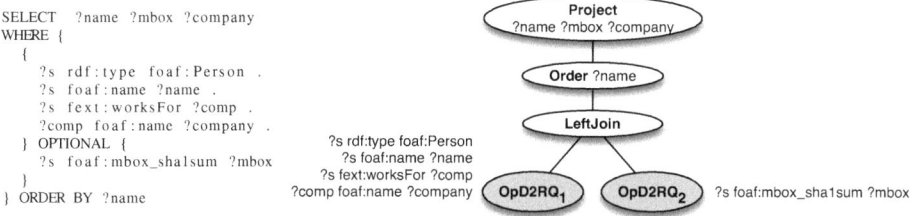

Figure 10.3: A SPARQL query and its corresponding D2RQ query plan.

```
SELECT DISTINCT
    'T3_company'.'ID',
    'T2_person'.'firstName',
    'T4_company'.'name',
    'T1_person'.'ID',
    'T2_person'.'lastName'
FROM
    'employee' AS 'T3_employee',
    'company' AS 'T3_company',
    'company' AS 'T4_company',
    'person' AS 'T2_person',
    'person' AS 'T3_person',
    'person' AS 'T1_person'
WHERE (
    'T1_person'.'ID' = 'T2_person'.'ID' AND
    'T2_person'.'ID' = 'T3_person'.'ID' AND
    'T3_company'.'ID' = 'T3_employee'.'company' AND
    'T3_company'.'ID' = 'T4_company'.'ID' AND
    'T3_employee'.'person' = 'T3_person'.'ID')
```

```
SELECT DISTINCT
    (SHA1('person'.'email')) AS
        exprff89995e,
    'person'.'ID' FROM 'person'
```

Figure 10.4: SQL queries for OpD2RQ$_1$ and OpD2RQ$_2$ shown in Figure 10.3, generated based on the mapping in Figure 10.2.

To give a quick example, for answering the simple triple pattern

```
{ ?s foaf:name ?n }
```

the D2RQ engine first determines relevant triple relations, then it tries to create a single SQL query based on the mapping (if it is not possible to express the virtual view by a single SQL query, multiple queries are used and combined with a SPARQL union operator), and finally the complete query is executed. An example query and its corresponding query plan are shown in Figure 10.3. As can be seen, instead of OpBGP operators, the query plan contains OpD2RQ operators, which generate SQL sub-plans and produce solution bindings based on the mapping specification. The corresponding SQL queries for the left and the right SQL sub-plan are depicted in Figure 10.4.

There are various ways to control RDF node generation from SQL results. Basically, it is possible to generate URI resources, blank nodes, and typed literals. There are several options for processing source values based on SQL expressions and functions and for creating URIs based on special string patterns. These features are controlled by specific properties of the D2RQ mapping vocabulary as shown in the small text lines beyond class maps and property bridges in Figure 10.2. A full description of the mapping facility is clearly out of scope and can be found on the project website at http://www4.wiwiss.fu-berlin.de/bizer/d2rq/.

In order to process higher-level SPARQL algebra operations such as filters, optionals, unions and solution modifiers, the D2RQ-Map engine reuses the query engine provided by *Jena ARQ*. As a consequence it is essential to optimize query plans by reordering triple patterns based on expected cardinalities and push down filters whenever possible into the generated SQL query. Several optimizations mentioned in Section 10.1 have been contributed to the D2RQ-Map open source project. A master thesis about RDB-to-RDF wrapping and the contributed optimizations to D2RQ-Map and D2R-Server was written by Herwig Leimer (2009) at the Johannes Kepler University Linz.

In order to integrate relational databases with SemWIQ, D2RQ-Map has been reused and optimized since it now features all the requirements discussed in Section 10.1. The evaluation of triple patterns can be compared to low-level access operations in SQL. Filters, joins, and other operations are applied in a higher stage in the query processing pipeline where intermediate bindings are streamed through until the result bindings can be returned as solutions. This way, D2RQ-Map perfectly fits into the SemWIQ query execution process.

10.2.2 D2RQ-Map Capabilities

D2RQ-Map uses a rather powerful mapping facility which is able to cope with the following aspects of heterogeneity discussed in Section 3.3.2.

- Technical heterogeneity is implicitly solved with the other aspects by accessing the underlying database via SQL and JDBC and providing a SPARQL interface to the user.

- Syntactical heterogeneity can be solved using SQL expressions and translation tables.

- Metamodel heterogeneity between the relational model and RDF is solved by the nature of D2RQ-Map.

- Structural heterogeneity can be solved in most cases. Schema information from the database can be wrapped to RDF if the RDBMS provides access to the metadata catalog via SQL. Vice versa, any RDF graph structure can be generated including classes, properties, custom RDF data types, etc.

- Schematic heterogeneity can be solved to some certain extent. Concerning the arity between source relations, it is possible to map binary $1:1$, $1:n$, $n:1$ and $n:n$ relationships. The latter can be achieved by using the d2rq:join property. Concerning correspondence arity as discussed in Section 3.5, $1:1$, $1:n$, $n:1$, and $n:n$ correspondences are possible. While $1:n$ can be achieved by multiple correspondences together with conditions (d2rq:condition, e.g. fragmenting employees by departments), $n:1$ correspondences can be achieved using SQL expressions (e.g. combining first and last name of people). $n:n$ correspondences can be created by a combination of both approaches.

- Semantic heterogeneity is implicitly solved by mapping to well-defined and publicly available RDF ontologies. Value-based translations can be achieved using translation tables.

10.3 Wrapping Spreadsheets

Since spreadsheets are frequently used by people in companies, organizations, and research institutions to share, exchange, and store data, XLWrap (Langegger and Wöß 2009c, Langegger and Wöß 2009a) has been developed as a spreadsheet wrapper for SemWIQ. Whenever there is no database in place, spreadsheets are often the primary fall-back tool for maintaining structured information. By contrast to a relational database, which has a fixed schema, data types, and integrity constraints, in case of a spreadsheet the implicit schema of the stored information has to be captured first when creating a formal mapping. In order to develop a generic mapping framework for spreadsheets, the spreadsheet paradigm has been analyzed and different ways of information representation have been examined first.

In this section the basic concept behind XLWrap is described. A full description can be found in Langegger and Wöß (2009c). In the following, the term *workbook* will be used to refer to a file of a spreadsheet application, and *worksheet* (or just *sheet*) is used to denote a single two-dimensional sheet of a workbook.

10.3.1 Information Representation in Spreadsheets

It is important to distinguish between the *information model* and the *representation model*, which is used to represent information within a spreadsheet. The *information model* is defined implicitly by the semantics of the entailed information, as for example, expenditures by category, year, and sub-division or personal information about employees. Concerning the *representation model*, three different layouts could be identified, whereas the third one is a hybrid approach of the first two:

Flat table: In this layout (depicted in Figure 10.5(a)) information is represented regardless of its dimensionality in a flat table with a single column (*or* row) heading. It is used to represent information such as data lists, e.g. persons with fixed properties such as name, mailbox, age, etc. Except for RDF123 (Han et al. 2008), all existing wrappers create exactly one RDF resource per row. Flat tables can also be used to represent information with multiple dimensions in so-called de-normalized tables which are also used for pivot tables and OLAP programs. Some cells of the header represent dimensions of the information model, the other header cells represent

10 SemWIQ Wrappers

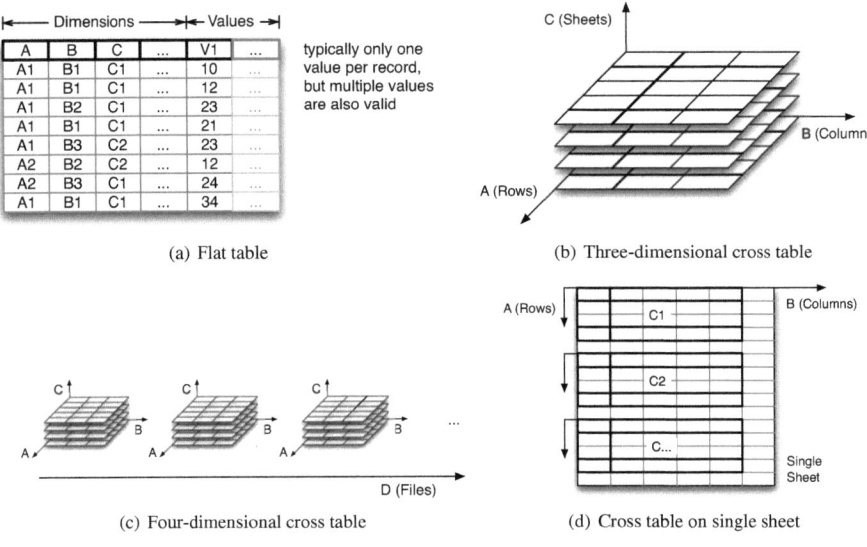

Figure 10.5: Information representation in spreadsheets.

values specific to each record. The domain values of dimensions repeatedly occur in the rows as shown in Figure 10.5(a).

Cross table: In this layout (shown in Figure 10.5(b)) the information is represented in a cross table, which may span multiple columns, rows, sheets, files, and directories (Figure 10.5(c)). Here, each *cell* represents a single instance. Instead of a single column/row header, cross tables have multiple headers, one per dimension. Along the sheet axis, the header is defined either by the sheet names or by text labels somewhere on the worksheet. Because a single sheet is already restricted to columns and rows, cross tables are often represented by repeating similar table layouts on the same sheet as depicted in Figure 10.5(d).

Hybrid layouts: There is also the possibility of combining flat and cross tables (e.g. denormalized tables can be repeated across several sheets or files).

Independent of the representation model, the wrapper must be able to translate the information model to any target graph corresponding to arbitrary global ontologies used in SemWIQ. All currently available spreadsheet wrappers are restricted to a simple flat table translation. More details on related work can be found in Langegger and Wöß (2009c).

Because in a spreadsheet application there is no explicit source schema S defined, it is not possible to define a mapping M based on value correspondences as described in Section 3.5. A generic mapping can only be defined if there are common representation patterns such as common table headers and dimension labels. In order to make this common patterns explicit and associate structured spreadsheet data with structured RDF graphs, so-called *graph templates* are used which is similar to XSL templates used to transform XML trees.

10.3.2 Definition of Spreadsheet Applications

In the following a definition for spreadsheet applications is given.

Definition 19 *A spreadsheet application A is defined as a set of named workbooks* w_i, $i \in \mathbb{N}_0$, *where* name(w_i) *is the canonical workbook filename denoted by its URI. A spreadsheet application has at least one workbook* w_0, *called the* base workbook *and optionally a set of* external workbooks w_i, $i \geq 1$, *which are referenced from* w_0 *by means of absolute cell references.*

Within companies it is very common that multiple spreadsheets are interlinked by external cell references. To be able to process external references in XLWrap mappings, this definition takes external workbooks into account. The URI scheme for local files is `file://`. Workbook files on the Web can be referenced by means of HTTP URIs.

Definition 20 *A workbook* $w_i \in A$ *is defined as a set of named worksheets* s_j, $j \in \mathbb{N}$, *where* name(s_j) *is the sheet name as specified in the application (a string).*

Beside single worksheets, it is also common to use multiple worksheets. As will be shown later, XLWrap supports a special sheet shift operation, which allows to repeatedly apply template mappings on multiple sheets.

Definition 21 *A worksheet* $s_j \in w_i$ *is defined as a matrix of cell values* $V = [v_{c,r}]_{n \times m}$ *where* $c \in \mathbb{N}_0$, $c < m$, *is the column index and* $r \in \mathbb{N}_0$, $r < n$, *is the row index of the corresponding worksheet table.* m, n *denote the total number of columns and rows used in worksheet* s_j.

Although there is a space limit for m and n in practice, there is no limitation enforced by this definition. The same applies to the number of worksheets in a workbook.

Definition 22 *A cell value* $v_{c,r}$ *has a* type annotation *denoted as* type($v_{c,r}$) $\rightarrow T$ *with* $T = \{t_{text}, t_{number}, t_{datetime}, t_{boolean}, t_{empty}\}$. *Additionally, a cell value may have a* formatting *(e.g. for number, currency, date/time formatting) and a* formula annotation *denoted as* formula($v_{c,r}$) $\rightarrow E$, *where* $e \in E$ *is a compositional expression according to a pre-defined grammar* G_E.

A cell formula, is not a specific type $\in T$. Instead, it is an annotation defining the expression which can be evaluated to reproduce or update $v_{c,r}$. Values with formula annotations are explicitly stored

10 SemWIQ Wrappers

in the corresponding workbook files. In our definition of spreadsheet applications, the grammar G_E supports *range references* denoted as e_{ref}. Range references are used to refer to other cells of the same spreadsheet, other sheets of the same workbook, or external workbooks. In Section 10.3.3 it will be described, how expressions and range references are also used for XLWrap mappings to map spreadsheet cells to RDF graphs. The proper definition of a *range reference* is given below.

Definition 23 *A range reference sub-expression e_{ref} is generally defined as a set of partial 7-tuples of the form $(w_i, s_{j1}, c_1, r_1, s_{j2}, c_2, r_2)$. These components specify a workbook, a start cell consisting of a sheet, column, row, as well as a target cell specified by a sheet, column, and row. Some tuple components are optional and may be left empty. If $|e_{ref}| > 1$, the range reference is called* multi range reference, *because it contains multiple single range references. In case of OpenOffice Calc, the general lexical representation of a single range reference is:*

$$((w_i \text{ "\#\$ " })? s_{j1} \text{ "." })? c_1 r_1 (":"(s_{j2} \text{ "." })? c_2 r_2)?$$

For multi range references, single range references are separated with a semicolon. The following two sub-types are defined:

- Cell reference, *which has the optional components w_i, s_{j1}, the mandatory components c_1, r_1, and component s_{j2}, c_2, r_2 left empty (e.g.* `A3`, `'Sheet 1'.A3`, *or* `file:foo.xls#$'Sheet 1'.A3`*)*

- Box reference, *which has the optional components w_i, s_{j1}, s_{j2} and the mandatory components c_1, r_1, c_2, r_2 (e.g.* `A3:B9`, *or* `file:foo.xls#$'Sheet 1'.A3:B28`*.*

Whenever the components w_i and s_{j1}, s_{j2} are omitted, the range reference is interpreted relative to the worksheet of its originating cell formula. Hence, a range reference can either be *absolute* or *relative* its base sheet or workbook file.

10.3.3 XLWrap Mappings

The RDF target graph is defined by means of template graphs which are repeatedly applied during the wrapping process. With XLWrap expressions it is possible to refer to arbitrary cells. In the following, XLWrap mappings are defined.

Definition 24 *An XLWrap mapping M is defined as a set of* map templates $m_k, k \in \mathbb{N}$.

Definition 25 *A map template $m_k = (w_k, s_k, C_k, G_k, F_k)$ consists of the following components: a base workbook $w_k \in w_i$, a base worksheet $s_k \in s_j$, a constant RDF graph C_k, an RDF template graph G_k, and a sequence of transform operations $F_k = (f_l), l \in \mathbb{N}$.*

10.3 Wrapping Spreadsheets

Definition 26 *A constant graph C_k and a template graph G_k are valid RDF graphs, according to the W3C specification, which may contain literals of the custom data type* `xl:Expr` *called* XLWrap *expressions*[3].

Definition 27 *A transform operation f_l can modify the template graph G_k and change range references in expressions.*

During the wrapping process, each map template $m_k \in M$ contributes a sub-graph $[[G_k]]$ to the overall result similar to RDF123 (Han et al. 2008), but with the difference that a graph template is not moved from the first row to the last one in a fixed direction, instead, it is moved based on the transformation sequence defined by (f_l). The bracket notation $[[\ldots]]$ is used to denote the application of a template graph including the evaluation of all XLWrap expressions. While C_k is evaluated and merged into the target graph once, the template graph G_k is subsequently transformed by (f_l) and evaluated multiple times. In the special case $|F_k| = 0$, no transformations are specified and G_k is applied once in its initial form.

Because by definition subjects and predicates cannot be literals, in order to specify XLWrap expressions for subjects or predicates, they have to be wrapped in blank nodes as part of the template graph. The special property `xl:uri` is then used to replace these blank nodes by URI resources in the target graph. Similarly, the property `xl:id` can be used to link blank nodes: XLWrap will produce blank nodes with equal local IDs in the target graph

XLWrap Expressions

XLWrap expressions are primarily used to refer to cells but it is also possible to combine multiple cell values based on a complete expression algebra similar to OpenOffice Calc or Microsoft Excel spreadsheet formulas (see Definition 22). Conditional expressions can be formulated using the special function `IF(condition; then-expr; else-expr)`.

Definition 28 *An XLWrap expression is defined as a compositional expression of basic expression symbols. XLWrap expressions are parsed from the lexical representation by the custom data type implementation*[4] *according to the grammar defined in Listing 10.1.*

XLWrap supports all standard arithmetic and also logical operators, string concatenation, and an extensible function library (additional implementations can be easily added at runtime). The most important functions for string manipulation, including SHA-1 hashing (which, for instance, is required for `foaf:mbox_sha1sum` property values in FOAF applications), type casting (to enforce specific literal data types in the RDF output), aggregate functions such as `SUM()`, which takes cell, box, and multi ranges as arguments, have already been implemented.

---
[3] The full namespace for the prefix `xl:` is `http://langegger.at/xlwrap/vocab#`.
[4] In *Jena* it is possible to register a custom data type handler by extending `BaseDatatype`.

10 SemWIQ Wrappers

```
XLExpression  =  "="? OrExpr <EOF>
OrExpr        =  AndExpr ( "||" AndExpr )*
AndExpr       =  Comparable ( "&&" Comparable )*
Comparable    =  Concatable ( CompOp Concatable )*
Concatable    =  Expr ( "&" Expr )*
Expr          =  Term ( ("+"|"-") Term)*
Term          =  Factor ( ("*"|"/") Factor)*
Factor        =  Atom ("^" Atom)*
Atom          =
    ("+"|"-"|"!")
    (
        <NUMBER> ("%")? |
        (<TRUE>|<FALSE>) |
        <STRING> |
        <CELLRANGE> |
        "(" Concatable ")" ("%")? |
        <FUNCIDENT> "(" ( Concatable ( (","|";") Concatable)* )? ")" ("%")?
    )
CompOp        =  "<=" | "<" | ">=" | ">" | ("!="|"<>") | ("=="|"=")
```

Listing 10.1: Grammar of XLWrap expressions

Transform Operations

The following transform operations are available in the current implementation:

- column shift: $f_{ColumnShift}(d, n, z, e_c)$

- row shift: $f_{RowShift}(d, n, z, e_c)$

- sheet shift: $f_{SheetShift}(d, n, z, e_c)$

- sheet repeat: $f_{SheetRepeat}((g_i), z, e_c)$

- file repeat: $f_{FileRepeat}((h_i), z, e_c)$

Common to all operations is z, a multi range reference, which can be used to restrict the transform operation on a set of ranges (default is *.*) and e_c can be a logical XLWrap expression, which is evaluated before a transformation is applied (default is *true*) – if *false*, this transformation stage is cancelled. For all the *shift* operations, d is the amount of columns/rows/sheets to shift (defaults to 1), n is the number of times to apply the operation (defaults to the maximum integer value of the runtime system), and for the repeat operations, (g_i) and (h_i), respectively, specify the set of sheets or files to apply the template for.

As mentioned along with Definition 23, a range reference can be *absolute* or *relative*. Relative range references are extended during evaluation by the base workbook w_k and base worksheet s_k defined in the mapping M. For example, "A3" may refer to "file:foo.xls#$Sheet1.A3" at runtime. The sheet/file repeat transformations will override the sheet/file component as needed, but absolute range references are never modified by transform operations.

10.3.4 Example

For a better understanding of XLWrap mappings a short example is provided. The source data for the example is printed in Table 10.1. The workbook w_0 used for this demonstration contains two sheets s_1, s_2 of information on revenues of a company. For each country the company operates in, revenues are organized in a cross table containing sold items and total revenue per product and year. As can be seen, data for 2008 is missing for Germany, and there is one more product for Germany.

Table 10.1: Source data for the discussed example ($s_1, s_2 \in w_0$).

Austria							
	2007		2008		2009		
product	items sold	revenue	items sold	revenue	items sold	revenue	
Product 1	342	7,866.00	376	8,648.00	490	11,760.00	
Product 2	4,333	1,005,256.00	5,655	1,328,925.00	3,493	838,320.00	
Product 3	3,312	1,136,016.00	4,566	1,598,100.00	5,993	1,917,760.00	
Product 4	45	19,350.00	56	24,304.00	54	23,328.00	
Totals	8,032	2,168,488.00	10,653	2,959,977.00	10,030	2,791,168.00	

Germany					
	2007		2009		
product	items sold	revenue	items sold	revenue	
Product1	2,431	55,913.00	3,419	82,056.00	
Product2	31,230	7,339,050.00	32,123	7,709,520.00	
Product3	23,121	8,092,350.00	31,039	9,932,480.00	
Product4	3,423	1,198,050.00	3,412	1,091,840.00	
Product5	121	52,514.00	312	134,784.00	
Totals	60,326	16,737,877.00	70,305	18,950,680.00	

Listing 10.2 shows a mapping formulated in the TriG syntax (Bizer and Cyganiak n.d.), which allows to specify multiple named graphs: while the default graph contains the main mapping specification, template graphs are defined as named graphs in the same file. After executing a complete dump, some parts of the target graph are shown in Listing 10.3.

XLWrap is capable of loading local files and downloading spreadsheet files from the Web. Currently, Excel files, Open Document spreadsheets, and also CSV files are supported. The layout of CSV files (delimiters, separators, white spaces) can be specified. CSV files are streamed in order to support large data files.

10.3.5 Processing SPARQL Queries

Concerning the execution of SPARQL queries there are two possible directions to follow: a fully virtual approach based on the general considerations described in Section 10.1 or a semi-materialized approach. While the first implementation of XLWrap was done based on the considerations of Section 10.1, a better performing solution has been implemented based on excessive caching.

10 SemWIQ Wrappers

```
@prefix rdf: <http://www.w3.org/1999/02/22-rdf-syntax-ns#> .
@prefix xl:  <http://langegger.at/xlwrap/vocab#> .
@prefix ex:  <http://example.org/> .
@prefix :    <http://myApplication/mapping#> .

{ [] a xl:Mapping ;
    xl:template [
        xl:fileName "files/testing/iswc09-example.xls" ;
        xl:sheetNumber "0" ;
        xl:templateGraph :Revenues ;
        xl:transform [
            a rdf:Seq ;
            rdf:_1 [ a xl:RowShift ;
                     xl:restriction "A4; B4:C4" ;
                     xl:condition "LEFT(A4, 7) == 'Product'" ;
                     xl:steps "1" ] ;
            rdf:_2 [ a xl:ColShift ;
                     xl:restriction "B2; B4:C4"^^xl:Expr ;
                     xl:condition "!EMPTY(B4:C4)" ;
                     xl:steps "2" ] ;
            rdf:_3 [ a xl:SheetShift ;
                     xl:restriction "#1.*"^^xl:Expr ;
                     xl:repeat "2" ] ;
        ]
    ] .
}

:Revenues {
    [ xl:uri "MAKEURI('Revenue_' & SHEETNAME(A1) & '_' & B2 & '_' & A4)"^^xl:Expr ] a ex:Revenue
    ;
    ex:country    "DBP_COUNTRY(SHEETNAME(A1))"^^xl:Expr ;
    ex:year       "DBP_YEAR(B2)"^^xl:Expr ;
    ex:product    "A4"^^xl:Expr ;
    ex:itemsSold  "B4"^^xl:Expr ;
    ex:revenue    "C4"^^xl:Expr .
}
```

Listing 10.2: Example mapping specified in TriG syntax.

```
ex:revenue_Austria_2007_Product1 a ex:Revenue ;
    ex:country <http://dbpedia.org/resource/Austria> ;
    ex:itemsSold "342"^^<http://www.w3.org/2001/XMLSchema#short> ;
    ex:product "Product1" ;
    ex:revenue "7866"^^<http://www.w3.org/2001/XMLSchema#int> ;
    ex:year <http://dbpedia.org/resource/2007> .
ex:revenue_Austria_2007_Product2 a ex:Revenue ;
    ex:country <http://dbpedia.org/resource/Austria> ;
    ex:itemsSold "4333"^^<http://www.w3.org/2001/XMLSchema#short> ;
    ex:product "Product2" ;
    ex:revenue "1005256"^^<http://www.w3.org/2001/XMLSchema#int> ;
    ex:year <http://dbpedia.org/resource/2007> .
ex:revenue_Austria_2007_Product3 ...
ex:revenue_Austria_2007_Product4 ...
ex:revenue_Austria_2008_Product1 ...
...
ex:revenue_Austria_2009_Product1 ...
...
ex:revenue_Germany_2007_Product1 ...
...
ex:revenue_Germany_2009_Product1 ...
...
ex:revenue_Germany_2009_Product5 ...
```

Listing 10.3: RDF graph for the given example spreadsheet and XLWrap mapping.

10.3 Wrapping Spreadsheets

In case of a fully virtual approach, for each triple pattern tp_i all map templates $m_k^{tp_i}$ that would contribute to the result must be selected. Next, all the associated transform operations $F_k^{tp_i}$ have to be applied subsequently to create a solution sequence μ_{tp_i}. Unfortunately, this generic approach of mapping-based evaluation does not scale and perform well in case of spreadsheets. For example, given a query pattern such as { ?s foaf:name 'Tom' }, without index structures, the wrapper would have to apply all transform operations and iterate over the complete sequence to look for objects with a value of 'Tom'.

Compared to a database management system, which is an operational layer on top of the actual database providing a structured query language and interfaces to other applications, spreadsheets are just files stored in a file system. When processing SPARQL queries on-the-fly, the wrapper would have to manage its own low-level index structures such as hash tables and B+ trees in order to achieve acceptable performance results when evaluating XLWrap map templates. These index structures would have to be updated by means of a notification mechanism (which is very difficult, if not impossible, to implement) or within pre-defined periods.

Optimized RDF-based Caching

Because single spreadsheets are typically rather small in size (compared to databases) and because spreadsheet files are modified occasionally on a per-file basis (if at all), a better approach is to completely wrap single spreadsheets and cache the results in a persistent RDF store such as *Jena TDB*. Although, this requires additional storage space for the cached RDF data, custom index structures that would be required otherwise, will also require additional storage.

XLWrap tracks any changes in mapping files and referenced workbook files, automatically reprocesses the corresponding mapping – which is usually a matter of seconds – and updates the cache accordingly. In this way, existing index structures implemented for *Jena TDB* can be reused and the performance for evaluating SPARQL queries is higher then following a complete virtual approach.

10.3.6 Capabilities of XLWrap

XLWrap is able to cope with the following heterogeneity aspects discussed in Section 3.3.2:

- Technical heterogeneity is implicitly solved because the access to the spreadsheet application is wrapped by XLWrap which provides a SPARQL interface to the SemWIQ mediator.

- Syntactical heterogeneity can be solved using XLWrap expressions, built-in functions, and custom functions.

- Metamodel heterogeneity between the implicit data model of the spreadsheet application and RDF is solved by the nature of XLWrap.

- Structural heterogeneity is solved based on the extensible set of transform operations which allows to subsequently apply arbitrary template graphs in a fully customized manner. However, if the structural complexity of the spreadsheet is very high (i.e. if there are only a few common patterns in the information model and its representation) it is required to specify a large number of specific map templates.

- Schematic heterogeneity does not occur because there is no explicit distinction between a schema and instance-level in spreadsheet applications.

- Semantic heterogeneity is implicitly solved by mapping to well-defined and publicly available RDF ontologies.

Several additional features and a revised mapping language have been discussed together with Richard Cyganiak (DERI Galway, IR) and Leigh Dodds (Talis, UK) at the Vienna Linked Data Camp 2009[5]. In addition to the template based mapping approach, it might be helpful to provide some brief procedural functions similar to XQuery or the XQuery-SPARQL integration approach presented by Polleres (2007).

---

[5] http://linkeddatacamp.org/wiki/XLWrap_state_and_feature_requests

11 Query Pattern Cardinality Estimation with RDFStats

One of the main contributions of this work is the query federation approach based on RDF graph statistics. In order to federate queries over a large number of data sources, it is impossible to access all sources at query time in order to determine whether they are relevant or not. RDFStats statistics are therefore used as data summaries for all the source graphs in order to federate and optimize global queries.

11.1 RDFStats Approach

Given a query sub-plan, the federator must be able to determine whether a data source is relevant or not as explained in Section 9.2.3. Additionally, the optimizer needs to know how much solution bindings can be expected for a given query sub-plan. These two requirements have been the starting point for the development of RDFStats.

Investigations towards RDF graph statistics generation have shown that Jena TDB is the only known SPARQL query processor making use of RDF statistics. All other stores are solely based on indexes, which they also use for calculating triple pattern cardinalities to optimize BGPs. Based on generated statistics, the TDB query engine is re-ordering triple patterns during the evaluation of basic graph patterns. TDB statistics include frequency counts for predicates (e.g. *(foaf:knows 12)*) and more detailed rules which are made up of triple patterns and a count estimates for the approximate number of matches the triple will yield. However, the TDB statistics are not created by default and they have to be generated manually each time the RDF dataset changes.

In relational database systems histograms are commonly used by query optimizers. Although newer approaches like wavelets have been introduced, histograms are still the favorite approximation method of all commercial database systems (Ioannidis 2003). A histogram on an attribute A is constructed by partitioning the source distribution of A into n mutually disjoint subsets called bins. The frequencies and values in each bin can then be approximated. Since histograms for database optimizers have been proposed (Kooi 1980), much research has been undertaken and many different approaches and algorithms have been published (Ioannidis 2003).

RDFStats consists of a statistics generator and a comprehensive API for managing and accessing

11 Query Pattern Cardinality Estimation with RDFStats

RDF graph statistics including estimation functions for SPARQL query pattern cardinalities. The generator collects RDF graph statistics from graphs behind local or remote SPARQL endpoints (but also from RDF graphs loaded from files) and generates several histograms. Because RDFStats may be useful for other query processors[1], it has been detached from SemWIQ as a separate project. The main features include:

- Two statistics generators are available, one for SPARQL endpoints and one for RDF documents (local files or web resources).

- Generators calculate one histogram over subject URIs, they count blank node subjects, and they create histograms for all properties (one histogram for each distinct property URI and object type).

- For the most important XML data types such as boolean, integer, float, dateTime, string, etc. specific histogram implementations and histogram builders exist. In case of strings, the OrderedStringHistogram is compressing strings into prefix-bins keeping the string's order and thus supporting range estimations. Similarly, the URIHistogram is compressing URIs into prefix-bins based on common domain names and path strings. For any unknown type, a default nominal-scaled generic single-bin histogram is used as long as no further specialized builder was registered at the HistogramBuilderFactory for that type.

- The extensible HistogramBuilder API allows to register further histogram builders and specific histogram implementations for custom types.

- A Base64 codec is used to encode and decode histogram data between serialized strings and Java objects. Histograms are stored in RDF as plain literals. This conversion is fully transparent and does not require any special attention when using the API.

- RDFStats provides the RDFStatsModel API for managing a number of statistics for different sources and the RDFStatsDataset API for accessing statistics of a particular data source.

- The RDFStatsUpdatableModel API provides operations for adding and updating statistics. It is based on a simple *multiple-read single-write* locking mechanism and can be used in multi-threaded applications such as SemWIQ.

- In order to estimate the expected cardinality of query patterns, the RDFStatsDataset API includes various functions defined by the interface QueryStatistics (Figure 11.4). Estimation also supports range queries and takes filter expressions into account (e.g. how many triples are there for instances of rev:Review and dc:date ≥ "2009-01-01"^^xsd:dateTime?).

---

[1] For instance, it has been used by Talis Information Ltd. to analyze data sets managed by the Talis platform and it is currently being used to implement a Grid-based query processor for SPARQL by colleagues from the Faculty of Informatics at the Polytechnic University of Madrid, Spain.

- The Histogram API (Figure 11.2) provides all the low-level histogram functions (including minimum, maximum, and cumulative sum in case of a ComparableDomainHistogram).
- RDFStats can be configured based on the Jena assembler mechanism to transparently persist statistic models (e.g. into files, RDBMS, Jena TDB, etc.).

11.2 Generation of RDF Statistics

There are many options on how and which kind of statistics to generate from RDF graphs. A simple approach used in Jena TDB is to record how often RDF properties are used, i.e. counting the number of triples (s, p', o) for all $p' \in P$ that exist in the graph. More details can be collected by generating histograms for each of the distribution of RDF property values, which is done by RDFStats. Additionally, a histogram is generated over all the subjects of the source graph. The generation process is based on several SPARQL queries issued against the source graph. It is described based on the flowchart in Figure 11.1.

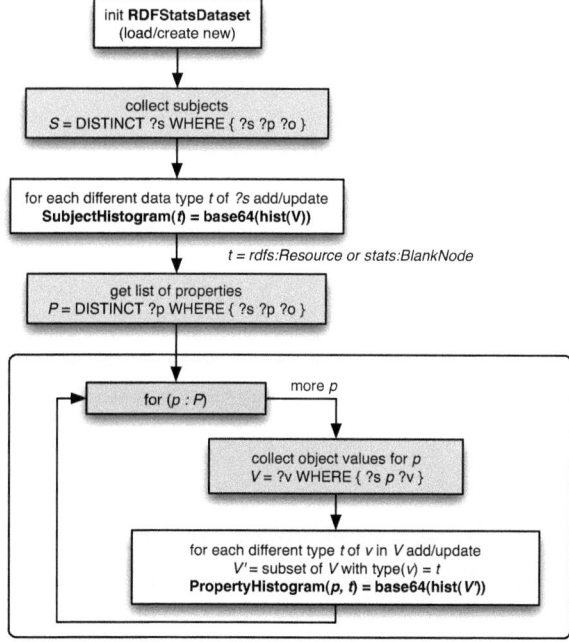

Figure 11.1: RDFStats generation process.

11 Query Pattern Cardinality Estimation with RDFStats

The process starts with the initialization of a new or already existing `RDFStatsDataset` instance, which manages the statistics for a specific RDF source, e.g. a SPARQL endpoint. Then the generator iterates over the set of distinct subjects occurring in the RDF graph using the SPARQL query pattern `DISTINCT ?s WHERE { ?s ?p ?o }`. Depending on the type *t* of the subject `?s`, its value is added to a different histogram. Generally, types are defined as follows:

Definition 29 *Given an RDF node n (which is either a URI, blank node, plain or typed literal), the type of n in the context of RDFStats is defined as:*

$$type(n) = \begin{cases} \texttt{rdfs:Resource} & \textit{if n is a URI node} \\ \texttt{stats:BlankNode} & \textit{if n is a blank node} \\ \texttt{xsd:string} & \textit{if n is a plain literal} \\ datatype(n) & \textit{if n is a typed literal} \end{cases}$$

Note: to denote blank nodes, the special type `stats:BlankNode` has been defined as part of the RDFStats vocabulary (Figure 11.3).

While for all the URI subjects retrieved, a `URIHistogram` is generated, blank node subjects are counted only and the sum is stored in a special `GenericSingleBinHistogram`. The obtained histograms are Base64 encoded and stored as RDF literals in the statistics graph using the RDFStats vocabulary shown in Figure 11.3.

Next, the generator creates histograms for each combination of property *p* and type *t* of retrieved object values. Using the SPARQL query `SELECT DISTINCT ?p WHERE { ?s ?p ?o }`, it iterates over properties *p* that exist in the source graph. By query `SELECT ?v WHERE { ?s p ?v }` the generator collects all values for *p*. For each combination of *p* and type *t* of object values, a histogram is generated. The histogram implementation to use depends on the type *t*. For the most important XSD types, a histogram implementation and the corresponding generator are already available. For custom literal data types, additional histogram and generator implementations may be registered at the `HistogramBuilderFactory`. To generate histograms for SPARQL endpoints or RDF documents the `RDFStatsGeneratorFactory` is used.

11.2.1 Histogram Generation Process

RDFStats separates the code used for the representation of histogram data and building histograms including encoding and decoding into two different sets of classes which implement the interfaces `Histogram` and `HistogramBuilder`. The APIs of both interfaces are depicted in Figure 11.2. The full type hierarchy is only shown for the histogram types implementing `Histogram`, but for each histogram type there must also be a corresponding builder implementation which can be registered at the `HistogramBuilderFactory`. This way, RDFStats can be easily extended with additional

11.2 Generation of RDF Statistics

histogram types and corresponding builders. The idea behind the code separation is basically that the builder collects usually unordered values first and then creates a histogram. If the source distribution is already ordered and if the counting of distinct values is disabled, histograms could also be generated on-the-fly and hence, safe memory.

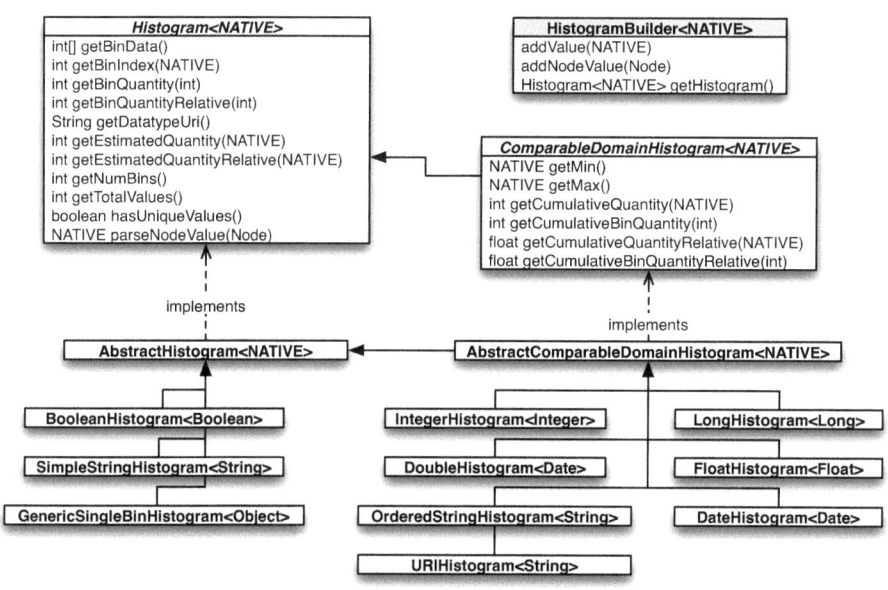

Figure 11.2: RDFStats Histogram API and class hierarchy.

Histograms can be generated for nominal and metric scales. The values of a metrical scaled source distribution are comparable. Examples are numbers, dates, but also short strings like names, which can be compared lexicographically. A nominal scale exists for boolean values. The special histogram implementation is provided for strings. The OrderedStringHistogram is repeatedly cutting strings from the right hand side in order to find common prefixes. Strings are compressed by half-length as long as the required amount of bins for distinct string prefixes exceeds a configurable value. In case of URIs, the URIHistogram is used, which is repeatedly cutting URIs to common prefixes based on path fragments separated by slashes. The compression algorithm is explained in the next section.

11.2.2 Order-preserving String Histogram

Automatically generating histograms for strings is not trivial if the lexicographical order of the original string values should be preserved. Especially for SemWIQ this information is very important in order to optimize range queries like `{ [] foaf:name ?n FILTER (?n > "M") }`.

In general, a string histogram can be thought as a map V of tuples (s, c_s). Each of these tuples represents a unique string label s and an associated bin with a quantity or cardinality s_c. During the construction phase, the occurrences of equal strings s are summed up leading to the integer c_s. In case of the `OrderedStringHistogram`, this set V is finally compressed by cutting down strings to common prefixes such that they can share bins. This compression is done by Algorithm 10 as will be explained briefly.

Algorithm 10 Algorithm for building an order-preserving string histogram.

Require: n, the preferred final histogram size
  function C   -P   -T   (V)
    V, a map: $String \rightarrow Integer$, collected distinct strings s with cardinality c_s
    $l_{max} \leftarrow$ G -M -S   -L   (V).
    if $|V| \leq n$ **then**
        return V
    end if
    $l \leftarrow l_{max}$
    repeat
        $W \leftarrow$ C   -M // a map: $String \rightarrow Integer$, intermediate tuples (s_{pfx}, c_{pfx})
        $l \leftarrow ($ $) l/2$ // cut strings by half length
        $b \leftarrow false$ // break condition
        for all $(s, c_s) \in V$ **do**
            $s_{pfx} \leftarrow$ L -T   (s, l)
            if C   -K (W, s_{pfx}) **then** // bin for s_{pfx} already exists in W
                $c_{pfx} \leftarrow$ G (W, s_{pfx})
                $c_s \leftarrow$ G (V, s)
                P $(W, s_{pfx}, c_{pfx} + c_s)$
            else // requires new bin in W for s_{pfx}
                if $|W| \leq n \lor l = 1$ **then**
                      $c_s \leftarrow$ G (V, s)
                      P (W, s_{pfx}, c_s)
                else // overflow
                      $b \leftarrow true$
                      Break
                end if
            end if
        end for
        if b **then**
            $V \leftarrow W$ // next state
        end if
    until $|V| \leq n \lor l = 1$
    return W
  end function

As can be seen at the beginning of Algorithm 10, it is only applied if $|V| > n$, otherwise V is just returned since no compression was necessary at all. The constant n is a configurable integer number which specifies how many bins a histogram should allocate. It is an approximate value in case of ordered string histograms. If $|V| > n$, the histogram will keep the full information (full-length bin labels). Otherwise, the compression is applied repeatedly until either $|V| \leq n$ or the maximum length of prefix labels l has reached 1. This means, that at least one character will be kept as a label. In the worst case, the histogram will need as many bins as distinct first characters exist. During each iteration, the intermediate set W is filled with trimmed prefixes s_{pfx} from V. The trim length l is initialized with the maximum length l_{max} found in the set of original strings, and divided by 2 at each iteration. As a result of trimming, prefixes will fall into equal bins leading to less bins required in total for W.

The URIHistogram implementation works similarly, with the difference, that strings are not cut by half of their length, instead, they are cut from the right hand side until the next slash occurs. In other words, they are subsequently compressed by common path fragments. In the worst case, the bin labels will be all the domain names occurring in the distribution.

11.2.3 Persisting Statistics

Basically, collected statistics can be stored into any Jena model. RDFStats provides an easy way to specify the target location of statistics based on an RDF configuration file. Additionally, RDFStats configurations may be integrated into other RDF-based configuration files which is used in case of SemWIQ.

The RDFStats vocabulary is depicted in Figure 11.3. A model may contain multiple instances of RDFStatsDataset, which is a sub-class of the SCOVO (Ayers et al. 2009) class Dataset. Each RDFStats dataset has a stats:sourceUrl and a stats:sourceType property, which must either be a stats:SPARQLEndpoint or a stats:RDFDocument. Depending on the source type, a different generator is used. During the statistics generation (Section 11.2) stats:SubjectHistogram and stats:PropertyHistogram items are created with different dimensions. Besides having an rdf:value, each instance has a property and a range dimension. The rdf:value of a histogram is a Base64 encoded string which is written and read by the corresponding histogram builders.

11.3 Using and Accessing Statistics

RDFStats provides means for accessing statistics on two different levels: at histogram level and at the dataset level. While the histogram API provides methods for accessing histogram data (see Figure 11.2), the dataset API includes graph and query pattern estimation functions.

Based on a simplified version of the SCOVO vocabulary (Ayers et al. 2009), which defines a dataset and multiple statistical items associated with it, RDFStats is able to store statistics for multiple source graphs as part of the same target statistics graph. The statistics graph is managed by the

11 Query Pattern Cardinality Estimation with RDFStats

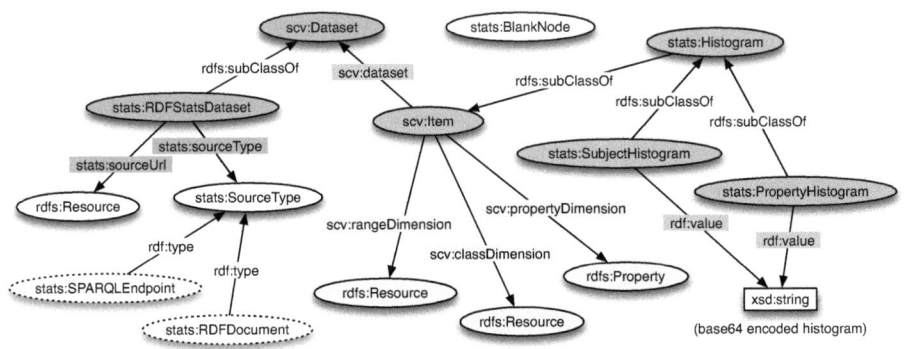

Figure 11.3: RDFStats vocabulary.

RDFStatsModel interface depicted in Figure 11.4. An RDFStatsDataset for a given source URL (which is either a SPARQL endpoint URI or an RDF document URL), is obtained by the method getDataset(String sourceUrl) from the RDFStats model. The RDFStatsDataset interface extends GraphStatistics, QueryStatistics, and JavaResourceView. The first two interfaces define several statistical functions as shown in the figure. The latter one provides methods for all RDF resources that are wrapped by a Java class (e.g. resources with the RDF type stats:RDFStatsDataset are wrapped by a Java class implementing the interface RDFStatsDataset as depicted). The factory class RDFStatsModelFactory, which is also shown in Figure 11.4, is used to initialize read-only and updatable RDFStats models.

11.3.1 Graph Statistics

The GraphStatistics interface defines methods for getting the set of occurring properties, total triples, total distinct subjects, URI subjects, anonymous (blank node) subjects, and the entropy of a property. The entropy of a property is calculated as the number of distinct object values divided by the number of total values for a specific property. The interface also defines a boolean function for checking if a specific subject does not exist in the source graph. And it provides two estimation functions for triple pattern cardinalities, with and without filter expressions. All these functions are implemented by RDFStatsDatasetImpl (Figure 11.4) based on the generated histograms.

In the following, the estimation of triple pattern cardinalities is described. A similar estimation strategy has been presented by Bernstein et al. (2007), however, they use simple selectivity constants instead of histograms. Given a triple pattern $t = (s, p, o)$, where each node s, p, and o is either a variable or a concrete value, there are basically 8 different pattern types to address. Based on the

11.3 Using and Accessing Statistics

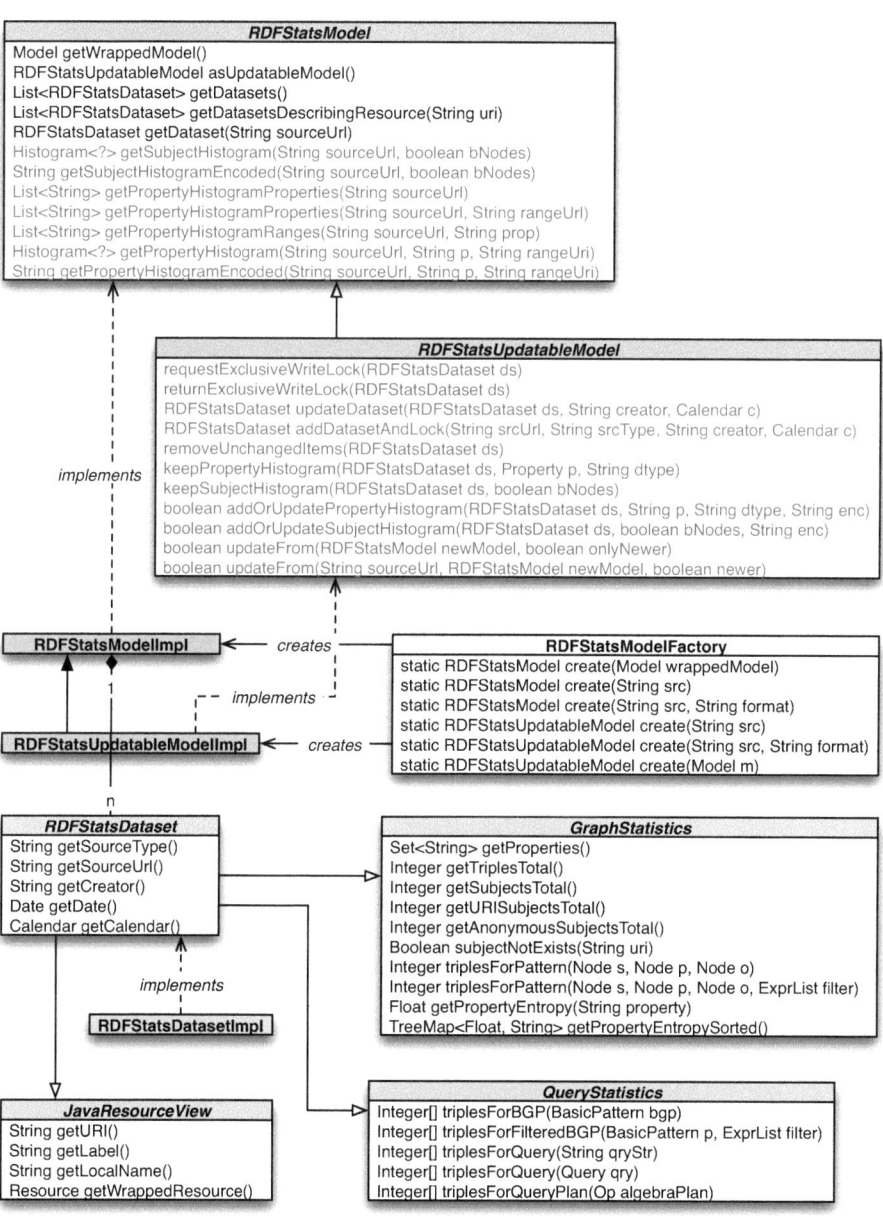

Figure 11.4: RDFStatsModel and RDFStatsDataset API.

pattern type, a different estimation function is used to estimate the expected cardinality of solution bindings. The apostrophe is used to denote concrete triple pattern nodes in the following. We write P for the set of different properties in the source graph and $R_{p'}$ for the set of different object types (as of Definition 29) for a specific property p'. Let h_S be the histogram over all subjects S occurring in the source graph and write $h_S(s')$ for the estimated values of s' based on the histogram h_S. Similarly, let $h_{p',r}$ be the property histogram for property p' and value type r. Write $h_{p',r}(o')$ for the estimated values of o' based on the histogram $h_{p',r}$. Additionally, write $\overline{h}_{p',r}(a,b)$ for the estimated cumulative sum of values between a and b based on the histogram $h_{p',r}$, and write $\overline{h}_S$ for the total values in histogram h_S.

The information obtained from histograms can be combined in order to calculate cardinality estimates c for the following triple pattern types:

1. (s', p', o'): $c = \begin{cases} sgn(h_{p',r}(o)) & \text{if } s' \text{ exists in } h_S(s') \\ 0 & \text{otherwise} \end{cases}$

2. (s', p', o): $c = \begin{cases} (\sum_{r \in R_{p'}} \overline{h}_{p',r}(-\inf, \inf))/\overline{h}_S & \text{if } s' \text{ exists in } h_S(s') \\ 0 & \text{otherwise} \end{cases}$

3. (s', p, o'): $c = \begin{cases} (\sum_{p' \in P} \sum_{r \in R_{p'}} h_{p',r}(o'))/\overline{h}_S & \text{if } s' \text{ exists in } h_S(s') \\ 0 & \text{otherwise} \end{cases}$

4. (s', p, o): $c = \begin{cases} (\sum_{p' \in P} \sum_{r \in R_{p'}} \overline{h}_{p',r}(-\inf, \inf))/\overline{h}_S & \text{if } s' \text{ exists in } h_S(s') \\ 0 & \text{otherwise} \end{cases}$

5. (s, p', o'): $h_{p'}(o')$

6. (s, p', o): $\sum_{r \in R_{p'}} \overline{h}_{p',r}(-\inf, \inf)$

7. (s, p, o'): $\sum_{p' \in P} h_{p', type(o')}(o')$

8. (s, p, o): $\sum_{p' \in P} \sum_{r \in R_{p'}} \overline{h}_{p',r}(-\inf, \inf)$

In the first case, the signum function is used because the triple pattern will either match and produce a single (empty) binding or it will not match. In all cases where the subject is concrete (1–4), it is checked if the subject s' exists in h_S. If not, no bindings will be produced. Additionally, in these cases the estimation calculated based on property histograms is divided by $\overline{h}_S$, which is the total number of distinct subjects in the source graph. If the type t of the subject s' is already known from a previous estimation, the cardinality for the pattern (s', rdf:type, t) is used instead of $\overline{h}_S$ to normalize the estimation. This approach addresses the fact, that usually different properties are used together with specific types. For example, given the pattern { ?s foaf:name ?n }, if there are 100.000 distinct subjects in total, but only 10 of them are FOAF persons, a division by $\overline{h}_S = 100.000$ would lead to underestimation. If ?s is known to be a FOAF person, a division by 10 will be more accurate.

In case 7, the function type() (see Definition 29) is used to determine the type r based on the object value o'.

Cardinality Estimation for Filtered Triple Patterns

If a preceding filter expression exists with a list of conjunctive expressions $E = e_1 \wedge e_2 \wedge \ldots \wedge e_n$, $n > 0$, the filter expression is taken into account when calculating histogram estimates. In this case, cumulative sums are calculated based on the range coverage of the filter expression as depicted in Figure 11.5. The CoverageBuilder visits all filter expressions starting with the root expression and recursively builds a specific range coverage data structure in bottom-up direction. For all low-level expression terms it initializes a new range coverage of the form (a, b), $a <= b$ where a, b may be inclusive or exclusive range bounds. In case of binary logical expression operation such as $\wedge, \vee$ the sub-coverages are merged accordingly, for the logical not operation the complement of the sub-coverage is created. The final coverage will be a simple sequence of range intervals. The estimated total value can be calculated by adding up single cumulative sums $\overline{h}_{p',r}(a, b)$ (as before) for each interval.

For example, consider the expression (?o = 10 || ?o >= 60) && ?o != 80. After pre-optimizing the expression, it becomes !(?o != 10 && ?o < 60) && ?o != 80. The corresponding coverage building process is depicted in Figure 11.5. The final estimation can be calculated as $c = h_{p',r}(10) + \overline{h}_{p',r}(60, \inf) - h_{p',r}(80)$.

11.3.2 Cardinality Estimation for Query Plans

The interface QueryStatistics (on the bottom of Figure 11.4) defines several functions which are used to calculate cardinality estimations for basic graph patterns and also complete algebra plans of a query. Because the current version of RDFStats does not include join selectivities, heuristics are used in order to estimate the cardinality of a BGP and other algebra operations.

In case of a BGP the cardinality estimations for triple patterns are combined in a special way. Basically, a BGP is a join over multiple triple patterns. Instead of applying the simple join heuristics used for the *Join* operator as described below, the following situations are taken into account:

- Given two triple patterns $t_1 = (s_1, p_1, o_1)$ and $t_2 = (s_2, p_2, o_2)$, if $s_1 = s_2$ and p_1, p_2, o_1, and o_2 are concrete: t_2 further restricts t_1 and the combined estimate will be the minimum of both triple

11 Query Pattern Cardinality Estimation with RDFStats

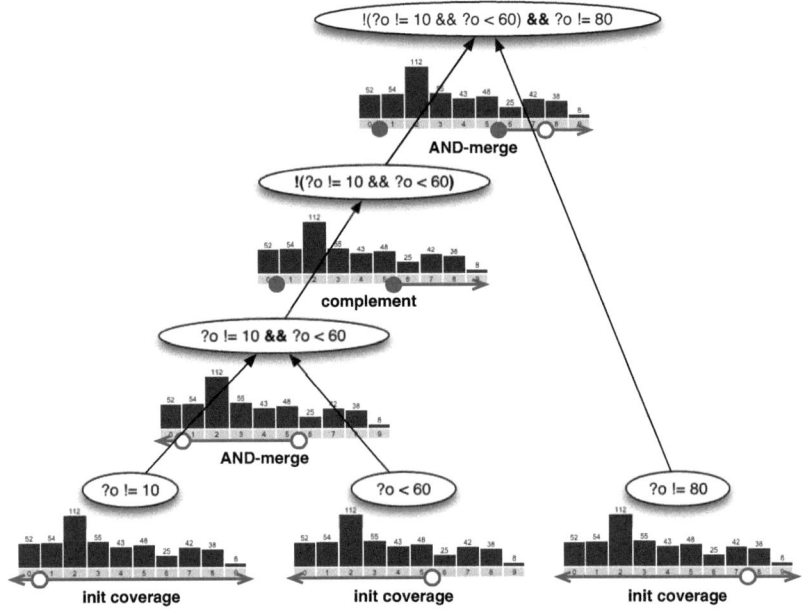

Figure 11.5: Range coverage for filter expression example.

pattern estimates: $c = \min(c_i)$, with c_i being the estimates for t_i. The cardinality of all these triple patterns is calculated first.

- For all other triple patterns t_i with $s_i = s_1$, their cardinality is estimated and if a type is known for s_i, the estimates are weighted by the fraction f, the corresponding class extension takes in the source graph. This approach addresses the fact, that typically different properties are used to describe instances of the same type. Although there may be intersections with other types, the weighted value is still better then the *Join* operator heuristic defined below. The fraction f is calculated as total triple count divided by the estimate for $(s, \texttt{rdf:type}, t)$.

The combination of all estimates for a BGP is then similar to the approach of Bastian Quilitz and Ulf Leser (2008):

$$c_{bgp} = \min(c_i) * \prod c_j$$

where c_i are the estimates for all triple patterns with concrete predicate and object and c_j are the estimates for all other triple patterns.

The cardinality estimation of a complete query plan is based on a bottom-up visitor which is starting from the root operator of a sub-plan and calculates intermediate estimates. Since the leaf operators are

11.3 Using and Accessing Statistics

always basic graph patterns, BGP estimates are calculated first. These estimates are further combined and modified by estimation functions for algebra operators. For all operators that have a single sub-operator, the sub-estimate c' is passed through by default. c^L and c^R are used to refer to the left and right sub-estimate in case of binary operators. The following formulas are used to calculate an average estimate and a lower and upper bound based on heuristics:

- *Filter*: $c_{min} = 0, c_{avg} = c'_{avg}/2, c_{max} = c'_{max}$
- *Distinct*: $c_{min} = 1, c_{avg} = c'_{avg} * \sum_{i=1}^{n} \frac{1}{2^i}, c_{max} = c'_{max}$, with n variables to project
- *Slice*: $c_{min} = \min(c'_{min}, n), c_{avg} = \min(c'_{avg}, n), c_{max} = \min(c'_{max}, n)$, with slice size n
- *Union*: $c_{min} = c^L_{min} + c^R_{min}, c_{avg} = c^L_{avg} + c^R_{avg}, c_{max} = c^L_{max} + c^R_{max}$
- *Join*: $c_{min} = 0, c_{avg} = c^L_{avg} * c^R_{avg} * s_{join}, c_{max} = c^L_{max} * c^R_{max}$, with selectivity $s_{join} = 0.5$ in case there are shared variables, $s_{join} = 1$ otherwise
- *LeftJoin*: $c_{min} = 0, c_{avg} = c^L_{avg} * s_{ljoin}, c_{max} = c^L_{max}$, with selectivity $s_{ljoin} = 0.5$ in case there are shared variables, $s_{ljoin} = 1$ otherwise

RDFStats provides an upper bound estimate, i.e. the max number of triples to expect from a data source. This enables a scalable selection of data sources during federation, because if the upper bound is zero, it can be guaranteed that no corresponding triples exist at all.

The formula for the *Filter* is only applied if the filter has not been taken into account already when processing the underlying BGP and filtered triple patterns as described before. Because a filter expression can be arbitrarily complex it is not always possible to calculate accurate estimates. A simple heuristic rule is to use the half of the previous average, assume 0 for the minimum and pass through the previous maximum estimate.

In case of the *Distinct* operator, the minimum must be 1 at least (all bindings are equal), the maximum is c'_{max} (all bindings are distinct), and the average is weighted based on the number of existing variables n according to the factor $\sum_{i=1}^{n} \frac{1}{2^i}$: the more variables exist, the lower is the chance that two bindings are equal and thus, c_{avg} will be higher. For instance, if $n = 1$ then $c_{avg} = c'_{avg} * \frac{1}{2}$ and if $n = 3$ then $c_{avg} = c'_{avg} * (\frac{1}{2} + \frac{1}{4} + \frac{1}{8})$. The estimation for *Slice* should be clear: all estimates are limited by n, which is the size of the slice.

For the *Union*, *Join*, and *LeftJoin* operators, estimates from the left and right sub-plans are combined. The *Union* should be clear also: estimates are simply added. In case of the *Join*, the minimum estimate is 0 (no compatible bindings at all) and the maximum estimate is the product (cross product, no shared variables). For the average estimate, a join selectivity of $s_{join} = 0.5$ is assumed if there are shared variables and 1 otherwise (cross product). The minimum *LeftJoin* estimate is again 0, but the maximum cannot be higher than c^L_{max}. In order to calculate the average estimate of the *LeftJoin* the selectivity s_{ljoin} is used, which is either 0.5 in case there are shared variables and 1 otherwise, in which case $c_{avg} = c_{avg}^L$.

To improve the cardinality estimation for higher level algebra operators, it will be required to compute several specific join selectivities for source graphs, which will be part of future work (see Section 14.2).

Part IV

Results

12 Demonstration and Evaluation

In this part of the thesis the *Semantic Web Integrator and Query Engine* is evaluated based on a case study. It will be demonstrated how SemWIQ can be used for the integration of datasets from the solar observation domain in order to create a *virtual observatory*. As part of the case study the advantages of the SemWIQ approach compared to traditional information integration will be discussed.

12.1 Case Study – Virtual Solar Observatory

The following case study relates to a real-world application (Langegger et al. 2007, Langegger et al. 2009) which has been developed for the Kanzelhöhe solar observatory as part of the Austrian Grid project, a national research project funded by the *Austrian Federal Ministry for Education, Science and Culture*. The Kanzelhöhe solar observatory is recording observations of the solar surface (chromosphere and photosphere) and various kinds of solar phenomena such as sunspots, magnetic activity, coronal loops, solar flares, etc. Scientists from the observatory near Villach, Carinthia cooperate with several other solar observation sites across Europe such as the Astrophysical Institute of Potsdam, the Hvar Observatory in Croatia, the Instituto de Astrofísica de Canarias in Spain and others. The goal of the astronomical physics community to create an infrastructure for sharing astronomical data based on Grid technology already dates back to the early 2000s. For instance, the *European Grid of Solar Observations* (Bentley and EGSO Consortium 2002) was developed between 2002–2005 as part of an EU-funded IST project with the aim to integrate solar observation datasets. However, the publications about the EGSO project are rather superficial and do not include any detailed information about the implementation of the system and the query processing approach. A similar initiative undertaken in the United States and supported by the NASA is the *Virtual Solar Observatory* project (Bogart et al. 2005). It is an XML-based integration system implemented in Perl which integrates XML data sources via SOAP. The system does not use any wrappers to address heterogeneity and it is not possible to execute distributed joins to combine data from different sources. In fact it is a rather simple approach of query federation and aggregation of result sets.

Starting in 2003, the Kanzelhöhe solar observatory took part in the Austrian Grid project together with the Institute for Application-Oriented Knowledge Processing at the Johannes Kepler University Linz (and about 20 other cooperation partners) with the goal of building a semantic integration middleware for astronomical datasets. Initially it was planned to develop the middleware for the Austrian

12 Demonstration and Evaluation

Grid as the *Grid-enabled Semantic Data Access Middleware* (G-SDAM) (Blöchl et al. 2005, Wöhrer et al. 2005). However, because the software was supposed to be highly relevant for the Semantic Web community, it was detached as a separate project called *SemWIQ*, which became an enabling sub-component of G-SDAM when used in a Grid environment. The Grid-integration of SemWIQ as part of G-SDAM is described in the master thesis of ThomasLeitner (2010).

12.1.1 Data Sources and Vocabularies

For the case study discussed in the following, three different astronomical datasets (DS1, DS2, DS4), one scientists dataset (DS3), and one publications dataset (DS5) are integrated via SemWIQ as shown in Figure 12.1. The icons in the figure indicate the type of data source: a relational database, a spreadsheet, or a native RDF data store. The databases and spreadsheets have been wrapped to RDF and all data is described based on the ontologies excerpted in Figure 12.2. The sizes of the data sources are shown in Table 12.1.

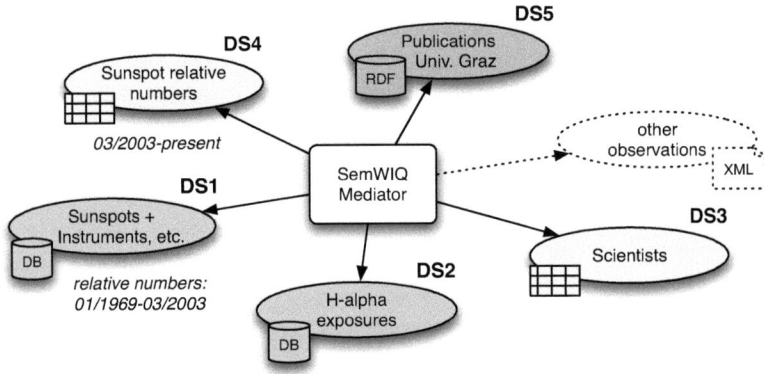

Figure 12.1: Solar observation datasets used for the case study.

Table 12.1: Sizes of the case study data sources DS1–5.

Data source	Triples	Things
DS1	89,104	5,293
DS2	128,880	8,592
DS3	89	17
DS4	84,851	4,974
DS5	420	35

12.1 Case Study – Virtual Solar Observatory

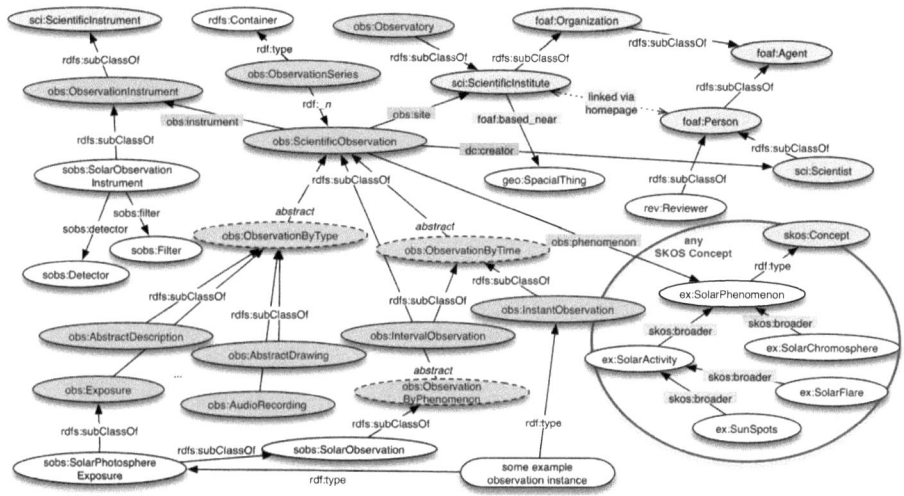

Figure 12.2: Domain ontologies for solar observation.

The ontologies include FOAF (*Friend-of-a-Friend*), SKOS (*Simple Knowledge Organization System*), the *Basic Geo Vocabulary* (Brickley n.d.), and a science, an observation, and a solar-observation vocabulary developed especially for this case study. Because there exists already a comprehensive SKOS taxonomy for astrophysical phenomena developed by IVOA Semantics WG (2009), which is part of the *International Virtual Observatory Alliance* (IVOA), observation records can be related to SKOS concepts as shown on the lower right of the figure. For the case study many external links have been created also to DBpedia (Auer et al. 2007) in order to provide readable descriptions for the corresponding astronomical concepts.

RDBMS-backed Sunspots and H-alpha Data Sources

The two RDBMS-backed astronomical datasets DS1 and DS2 (Figure 12.1) are wrapped by the *semwiq-endpoint* component based on D2RQ-Map (which has been described in Section 10.2). An Entity-Relationship diagram of the sunspots database is shown in Figure 12.3. The diagram only includes foreign-key relationships, but no attributes. Relevant attributes which are mapped to RDF are part of the mapping in Appendix A.1. The dashed lines indicate implicit relationships based on time. The most relevant entities are marked with bold edges: *exposure*, *detector*, *filter*, *instrument*, and *relative_numbers*. The *exposures* table contains digital scans of manually drawn sunspot diagrams as shown in Figure 12.4(a) (the example picture is from 2001, which was a year within a phase of

12 Demonstration and Evaluation

high activity). The sunspot drawing is the only continuous kind of solar observation that is still done manually. Several approaches have been undertaken to automatically cluster and classify spots and groups, however, none of the algorithms could reach the desired accuracy, which is why the scientists still make manual observations. The observation site is occupied daily and the sunspot observation is recorded preferably in the morning hours, but otherwise as soon as the sky is clear. Clear sky is an important requirement for observations based on visible light. The integration of sunspot observations from different observations sites across Europe is therefore important in order to obtain synoptic data series.

Besides the digitized sunspot drawings, the *relative_numbers* table of the sunspots database stores so-called *relative numbers*, which include the number of spots and groups observed, weather conditions (clearness of the sky), several other attributes and an optional short comment added by the observer. The relative numbers complement the sunspot scans. The RDBMS-backed data source contributes relative numbers recorded from January 1969 until July 1988. Newer sunspot relative numbers are stored in a spreadsheet wrapped by data source DS4 (as shown in Figure 12.1). The *detector*, *filter*, and *instrument* tables contain information on the various observation instruments used throughout the observatory and their configuration at a given period of time. A specific instrument configuration is associated with each observation record. The other tables shown in the diagram are not relevant for integration, which is why they are not mapped in the following.

Scientists at Kanzelhöhe use a very similar database model to store H-alpha observation records, which are integrated as a separate data source (DS2). The only difference in the model is the missing table for sunspot relative numbers. There is also an *exposures* table, which contains pictures taken with a special H-alpha telescope. An example picture is shown in Figure 12.4(b). It filters a red visible spectral line created by hydrogen at a specific wavelength. Besides the relationships to instruments, filters, and detectors as in case of the sunspots model (Figure 12.3), the attributes of H-alpha exposures include date, exposure time, centering coordinates of the telescope axis, scaling attributes of the viewport, width and height of the exposure in pixels, and the path to the file in the local archive. All multimedia files such as exposures and videos of flares are published on the website of the observatory at http://www.kso.ac.at. In order to link directly to these files, the virtual RDF target graph contains resolvable HTTP URIs pointing to the published files.

Unfortunately, the database model used at solar observatory is not well designed. It is not normalized and a major amount of common tables has been duplicated to each observation station connected to the network. Moreover, we have found several inconsistent records due to the fact that MySQL is used with the MyISAM storage engine that does not support referential integrity. Nevertheless, since a bad database design frequently occur in organizations and real-world applications, it could be regarded as an additional challenge to cope with. An important fact is, that the database model cannot be altered. The database is fully autonomous and issues with inconsistency have to be solved by wrappers whenever possible.

12.1 Case Study – Virtual Solar Observatory

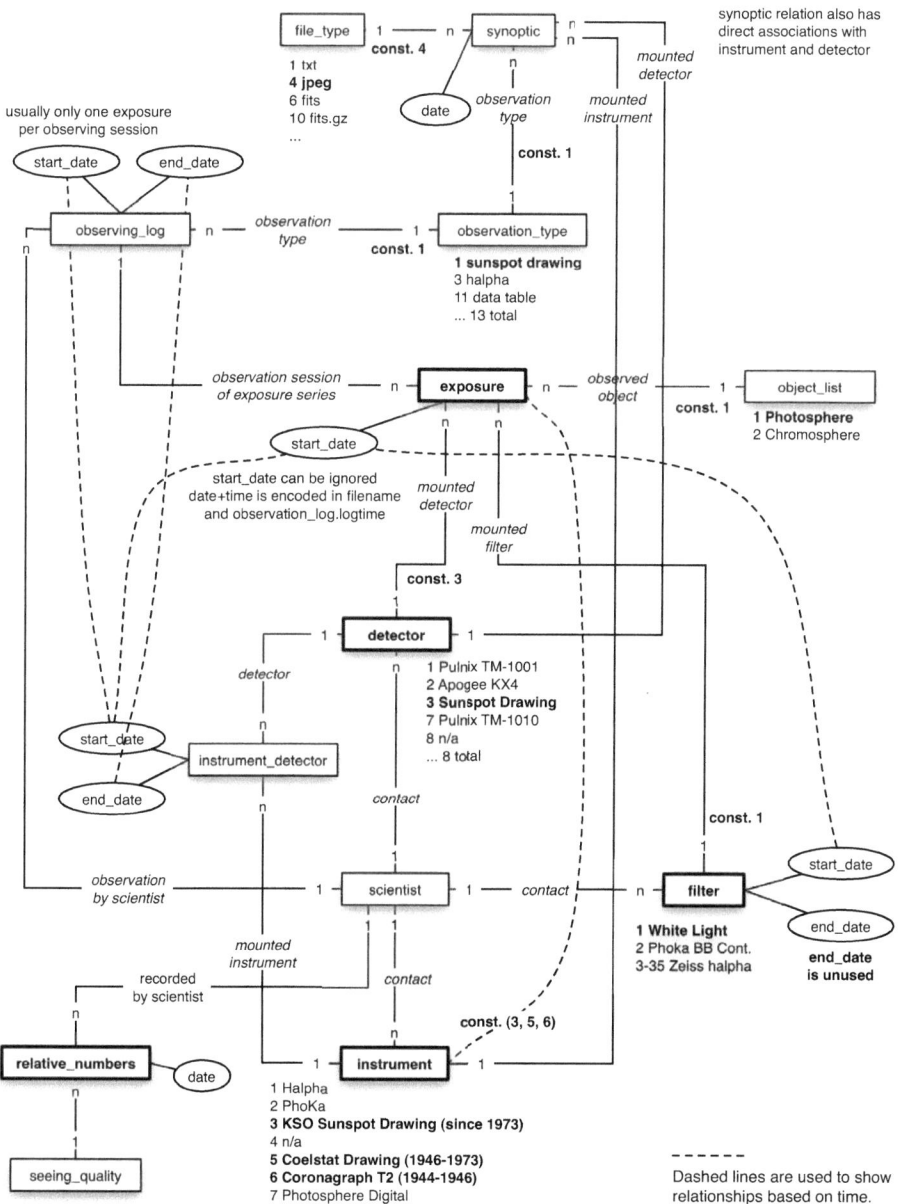

Figure 12.3: ER diagram of the Kanzelhöhe solar observatory's sunspots database (DS1).

12 Demonstration and Evaluation

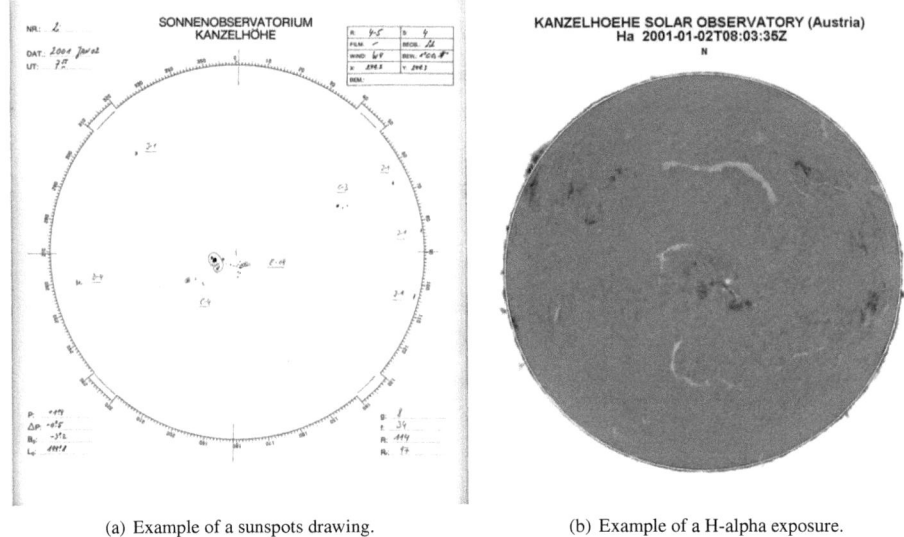

(a) Example of a sunspots drawing.

(b) Example of a H-alpha exposure.

Figure 12.4: Example exposures from the Kanzelhöhe solar observatory.

The D2RQ mapping for the sunspots dataset (DS1) is printed in Appendix A.1. The mapping for the H-alpha dataset is very similar. The duplicated instrument and filter configuration tables are not mapped again and hence, the wrapper only exports the *exposure* table. These exposures are digitized images of the sun's chromosphere, automatically captured by the H-alpha patrol device on a daily base.

Spreadsheet-based Scientists Data Source

A spreadsheet file in Microsoft Excel format which contains personal information about scientists working at the organization is provided by data source DS3. The spreadsheet contains a simple row-based table on the first sheet which has the following structure:

ID	Contact	First name	Last name	Address	City	State	ZIP	Email	Internet suffix	Retired
...	...	...	...	...	...	...	...	...	...	...

It is wrapped by XLWrap and the corresponding mapping specification is printed in Appendix A.2.

Spreadsheet-based Sunspot Relative Numbers

The recordings of sunspot relative numbers starting from July 19th 1988 are stored in a spreadsheet which is wrapped via XLWrap as a separate data source (DS4). The spreadsheet contains a single

12.1 Case Study – Virtual Solar Observatory

sheet with the following table structure:

id	date	groups	spots	ruhe	tinygrps	remarks	R	seeing10	scientist_key
5001	19.07.88 07:40	7	76	45	2		107	30	5
5002	20.07.88 11:40	6	42	40	2		81	35	5
5003	21.07.88 06:30	10	80	25	5		113	20	1
5004	22.07.88 10:25	7	48	30	0		86	30	1
5005	23.07.88 06:20	9	45	30	2		99	30	1
...	...	...	...	...	...	...	...	...	...

The XLWrap mapping for this spreadsheet generates the same target graph than the D2RQ mapping creates for the database records of sunspot relative numbers between January 1969 and July 1988. The XLWrap mapping is printed in Appendix A.3.

Native RDF Data Source for Publications

The Kanzelhöhe solar observatory is maintained by the *Institute for Geophysics, Astrophysics, and Meteorology* (IGAM) at the Karl-Franzens University of Graz. Data source DS5 (Figure 12.1) contributes publications meta data about papers written by scientists from the university. The dataset has been converted to RDF before and was loaded into a Jena TDB store. It is also served by the *semwiq-endpoint* component, however, no wrapper is configured as part of the Joseki configuration. The publications are described using the *Semantic Web for Research Communities* vocabulary (Sure et al. 2005) and the *Semantic Web Conference Ontology* (Möller et al. 2007). An example publication from the dataset is printed in Listing 12.1. The author URIs refer to the scientists data source.

```
@prefix swrc:   <http://swrc.ontoware.org/ontology#> .
@prefix swc:    <http://data.semanticweb.org/ns/swc/ontology#> .
@prefix s:      <http://semwiqdemo:8093/resource/> .
@prefix dc:     <http://purl.org/dc/elements/1.1/> .
@prefix :       <http://semwiqdemo:8094/resource/> .

:InCollection_PKM00
    a         swrc:InCollection , swc:Paper ;
    rdfs:label "Signatures of large-scale changes associated with the May 2" ;
    swc:isPartOf :Collection_PDM00 ;
    dc:creator s:DMaia , s:NVilmer , s:WOtruba , s:SPohjolainen , s:MPick , s:JKhan ;
    dc:title "Signatures of large-scale changes associated with the May 2" ;
    swrc:author s:DMaia , s:NVilmer , s:WOtruba , s:SPohjolainen , s:JKhan , s:MPick ;
    swrc:pages "1404ff" ;
    swrc:year 2000 .
...
```

Listing 12.1: Excerpt of the publications data source.

12.1.2 Setup Tasks

Setting up an information integration system based on SemWIQ is a matter of the following tasks:

12 Demonstration and Evaluation

1. Depending on the application scenario, the following SemWIQ components have to be downloaded from the SourceForge repository at http://semwiq.sourceforge.net:
   a) When using the mediator in a Jena-based Semantic Web application, the *semwiq-mediator* package is needed.
   b) In order to set up a mediator which is accessible via a web frontend and which provides a SPARQL endpoint for the virtually integrated dataset, the *semwiq-webapp* package is needed. It builds upon the (already bundled) *semwiq-mediator* package.

   Regarding the wrapped (or native RDF) data sources, the *semwiq-endpoint* package is required. It provides all the SPARQL extensions, integrates RDFStats (Langegger and Wöß 2009b) into Joseki (Jena Community 2009b), integrates Snorql from D2R-Server (Chris Bizer and Richard Cyganiak 2006) as a HTML-based query interface, and includes Pubby (Cyganiak and Bizer 2009) as a Linked Data frontend.

2. Depending on the information systems to integrate, additional wrapper libraries may be required:
   a) In case of a relational database system, the D2RQ-Map library is needed.
   b) For spreadsheets, the XLWrap library (Langegger and Wöß 2009c) is needed.
   c) For any other data source, existing wrappers may be used as long as they support the Jena assembler mechanism (Jena Community 2009a).

3. For each data source to integrate, an instance of *semwiq-endpoint* is prepared. The dependent wrapper libraries can be copied into the lib directory of the SemWIQ endpoint component to be found by the Jena assembler.

4. For each wrapped data source, a specific mapping is necessary. In case of a relational database system, it will be a D2RQ-Map mapping file (Section 10.2) and in case of a spreadsheet (or a collection of spreadsheets), it will be an XLWrap mapping file (Section 10.3). The corresponding manuals should be used in order to create the mapping.

5. Once all the *semwiq-endpoint* instances have been created, they can be started. The endpoints will be initialized based on Joseki configurations. The wrapped Jena dataset is automatically assembled at runtime based on the Jena assembler mechanism. The console log will print the SPARQL endpoint URI, which is used for its registration at the mediator in the following step.

6. Finally, the *semwiq-mediator* is configured and launched and the wrapped (or native RDF) data sources are registered by their SPARQL endpoint URIs.

The data source registry will automatically fetch the required statistics based on the SPARQL extensions. Alternatively, the SemWIQ mediator can be configured to remotely generate RDFStats,

12.1 Case Study – Virtual Solar Observatory

which is however only feasible if the data source is either relatively small in size or it is situated in the same local area network as the mediator. If the instance-based federator is used, it will automatically download all the vocabularies used by registered data sources from the web into a cache. The cache is later used for automatic type detection. Adding additional data sources does not require any modifications at the data source or at the mediator. The data source registry will fetch the corresponding statistics and, thus, the federator will take the new data source into account. Upon unregistration, the corresponding statistics are deleted from the central metadata catalog.

Case Study Setup

For each of the five data sources depicted in Figure 12.1, a separate instance of *semwiq-endpoint* is used with different wrapper libraries: for the sunspots and the H-alpha databases the D2RQ-Map libraries are used and in case of the two spreadsheets, the XLWrap library is used. No additional library is necessary for the publications data source, which is a native RDF file served by *semwiq-endpoint* via SPARQL.

Because there may be potential links between the different datasets, e.g. dc:creator of a observation record should be correctly linked to the corresponding scientist, it might be helpful to use record linkage tools. There are general tools such as *Febrl* (Christen 2008), which can be used for record linkage tasks in database systems, but there are also Semantic Web specific tools such as *Silk* (Volz et al. 2009). Currently, the integration of record linkage and data cleansing tools into SemWIQ is out of scope. Because each source information system might use a different metamodel, it will be necessary to implement specialized plugins into a generic mapping tool.

Once the endpoints and the mediator web application are running, the data sources can be registered at the mediator via a web front-end. After the registration of a new data source, it will be considered by the federator for upcoming queries. Besides running in a web application, the SemWIQ mediator can be transparently used in any Jena-based Semantic Web application as a Jena dataset. There is also a Java Swing client distributed as part of the *semwiq-mediator* package, which is suitable for testing and debugging. Both, the web application and the Java Swing client provide buttons to register and un-register data sources. If SemWIQ is embedded into an application, the functionality is provided via the API shown in Figure 9.9 on page 160.

A data source is registered based on the corresponding SPARQL endpoint URI. All other information such as voiD meta data and RDFStats statistics are automatically retrieved from the endpoint by issuing a DESCRIBE DATASET query. For each data source, it is possible to specify a specific monitoring profile, which allows fine-grained monitoring control on a per-data source basis. The profile defines how the statistics are fetched. They can be either downloaded as part of voiD meta data (which is the default setting), as a compressed file from the endpoint, or they can be generated remotely via the SPARQL endpoint (which is not suggested in case of large datasets). The latter option can be used, if RDFStats is not available at the wrapper (e.g. because there is no access to the host to deploy it). The profile also defines a polling interval in seconds for the monitor.

12.2 Evaluation

The most important aspects and goals of the approach have been summarized as part of Section 1.1. The system is very flexible, since it is based on open data and protocol standards. SemWIQ is currently the only generic mediator framework based on Semantic Web technology, that can be used for a broad range of different scenarios. Although DARQ (Bastian Quilitz and Ulf Leser 2008) can be used as a generic SPARQL federator, queries are not optimized across wrappers, only simple selectivities are used (but not automatically generated), and it has no explicit registry component. As pointed out in the related work part, most of the research projects during the last decade have been focused on very specific needs of a particular application domain. SemWIQ is currently only limited in terms of availability of wrappers for legacy information sources. However, there already exists a broad range of RDF wrapping technology as listed on the Semantic Web Interest Groups's community Wiki (Semantic Web Interest Group n.d.). SemWIQ is very flexible also with respect to adding and removing data sources. There is no global common schema that has to be managed as in traditional RDBMS-based commercial systems. Once a data source is registered at the mediator by its SPARQL endpoint URI, statistics and metadata are automatically exchanged, and the data source becomes available as part of the virtual global RDF graph.

Compared to traditional approaches based on relational database systems or XML, there are many aspects of Semantic Web technologies, which make them well suited for the integration of data from globally distributed, heterogeneous, and autonomous data sources. The *Resource Description Framework* is highly applicable for the global data model of an information integration system as shown in Section 8.1.1. Although RDF graphs may become rather complex, including schema information and ontological assertions, it is possible to denote them as simple sets of triples which facilitates RDF data management and query processing.

12.2.1 Sample Queries

In the following, some example queries listed in Table 12.2 are used to demonstrate the capabilities of SemWIQ. For each of the queries, the corresponding global query plan and the query results are provided. Query plans contain *Service* operators, which delegate sub-plans to registered data sources. In the following figures, a port number is shown for each *Service* operator. The last digit of each port number corresponds to the data source number as depicted in Figure 12.1. Each query will be discussed in detail.

12.2 Evaluation

Table 12.2: Example queries.

#	Description	SPARQL query
1	What kind of information is there available?	```SELECT DISTINCT ?type WHERE {
[] rdf:type ?type }```
2	What kinds of observations are there available?	```SELECT DISTINCT ?obs WHERE {
[] rdf:type ?obs, obs:ScientificObservation }```
3	Retrieve sunspot relative number records from January 2001 including the creator and a time stamp.	```SELECT * WHERE {
?s rdf:type sobs:SunspotRelativeNumbers ;
dc:creator ?creator ;
obs:dateTime ?dt .
FILTER (?dt > "2001-01-01T00:00:00"^^xsd:dateTime
&& ?dt < "2001-01-31T23:59:59"^^xsd:dateTime)
} ORDER BY ?dt```
4	Get all information about a specific observation record (SELECT query and DESCRIBE variant).	```SELECT * WHERE {
  <http://semwiqdemo:8094/resource/
      SunspotRelativeNumbers_8427>
    ?property ?value }

DESCRIBE <http://semwiqdemo:8094/resource/
      SunspotRelativeNumbers_8427>``` |
| 5 | Get information about the scientist who made the observation. | ```SELECT ?name ?mbox WHERE {
  <http://semwiqdemo:8094/resource/
      SunspotRelativeNumbers_8427>
    dc:creator ?creator .
  ?creator foaf:name ?name .
  OPTIONAL { ?creator foaf:mbox_sha1sum ?mbox } }``` |
| 6 | Get publications of the scientist since the year 2000 and if applicable, include title of the proceedings or collection. | ```SELECT ?year ?title ?bookTitle WHERE {
  ?pub a swc:Paper ;
     dc:creator <http://semwiqdemo:8093/resource/WOtruba
         > ;
     dc:title ?title ;
     swrc:year ?year ;
  FILTER (?year >= 2000)
  OPTIONAL { ?pub swc:isPartOf ?book .
      ?book dc:title ?bookTitle }
} ORDER BY ?year ?title``` |
| 7 | Get publications that relate to the observation record retrieved by Query 4. | ```SELECT ?title ?s WHERE {
  <http://semwiqdemo:8094/resource/
      SunspotRelativeNumbers_8427> dc:subject ?s.
  ?pub a swc:Paper ;
     dc:subject ?s ;
     dc:title ?title .
} ORDER BY ?title``` |
| 8 | Check if there are any observations of the solar chromosphere done with a Pulnix TM-1010 detector. | ```ASK { ?s a obs:ScientificObservation ;
     obs:phenomenon <http://www.astro.physik.uni-
         goettingen.de/~hessman/rdf/IAU93#
         Chromosphere> ;
     sobs:detector ?det .
  ?det a sobs:Detector ; dc:title ?title .
  FILTER (?title = 'Pulnix TM-1010') }``` |

207

Query 1

This is a very typical query for the purpose of exploring a dataset. It selects the distinct set of classes which are actually used in the integrated dataset (the virtual global RDF graph). Since triples with rdf:type as property are used in all five data sources of the case study, the federator will delegate a sub-query with the triple pattern to all of them. An EXPLAIN query reveals the global query plan as depicted in Figure 12.5. In this case, the triple-based federation algorithm is used, although the instance-based variant would lead to the same result. It can be seen, that the federation algorithm creates a union sequence with a *Service* operator for each relevant data source. The distinct projection on ?type returns the distinct set of used classes in the virtual graph as depicted in Table 12.3.

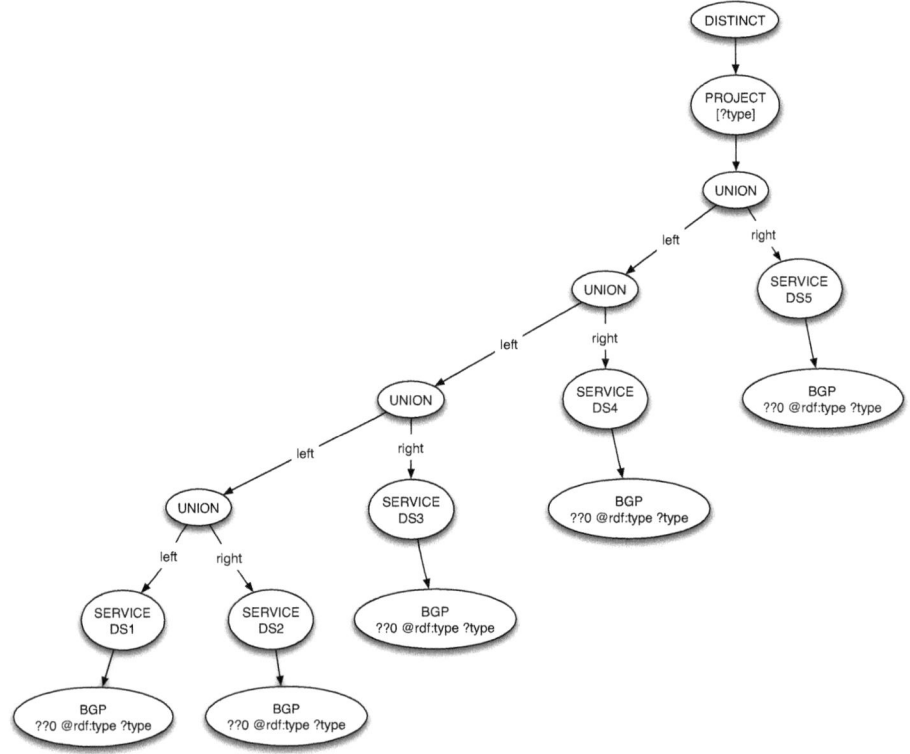

Figure 12.5: Plan for Query 1 (using triple-based federator).

Table 12.3: Results of Query 1.

type
sobs:Filter
sobs:SunspotRelativeNumbers
sobs:SunspotDrawing
sobs:SolarObservationInstrument
sobs:Detector
sobs:SunExposure
sci:Scientist
swrc:University
swrc:Institute
swrc:InCollection
swc:Paper
swrc:InProceedings
swrc:Article
swrc:Collection
swrc:Proceedings

Query 2

The second example query demonstrates the query-time subsumption capability of the instance-based federator. Consider, a scientist would like to explore what kinds of observations the integrated system knows of. The query is very similar to Query 1: it basically selects a list of classes ?obs, however, here the result is further restricted to resources that additionally have a rdf:type of obs:ScientificObservation, i.e. all known subclasses of obs:ScientificObservation. As described in Section 9.4, the federation algorithm will include a sub-plan for all interesting data sources which in this case are DS1, DS2, and DS4. Data source DS1 is relevant, because it contributes sobs:SunspotRelativeNumbers and sobs:SunspotDrawing resources, DS2 is relevant because it contains sobs:SunExposure resources, and data source DS4 contributes an extension of sobs:SunspotRelativeNumbers as well. The corresponding query plan is depicted in Figure 12.6. The result set is shown in Table 12.4.

Table 12.4: Results of Query 2.

obs
sobs:SunspotRelativeNumbers
sobs:SunspotDrawing
sobs:SunExposure

12 Demonstration and Evaluation

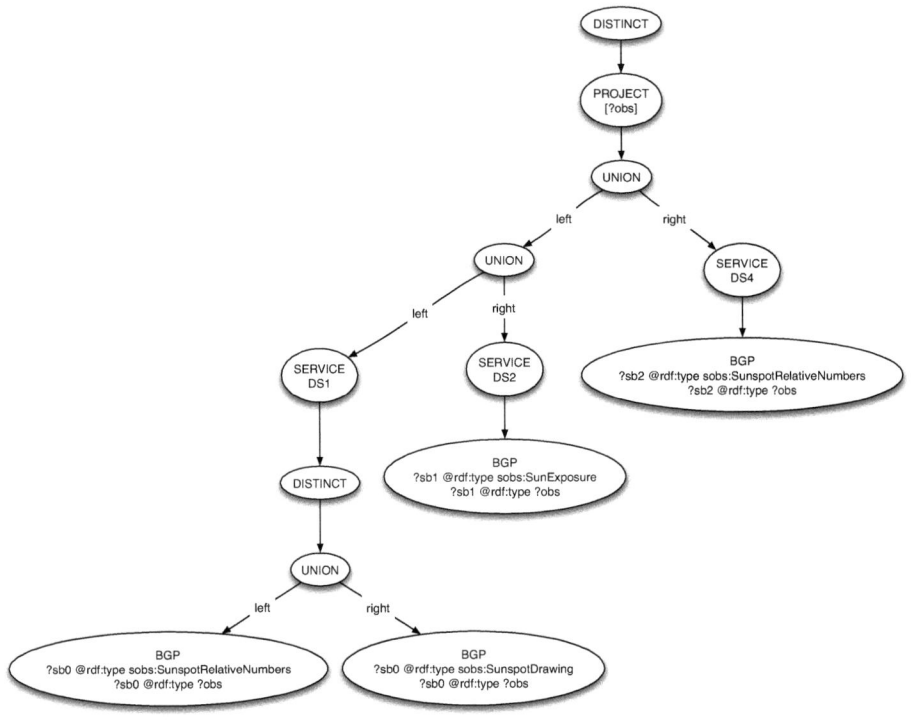

Figure 12.6: Plan for Query 2 (using instance-based federator).

Query 3

It is assumed, that the scientist wants to check the availability of observation records of the type sobs:SunspotRelativeNumbers for January 2001, which was a period of rather high solar activity. Additionally, the scientist would like to know about the creator of the record as well as the date and time the record was created. This can be achieved by Query 3, which contains a filter expression for the desired time period from January 1–31, 2001. The query also contains an ORDER BY clause in order to sort the results based on the time stamp ?dt.

The query plan for Query 3, shown in Figure 12.7 is already rather complex. Below the *Order* operator, the query plan contains a 2-way *Sequence*, which is a substitution-based join as explained in Section 9.2.5. The first sequence sub-plan (*Union* on the left hand side of the figure) selects all resources that have a obs:dateTime property within the desired time period, January 1–31, 2001. Obviously there are only two interesting data sources, DS1 and DS4, which contain matching triples.

12.2 Evaluation

Thus, a *Union* has been created to concatenate the results obtained from DS1 and DS4. As can be seen in the query plan, the *Filter* has been pushed down beyond the service operator in order to execute it already at the local data source and hence, utilize any existing indexes.

The second sequence sub-plan (*Union* in the center of the figure) restricts all bindings for ?s to resources that match the pattern { ?s rdf:type sobs:SunspotRelativeNumbers }. Apparently, the estimated result cardinality of the first sequence sub-plan was lower than the one of this sub-plan, which is why the other was executed first. Assuming the first sub-plan returned 100 bindings for ?s, the row-blocking based query execution (see Section 9.2.5) only requires one sub-query with 100 initial bindings for the second sub-plan in order to process this distributed 2-way join. Finally, the third sequence sub-plan (*Union* on the right hand side of the figure), which is a three-way *Union*, adds ?creator bindings to each one of the intermediate solutions, as long as the pattern matches. Obviously, the triple pattern { ?s dc:creator ?creator } had the biggest estimated cardinalty, which is why it is the last sub-plan of the sequence.

The result of Query 3 is shown in Table 12.5. It contains a total of 17 solutions sorted by the time stamp variable ?dt. It can be seen that the observations have been recorded by different scientists based on their weekly schedules. Query 5 and 6 will be used later in order to retrieve details about scientists.

Table 12.5: Results of Query 3.

s	creator	dt
ds4:SunspotRelativeNumbers_8426	ds3:ASchroll	"2001-01-02T07:55:00Z"^^xsd:dateTime
ds4:SunspotRelativeNumbers_8427	ds3:WOtruba	"2001-01-04T11:33:00Z"^^xsd:dateTime
ds4:SunspotRelativeNumbers_8428	ds3:WOtruba	"2001-01-05T09:36:00Z"^^xsd:dateTime
ds4:SunspotRelativeNumbers_8429	ds3:WOtruba	"2001-01-06T10:30:00Z"^^xsd:dateTime
ds4:SunspotRelativeNumbers_8430	ds3:WOtruba	"2001-01-09T09:35:00Z"^^xsd:dateTime
ds4:SunspotRelativeNumbers_8431	ds3:WOtruba	"2001-01-10T08:44:00Z"^^xsd:dateTime
ds4:SunspotRelativeNumbers_8432	ds3:HFreislich	"2001-01-11T09:20:00Z"^^xsd:dateTime
ds4:SunspotRelativeNumbers_8433	ds3:HFreislich	"2001-01-12T09:25:00Z"^^xsd:dateTime
ds4:SunspotRelativeNumbers_8434	ds3:HFreislich	"2001-01-14T11:25:00Z"^^xsd:dateTime
ds4:SunspotRelativeNumbers_8435	ds3:HFreislich	"2001-01-15T10:45:00Z"^^xsd:dateTime
ds4:SunspotRelativeNumbers_8436	ds3:HFreislich	"2001-01-16T12:07:00Z"^^xsd:dateTime
ds4:SunspotRelativeNumbers_8437	ds3:HFreislich	"2001-01-17T08:23:00Z"^^xsd:dateTime
ds4:SunspotRelativeNumbers_8438	ds3:ASchroll	"2001-01-19T09:40:00Z"^^xsd:dateTime
ds4:SunspotRelativeNumbers_8439	ds3:ASchroll	"2001-01-20T08:00:00Z"^^xsd:dateTime
ds4:SunspotRelativeNumbers_8440	ds3:ASchroll	"2001-01-23T10:50:00Z"^^xsd:dateTime
ds4:SunspotRelativeNumbers_8441	ds3:WOtruba	"2001-01-26T10:00:00Z"^^xsd:dateTime
ds4:SunspotRelativeNumbers_8442	ds3:WOtruba	"2001-01-28T13:50:00Z"^^xsd:dateTime

Query 4

Query 4 retrieves details on a specific observation record. Basically, this can be achieved by two different query forms: SELECT and DESCRIBE. While the first form returns a query solution as usual,

12 Demonstration and Evaluation

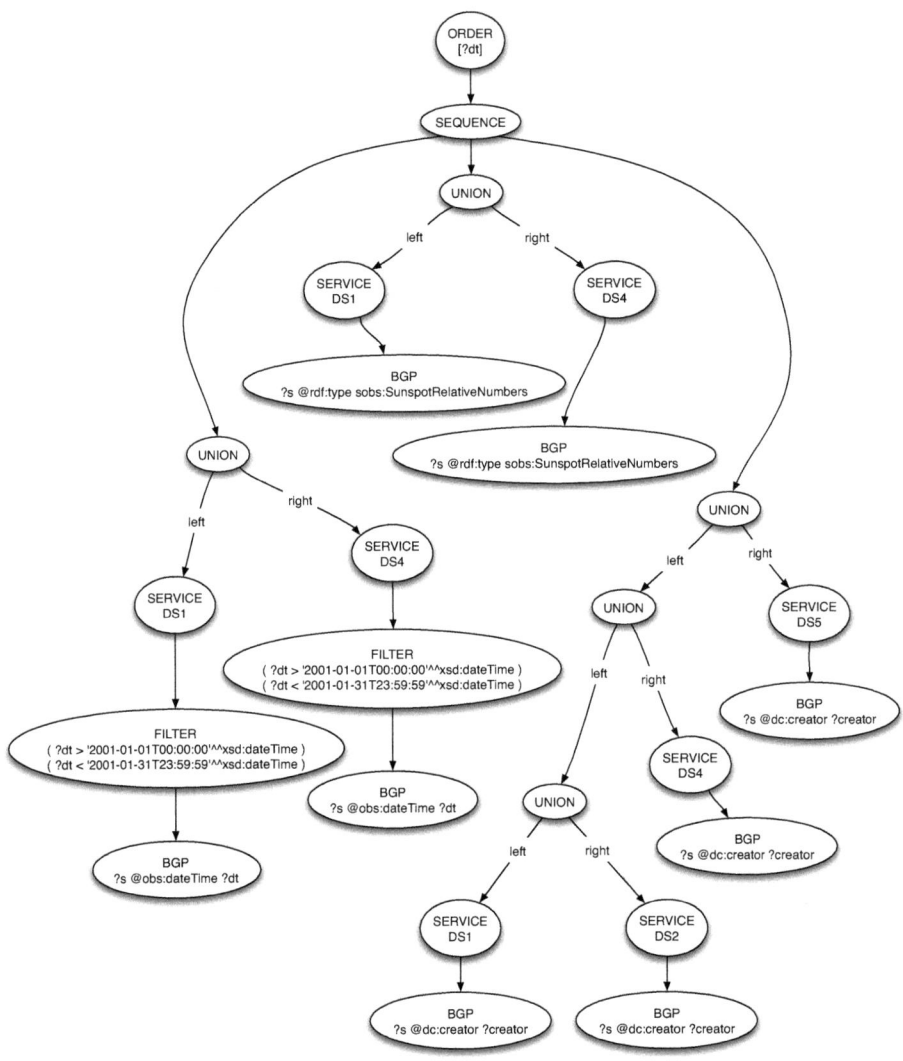

Figure 12.7: Plan for Query 3 (using triple-based federator).

the DESCRIBE variant returns an RDF graph which contains all the triples known for a specific resource as the subject. The SELECT variant of Query 4 explicitly contains a single triple pattern with the observation record's URI as a subject, and the variables ?property and ?value) as property and object. As a consequence, this query will return all matching triples about the specific resource as shown in Table 12.6. The corresponding query plan is depicted in Figure 12.8. Because the resource is only known at DS4, the resulting plan is very simple. The DESCRIBE variant for Query 4 returns the same information, however, in the form of an RDF graph consisting of all matching triples. This DESCRIBE query result is printed in Listing 12.2.

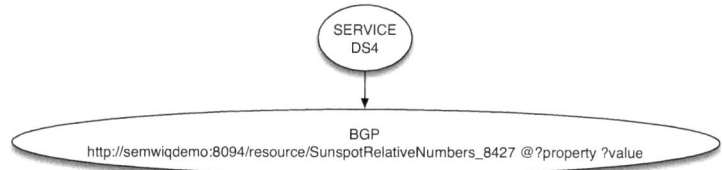

Figure 12.8: Plan for Query 4 (using triple-based federator).

Table 12.6: Results of Query 4.

property	value
sobs:rValue	81
obs:phenomenon	astro:SunspotNumbers
obs:phenomenon	astro:SolarSurface
obs:phenomenon	astro:SunspotGroups
obs:phenomenon	astro:Sunspots
obs:phenomenon	astro:Sun
obs:phenomenon	astro:Photosphere
dc:subject	dbpedia:Sun
dc:subject	dbpedia:Sunspot
dc:subject	dbpedia:Photosphere
dc:creator	<http://semwiqdemo:8093/resource/WOtruba>
sobs:seeingQuality	25
sobs:spots	39
obs:dateTime	"2001-01-04T11:33:00Z"^^xsd:dateTime
sobs:groups	8
rdf:type	sobs:SunspotRelativeNumbers
obs:site	<http://www.kso.ac.at/>

Query 5

Consider, a scientist using SemWIQ would like to contact the scientist who recorded a specific observation. Query 5 shows such an example. It retrieves the name and, optionally, the e-mail address

12 Demonstration and Evaluation

```
<http://semwiqdemo:8094/resource/SunspotRelativeNumbers_8427>
        a       sobs:SunspotRelativeNumbers ;
        dc:creator <http://semwiqdemo:8093/resource/WOtruba> ;
        sobs:groups 8 ;
        sobs:rValue 81 ;
        sobs:seeingQuality 25 ;
        sobs:spots 39 ;
        obs:dateTime "2001-01-04T11:33:00Z"^^xsd:dateTime ;
        obs:site <http://www.kso.ac.at/> ;
        dc:subject <http://dbpedia.org/resource/Sun>, <http://dbpedia.org/resource/Sunspot>, <http://
                dbpedia.org/resource/Photosphere> ;
        obs:phenomenon <http://www.astro.physik.uni-goettingen.de/~hessman/rdf/IAU93#SolarSurface> , <
                http://www.astro.physik.uni-goettingen.de/~hessman/rdf/IAU93#SunspotGroups> , <http://www.
                astro.physik.uni-goettingen.de/~hessman/rdf/IAU93#SunspotNumbers> , <http://www.astro.
                physik.uni-goettingen.de/~hessman/rdf/IAU93#Sun> , <http://www.astro.physik.uni-goettingen
                .de/~hessman/rdf/IAU93#Sunspots> , <http://www.astro.physik.uni-goettingen.de/~hessman/rdf
                /IAU93#Photosphere> .
```

Listing 12.2: Results of the DESCRIBE variant for Query 4.

of the creator of the sunspot relative numbers record from January 4th, 2001. The e-mail address is obtained using an OPTIONAL pattern, since otherwise the query would not return any results in case there was no e-mail address available. Actually, the full e-mail address is not retrieved because of privacy reasons. Within the Semantic Web it is very common to provide only a SHA1 checksum in order to match the e-mail address from a list of already known addresses (i.e. local address book). There is only one result because the observation has only one creator:

name	mbox
Wolfgang Otruba	7d7f16c9b0c26fb0621539382eed66df7d3d5eca

The corresponding query plan is depicted in Figure 12.9. After the root projection for ?name, ?mbox, there is a *Conditional* operator, which is effectively a substitute-based *LeftJoin* (see Section 9.2.5). Its left sub-plan consists of a 2-way *Sequence* over two other sub-plans and the right sub-plan of the *Conditional* consists of a single *Service* fetching the optional foaf:mbox_sha1sum from DS3. Query execution starts from the left with obtaining the creator for the sunspot relative numbers record at DS4. All bindings for ?creator (which is actually a single one because the record was created by one scientist) are merged with the bindings for ?creator and ?name obtained from DS3. Finally, after executing the *Conditional*, the result also contains optional bindings for ?mbox.

Query 6

Next, consider the user wants to explore recent publications of the scientist who made the observation from January 4th, 2001. Query 6 retrieves the title, year, and optionally the book title (in case of proceedings or journal contributions) of all publications where the observer appears as a co-author since the year 2000. Additionally, the results are ordered by year and title.

The query plan for Query 6 is depicted in Figure 12.10. It is has become very complex now. The plan has a projection as root node, selecting only the variables ?year, ?title, and ?bookTitle,

12.2 Evaluation

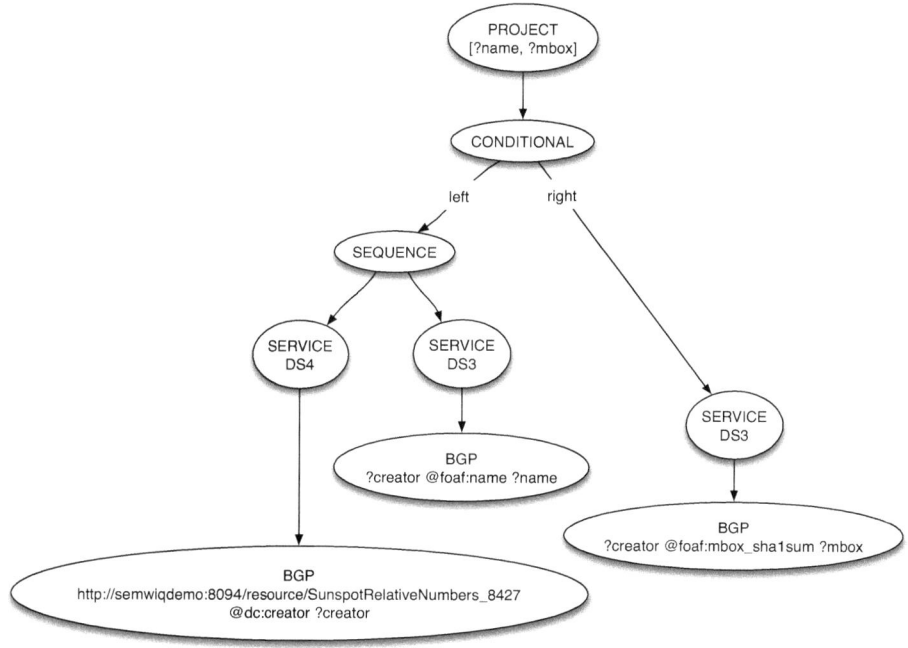

Figure 12.9: Plan for Query 5 (using triple-based federator).

sorted with an *Order* operator by ?year and ?title. Next, the plan contains a *Conditional* operator with a left and right sub-plan denoted as s_L and s_R in the following. Both are *Sequence* operators, which is a substitute-based *Join* as already known. s_L is a three-way join executed from the left with the sub-plans q_1, q_2, q_3. Query evaluation starts with q_1, which returns all available publications since the year 2000 from DS5. Note that only DS5 contains relevant information, otherwise there would be a *Union* over several *Service* sub-plans. Next, solution bindings from q_1 with variables ?pub, ?year are passed on to the execution of q_2, which adds a binding for ?title in case of compatible bindings (*merge*, Section 4.4.3). It can be seen, that q_2 is a *Union* over sub-plans delegated to DS1 and DS5, because both data sources are interesting for the corresponding pattern. The third sub-plan q_3 is a *Union* sequence over four data sources, DS1, DS2, DS4, and DS5. Although all of them know about resources Wolfgang Otruba is dc:author of in general, at execution time only bindings from DS5 will be relevant and merged. All other sub-plans will not have a match because the values for ?pub selected by q_1 also came from DS5.

The right *Conditional* sub-plan s_R is a *Sequence* over two sub-plans. The first sub-plan (left hand

215

12 Demonstration and Evaluation

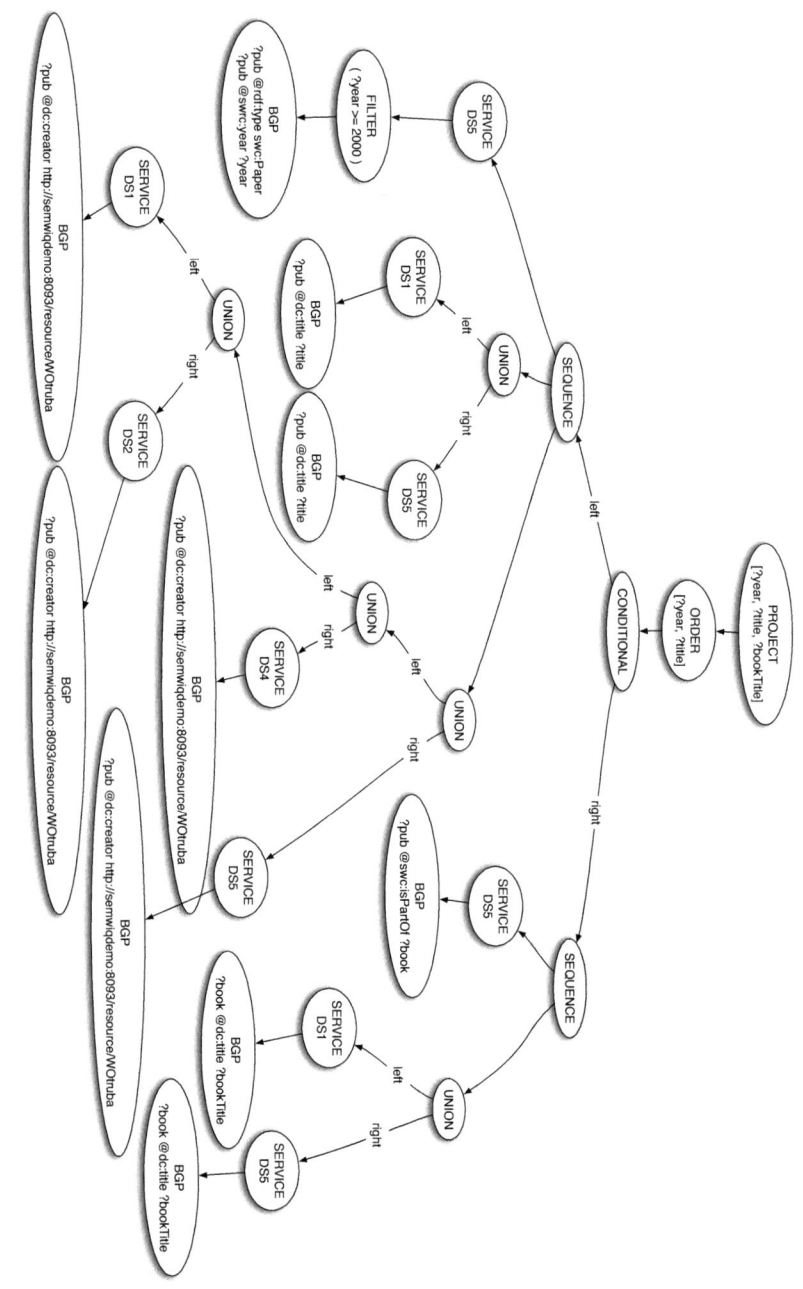

Figure 12.10: Plan for Query 6 (using triple-based federator).

216

12.2 Evaluation

side) selects any books a publication might be part of (`swc:isPartOf` property). The solution bindings are then joined against the right sub-plan, which merges the corresponding `dc:title`. In this case, DS1 and DS5 are considered as relevant, since both contain matching triples. However, in the end only DS5 will contribute any book titles. After executing the *Conditional* operator, any book titles will be merged optionally to the final result bindings.

The result of Query 6 is printed in Table 12.7. Almost all publications have a book title, there is only one from the year 2000 which has none. Wolfgang Otruba, which is the creator of the observation from January 4th, 2001 is appearing as a co-author of all the publications in the table.

Table 12.7: Results of Query 6.

year	title	booktitle
2000	Automatic image processing in the frame of a solar flare alerting system	-
2000	Evaluation of a low-end architecture for colloborative software development, remote sensing, and data analysis from multiple sites	Advanced Global Communications Technologies for Astronomy, Proceedings of SPIE
2000	Signatures of large-scale changes associated with the May 2	AAS/Solar Physics Division Meeting, 32, (2000)
2000	Statistical properties relevant to solar flare prediction	Hvar Observatory Bulletin Vol. 24
2000	Statistical properties relevant to solar flare prediction	Hvar Observatory Bulletin Vol. 24
2001	Observations of NOAA 8210 Using MOF and DHC of Kanzelhöhe Solar Observatory	The Dynamic Sun, Proceedings of the Summerschool and Workshop held at the Kanzelhöhe
2005	Loop-top altitude decrease in an X-class flare	Hvar Observatory Bulletin
2006	Hemispheric Sunspot Numbers 1945-2004: data merging from two observatories	Central European Astrophysics Bulletin
2006	Hemispheric sunspot numbers Rn and Rs from 1945-2004: catalogue and N-S asymmetry analysis for solar cycles 18-23	Astronomy & Astrophysics
2006	Solar Monitoring Program at Kanzelhöhe Observatory	Sun and Geosphere
2006	X-ray sources and magnetic reconnection in the X3.9 flare of 2003 November 3	Astronomy & Astrophysics
2007	KEAS::Grid	Central European Astrophysics Bulletin

Query 7

Because observations and publications have been tagged with keywords (using `dc:subject`), it is now possible to find related publications for given observations and vice-versa. Query 7 shows an example of the first use case: for a given observation record, which is the sunspot relative numbers observation from January 4th, 2001, it finds the title and subjects of related publications.

The query plan is shown in Figure 12.11. It consists of a *Project* and *Order* followed by a 4-way *Sequence*. The first sub-plan (left hand side) selects all papers and binds their URIs to ?pub. Next, a *Union* over DS1 and DS5 joins `dc:title` bindings, and in a further step, `dc:subject` bindings are joined from DS1, DS2, and DS4. Finally, the solution bindings are joined against all `dc:subject`

12 Demonstration and Evaluation

properties from the specific observation. Table 12.8 contains the results. There are three different related publications, two of them matching based on two subjects.

Table 12.8: Results of Query 7.

title	s
Hemispheric Sunspot Numbers 1945-2004: data merging from two observatories	dbpedia:Sun
Hemispheric Sunspot Numbers 1945-2004: data merging from two observatories	dbpedia:Sunspot
Hemispheric sunspot numbers Rn and Rs from 1945-2004: catalogue and N-S asymmetry analysis for solar cycles 18-23	dbpedia:Sun
Hemispheric sunspot numbers Rn and Rs from 1945-2004: catalogue and N-S asymmetry analysis for solar cycles 18-23	dbpedia:Sunspot
High Cadence Digital Full Disk H-alpha; Patrol Device at Kanzelhöhe	dbpedia:Sun

Query 8

The last query is an ASK query used to check if there are any observations of the solar chromosphere recorded with a specific detector (e.g. Pulnix TM-1010). The instance-based federator is used, because subsumption reasoning is required. Basically, also for ASK queries, a query plan is compiled as depicted in Figure 12.12. It is executed as usual, however, the query engine can already stop evaluation once a result has been found. In some cases this might be more efficient for such boolean query forms. In our example, the result is *true*.

Query execution starts with retrieving the URI for the detector named "Pulnix TM-1010" from DS1 (bound to ?det). The right sub-plan of the *Sequence* joins any observations (*interesting* sub-classes of obs:ScientificObservation) that have a property obs:detector with the corresponding URI as a value (matching ?det). Additionally, a observation record must have a matching obs:phenomenon value, which is a SKOS concept for *Chromoshpere* as part of the IVOA (*International Virtual Observatory Alliance*) taxonomy.

12.2 Evaluation

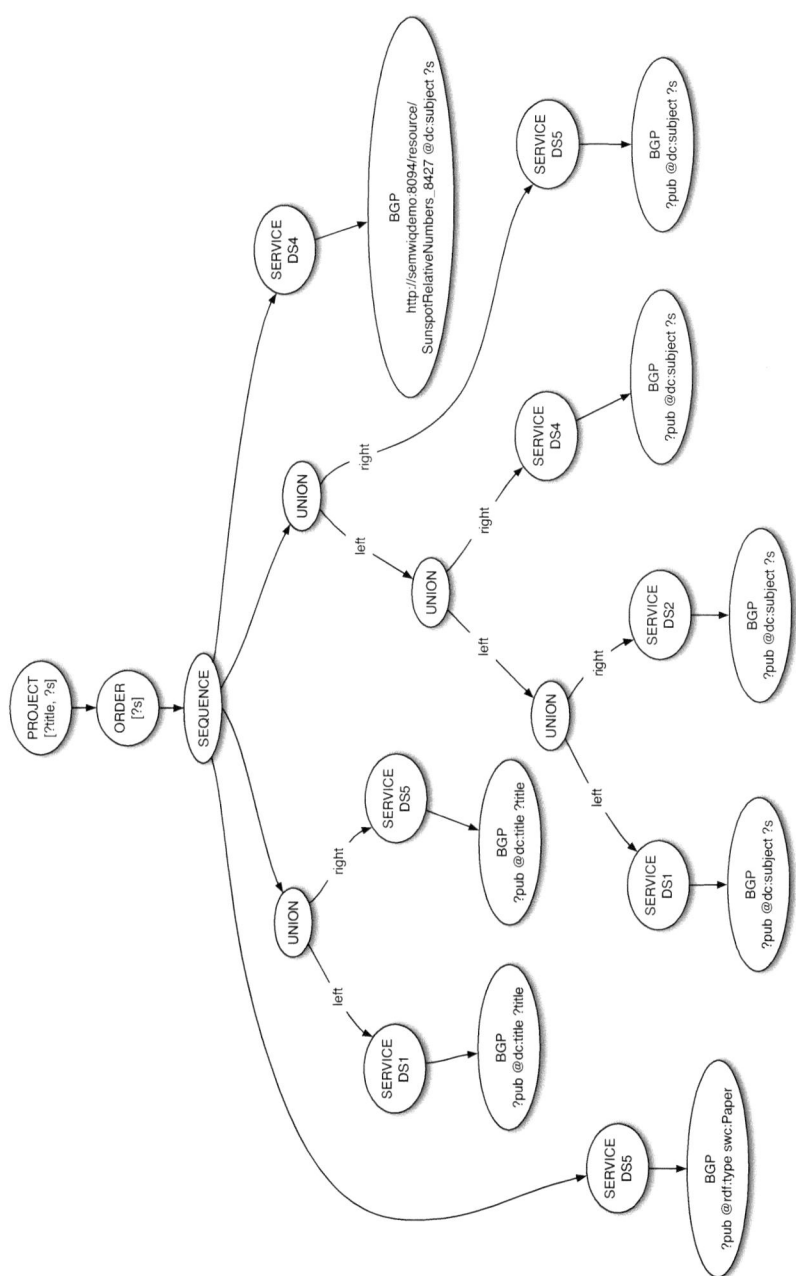

Figure 12.11: Plan for Query 7 (using triple-based federator).

12 Demonstration and Evaluation

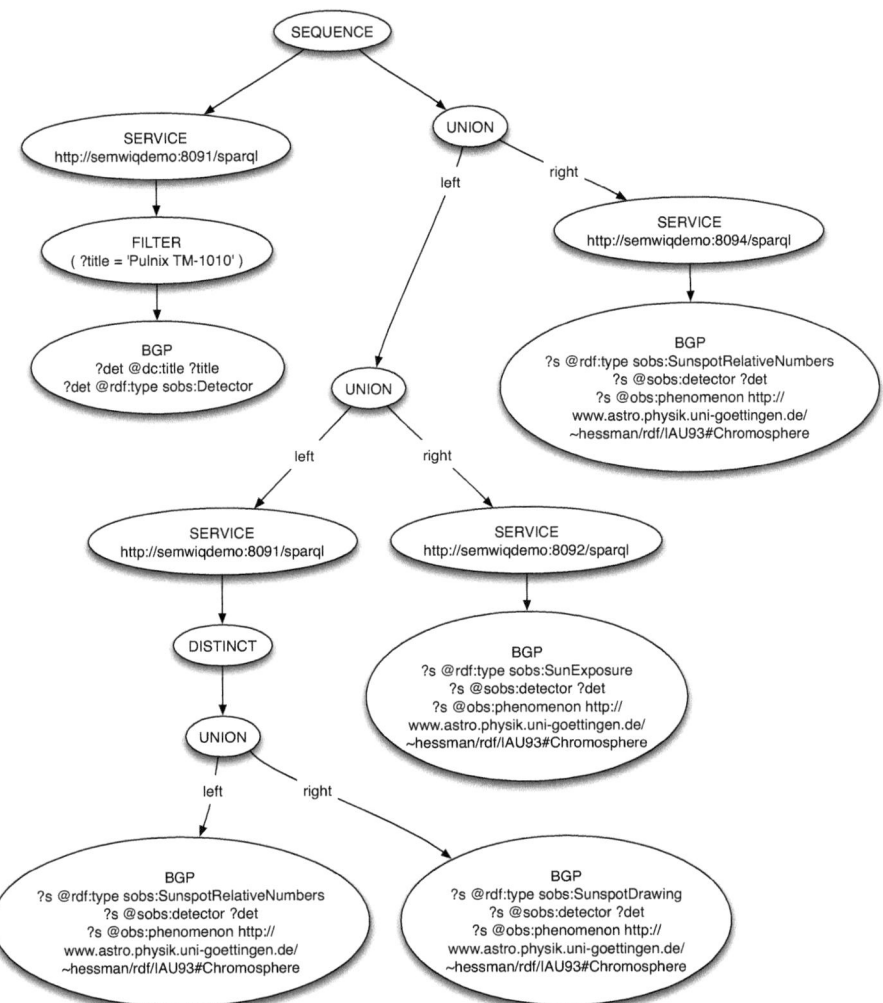

Figure 12.12: Plan for Query 8 (using instance-based federator).

12.2.2 Performance

As described in Chapter 9, the SemWIQ query optimizer consists of two optimization phases: pre-optimization before federation, and post-optimization afterwards. One of the most important logical optimization steps is the push-down of filter expressions, which also involves the transformation and simplification of filter expressions. Currently, only the most important rules have been implemented, such as De Morgan's Law, the Distributive Law, and the Associative Law. The optimizer does not eliminate any redundant or unsatisfiable expressions at the moment.

The execution of joins is based on the substitute algorithm and row blocking via SPARQL as explained in Section 9.2.5. The optimization is currently done by re-ordering the sub-plans of a join sequence based on expected cardinalities. There are still some situations which would require additional optimization of course. Basically, query optimization is a huge research topic of its own. Improvements to the optimizer will be added in future as described in Section 14.2.

In order to provide some quantitative results, time measures for the previous example queries are provided in Table 12.9. The measures include times for the pre-optimization, federation, and post-optimization phases, the total plan compilation time, as well as the time until the first result was received and the total query execution time. The measures where obtained by executing the queries from the case study described before. The mediator was running on a Apple Macbook with a 2.16 GHz Intel Core 2 Duo CPU, 2 GB RAM, and Mac OS X. The five endpoints where running on two equally equipped Linux workstations, each one with two 1.6 GHz AMD Opteron CPUs and 2 GB RAM (DS1–3 on one host and DS4–5 on the other one). The Macbook was connected to the endpoints over a 2 Mbit internet connection. All queries where executed three times after one warm-up query. The average of the three sample measures are printed in Table 12.9.

Table 12.9: Query execution time measures.

Query	Pre-opt	Federate	Post-opt	Compile	1st result	Exec time	Total
1	<1 ms	17 ms	6 ms	23 ms	102 ms	17250 ms	17273 ms
2	1 ms	362 ms	9 ms	372 ms	459 ms	30573 ms	33944 ms
3	<1 ms	52 ms	23 ms	75 ms	2126 ms	2126 ms	2201 ms
4	<1 ms	28 ms	1 ms	29 ms	358 ms	367 ms	396 ms
5	<1 ms	41 ms	6 ms	47 ms	493 ms	496 ms	543 ms
6	<1 ms	74 ms	29 ms	103 ms	1108 ms	1109 ms	1212 ms
7	<1 ms	54 ms	20 ms	74 ms	2391 ms	2391 ms	2465 ms
8	<1 ms	223 ms	16 ms	239 ms	-	481 ms	720 ms

The pre-optimization step is typically very fast (<1 ms). It only involves traversing relatively small initial query plans and filter expressions. The federation step is a bit more complex, since RDFStats statistics are accessed. RDFStats calculation times heavily depend on the RDF store used (Jena TDB in this case, which features an efficient LRU cache). When using the subsumption reasoning feature of the instance-based federator (Query 2 and 8), the federator is slower. This is because RDFStats statistics are accessed much more often and query plans usually become rather large. Post-optimization times correlate with the number of *Sequence* operators and their sub-plans, because the most costly step is the statistics-based cardinality estimation during join optimization.

Concerning the time until the first result is received, it can be seen that this value is sometimes nearly equal to the total execution time (Queries 3-7). One reason for this is that *Order* often needs to be processed at the mediator, in which case it is not possible to stream results directly to the client (Queries 3, 6, and 7). Another reason might be, that the overall results are obtained by the same bindings block because of the row-blocking feature (Query 4 and 5).

Execution performance is rather bad in case of Query 1 and Query 2 which is mainly because the *Distinct* operation is executed at the mediator and a lot of bindings have to be retrieved. Such queries will be optimized as part of future work (see Section 14.2). Basically, it is possible to copy down *Distinct* operations in many cases and execute them twice, once at the remote data sources in order to reduce the amount of transferred bindings and a second time at the mediator as part of the global plan.

12.2.3 Navigation based on Linked Data Principles

Accessing information in a information integration system has to be supported by various means of searching and browsing. While the mediator acts as the central point of access and search gateway, the *Linked Data* principles introduced in Section 4.5 can be used to support the browsing aspect. Similarly to the traditional World Wide Web, where documents and multimedia resources can be browsed based on hyperlinks, RDF graphs can be browsed as *Linked Data*. For each thing (RDF resource), that has a URI, the corresponding web server may either provide an HTML page for human users or plain RDF triples. In the second case, a special *Linked Data* browser can be used to render a suitable page with navigable links.

This paradigm has been implemented in SemWIQ also. Because the *semwiq-endpoint* package integrates the *Linked Data Interface* Pubby (Cyganiak and Bizer 2009), it is possible to browse SemWIQ data sources directly. Additionally, the *semwiq-webapp* component provides a browser based on *Snorql* from D2R-Server (Chris Bizer and Richard Cyganiak 2006), which can be used to browse query results based on hyperlinks. The user may start with a global query for sunspot observations. When scrolling through the results, (s)he may select a specific observation record which is linked to other things such as its creator, the observation instrument, detector, filters, observation site, subject terms, publications, etc. The user does not necessarily have to formulate further queries, but can navigate through the distributed graph directly. Additional links from and to other datasets on the *Web of Data* can be added any time to increase the overall benefit. This way of Semantic Web-based data integration opens numerous ways of adding and merging information on the Web, all due to interoperability of open data and standards.

12.2 Evaluation

Given the case study setup, consider a scientist has used Query 1 to get a list of classes as shown in Table 12.3. The SemWIQ web application renders an HTML page as shown by screenshot (1) in Figure 12.13. All result values are clickable and additionally, there are two icons on the right side of each value. The first icon (a box with an arrow) is only shown if the value is a URI, but not in case of a literal. It directly points to the URI such that the browser will try to resolve it when clicked. The other icon which looks like a box in a box is used for provenance as described in Section 9.2.6: when moving the mouse over the icon, a tooltip with the origin (SPARQL endpoint URI) of the value appears. By clicking directly on a value (or the first icon in case of a URI value) the user can start browsing. For example, if the scientist would like to see which conference proceedings are known, (s)he can click on the result value `swrc:Proceedings`. The arrow in the figure points to another screenshot which shows the rendered result page (2). Three proceedings are known and the example continues with a click on the second result which brings up all information known about the proceeding entitled "The Dynamic Sun [...]" from 2001 (3). As part of the virtual dataset just one paper is known as part of the proceeding and a click on the corresponding link brings us to screenshot (4). Besides general details, all the authors are listed. It is now assumed, that the scientist would like to know more about Mr. Otruba (5), who is working at the Kanzelhöhe solar observatory. There is a lot of information about different observations recorded by Mr. Otruba (the screenshot is cropped). A click on a specific observation record shows all the details and a link to a FITS file (*Flexible Image Transport System*, a file format for astronomical observations (International Astronomical Union 2008)) via `obs:fileUri`. The information is virtually combined from different registered data sources while browsing.

When clicking on the external link icon, the URI of the corresponding resource value is resolved. If the URI points to a resource served by a SemWIQ endpoint, an HTML page will be rendered providing all details about the resource. Vocabulary concepts can be resolved in order to get a human readable description and detailed documentation. All ontological concepts such as terms pointing to DBpedia can be resolved to get a meaningful description. For instance, consider the user wants to know, what the `dc:subject` `http://dbpedia.org/resource/H-alpha` of the observation in screenshot (6) means. By clicking the icon, the browser will resolve the URI and provide the information depicted in Figure 12.14.

12 Demonstration and Evaluation

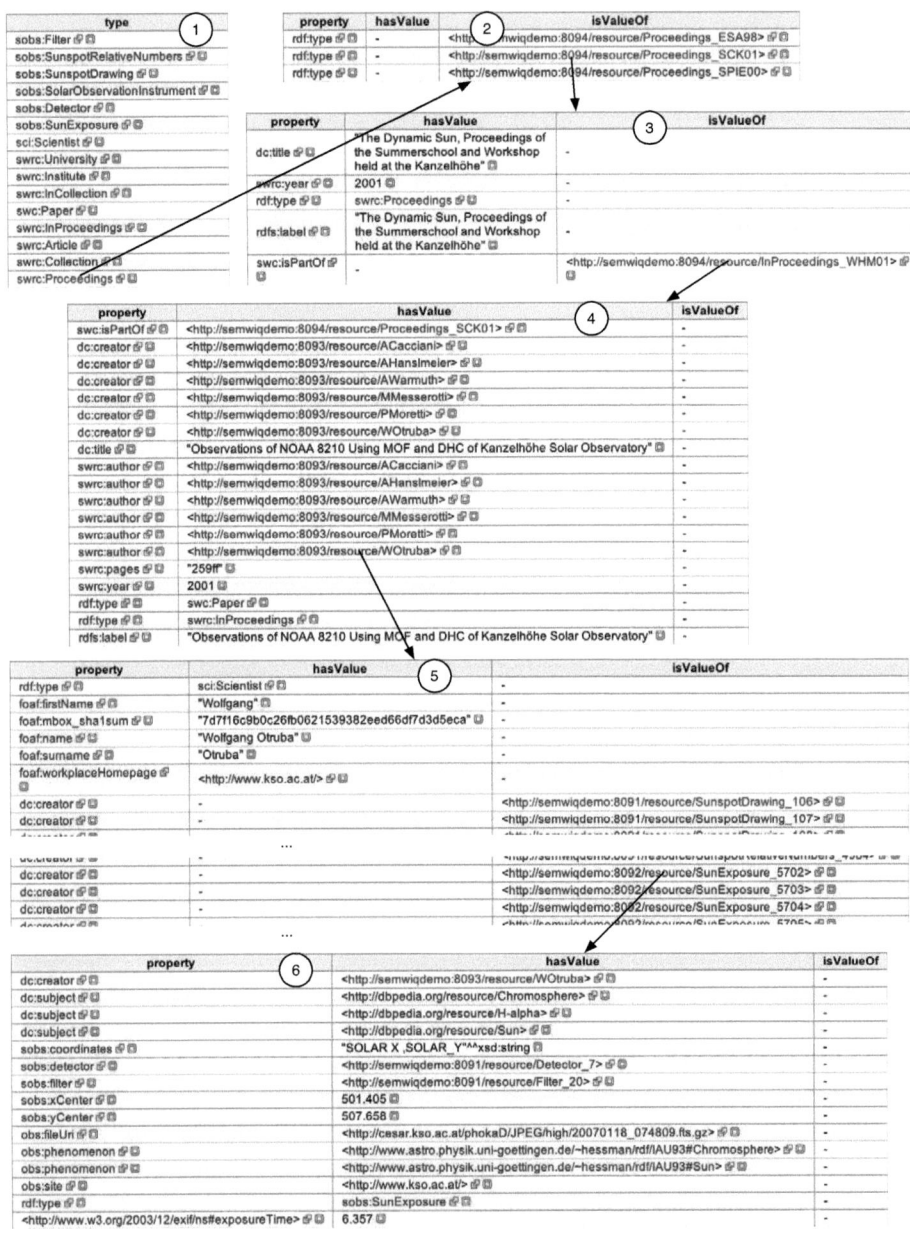

Figure 12.13: Browsing Linked Data with SemWIQ (screenshots).

12.2 Evaluation

About: H-alpha
An Entity in Data Space: dbpedia.org

In physics and astronomy, H-alpha, also written Hα, is a specific red visible spectral line created by hydrogen with a wavelength of 6562.8 Å. According to the Bohr model of the atom, electrons exist in quantized energy levels surrounding the atom's nucleus. These energy levels are described by the principal quantum number n = 1, 2, 3, ... Electrons may only exist in these states, and may only transit between these states.

Property	Value
dbpedia-owl:thumbnail	• http://upload.wikimedia.org/wikipedia/commons/thumb/5/55/Bohr-atom-PAR.svg/200px-Bohr-atom-PAR.svg.png
dbpprop:abstract	• In physics and astronomy, H-alpha, also written Hα, is a specific red visible spectral line created by hydrogen with a wavelength of 6562.8 Å. According to the Bohr model of the atom, electrons exist in quantized energy levels surrounding the atom's nucleus. These energy levels are described by the principal quantum number n = 1, 2, 3, ... Electrons may only exist in these states, and may only transit between these states. The set of transitions from n ≥ 3 to n = 2 is called the Balmer series and its members are named sequentially by Greek letters: n = 3 to n = 2 is called Balmer-alpha or H-alpha, n = 4 to n = 2 is called H-beta, n = 5 to n = 2 is called H-gamma, etc. For the Lyman series the naming convention is: n = 2 to n = 1 is called Lyman-alpha, n = 3 to n = 1 is called Lyman-beta, etc. H-alpha has a wavelength of 6562.81 Å, is visible in the red part of the electromagnetic spectrum, and is the easiest way for astronomers to trace the ionized hydrogen content of gas clouds. Since it takes nearly as much energy to excite the hydrogen atom's electron from n = 1 to n = 3 as it does to ionize the hydrogen atom, the probability of the electron being excited to n = 3 without being removed from the atom is very small. Instead, after being ionized, the electron and proton recombine to form a new hydrogen atom. In the new atom, the electron may begin in any energy level, and subsequently cascades to the ground state (n = 1), emitting photons with each transition. Approximately half the time, this cascade will include the n = 3 to n = 2 transition and the atom will emit H-alpha light. Therefore, the H-alpha line occurs where hydrogen is being ionized. The H-alpha line saturates (self-absorbs) relatively easily because hydrogen is the primary component of nebulae, so while it can indicate the shape and extent of the cloud, it cannot be used to accurately determine the cloud's mass. Instead, molecules such as carbon dioxide, carbon monoxide, formaldehyde, ammonia, or methyl cyanide are typically used to determine the mass of a cloud.
dbpprop:hasPhotoCollection	http://www4.wiwiss.fu-berlin.de/flickrwrappr/photos/H-alpha
rdfs:comment	• In physics and astronomy, H-alpha, also written Hα, is a specific red visible spectral line created by hydrogen with a wavelength of 6562.8 Å. According to the Bohr model of the atom, electrons exist in quantized energy levels surrounding the atom's nucleus. These energy levels are described by the principal quantum number n = 1, 2, 3, ... Electrons may only exist in these states, and may only transit between these states.
rdfs:label	• H-alpha
owl:sameAs	• freebase:H-alpha
skos:subject	• dbpedia:Category:Hydrogen_physics • dbpedia:Category:Astronomical_spectroscopy • dbpedia:Category:Atomic_physics

Figure 12.14: DBpedia page for `http://dbpedia.org/resource/H-alpha`.

225

12 Demonstration and Evaluation

13 Conclusion

In this PhD thesis a novel approach for virtual information integration based on Semantic Web concepts is presented. Compared to traditional information integration systems, which are typically based on relational database systems, SemWIQ follows a concept-based approach. All the information integrated via SemWIQ is mapped to distributed ontologies which can be easily extended and published on the web. Thus, data is described based on its meaning, instead of a functional data model. The meta model used for the representation of ontologies as well as integrated information is the Resource Description Framework (RDF). It is a standardized knowledge representation model used in the Semantic Web and it has several characteristics which make it well suited as a global meta model for information integration.

The system is based on a mediator-wrapper architecture: the SemWIQ mediator delegates subqueries to several wrapped endpoints, which translate data from heterogeneous data sources to RDF. By contrast to other recent approaches, source data is not just mapped to RDF ontologies, it is fully translated and processed in RDF. In order to accurately represent all the integrated information from different kinds of information systems (relational databases, XML files and databases, spreadsheets, CSV files, web services, etc.), the global metamodel requires a high level of expressiveness. RDF provides high expressiveness, but its core is still simple enough to facilitate query processing. It is a reflexive graph-based model, which can be extended by higher level concepts and additional meaning represented in RDF itself.

In SemWIQ, global queries are formulated in SPARQL, which is a standardized query language for RDF graphs. It has similar capabilities to SQL, but since it is based on graph pattern matching, query formulation is based on RDF graphs and thus, very close to human conception of knowledge. In order to provide acceptable performance and an extensible framework for query optimization, the SemWIQ mediator is based on a holistic, pipelined query processing approach.

One of the major contributions of this work is a scalable federation approach based on RDF statistics which are generated by the RDFStats sub-component. It features a statistics generator for RDF graphs, which is generating several histograms for subject URIs and property values. Based on these histograms and several estimation functions, the mediator is able to federate a global query plan *offline*, i.e. without explicitly accessing each registered data source. RDFStats statistics are also used for query optimization and it will be used for the adaptive SPARQL query builder described in Section 14.1. Two further contributions are the optimization of D2R-Server (Chris Bizer and Richard

13 Conclusion

Cyganiak 2006), which is used to wrap relational database systems and the development of XLWrap (Langegger and Wöß 2009c), which is currently the only existing spreadsheet-to-RDF wrapper that is able to wrap any spreadsheet layout (including multi-dimensional cross tables) to arbitrary RDF graphs. The optimization of D2R-Server was very important, since the performance of wrappers greatly affects the overall query processing performance.

The proposed approach is very flexible, since no explicit global schema needs to be maintained and data sources can be easily added and removed. Adding a data source is a matter of registering the URL of the wrapper's SPARQL endpoint at the mediator. There is no integrated global schema which has to be altered. The system is basically not limited in terms of number of data sources or ontological concepts used to represent information. Once a new data source is registered and RDFStats statistics are available to the mediator, the federator considers the new data source for future queries. It will only delegate a sub-query, if the data source would contribute any sub-results, which is estimated based on statistics.

Although the case study just showed one possible use case, SemWIQ can be used for many other data sharing scenarios as long as wrappers exist for the corresponding source information systems. Otherwise, a wrapper may be created as explained in Section 10.1. Combined with latest research towards new graphical user interfaces for linked data on the Semantic Web, the proposed approach is well suited for large-scale collaborative knowledge sharing in research as well as in the industry. As part of a national research project, SemWIQ has been integrated into the *Grid-enabled Semantic Data Access Middleware* (G-SDAM) in order to enable semantic data integration for the Austrian Grid (Austrian Grid Consortium n.d.).

The content of the PhD thesis is summarized in short. In Part I the fundamental aspects of data, information, and knowledge are introduced and the concepts of data modeling and metamodels are discussed (Chapter 2). It is shown that different data models share a common ontological basis which is very important for the integration of information maintained by heterogeneous systems. In Chapter 3, an introduction to the topic of information integration is provided including a discussion on some of the challenges such as different aspects of heterogeneity. A reference architecture of information integration systems is presented and different techniques for model mapping are discussed. Additionally, a Semantic Web primer (Chapter 4) is provided as part of the background part to introduce the most important concepts such as the *Resource Description Framework* (RDF), the *SPARQL Protocol and RDF Query Language*, and the idea of *Linked Data*.

In Part II a selection of relevant related work is presented. After the general overview in Chapter 5, the mediator-wrapper architecture and some of the early approaches developed during the 1990ies are presented in Chapter 6. In Chapter 7 recent approaches based on Semantic Web concepts and ontologies are introduced including generic systems and systems developed for specific use cases in applied research projects.

The SemWIQ approach is presented in Part III starting with an overview (Chapter 8) introducing the general approach, the architecture, and the query processor. Details on the SemWIQ mediator, extensions to SPARQL, the two federators (triple-based and instance-based), and some implementation notes are given in Chapter 9. In Chapter 10 general considerations concerning SPARQL wrappers are provided. Additionally, the optimized version of D2R-Server, which is used for relational database systems, and XLWrap, a flexible wrapper for spreadsheets, are described. One of the main contributions, the RDFStats statistics generator and query pattern cardinality estimation component is introduced in Chapter 11.

In order to demonstrate the capabilities of the system, a case study in the area of solar astronomy is developed and described in Chapter 12. Based on eight different example queries various features of SemWIQ including query-time subsumption reasoning supported by the instance-based federator are demonstrated. For each of the queries the corresponding global query plan is depicted and the result is shown and discussed. The set of queries includes SELECT, DESCRIBE, and ASK variants with different operators such as *Project, Distinct, Filter, Join, LeftJoin, Union*, etc. As part of the evaluation some performance measures are provided. Additionally, it is shown how novel concepts of browsable Linked Data can be used in order to navigate based on semantic links and explore the virtual global dataset.

13 Conclusion

14 Future Directions

In the following, two future plans are highlighted: the development of a graphical query builder and results visualization tool (Section 14.1) and further query optimization including support for distributed query processing by utilizing grid resources (Section 14.2). A significant amount of feedback and feature requests have been received also for XLWrap (Langegger and Wöß 2009c), which will be continuously extended in future as well. Especially because of the growing interest on opening government data as *Linked Data*, XLWrap has gained increasing interest since most governmental data is currently stored in spreadsheets.

14.1 Graphical Query Builder and Results Visualization

Although a declarative query language like SPARQL provides the most expressiveness, for scientists the formulation of such queries is often inappropriate. What they are demanding for is a rich and adaptive graphical user interface with drag-and-drop functionality. Such a GUI should combine querying and browsing capabilities and integrate special pluggable visualization components for specific kinds of data and multimedia content. In order to support a broad range of different platforms, it is best to implement such a tool as a web application running in a web browser.

A graphical SPARQL query builder has been developed as part the master thesis by Rambichler (2009). The query builder allows users to drag ontological items from a vocabulary toolbox into a working area and hence, construct queries graphically. Because SPARQL graph patterns can be represented as graphs, a query can be constructed by dragging concepts from the toolbox and building a query graph pattern based on the WYSIWYG paradigm. A screenshot of the current prototype is depicted in Figure 14.1. The tool is running in a web browser (in the figure it is the Google Web Toolkit debugger) and thus, it can be accessed from any workstation independent of the platform an operating system which is a very important aspect when the tool is used for scientific purposes.

On the left hand side there is the property editor (1) and the vocabulary toolbox (2). Queries are built inside of the working area (3), which is separated into three sections: the actual space where graph patterns are constructed, a section which allows to add solution modifiers to the query, and a section which provides ordering options. The property editor is automatically adapting to the current selection. It allows to change the type of a graph node and to edit certain attributes such as the URI (in case of URI resources) or data types and language tags (in case of literals). The vocabulary toolbox

14 Future Directions

contains a tree of ontology concepts such as classes and properties, which may be dragged into the working area. Vocabularies can be easily loaded and unloaded. Classes are organized based on the defined sub-class hierarchy.

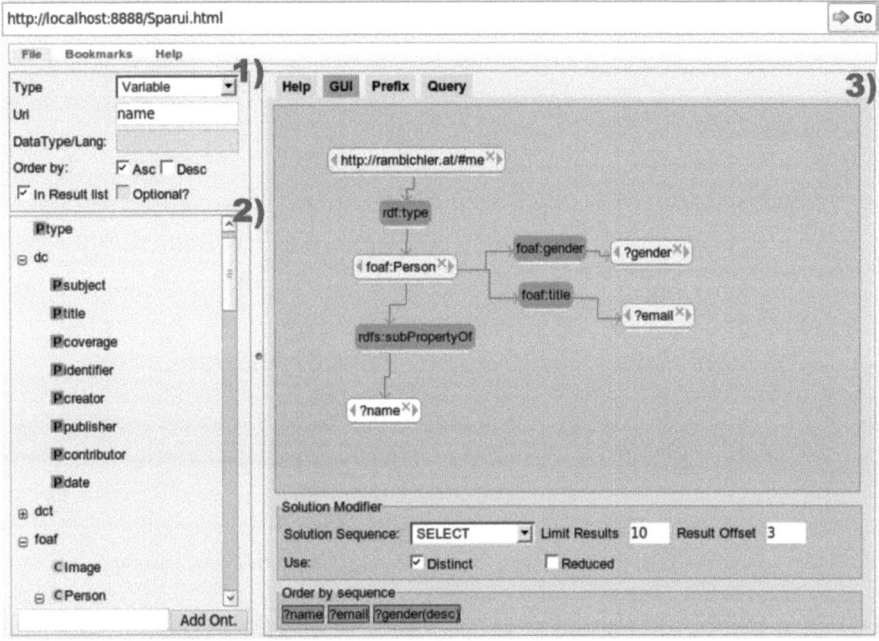

Figure 14.1: SPARUI – A Graphical Query Builder for SemWIQ (Rambichler 2009).

Currently the vocabularies must be loaded manually. However, in a future version the editor will automatically load the vocabularies used in the virtual global dataset based on information obtained from RDFStats statistics. Additionally, based on existing statistics, the editor will automatically adapt and provide only those properties and classes at a given point which would make sense to add to the query pattern. This is possible, because RDFStats estimation functions can be used to predict if a certain pattern will bring any results without executing the query. Furthermore, ontological concepts will be ranked based on their relevance which can also be obtained from RDFStats statistics.

14.2 Query Optimization

Future work regarding the federated query processor includes the refinement of the cost model, further algebraic simplification of filter expressions, and alternative join methods. Especially when used in grid environments it would be feasible to utilize existing grid resources to process expensive join operations. The parallel execution of bushy join plans is used by state-of-the-art distributed database systems such as Oracle or IBM DB2. However, such a distribute query processing approach requires a special infrastructure with a number of addressable nodes used for parallel join processing. In case of the public Semantic Web and the *Web of Data* as outlined in Section 4.5, which consists of distributed and fully autonomous hosts, it is not possible to delegate join processing sub-tasks to some of these hosts. A possible solution would be to integrate SemWIQ mediators into existing grid infrastructures and utilize available grid resources. Existing distributed query processing middleware such as OGSA-DQP (Alpdemir et al. 2003) can then be used by the SemWIQ query processor. The integration of SemWIQ into the Austrian Grid infrastructure is currently in progress as part of a further master thesis (Leitner 2010).

The current cost model is based on the assumption that transferring data is the most expensive part during query processing. Thus, costs are calculated based on the expected cardinalities of intermediate solution bindings. Current Semantic Web query processors such as Jena ARQ are still quite simple too and do not use cost models similar to relational database query processors. The costs for filtering, projecting, and sorting intermediate solutions are not taken into account. In order to reuse relevant algorithms from traditional database optimizers developed during the last decades, the definition of a fine-grained cost-model will be the first step.

The current RDFStats approach is based on histograms over all subjects of the source graph and histograms over all the property values as described in Chapter 11. In order to improve the estimation accuracy for joins, it would be required to pre-process certain join selectivity factors. However, it is clearly impossible to process and store selectivity factors for all possible combinations of edge sequences in an RDF graph. Hence, a more sophisticated approach which takes query logs and other heuristics into account will be required. Future research into this direction is planned in cooperation with Jürgen Umbrich from DERI Galway. These research plans will also include experiments towards multi-dimensional histograms over clustered subjects and properties as dimensions.

14 Future Directions

Appendix

A Mapping Specifications for the Use-Case Demo

A.1 D2RQ Mapping for the KSO Sunspots Database

```
@prefix d2rq: <http://www.wiwiss.fu-berlin.de/suhl/bizer/D2RQ/0.1#> .
@prefix jdbc: <http://d2rq.org/terms/jdbc/> .

@prefix rdf: <http://www.w3.org/1999/02/22-rdf-syntax-ns#> .
@prefix rdfs: <http://www.w3.org/2000/01/rdf-schema#> .
@prefix xsd: <http://www.w3.org/2001/XMLSchema#> .
@prefix dc: <http://purl.org/dc/elements/1.1/> .
@prefix foaf: <http://xmlns.com/foaf/0.1/> .
@prefix vcard: <http://www.w3.org/2006/vcard/ns#> .
@prefix geo: <http://www.w3.org/2003/01/geo/wgs84_pos#> .
@prefix exif: <http://www.w3.org/2003/12/exif/ns#> .

@prefix sci: <http://semwiq.faw.uni-linz.ac.at/global/science/science.owl#> .
@prefix obs: <http://semwiq.faw.uni-linz.ac.at/global/science/observation.owl#> .
@prefix sobs: <http://semwiq.faw.uni-linz.ac.at/global/science/astronomy/solar-observation.owl#> .

@prefix : <http://semwiqdemo:8091/resource/> .

:database a d2rq:Database;
        d2rq:jdbcDriver "com.mysql.jdbc.Driver";
        d2rq:jdbcDSN "jdbc:mysql://localhost/db_keas_sunspots?autoReconnect=true";
        d2rq:username "kso";
        d2rq:password "kso";
        jdbc:keepAlive "3600";
        .

######## SUNSPOT RELATIVE NUMBERS ###########

:SunspotRelativeNumbers a d2rq:ClassMap;
        d2rq:dataStorage :database;
    d2rq:uriPattern "SunspotRelativeNumbers_@@tbl_sunspots_relative_numbers.
        sunspots_relative_numbers_key@@";
        d2rq:class sobs:SunspotRelativeNumbers;
        d2rq:additionalProperty [
                a d2rq:AdditionalProperty;
                d2rq:propertyName obs:phenomenon;
                d2rq:propertyValue <http://www.astro.physik.uni-goettingen.de/~hessman/rdf/IAU93#Sun
                    >;
        ];
```

A Mapping Specifications for the Use-Case Demo

```
        d2rq:additionalProperty [
                a d2rq:AdditionalProperty;
                d2rq:propertyName obs:phenomenon;
                d2rq:propertyValue <http://www.astro.physik.uni-goettingen.de/~hessman/rdf/IAU93#
                    Sunspots>;
        ];
        d2rq:additionalProperty [
                a d2rq:AdditionalProperty;
                d2rq:propertyName obs:phenomenon;
                d2rq:propertyValue <http://www.astro.physik.uni-goettingen.de/~hessman/rdf/IAU93#
                    SolarSurface>;
        ];
        d2rq:additionalProperty [
                a d2rq:AdditionalProperty;
                d2rq:propertyName obs:phenomenon;
                d2rq:propertyValue <http://www.astro.physik.uni-goettingen.de/~hessman/rdf/IAU93#
                    SunspotGroups>;
        ];
        d2rq:additionalProperty [
                a d2rq:AdditionalProperty;
                d2rq:propertyName obs:phenomenon;
                d2rq:propertyValue <http://www.astro.physik.uni-goettingen.de/~hessman/rdf/IAU93#
                    SunspotNumbers>;
        ];
        d2rq:additionalProperty [
                a d2rq:AdditionalProperty;
                d2rq:propertyName obs:phenomenon;
                d2rq:propertyValue <http://www.astro.physik.uni-goettingen.de/~hessman/rdf/IAU93#
                    Photosphere>;
        ];
        d2rq:additionalProperty [
                a d2rq:AdditionalProperty;
                d2rq:propertyName obs:site ;
                d2rq:propertyValue <http://www.kso.ac.at/> ;
        ];
        .
:spots a d2rq:PropertyBridge;
        d2rq:belongsToClassMap :SunspotRelativeNumbers;
        d2rq:property sobs:spots;
        d2rq:column "tbl_sunspots_relative_numbers.spots";
        d2rq:datatype xsd:long;
        .
:groups a d2rq:PropertyBridge;
        d2rq:belongsToClassMap :SunspotRelativeNumbers;
        d2rq:property sobs:groups;
        d2rq:column "tbl_sunspots_relative_numbers.groups";
        d2rq:datatype xsd:long;
        .
:rValue a d2rq:PropertyBridge;
        d2rq:belongsToClassMap :SunspotRelativeNumbers;
        d2rq:property sobs:rValue;
        d2rq:column "tbl_sunspots_relative_numbers.R";
        d2rq:datatype xsd:int;
        .
:seeingQuality a d2rq:PropertyBridge;
        d2rq:belongsToClassMap :SunspotRelativeNumbers;
        d2rq:property sobs:seeingQuality;
```

A.1 D2RQ Mapping for the KSO Sunspots Database

```
        d2rq:join "tbl_sunspots_relative_numbers.seeing_key=tbl_sunspots_seeing_quality.seeing10";
        d2rq:column "tbl_sunspots_seeing_quality.quality";
        d2rq:datatype xsd:int;
        .
:dateTime a d2rq:PropertyBridge;
        d2rq:belongsToClassMap :SunspotRelativeNumbers;
        d2rq:property obs:dateTime;
        d2rq:column "tbl_sunspots_relative_numbers.date";
        d2rq:datatype xsd:dateTime;
        .
:description a d2rq:PropertyBridge;
        d2rq:belongsToClassMap :SunspotRelativeNumbers;
        d2rq:property rdfs:description;
        d2rq:column "tbl_sunspots_relative_numbers.remarks";
        d2rq:datatype xsd:string;
        .
:creator a d2rq:PropertyBridge;
        d2rq:belongsToClassMap :SunspotRelativeNumbers;
        d2rq:property dc:creator;
        d2rq:join "tbl_sunspots_relative_numbers.scientist_key = tbl_sunspots_scientist.
            scientist_key";
        d2rq:uriSqlExpression "CONCAT('http://semwiqdemo:8093/resource/', LEFT(
            tbl_sunspots_scientist.first_name, 1), tbl_sunspots_scientist.last_name)" ;
        .

########## SUNSPOT DRAWINGS ###########

:SunspotDrawing a d2rq:ClassMap;
        d2rq:dataStorage :database;
        d2rq:class sobs:SunspotDrawing;
    d2rq:uriPattern "SunspotDrawing_@@tbl_sunspots_exposure.exposure_key@@";
        d2rq:additionalProperty [
                a d2rq:AdditionalProperty;
                d2rq:propertyName obs:phenomenon;
                d2rq:propertyValue <http://www.astro.physik.uni-goettingen.de/~hessman/rdf/IAU93#Sun
                    >;
        ];
        d2rq:additionalProperty [
                a d2rq:AdditionalProperty;
                d2rq:propertyName obs:phenomenon;
                d2rq:propertyValue <http://www.astro.physik.uni-goettingen.de/~hessman/rdf/IAU93#
                    Sunspots>;
        ];
        d2rq:additionalProperty [
                a d2rq:AdditionalProperty;
                d2rq:propertyName obs:phenomenon;
                d2rq:propertyValue <http://www.astro.physik.uni-goettingen.de/~hessman/rdf/IAU93#
                    SolarSurface>;
        ];
        d2rq:additionalProperty [
                a d2rq:AdditionalProperty;
                d2rq:propertyName obs:phenomenon;
                d2rq:propertyValue <http://www.astro.physik.uni-goettingen.de/~hessman/rdf/IAU93#
                    SunspotGroups>;
        ];
        d2rq:additionalProperty [
                a d2rq:AdditionalProperty;
```

A Mapping Specifications for the Use-Case Demo

```
                d2rq:propertyName obs:phenomenon;
                d2rq:propertyValue <http://www.astro.physik.uni-goettingen.de/~hessman/rdf/IAU93#
                    SunspotNumbers>;
        ];
        d2rq:additionalProperty [
                a d2rq:AdditionalProperty;
                d2rq:propertyName obs:phenomenon;
                d2rq:propertyValue <http://www.astro.physik.uni-goettingen.de/~hessman/rdf/IAU93#
                    Photosphere>;
        ];
        d2rq:additionalProperty [
                a d2rq:AdditionalProperty;
                d2rq:propertyName obs:site ;
                d2rq:propertyValue <http://www.kso.ac.at/>;
        ]
        .
:creatorDrawings a d2rq:PropertyBridge;
        d2rq:belongsToClassMap :SunspotDrawing;
        d2rq:property dc:creator;
        d2rq:join "tbl_sunspots_exposure.observing_log_key = tbl_sunspots_observing_log.
            observing_log_key" ;
        d2rq:uriSqlExpression "CONCAT('http://semwiqdemo:8093/resource/', LEFT(
            tbl_sunspots_scientist.first_name, 1), tbl_sunspots_scientist.last_name)" ;
        .
:filter a d2rq:PropertyBridge;
    d2rq:belongsToClassMap :SunspotDrawing;
    d2rq:property sobs:filter;
    d2rq:join "tbl_sunspots_exposure.filter_key = tbl_sunspots_filter.filter_key";
        d2rq:refersToClassMap :Filter;
        .
:detector a d2rq:PropertyBridge;
    d2rq:belongsToClassMap :SunspotDrawing;
    d2rq:property sobs:detector;
    d2rq:join "tbl_sunspots_exposure.detector_key = tbl_sunspots_detector.detector_key";
        d2rq:refersToClassMap :Detector;
        .
:xCenter a d2rq:PropertyBridge;
        d2rq:belongsToClassMap :SunspotDrawing;
        d2rq:property sobs:xCenter;
        d2rq:column "tbl_sunspots_exposure.xcen";
        d2rq:datatype xsd:float;
        .
:yCenter a d2rq:PropertyBridge;
        d2rq:belongsToClassMap :SunspotDrawing;
        d2rq:property sobs:yCenter;
        d2rq:column "tbl_sunspots_exposure.ycen";
        d2rq:datatype xsd:float;
        .
:exposureTime a d2rq:PropertyBridge;
        d2rq:belongsToClassMap :SunspotDrawing;
        d2rq:property exif:exposureTime;
        d2rq:column "tbl_sunspots_exposure.exposure_time";
        d2rq:datatype xsd:float;
        .
:fileUri a d2rq:PropertyBridge;
        d2rq:belongsToClassMap :SunspotDrawing;
        d2rq:property obs:fileUri;
```

A.1 D2RQ Mapping for the KSO Sunspots Database

```
        d2rq:uriSqlExpression "CONCAT('http://cesar.kso.ac.at/sunspot_drawings/', YEAR(
            tbl_sunspots_exposure.start_date), '/', tbl_sunspots_exposure.filename)";
:drawingTime a d2rq:PropertyBridge;
        d2rq:belongsToClassMap :SunspotDrawing;
        d2rq:property obs:dateTime;
        d2rq:sqlExpression "TIMESTAMP(CONCAT(SUBSTRING(filename, 15, 4), '-', SUBSTRING(filename,
            19, 2), '-', SUBSTRING(filename, 21,2), ' ', SUBSTRING(filename, 24,2), ':', SUBSTRING(
            filename, 26,2)))";
        d2rq:datatype xsd:dateTime;
        .

########## FILTER #############

:Filter a d2rq:ClassMap;
    d2rq:dataStorage :database;
    d2rq:uriPattern "Filter_@@tbl_sunspots_filter.filter_key@@";
    d2rq:class sobs:Filter;
    .
:filterName a d2rq:PropertyBridge;
        d2rq:belongsToClassMap :Filter;
        d2rq:property rdfs:label, dc:title;
        d2rq:column "tbl_sunspots_filter.name";
        .
:filterId a d2rq:PropertyBridge ;
        d2rq:belongsToClassMap :Filter ;
        d2rq:property dc:identifier ;
        d2rq:column "tbl_sunspots_filter.filter" ;
        .
:equivWidth a d2rq:PropertyBridge;
    d2rq:belongsToClassMap :Filter;
    d2rq:property sobs:equivWidth;
    d2rq:datatype xsd:float;
    d2rq:column "tbl_sunspots_filter.equivalent_width";
    .
:fullWithAtHalfMax a d2rq:PropertyBridge;
    d2rq:belongsToClassMap :Filter;
    d2rq:property sobs:fullWithAtHalfMax;
    d2rq:datatype xsd:float;
    d2rq:column "tbl_sunspots_filter.fwhm";
    .
:waveLength a d2rq:PropertyBridge;
    d2rq:belongsToClassMap :Filter;
    d2rq:property sobs:waveLength;
    d2rq:datatype xsd:float;
    d2rq:column "tbl_sunspots_filter.wavelnth";
    .
:Angstrom a d2rq:PropertyBridge;
    d2rq:belongsToClassMap :Filter;
    d2rq:property sobs:waveUnit ;
    d2rq:uriPattern "http://dbpedia.org/resource/Angstrom";
    d2rq:condition "(tbl_sunspots_filter.waveunit = 'Ang')";
    .
:NanoMeters a d2rq:PropertyBridge;
    d2rq:belongsToClassMap :Filter;
    d2rq:property sobs:waveUnit ;
    d2rq:uriPattern "http://dbpedia.org/resource/Nanometer";
```

A Mapping Specifications for the Use-Case Demo

```
    d2rq:condition "(tbl_sunspots_filter.waveunit = 'nm')";
    .

######### DETECTOR #########

:Detector a d2rq:ClassMap;
    d2rq:dataStorage :database;
    d2rq:uriPattern "Detector_@@tbl_sunspots_detector.detector_key@@";
    d2rq:class sobs:Detector;
:detectorName a d2rq:PropertyBridge ;
        d2rq:belongsToClassMap :Detector ;
        d2rq:property rdfs:label, dc:title ;
        d2rq:column "tbl_sunspots_detector.name" ;
    .
:detectorId a d2rq:PropertyBridge ;
        d2rq:belongsToClassMap :Detector ;
        d2rq:property dc:identifier ;
        d2rq:column "tbl_sunspots_detector.detector" ;
    .
:parallelAxis a d2rq:PropertyBridge;
    d2rq:belongsToClassMap :Detector;
    d2rq:property sobs:parallelAxis ;
    d2rq:column "tbl_sunspots_detector.parallel_axis";
    d2rq:datatype xsd:float;
    .
:serialAxis a d2rq:PropertyBridge;
    d2rq:belongsToClassMap :Detector;
    d2rq:property sobs:serialAxis;
    d2rq:column "tbl_sunspots_detector.serial_axis";
    d2rq:datatype xsd:float;
    .

########### INSTRUMENT #############

:SolarObservationInstrument a d2rq:ClassMap;
    d2rq:dataStorage :database;
    d2rq:class sobs:SolarObservationInstrument;
    d2rq:uriPattern "Instrument_@@tbl_sunspots_instrument.instrument_key@@";
    .
:instrumentName a d2rq:PropertyBridge ;
        d2rq:belongsToClassMap :SolarObservationInstrument ;
        d2rq:property rdfs:label, dc:title ;
        d2rq:column "tbl_sunspots_instrument.name" ;
    .
:instrumentId a d2rq:PropertyBridge ;
        d2rq:belongsToClassMap :SolarObservationInstrument ;
        d2rq:property dc:identifier ;
        d2rq:column "tbl_sunspots_instrument.instrument" ;
    .
:instrumentContact a d2rq:PropertyBridge ;
        d2rq:belongsToClassMap :SolarObservationInstrument ;
        d2rq:property sci:contactPerson ;
        d2rq:uriPattern "http://semwiqdemo:8093/resource/Scientist_@@tbl_sunspots_instrument.
            contact@@" ;
    .
```

A.2 XLWrap Mapping for the Scientists Spreadsheet

```
@prefix rdfs:     <http://www.w3.org/2000/01/rdf-schema#> .
@prefix rdf:      <http://www.w3.org/1999/02/22-rdf-syntax-ns#> .
@prefix xsd:      <http://www.w3.org/2001/XMLSchema#> .
@prefix foaf:     <http://xmlns.com/foaf/0.1/> .
@prefix sci:      <http://semwiq.faw.uni-linz.ac.at/global/science/science.owl#> .

@prefix xl:            <http://purl.org/NET/xlwrap#> .
@prefix :              <http://example.org/> .

{ [] a xl:Mapping ;
        xl:offline "false"^^xsd:boolean ;

        xl:template [
                xl:fileName "semwiq-usecase-demo/scientists/scientists.xls" ;
                xl:templateGraph :Scientists ;
                xl:transform [
                        rdf:type xl:RowShift ;
                        xl:breakCondition "ALLEMPTY(A2)"^^xl:Expr
                ] ;
        ] .
}

:Scientists {
#       [ xl:uri "'http://www.kso.ac.at/staff/id_' & A2"^^xl:Expr ] rdf:type sci:Scientist ;
        [ xl:uri "'http://semwiqdemo:8093/resource/' & LEFT(C2, 1) & D2"^^xl:Expr ] rdf:type sci:
            Scientist ;
                foaf:name "TRIM(C2 & ' ' & D2)"^^xl:Expr ;
                foaf:firstName "C2"^^xl:Expr ;
                foaf:surname "D2"^^xl:Expr ;
                foaf:mbox_sha1sum "SHA(I2)"^^xl:Expr ;
                foaf:workplaceHomepage <http://www.kso.ac.at/> ;
                sci:retired "BOOLEAN(K2)"^^xl:Expr ;
            .
}
```

A Mapping Specifications for the Use-Case Demo

A.3 XLWrap Mapping for the Sunspots Relative Numbers Spreadsheet

```
@prefix rdfs:      <http://www.w3.org/2000/01/rdf-schema#> .
@prefix rdf:       <http://www.w3.org/1999/02/22-rdf-syntax-ns#> .
@prefix xsd:       <http://www.w3.org/2001/XMLSchema#> .
@prefix foaf:      <http://xmlns.com/foaf/0.1/> .
@prefix dc:        <http://purl.org/dc/elements/1.1/> .
@prefix sci:       <http://semwiq.faw.uni-linz.ac.at/global/science/science.owl#> .
@prefix obs:       <http://semwiq.faw.uni-linz.ac.at/global/science/observation.owl#> .
@prefix sobs:      <http://semwiq.faw.uni-linz.ac.at/global/science/astronomy/solar-observation.owl#> .
@prefix xl:        <http://purl.org/NET/xlwrap#> .
@prefix :          <http://example.org/> .

{ [] a xl:Mapping ;
    xl:offline "false"^^xsd:boolean ;

    xl:template [
        xl:fileName "semwiq-usecase-demo/sunspots/sunspots.csv" ;
        xl:templateGraph :Sunspots ;
        xl:transform [
            rdf:type xl:RowShift ;
            xl:breakCondition "ALLEMPTY(A2)"^^xl:Expr
        ] ;
    ] .
}

:Sunspots {
    [ xl:uri "'http://semwiqdemo:8094/resource/SunspotRelativeNumbers_' & A2"^^xl:Expr ] rdf:
        type sobs:SunspotRelativeNumbers ;
        sobs:groups "C2"^^xl:Expr ;
        sobs:spots "D2"^^xl:Expr ;
        rdfs:comment "G2"^^xl:Expr ;
        sobs:rValue "H2"^^xl:Expr ;
        sobs:seeingQuality "K2"^^xl:Expr ;
        dc:creator [ xl:uri "'http://semwiqdemo:8093/resource/' & URLENCODE(LEFT(N2, 1) & O2
            )"^^xl:Expr ] ;
    .
}
```

Bibliography

Alexander, K., Cyganiak, R., Hausenblas, M. and Zhao, J.: 2009, Describing Linked Datasets, *in* C. Bizer, T. Heath, T. Berners-Lee and K. Idehen (eds), *Proceedings of the WWW2009 Workshop on Linked Data on the Web (LDOW2009)*, CEUR Workshop Proceedings.

Alpdemir, N., Mukherjee, A., Gounaris, A., Paton, N., Watson, P., Fern, A. and Smith, J.: 2003, OGSA-DQP: A Service-Based Distributed Query Processor for the Grid, *in* E. Bertino, S. Christodoulakis, D. Plexousakis, V. Christophides, M. Koubarakis, K. Böhm and E. Ferrari (eds), *Proceedings of the 7th International Conference on Extending Database Technology*, Vol. 2992 of *LNCS*, Springer, Berlin, Heidelberg, pp. 858–861.

Arenas, M., Gutierrez, C., Parsia, B., Pérez, J., Polleres, A. and Seaborne, A.: 2007, SPARQL – Where are we? – Current state, theory and practice, *Tutorial at the European Semantic Web Conference (ESWC 2007), Innsbruck, Austria*.

Arens, Y. and Knoblock, C.: 1993, SIMS: Retrieving and integrating information from multiple sources, *Proceedings of the 1993 ACM SIGMOD International Conference on Management of data*, ACM, New York, pp. 562–563.

Ashish, N.: 2005, Semantic-Web Technology: Applications at NASA, NASA Report, http://ti.arc.nasa.gov/m/pub/879h/0879%20(Ashish).pdf. Last visit in Dec 2009.

Astrahan, M., Blasgen, M., Chamberlin, D., Eswaran, K., Gray, J., Griffiths, P., King, W., Lorie, R., McJones, P., Mehl, J., Putzolu, G., Traiger, I., Wade, B. and Watson, V.: 1976, System R: relational approach to database management, *ACM Transactions on Database Systems* **1**(2), 97–137.

Auer, S., Bizer, C., Lehmann, J., Kobilarov, G., Cyganiak, R. and Ives, Z.: 2007, DBpedia: A Nucleus for a Web of Open Data, *in* K. e. a. Aberer (ed.), *Proceedings of the 6th International Semantic Web Conference (ISWC'07)*, Vol. 4825 of *LNCS*, Springer, Berlin, Heidelberg, pp. 715–728.

Auer, S., Dietzold, S. and Riechert, T.: 2006, OntoWiki – A Tool for Social, Semantic Collaboration, *in* I. C. et al. (ed.), *Proceedings of the 5th International Semantic Web Conference*, Springer, Berlin, Heidelberg.

Bibliography

Austrian Grid Consortium: n.d., Austrian Grid Website, http://www.austriangrid.at. Last visit: Feb 2009.

Ayadi, N. Y., Lacroix, Z. and Vidal, M.-E.: 2008, BiOnMap: a deductive approach for resource discovery, *Proceedings of iiWAS 2008*, pp. 477–482.

Ayers, D., Feigenbaum, L., Halb, W., Hausenblas, M., Heath, T. and Raimond, Y.: 2009, The Statistical Core Vocabulary (SCOVO), http://purl.org/NET/scovo. Last visit in Feb 2009.

Baru, C., Gupta, A., Ludäscher, B., Marciano, R., Papakonstantinou, Y., Velikhov, P. and Chu, V.: 1999, XML-based information mediation with MIX, *SIGMOD Record* **28**(2), 597–599.

Basca, C., Corlosquet, S., Cyganiak, R., Fernández, S. and Schandl, T.: 2008, Neologism: Easy Vocabulary Publishing, *Workshop Proceedings of ESWC 2008, 4th Workshop on Scripting for the Semantic Web*, Springer, Berlin, Heidelberg.

Bastian Quilitz and Ulf Leser: 2008, Querying Distributed RDF Data Sources with SPARQL, *Procceedings of the European Semantic Web Conference (ESWC2008)*, Springer, Berlin, Heidelberg.

Batini, C., Lenzerini, M. and Navathe, S.: 1986, A comparative analysis of methodologies for database schema integration, *ACM Computing Surveys* **18**(4), 323–364.

Bayardo, R. J., Bohrer, W., Brice, R., Cichocki, A., Fowler, J., Helal, A., Kashyap, V., Ksiezyk, T., Martin, G., Nodine, M., Rashid, M., Rusinkiewicz, M., Shea, R., Unnikrishnan, C., Unruh, A. and Woelk, D.: 1997, InfoSleuth: agent-based semantic integration of information in open and dynamic environments, *SIGMOD '97: Proceedings of the 1997 ACM SIGMOD international conference on Management of data*, ACM, New York, NY, USA, pp. 195–206.

Beckett, D.: 2007, Turtle – Terse RDF Triple Language, http://www.dajobe.org/2004/01/turtle/.

Bentley, B. and EGSO Consortium: 2002, EGSO - The European Grid of Solar Observations, *in* A. Wilson (ed.), *Proceedings of the 10th European Solar Physics Meeting "Solar Variability: From the Core to Outer Frontiers" Prague, Czech Republic, EGSO - The European Grid of Solar ObservationsBob Bentley et. al.in Proceedings of the 10th European Solar Physics Meeting "Solar Variability: From the Core to Outer Frontiers" Prague*. ESA Publication SP-506.

Berkley, C., Bowers, S., Jones, M., Ludäscher, B., Schildhauer, M. and Tao, J.: 2005, Incorporating semantics in scientific workflow authoring, *SSDBM'2005: Proceedings of the 17th international conference on Scientific and statistical database management*, Lawrence Berkeley Laboratory, Berkeley, CA, US, pp. 75–78.

Berners-Lee, T.: 2006, Linked Data, http://www.w3.org/DesignIssues/LinkedData.html.

Bibliography

Berners-Lee, T.: n.d., Plenary talk by Tim BL at WWWF94: Overview, http://www.w3.org/Talks/WWW94Tim/.

Berners-Lee, T., Chen, Y., Chilton, L. and Connolly, D. e. a.: 2006, Tabulator: Exploring and analyzing linked data on the Semantic Web, *Proceedings of the ISWC Workshop on Semantic Web User Interaction*, CEUR Workshop Proceedings.

Bernstein, A., Kiefer, C. and Stocker, M.: 2007, OptARQ: A SPARQL Optimization Approach based on Triple Pattern Selectivity Estimation, *Technical Report ifi-2007.03*, University of Zürich, Department of Informatics.

Bizer, C. and Cyganiak, R.: 2007, D2RQ – Lessons Learned, (Position paper for the W3C Workshop on RDF Access to Relational Databases, http://www.w3.org/2007/03/RdfRDB/papers/d2rq-positionpaper/). Last visit: Sep 2008.

Bizer, C. and Cyganiak, R.: n.d., The TriG Syntax, http://www4.wiwiss.fu-berlin.de/bizer/TriG/. Last visit in Dec 2009.

Bizer, C., Cyganiak, R. and Heath, T.: 2007, How to Publish Linked Data on the Web, http://sites.wiwiss.fu-berlin.de/suhl/bizer/pub/LinkedDataTutorial/. Last visit: Dec 12, 2007.

Bizer, C., Gauß, T., Cyganiak, R. and Hartig, O.: 2009, Semantic Web Client Library - Querying the complete Semantic Web with SPARQL, http://www4.wiwiss.fu-berlin.de/bizer/ng4j/semwebclient/. Last visit in March 2009.

Blöchl, M., Gruber, G., Langegger, A. and Wöß, W.: 2005, G-SDAM: Seamless semantic data interchange for Grid Computing, *Proceedings of the 1st Austrian Grid Symposium*.

Blöchl, M., Langegger, A. and Wöß, W.: 2006, Registration of Heterogeneous Data Sources in the Case of the Grid Semantic Data Access Middleware (G-SDAM), *Proceedings of the Austrian Grid Symposium (AGS'06)*, OCG.

Bodenreider, O.: 2008, Ontologies and Data Integration in Biomedicine: Success Stories and Challenging Issues, *DILS '08: Proceedings of the 5th international workshop on Data Integration in the Life Sciences*, Springer, Berlin, Heidelberg, pp. 1–4.

Bogart, R. S., Tian, K. Q., Davey, A., Dimitoglou, G., Gurman, J. B., Hill, F., Hourclé, J., Martens, P. C., Suárez-Sola, I., Wampler, S. and Yoshimura, K.: 2005, Building a Virtual Solar Observatory: Lessons Learned, *American Geophysical Union Spring Meeting Abstracts* .

Brickley, D.: n.d., Basic Geo (WGS84 lat/long) Vocabulary - W3C Semantic Web Interest Group, http://www.w3.org/2003/01/geo/#documents. Last visit in Dec 2009.

Bibliography

Brickley, D. and Miller, L.: 2007, FOAF Vocabulary Specification, http://xmlns.com/foaf/spec/.

Bush, V.: 1945, As We May Think, *The Atlantic Monthly* **176**(1), 101–108.

Calvanese, D., Giacomo, G., Lembo, D., Lenzerini, M. and Rosati, R.: 2009, Conceptual Modeling for Data Integration, *Conceptual Modeling: Foundations and Applications: Essays in Honor of John Mylopoulos* pp. 173–197.

Carey, M., Haas, L., Schwarz, P., Arya, M., Cody, W., Fagin, R., Flickner, M., Luniewski, A., Niblack, W., Petkovic, D., Thomas, J., Williams, J. and Wimmers, E.: 1995, Towards heterogeneous multimedia information systems: the Garlic approach, *RIDE '95: Proceedings of the 5th International Workshop on Research Issues in Data Engineering-Distributed Object Management (RIDE-DOM'95)*, IEEE Computer Society, Washington, DC, p. 124.

Carey, M. J., Haas, L. M., Maganty, V. and Williams, J. H.: 1996, PESTO: An Integrated Query/Browser for Object Databases, *VLDB '96: Proceedings of the 22th International Conference on Very Large Data Bases*, Morgan Kaufmann Publishers Inc., San Francisco, CA, USA, pp. 203–214.

Carroll, J., Dickinson, I., Dollin, C., Reynolds, D., Seaborne, A. and Wilkinson, K.: 2004, Jena: Implementing the Semantic Web Recommendations, *Proceedings of the International World Wide Web Conference*, Hewlett Packard Labs, p. 74.

Cattell, R.: 1993, *The Object Database Standard: ODMG-93 (Release 1.1)*, Morgan Kaufmann Publishers Inc., San Francisco, CA, USA.

Chawathe, S. S., Garcia-Molina, H., Hammer, J., Ireland, K., Papakonstantinou, Y., Ullman, J. D. and Widom, J.: 1994, The TSIMMIS Project: Integration of Heterogeneous Information Sources, *Proceedings of IPSJ Conference*, pp. 7–18.

Chen, H., Wu, Z. and Mao, Y.: 2005, Rewriting Queries Using Views for RDF-Based Relational Integration, *17th IEEE International Conference on Tools with Artificial Intelligence (ICTAI'05)*, IEEE Computer Society, Los Alamitos, CA, pp. 260–264.

Chris Bizer and Richard Cyganiak: 2006, D2R Server – Publishing Relational Databases on the Semantic Web, *5th International Semantic Web Conference*.

Christen, P.: 2008, Febrl – an open source data cleaning, deduplication and record linkage system with a graphical user interface, *KDD '08: Proceeding of the 14th ACM SIGKDD international conference on Knowledge discovery and data mining*, ACM, New York, NY, USA, pp. 1065–1068.

Collet, C., Huhns, M. N. and Shen, W.-M.: 1991, Resource Integration Using a Large Knowledge Base in Carnot, *Computer* **24**(12), 55–62.

Connolly, D.: 2007, Gleaning Resource Descriptions from Dialects of Languages (GRDDL), W3C Recommendation, http://www.w3.org/TR/grddl/. Last visit in Dec 2009.

Coulouris, G., Dollimore, J. and Kindberg, T.: 2005, *Distributed Systems – Concepts and Design*, 4 edn, Pearson Education Ltd.

Cyganiak, R. and Bizer, C.: 2009, Pubby – A Linked Data Frontend for SPARQL Endpoints, http://www4.wiwiss.fu-berlin.de/pubby/. Last visit in March 2009.

de Laborda, C. P. and Conrad, S.: 2006, Bringing Relational Data into the SemanticWeb using SPARQL and Relational.OWL, *ICDEW '06: Proceedings of the 22nd International Conference on Data Engineering Workshops*, IEEE Computer Society, Washington, DC, USA, p. 55.

Dimitrov, D. A., Heflin, J., Qasem, A. and Wang, N.: 2006, Information integration via an end-toend distributed semantic web system, *The Semantic Web - ISWC 2006, 5th International Semantic Web Conference, ISWC 2006*, Springer, pp. 764–777.

Ding, L., Finin, T., Joshi, A., Pan, R., Cost, R. S., Peng, Y., Reddivari, P., Doshi, V. and Sachs, J.: 2004, Swoogle: a search and metadata engine for the semantic web, *CIKM '04: Proceedings of the thirteenth ACM international conference on Information and knowledge management*, ACM, New York, NY, USA, pp. 652–659.

Erling, O.: 2008, Requirements for Relational-to-RDF Mapping, Blog post at http://www.openlinksw.com/weblog/oerling/?id=1434. Last visit in Dec 2009.

Erling, O. and Mikhailov, I.: 2007, RDF Support in the Virtuoso DBMS, *CSSW*, pp. 59–68.

EURO VO Consortium: 2008, The European Virtual Observatory EURO-VO, http://www.euro-vo.org. Last visit in Dec 2009.

Farquhar, A., Fikes, R. and Rice, J.: 1996, The Ontolingua Server: A Tool for Collaborative Ontology Construction, *Knowledge systems*, Standfoard University, AI Laboratory.

Farquhar, A., Fikes, R. and Rice, J.: 1997, The Ontolingua Server: a tool for collaborative ontology construction, *International Journal of Human-Computer Studies* **46**(6), 707–727.

Feigenbaum, L., Herman, I., Hongsermeier, T., Neumann, E. and Stephens, S.: 2007, The Semantic Web in Action, *Scientific American* **297**, 90–97.

Fellbaum, C.: 1998, *WordNet An Electronic Lexical Database*, MIT Press.

Bibliography

Fensel, D. and van Harmelen, F.: 2007, Unifying Reasoning and Search to Web Scale, *IEEE Internet Computing* **11**(2), 96–95.

Fielding, R. T.: 2000, *Architectural Styles and the Design of Network-based Software Architectures*, Phd thesis, University of California, Irvine.

Finin, T., Fritzson, R., McKay, D. and McEntire, R.: 1994, KQML as an agent communication language, *CIKM '94: Proceedings of the third international conference on Information and knowledge management*, ACM, New York, NY, USA, pp. 456–463.

Flatscher, R. G.: 2002, Metamodeling in EIA/CDIF – meta-metamodel and metamodels, *ACM Transactions on Modeling and Computer Simulation* **12**(4), 322–342.

Fowler, J., Perry, B., Nodine, M. H. and Bargmeyer, B.: 1999, Agent-Based Semantic Interoperability in InfoSleuth, *SIGMOD Record* **28**(1), 60–67.

Fox, P., Cinquini, L., McGuinness, D., West, P., Garcia, J., Benedict, J. and Zednik, S.: 2007, Semantic web services for interdisciplinary scientific data query and retrieval, *Proceedings of the AAAI Semantic e-Science Workshop, WS-07-11*.

Fox, P., McGuinness, D., Cinquini, L., West, P., Garcia, J., Benedict, J. and Middleton, D.: 2009, Ontology-supported scientific data frameworks: The Virtual Solar-Terrestrial Observatory experience, *Computers & Geosciences* **35**(4), 724–738.

Fox, P., McGuinness, D., Raskin, R. and Sinha, K.: 2007, A volcano erupts: semantically mediated integration of heterogeneous volcanic and atmospheric data, *CIMS '07: Proceedings of the ACM first workshop on CyberInfrastructure: information management in eScience*, ACM, New York, NY, USA, pp. 1–6.

Franklin, M., Halevy, A. and Maier, D.: 2005, From databases to dataspaces: a new abstraction for information management, *SIGMOD Record* **34**(4), 27–33.

Freytag, J. C.: 1987, A rule-based view of query optimization, *SIGMOD '87: Proceedings of the 1987 ACM SIGMOD international conference on Management of data*, ACM, New York, NY, USA, pp. 173–180.

Garcia-Molina, H., Papakonstantinou, Y., Quass, D., Rajaraman, A., Sagiv, Y., Ullman, J., Vassalos, V. and Widom, J.: 1997, The TSIMMIS Approach to Mediation: Data Models and Languages, *Journal of Intelligent Information Systems* **8**(2), 117–132.

Gardarin, G., Finance, B. and Fankhauser, P.: 1997, Federating object-oriented and relational databases: the IRO-DB experience, *2nd IFCIS International Conference on Cooperative Information Systems (CoopIS'97)* .

Gibbins, N. and Shadbolt, N.: 2009, Resource Description Framework (RDF), *Encyclopedia of Library and Information Sciences, University of Southampton, UK* .

Goh, C. H., Bressan, S., Madnick, S. and Siegel, M.: 1999, Context interchange: new features and formalisms for the intelligent integration of information, *ACM Transactions on Information Systems* **17**(3), 270–293.

Golbeck, J., Khan, T., Sanghavi, N. and Thakker, N.: 2009, Multiple Personalities on the Web: A Study of Shared Mboxes in FOAF, *Social Data on the Web (SDOW2009), Workshop at the 8th International Semantic Web Conference,*.

Gong, L.: 2001, JXTA: A Network Programming Environment, *IEEE Internet Computing* **5**(3), 88–95.

Graefe, G. and DeWitt, D. J.: 1987, The EXODUS optimizer generator, *SIGMOD '87: Proceedings of the 1987 ACM SIGMOD international conference on Management of data*, ACM, New York, NY, USA, pp. 160–172.

Groza, T., Handschuh, S., Moeller, K., Grimnes, G., Sauermann, L., Minack, E., Mesnage, C., Jazayeri, M., Reif, G. and Gudjonsdottir, R.: 2007, The NEPOMUK Project – On the way to the Social Semantic Desktop, *in* T. Pellegrini and S. Schaffert (eds), *Proceedings of I-Semantics' 07*, pp. 201–211.

Gruber, T.: 1993, A translation approach to portable ontology specifications, *Journal of Knowledge Acquisistion* **5**(2), 199–220.

Haas, L. M., Hernández, M. A., Ho, H., Popa, L. and Roth, M.: 2005, Clio grows up: from research prototype to industrial tool, *SIGMOD '05: Proceedings of the 2005 ACM SIGMOD international conference on Management of data*, ACM, New York, NY, USA, pp. 805–810.

Halevy, A. Y., Ashish, N., Bitton, D., Carey, M., Draper, D., Pollock, J., Rosenthal, A. and Sikka, V.: 2005, Enterprise information integration: successes, challenges and controversies, *SIGMOD '05: Proceedings of the 2005 ACM SIGMOD international conference on Management of data*, ACM, New York, NY, USA, pp. 778–787.

Han, L., Finin, T., Parr, C., Sachs, J. and Joshi, A.: 2008, RDF123: From Spreadsheets to RDF, *in* A. Sheth, S. Staab, M. Dean, M. Paolucci, D. Maynard, T. Finin and K. Thirunarayan (eds), *7th International Semantic Web Conference (ISWC2008)*, Vol. 5318 of *LNCS*, Springer, Berlin, Heidelberg, pp. 451–466.

Harris, S., Lamb, N. and Shadbolt, N.: 2009, 4store: The Design and Implementation of a Clustered RDF Store, *The 5th International Workshop on Scalable Semantic Web Knowledge Base Systems (SSWS2009), CEUR Workshop Proceedings*, Vol. 517, Garlik Ltd.

Harth, A., Umbrich, J. and Decker, S.: 2006, MultiCrawler: A Pipelined Architecture for Crawling and Indexing Semantic Web Data, *5th International Semantic Web Conference, Athens, USA*.

Harth, A., Umbrich, J., Hogan, A. and Decker, S.: 2007, YARS2: A Federated Repository for Querying Graph Structured Data from the Web, *ISWC/ASWC*, pp. 211–224.

Hartig, O., Bizer, C. and Freytag, J.-C.: 2009, Executing SPARQL Queries over the Web of Linked Data, *8th International Semantic Web Conference (ISWC2009)*.

Hayes, P. and McBrien, B.: 2004, RDF Semantics W3C Recommendation, http://www.w3.org/TR/rdf-mt/.

Hernandez, M. J.: 2003, *Database Design for Mere Mortals(R): A Hands-On Guide to Relational Database Design (2nd Edition)*, 2. edn, Addison-Wesley.

Horrocks, I., Parsia, B., Schneider, P. P. and Hendler, J.: 2005, Semantic Web Architecture: Stack or Two Towers?, in F. Fages and S. Soliman (eds), *Principles and Practice of Semantic Web Reasoning (PPSWR 2005)*, Vol. 3703 of *LNCS*, Springer, Berlin, Heidelberg, pp. 37–41.

Horrocks, I., Patel-Schneider, P. F., Boley, H., Tabet, S., Grosof, B. and Dean, M.: 2004, SWRL: A Semantic Web Rule Language Combining OWL and RuleML, http://www.w3.org/Submission/SWRL/. Last visit in Dec 2009.

Hull, D., Wolstencroft, K., Stevens, R., Goble, C., Pocock, M., Li, P. and Oinn, T.: 2006, Taverna: a tool for building and running workflows of services, *Nucleic Acids Research* **34**, 729–732.

Idehen, K. and Blakeley, C.: 2007, Virtuoso Sponger Whitepaper v1.0 (Virtuoso 5.0), *Technical report*, OpenLink Software. White Paper.

International Astronomical Union: 2008, Definition of the Flexible Image Transport System (FITS), http://fits.gsfc.nasa.gov/standard30/fits_standard30.pdf. Last visit in Dec 2009.

Ioannidis, Y.: 2003, The History of Histograms (Abridged), *VLDB '2003: Proceedings of the 29th international conference on Very large data bases*, VLDB Endowment, pp. 19–30.

Ioannidis, Y. E. and Kang, Y. C.: 1991, Left-deep vs. bushy trees: an analysis of strategy spaces and its implications for query optimization, *SIGMOD '91: Proceedings of the 1991 ACM SIGMOD international conference on Management of data*, ACM, New York, NY, USA, pp. 168–177.

IVOA Semantics WG: 2009, IVOAT Thesaurus, www.ivoa.net/rdf/Vocabularies/IVOAT. Last visit in Dec 2009.

JBoss Community: n.d., JBoss Drools Homepage - The Business Logic integration Platform, http://www.jboss.org/drools/. Last visit in Dec 2009.

Jena Community: 2009a, Jena – A Semantic Web Framework for Java, http://jena.sourceforge.net/. Last visit in March 2009.

Jena Community: 2009b, Joseki – A SPARQL Server for Jena, http://www.joseki.org/. Last visit: June 2009.

Josifovski, V., Schwarz, P., Haas, L. and Lin, E.: 2002, Garlic: a new flavor of federated query processing for DB2, *SIGMOD '02: Proceedings of the 2002 ACM SIGMOD international conference on Management of data*, ACM, New York, NY, USA, pp. 524–532.

Karnstedt, M., Sattler, K.-U., Geist, I. and Höpfner, H.: 2003, Semantic Caching in Ontology-based Mediator Systems, *Berliner XML Tage*, pp. 155–169.

Kemper, A. and Eickler, A.: 2006, *Datenbanksysteme: Eine Einführung (6. Auflage)*, 6. edn, Oldenbourg, München, Germany.

Khare, R. and Çelik, T.: 2006, Microformats A Pragmatic Path to the Semantic Web, *Technical Report 06-01*, CommerceNet Labs.

Kifer, M., Lausen, G. and Wu, J.: 1995, Logical foundations of object-oriented and frame-based languages, *ACM Journal* **42**(4), 741–843.

Kirk, T., Levy, A. Y., Sagiv, Y. and Srivastava, D.: 1995, The Information Manifold, *Proceedings of the AAAI 1995 Spring Symp. on Information Gathering from Heterogeneous, Distributed Enviroments*, pp. 85–91.

Kooi, R.: 1980, *The Optimization of Queries in Relational Databases*, Phd thesis, Case Western Reserve University Cleveland, USA.

Kossmann, D.: 2000, The State of the Art in Distributed Query Processing, *ACM Computing Surveys* **32**(4), 422–469.

Lacroix, Z., Raschid, L. and Vidal, M. E.: 2006, Semantic Model to Integrate Biological Resources, *ICDEW '06: Proceedings of the 22nd International Conference on Data Engineering Workshops*, IEEE Computer Society, Washington, DC, USA, p. 63.

Langegger, A.: 2007, Semantische Datenintegration in eScience Grids – Chancen im E-Business, Invited Talk at the Austrian Federal Economic Chamber, Arbeitskreis Semantic Web, ebSemantics.

Langegger, A., Blöchl, M. and Wöß, W.: 2007, Sharing Data on the Grid using Ontologies and Distributed SPARQL Queries, *DEXA '07: Proceedings of the 18th International Conference on Database and Expert Systems Applications (DEXA 2007)*, IEEE Computer Society, Washington, DC, USA, pp. 450–454.

Langegger, A., Leitner, T. and Wöß, W.: 2009, Providing Semantic Data Integration as a Grid Service, *3rd Austrian Grid Symposium 2009, Linz*, OCG.

Langegger, A. and Wöß, W.: 2008, SemWIQ – Semantic Web Integrator and Query Engine, *in* H.-G. Hegering, A. Lehmann, H.-J. Ohlbach and C. Scheideler (eds), *Beiträge der 38. Jahrestagung der Gesellschaft für Informatik e.V. (GI)*, Vol. 1, Bonner Köllen Verlag.

Langegger, A. and Wöß, W.: 2009a, Querying and Semantically Integrating Spreadsheet Collections with XLWrap-Server – Use Cases and Mapping Design Patterns, *Poster & Demo Session at the 8th International Semantic Web Conference (ISWC2009), Washington D.C.*

Langegger, A. and Wöß, W.: 2009b, RDFStats – An Extensible RDF Statistics Generator and Library, *Workshop Proceedings of the DEXA Conference 2009*, IEEE Computer Society Press.

Langegger, A. and Wöß, W.: 2009c, XLWrap – Querying and Integrating Arbitrary Spreadsheets with SPARQL, *in* A. Bernstein, D. Karger, T. Heath, L. Feigenbaum, D. Maynard, E. Motta and K. Thirunarayan (eds), *Proceedings of the 8th International Semantic Web Conference (ISWC2009), Washington D.C.*, Vol. 5823 of *LNCS*, Springer, Berlin, Heidelberg.

Langegger, A., Wöß, W. and Blöchl, M.: 2008a, A Semantic Web middleware for Virtual Data Integration on the Web, *Proceedings of the European Semantic Web Conference 2008, Tenerife*.

Langegger, A., Wöß, W. and Blöchl, M.: 2008b, A Semantic Web Middleware for Virtual Data Integration on the Web (Poster), *CEUR-WS Proceedings of the European Semantic Web Conference (ESWC'08)*, CEUR.

Laura M. Haas, Donald Kossmann, Edward L. Wimmers and Jun Yang: 1997, Optimizing Queries Across Diverse Data Sources, *Proceedings of the 23th International Conference on Very Large Databases*, VLDB Endowment, Saratoga, Calif., Athens, pp. 276–285.

Legler, F.: 2005, *Datentransformation mittels Schema Mapping*, master thesis, Humboldt-Universität zu Berlin, Berlin.

Leimer, H.: 2009, *Transformation von Daten relationaler Datenbanken in das Resource Description Framework*, master thesis, Johannes Kepler University Linz, Linz.

Leitner, T.: 2010, *Semantic Data Integration for Grid Environments*, master thesis, Johannes Kepler University Linz.

Lenat, D. B.: 1995, CYC: a large-scale investment in knowledge infrastructure, *Communications of the ACM* **38**(11), 33–38.

Lenzerini, M.: 2002, Data integration: a theoretical perspective, *PODS '02: Proceedings of the twenty-first ACM SIGMOD-SIGACT-SIGART symposium on Principles of database systems*, ACM, New York, NY, USA, pp. 233–246.

Leser, U. and Naumann, F.: 2007, *Informationsintegration – Architekturen und Methoden zur Integration verteilter und heterogener Datenquellen*, 1 edn, dpunkt.verlag.

Lin, J. and Mendelzon, A. O.: 1998, Merging Databases under Constraints, *International Journal of Cooperative Information Systems* **7**(1), 55–76.

Lohman, G. M.: 1988, Grammar-like functional rules for representing query optimization alternatives, *SIGMOD '88: Proceedings of the 1988 ACM SIGMOD international conference on Management of data*, ACM Press, New York, NY, USA, pp. 18–27.

Mackert, L. F. and Lohman, G. M.: 1986, R* optimizer validation and performance evaluation for local queries, *SIGMOD '86: Proceedings of the 1986 ACM SIGMOD international conference on Management of data*, ACM, New York, NY, USA, pp. 84–95.

Martín, L., Anguita, A., Maojo, V., Bonsma, E., Bucur, A. I. D., Vrijnsen, J., Brochhausen, M., Cocos, C., Stenzhorn, H., Tsiknakis, M., Doerr, M. and Kondylakis, H.: 2008, Ontology Based Integration of Distributed and Heterogeneous Data Sources in ACGT, *in* L. Azevedo and A. R. Londral (eds), *Proceedings of the First International Conference on Health Informatics (HEALTHINF 2008)*, INSTICC - Institute for Systems and Technologies of Information, Control and Communication, pp. 301–306.

Marx, V.: 2009, Pharmas Nudge Semantic Web Technology Toward Practical Drug Discovery Applications, BioInform Newsletter, http://www.genomeweb.com/print/912896. Last visit in Dec 2009.

McGuinness, D. L.: 2003, Ontologies Come of Age, *in* D. Fensel, J. Hendler, H. Lieberman and W. Wahlster (eds), *Spinning the Semantic Web: Bringing the World Wide Web to Its Full Potential*, MIT Press.

McGuinness, D. and van Harmelen, F.: 2004, OWL Web Ontology Language – Overview, http://www.w3.org/TR/owl-features/.

Melnik, S., Garcia-Molina, H. and Rahm, E.: 2001, Similarity Flooding: A Versatile Graph Matching Algorithm (Extended Technical Report), *Technical Report 2001-25*, Stanford InfoLab.

Bibliography

Miles, A. and Bechhofer, S.: 2009, SKOS Simple Knowledge Organization System Reference – W3C Candidate Recommendation, http://www.w3.org/TR/skos-reference.

Minsky, M.: 1974, A Framework for Representing Knowledge, *Technical Report AIM-306*, MIT, Cambridge, MA, USA.

Möller, K., Bechhofer, S. and Heath, T.: 2007, Semantic Web Conference Ontology, http://data.semanticweb.org/ns/swc/ontology. Last visit in Dec 2009.

Motik, B.: 2007, On the Properties of Metamodeling in OWL, *Journal of Logic and Computation* **17**(4), 617–637.

Naacke, H., Gardarin, G. and Tomasic, A.: 1998, Leveraging Mediator Cost Models with Heterogeneous Data Sources, *ICDE '98: Proceedings of the Fourteenth International Conference on Data Engineering*, IEEE Computer Society, Washington, DC, USA, pp. 351–360.

Netscape Communications Corp.: 2009, Open Directory Project, http://www.dmoz.org. Last visit in Dec 2009.

Newman, A.: 2006, *Querying the Semantic Web using a Relational Based SPARQL*, bachelor thesis, School of Information Technology and Electrical Engineering, University of Queensland.

Noy, N., Shah, N., Dai, B., Dorf, M., Griffith, N., Jonquet, C., Montegut, M., Rubin, D., Youn, C. and Musen, M. A.: 2008, BioPortal: A Web Repository for Biomedical Ontologies and Data Resources, *in* C. Bizer and A. Joshi (eds), *7th International Semantic Web Conference (ISWC2008) Posters & Demos*, Vol. 401, CEUR-WS.org.

Özsu, T. and Valduriez, P.: 1999, *Principles of Distributed Database Systems, Second Edition*, 2 edn, Prentice Hall.

Papakonstantinou, Y., Garcia-Molina, H. and Ullman, J. D.: 1996, MedMaker: A Mediation System Based on Declarative Specifications, *ICDE '96: Proceedings of the Twelfth International Conference on Data Engineering*, IEEE Computer Society, Washington, DC, USA, pp. 132–141.

Papakonstantinou, Y., Garcia-Molina, H. and Widom, J.: 1995, Object Exchange Across Heterogeneous Information Sources, *ICDE '95: Proceedings of the Eleventh International Conference on Data Engineering*, IEEE Computer Society, Washington, DC, USA, pp. 251–260.

Patel-Schneider, P. F., Hayes, P. and Horrocks, I.: 2004, OWL Web Ontology Language – Semantics and Abstract Syntax, http://www.w3.org/TR/owl-semantics/.

Patil, R. S., Fikes, R. E., Patel-Schneider, P. F., McKay, D., Finin, T., Gruber, T. R. and Neches, R.: 1992, The DARPA Knowledge Sharing Effort: Progress report, *in* C. Rich, B. Nebel and

W. Swartout (eds), *Principles of Knowledge Representation and Reasoning: Proceedings of the Third International Conference*, Morgan Kaufmann, Cambridge.

Peckham, J. and Maryanski, F.: 1988, Semantic data models, *ACM Computing Surveys* **20**(3), 153–189.

Pérez, J., Arenas, M. and Gutierrez, C.: 2006, Semantics and Complexity of SPARQL, *in* I. Cruz, S. Decker, D. Allemang, C. Preist, D. Schwabe, P. Mika, M. Uschold and L. Aroyo (eds), *5th International Semantic Web Conference, Athens, USA,*, Vol. 4273 of *LNCS*, Springer, Berlin, Heidelberg.

Polleres, A.: 2007, From SPARQL to rules (and back), *WWW '07: Proceedings of the 16th international conference on World Wide Web*, ACM, New York, NY, USA, pp. 787–796.

Predoiu, L., Feier, C., Scharffe, F., de Bruijn, J., Martín-Recuerda, F., Manov, D. and Ehrig, M.: 2006, State of the Art Survey on Ontology Merging and Aligning, *SEKT EU Project Deliverable 4.2.2*, DERI Innsbruck (now STI Innsbruck).

Prud'hommeaux, E.: 2007, Federated SPARQL, http://www.w3.org/2007/05/SPARQLfed/. Last visit: Sep 2008.

Prud'hommeaux, E. and Seaborne, A.: 2008, SPARQL Query Language for RDF, W3C Recommendation, http://www.w3.org/TR/rdf-sparql-query/. Last visit: March 2009.

Qasem, A., Dimitrov, A. and Heflin, J.: 2008, ISENS: A Multi-ontology Query System for the Semantic Deep Web, *Fifth IEEE Conference on Enterprise Computing, E-Commerce and E-Services* pp. 396–399.

Rambichler, M.: 2009, *Entwicklung eines grafischen Query Builders für verteilte SPARQL-Abfragen (in progress)*, master thesis, Johannes Kepler University Linz, Linz, Austria.

Raskin, R. and Pan, M.: 2003, Semantic Web for Earth and Environmental Terminology (SWEET), *in* N. Ashish and C. Goble (eds), *ISWC 2003 Workshop: Semantic Web Technologies for Searching and Retrieving Scientific Data, CEUR Workshop Proceedings*, Vol. 83.

Resnick, P. and Miller, J.: 1996, PICS: Internet access controls without censorship, *Communications of the ACM* **39**(10), 87–93.

Richard Cyganiak: 2005, A Relational Algebra for SPARQL, *Technical Report HPL-2005-170*, HP Labs, Bristol, UK.

Rodríguez, J. B., Corcho, O. and Gómez-Pérez, A.: 2004, R2O, an Extensible and Semantically Based Databaseto-ontology Mapping Language.

Russell, S. and Norvig, P.: 2003, *Artificial Intelligence: A Modern Approach*, 2 edn, Prentice Hall.

Ruttenberg, A., Rees, J., Samwald, M. and Marshall, S. S.: 2009, Life sciences on the Semantic Web: the Neurocommons and beyond, *Briefings in bioinformatics* .

Sattler, K.-U., Geist, I., Habrecht, R. and Schallehn, E.: 2003, Konzeptbasierte Anfrageverarbeitung in Mediatorsystemen, *BTW*, pp. 78–97.

Sattler, K.-U., Geist, I. and Schallehn, E.: 2005, Concept-based querying in mediator systems, *The VLDB Journal* **14**(1), 97–111.

Sauermann, L. and Cyganiak, R.: 2007, Cool URIs for the Semantic Web - W3C Working Draft, http://www.w3.org/TR/cooluris. Last visit: Oct 2008.

Schmitt, I. and Saake, G.: 2005, A comprehensive database schema integration method based on the theory of formal concepts, *Acta Informatica* **41**(7), 475–524.

Seaborne, A.: 2007, SPARQL S-expressions, http://seaborne.blogspot.com/2007/04/sparql-s-expressions.html.

Selinger, P. G., Astrahan, M. M., Chamberlin, D. D., Lorie, R. A. and Price, T. G.: 1979, Access path selection in a relational database management system, *SIGMOD '79: Proceedings of the 1979 ACM SIGMOD international conference on Management of data*, ACM, New York, NY, USA, pp. 23–34.

Semantic Web Interest Group: n.d., ESW Wiki, http://esw.w3.org/topic/. Last visit in Dec 2009.

Sharma, N.: 2008, The Origin of the Data Information Knowledge Wisdom Hierarchy, http://www-personal.si.umich.edu/~nsharma/dikw_origin.htm. Last visit: Nov 2008.

Sheth, A. P. and Larson, J. A.: 1990, Federated database systems for managing distributed, heterogeneous, and autonomous databases, *ACM Computing Surveys* **22**(3), 183–236.

Slater, T., Bouton, C. and Huang, E. S.: 2008, Beyond data integration, *Drug Discovery Today* **13**(13–14), 584–589.

Smith, M. K., Welty, C. and McGuinness, D.: 2004, OWL Web Ontology Language – Guide, http://www.w3.org/TR/owl-guide/.

Spaccapietra, S., Parent, C. and Dupont, Y.: 1992, Model independent assertions for integration of heterogeneous schemas, *The VLDB Journal* **1**(1), 81–126.

Staab, S. and Studer, R.: 2004, *Handbook on Ontologies*, International Handbooks on Information Systems, Springer, Berlin, Heidelberg.

Steer, D.: n.d., SquirrelRDF Homepage, http://jena.sourceforge.net/SquirrelRDF/. Last visit in Dec 2009.

Sure, Y., Bloehdorn, S., Haase, P., Hartmann, J. and Oberle, D.: 2005, The SWRC Ontology - Semantic Web for Research Communities, *in* C. Bento, A. Cardoso and G. Dias (eds), *Proceedings of the 12th Portuguese Conference on Artificial Intelligence - Progress in Artificial Intelligence (EPIA 2005)*, Vol. 3803 of *LNCS*, Springer, Berlin, Heidelberg, pp. 218 – 231.

Swick, R.: 2002, W3C Metadata Activity Statement, http://www.w3.org/Metadata/Activity. Last visit in Dec 2009.

Telcordia Technologies, Inc.: 2005, InfoSleuth Example Applications, http://www.argreenhouse.com/InfoSleuth/application_cases.shtml. Last visit in Dec 2009.

Thompson, B., Personick, M., Bebee, B., Parsia, B. and Cutcher, M.: 2006, A high performance RDFS store using a Generic Object Model, *XTech 2006 - Building Web 2.0*.

Tim Berners Lee: 1998, Notation 3, http://www.w3.org/DesignIssues/Notation3. Last visit: Dec 2008.

Tim Berners Lee: 2000, Issue rdfms-literalsubjects: Should the subjects of RDF statements be allowed to be literals?, http://www.w3.org/2000/03/rdf-tracking/#rdfms-literalsubjects.

Tim Berners Lee, James Hendler and Ora Lassila: 2001, The Semantic Web – A new form of Web content that is meaningful to computers will unleash a revolution of new possibilities, *Scientific American*.

Tomasic, A., Raschid, L. and Valduriez, P.: 1996, Scaling heterogeneous databases and the design of Disco, *Proceedings of the 16th International Conference on Distributed Computing Systems (ICDCS 1996), Hong Kong*, IEEE Computer Society, Los Alamitos, CA, USA, p. 449.

Tummarello, G., Delbru, R. and Oren, E.: 2007, Sindice.com: Weaving the Open Linked Data, *Proceedings of the 6th International Semantic Web Conference (ISWC)*.

Ullman, J. D.: 2000, Information integration using logical views, *Theoretical Computer Science* **239**(2), 189–210.

Uschold, M. and Gruninger, M.: 2004, Ontologies and semantics for seamless connectivity, *SIGMOD Record* **33**(4), 58–64.

Bibliography

Volz, J., Bizer, C., Gaedke, M. and Kobilarov, G.: 2009, Silk - A Link Discovery Framework for the Web of Data, *Proceedings of the WWW2009 Workshop on Linked Data on the Web (LDOW2009)*, CEUR Workshop Proceedings.

W3C SWIG: 2009, Linking Open Data W3C SWEO Community Project, http://esw.w3.org/topic/SweoIG/TaskForces/CommunityProjects/LinkingOpenData. Last visit in Dec 2009.

Wang, H., Rector, A., Drummond, N., Horridge, M., Seidenberg, J., Noy, N., Musen, M., Redmond, T., Rubin, D., Tu, S. and Tudorache, T.: 2006, Frames and OWL Side by Side, *Protege Conference 2006, Standford University, USA*, Stanford University.

Wiederhold, G.: 1992, Mediators in the Architecture of Future Information Systems, *IEEE Computer* **25**(3), 38–49.

Wilkinson, M., Schoof, H., Ernst, R. and Haase, D.: 2005, BioMOBY Successfully Integrates Distributed Heterogenous Bioinformatics Web Services – The PlaNet exemplar case, *Plant Physiology* **138**(1), 5–17.

Wöhrer, A., Blöchl, M., Brezany, P., Gruber, G., Langegger, A., Schentz, H. and Wöß, W.: 2005, Towards Semantic Data Integration for Advanced Data Analysis of Grid Data Repositories, *Proceedings of the Austrian Grid Symposium (AGS'05)*, OCG.

Wong, E. and Youssefi, K.: 1976, Decomposition - A Strategy for Query Processing, *ACM Transactions on Database Systems* **1**(3), 223–241.

Yuan, J.: 2006, Semantic-Based Dynamic Enterprise Information Integration, *in* M. Zongmin (ed.), *Database Modeling for Industrial Data Management*, Idea Group Inc., Hershey, Pennsylvania, chapter VI.

Yuan, J., Bahrami, A., Wang, C., Murray, M. and Hunt, A.: 2006, A semantic information integration tool suite, *VLDB '06: Proceedings of the 32nd international conference on Very large data bases*, VLDB Endowment, pp. 1171–1174.

I want morebooks!

Buy your books fast and straightforward online - at one of the world's fastest growing online book stores! Environmentally sound due to Print-on-Demand technologies.

Buy your books online at

www.get-morebooks.com

Kaufen Sie Ihre Bücher schnell und unkompliziert online – auf einer der am schnellsten wachsenden Buchhandelsplattformen weltweit!
Dank Print-On-Demand umwelt- und ressourcenschonend produziert.

Bücher schneller online kaufen

www.morebooks.de

OmniScriptum Marketing DEU GmbH
Heinrich-Böcking-Str. 6-8
D - 66121 Saarbrücken
Telefax: +49 681 93 81 567-9

info@omniscriptum.com
www.omniscriptum.com

Printed by Books on Demand GmbH, Norderstedt / Germany